Global Faith,
Worldly Power

GLOBAL FAITH, WORLDLY POWER

Evangelical Internationalism and U.S. Empire

Edited by John Corrigan,
Melani McAlister, and Axel R. Schäfer

The University of North Carolina Press

Chapel Hill

Designed by Jamison Cockerham
Set in Scala, Futura Now, and Sentinel
by Jamie McKee, MacKey Composition

Manufactured in the United States of America

Cover illustrations: © iStockphoto

Complete Library of Congress Cataloging-in-Publication Data is available at
https://lccn.loc.gov/2022016268.
978–1–4696–7058–4 (cloth: alk. paper)
978–1–4696–7059–1 (pbk.: alk. paper)
978–1–4696–7060–7 (ebook)

An earlier version of chapter 7 appeared in Helen Jin Kim, *Race for Revival: How Cold War South Korea Shaped the American Evangelical Empire* (New York: Oxford Publishing Limited), 22–36.

publication supported by a grant
from Figure Foundation

CONTENTS

ILLUSTRATIONS

Global Faith,
Worldly Power

U.S. Evangelical Ambitions in Transnational Context

Melani McAlister, Axel R. Schäfer,
and John Corrigan

Evangelicals, empire, and power. Theologically conservative Protestants in the United States have encountered the world, mobilized—and sometimes challenged—the U.S. state, and positioned themselves in times of international crisis. This book takes as its starting point the grand American evangelical venture to convert the world, but it moves from that missionary presumption to examine how biblical imperatives have intersected with worldly imaginaries. We focus on U.S. evangelicals—a group that many observers, out of long habit, assume to have little or no investment in the world beyond their borders. Our aim is to counter that assumption: both to explore the complex ways that theologically conservative Protestantism has mattered on the international stage and to show how global realities have refashioned the experience of U.S. evangelicals.

We include evangelicals across lines of race here: white and Black, Asian and Latinx. While these groups often differ significantly in their politics, they are involved in overlapping networks, connect across denominations, listen to some of the same famous preachers, and navigate similar, if far from identical, questions about the intersections of faith and politics. The project is attentive to the racial and ethnic diversity of a movement in which race remains a central tension. It also examines how the globalization of the faith—long a goal of the missionary imperative—has had a boomerang impact, reshaping U.S. evangelical life.[1]

We further explore how these diverse evangelicals have engaged various regions of the world: Latin America, the Caribbean, Asia, Africa, and Europe. To make possible this kind of expansive reach, we brought together some of the world's finest scholars of U.S. evangelicalism in its global context. Contributors include historians of U.S. religion, Latin Americanists, scholars of Middle East studies, Africanists, Caribbean historians, and specialists in Europe. In the last ten years, there has been an explosion of work that brings evangelicals into full view as transnational political actors, showing their impact on debates about humanitarianism and human rights, religious freedom, gender and sexuality, and U.S. foreign policy, among other topics. Much of that scholarship was written by the contributors to this volume. In conversation with each other, we are able to provide a geographic reach and a depth of understanding that a single individual simply could not.

Our argument here is not that evangelicals, of any race, are *not* politically conservative, nationalist, or solipsistic. While it is certainly true that there are liberal and even radical evangelicals in the United States and globally, across a number range of demographic lines, the point of this collection is not a recuperative one. It is instead a call for us to examine and understand the complex ways that evangelical forms of practice and power work and how much they exist within—and help to construct—a cultural and political universe of border-crossing, media-blended, and institutional and political diversity. Any such project must also reckon with the realities of U.S. state and non-state forms of power within evangelicalism.

U.S. Evangelicals Are Global

At the turn of the twenty-first century, a range of evangelical activists and journalistic observers began to note the seemingly new enthusiasm of American evangelical churches for political and humanitarian causes in the Global South. In 2002, *New York Times* columnist Nicholas Kristof touted American evangelicals as the "new internationalists," citing their interest in global poverty and funding for AIDS programs overseas.[2] By 2020, the conversation about evangelicals and foreign policy often focused less on surprise at their internationalism than on a lack of surprise at their decidedly partial global investments. President Donald Trump and Vice President Mike Pence, for example, made determined efforts to reach out to Christian conservatives by single-mindedly supporting minority Christian populations in the Middle East and backing noticeably one-sided visions of international religious freedom.[3] Whether in the form of Kristof's warm embrace or as an angry outpouring at perceived hypocrisy, many of these recent observations about evangelical investments seemed to imply that, for better or worse, theologically conservative Christians had moved, at last, onto the global stage.

This approach to understanding evangelicalism, however, is based on a misreading of the movement's far longer and more complicated globalizing history. From the colonial period to the Civil War, theologically conservative Protestants were deeply invested in missionary work, national expansion and Indian removal, debates over slavery, and various forms of humanitarianism that crossed colonial or national lines. Their border-crossing investments only increased over time. In the 1890s, Christians of all stripes organized on behalf of Armenian Christians in the Ottoman Empire, offering not only humanitarian donations but also political commentary aimed against the "infidel Turks."[4] At the end of the First World War, Southern Baptist minister George W. Truett pronounced that Baptists were the paradigmatic exemplars of Woodrow Wilson's vision of America as a beacon of democracy—while insisting that Catholics could never embody such Americanism.[5] During the Cold War, U.S. evangelicals were outspoken anti-communists who depicted the standoff as a patriotic battle against enemies who needed to be defeated not only militarily but also spiritually and culturally. In the second half of the twentieth century, as Jonathan Herzog has argued, efforts to mobilize the resources of religion for the exercise of America's global power were very much at the heart of the "spiritual-industrial complex" that tied church and state ever closer to each other, particularly but not solely on the issue of the communist threat.[6] The issue of decolonization, however, often put Black and white evangelicals at odds, with African Methodist Episcopal and other Black churches strongly supporting African nationalism, while white evangelicals typically held a distinctly more ambivalent stance.

Despite the global cultural, racial, and theological complexity that has long shaped evangelicalism, two generations of scholarship, starting in the 1980s, focused primarily on the *domestic* politics of the religious right, with white evangelicals at its heart.[7] As historians and others recognized the rising political and cultural power of white evangelicals, they began to look back into the late nineteenth century to tell a story—one now entirely canonical—of a group of believers who, marginalized by the liberal historicist and modernist theology of the late nineteenth century, were captivated by a new type of orthodoxy. It centered both on *The Fundamentals*, a series of manifestos published starting in 1910 that spoke out against the "higher criticism" of the Bible and in favor of the absolute authority of the scriptures, and on the Scofield Reference Bible of 1909, which gave Americans' biblical literalism its premillennial and dispensationalist cast. Historians went on to trace how "fundamentalists" were then angered by mainstream press parodies of the Scopes trial of 1925, when dashing lawyer Clarence Darrow brilliantly defended the teaching of evolution in schools in the small town of Dayton, Tennessee, against the rhetorical prowess of evangelical standard-bearer and three-time Democratic presidential candidate William Jennings Bryan.[8]

Afterward, according to this account, fundamentalists retreated into pietism and political quietude, waiting out two world wars and the Depression with little to say about politics of any sort. After World War II, a younger cohort tried to wrench control of the narrative, styling themselves "neo-evangelicals." They developed new, more savvy institutions, founding the National Association of Evangelicals in 1942, Fuller Theological Seminary in 1947, and *Christianity Today* in 1956. At the same time, most of them remained firmly traditional in theology and generally conservative in their politics. They sought to create a broad interdenominational evangelical base and to dispense with the gloom and doom of prewar fundamentalism. (Even the name "neo-evangelicals," only partially adopted, distinguished them from the stricter and more separatist "fundamentalists" of a previous generation.) Their focus on foreign missions, religious broadcasting, Christian schools, the military chaplaincy, and church-state issues gave a new boost to this-worldly evangelical social and political action. They also recognized that evangelicalism was not confined to the geographical backwaters of small towns and rural constituencies and in fact was present in strength in urban areas, where its membership numbered white-collar workers and an emerging entrepreneurial class.[9]

This new generation was only partly successful in the rebranding of white conservative Protestantism, however—especially on issues of race. There was unquestionably a divide between someone like Billy Graham, the midcentury's best-known neo-evangelical, who was at once deeply anti-communist and a relative moderate on race relations, and Jerry Falwell Sr., who, having little truck with the loosely ecumenical approach of Graham, made his name criticizing integration and supporting the South African apartheid state. But white evangelicals overall, although divided on the acceptability of legal segregation, generally worshipped and organized themselves in segregated institutions. And ultimately it was a new generation of deeply right-wing leaders—Falwell, Pat Robertson, Jimmy Swaggart, James Hagee, Ralph Reed—who came to define the religious right of the 1970s and 1980s. They promoted themselves as a vanguard fighting feminism, racial liberalism, abortion rights, and theological liberalism of all types. The Moral Majority that Falwell founded in 1978 changed the face of American politics and did indeed herald a sharp rightward turn that gave political heft to a variety of social and religious anxieties. Falwell, who personified the image of the 1980s televangelist, cast his long shadow well into the twenty-first century when his son Jerry Falwell Jr., president of Liberty University, became an early and vocal supporter of Donald Trump during the 2016 election.

It is not that this story of the rise of the religious right is wrong, then, but it misses a great deal. It ignores the rising numbers of Asian American, Latinx, Black, Arab, and other evangelicals who identify with many of the same theologies of white evangelicals but who disagree (in various ways) with their political prescriptions. In 2016, Black Protestants made up 8 percent of the U.S. population, Latinx Protestants 4 percent, and "Asian, mixed-race, or other" Protestants 3 percent. Most of these Protestants identified themselves with theologically conservative churches, if not necessarily with the label "evangelical."[10] The focus on the Right also makes all but invisible the deep and often profound political debates in what is a significantly but not entirely conservative community. And it tells us almost nothing about what is arguably the most important transformation in evangelical life: the increasing globalization of Protestant Christianity, and with it the dawning awareness that white U.S. evangelicals are, as of the early years of the twenty-first century, a minority on the evangelical world stage.[11]

This volume aims to trace an alternative history of evangelical internationalism, one that puts internationalism at the center and that accounts for the racial diversity of the U.S. and global evangelical communities. The first section, on America's missionary impulse, examines the nineteenth and early twentieth centuries, a time when missionary activities—both proselytizing and humanitarian—were at the heart of how U.S. evangelicals engaged the world beyond their borders. It highlights the role of missionaries as non-state actors but also attends to the multiple ways they depended on the reach of U.S. state power. The second section focuses on the Cold War and the rise of global Christianity. It explores how evangelicals participated in networks with believers around the world, beginning to see them as part of a community of fellow believers, not just missionary objects. Yet it also shows their continued investments in nationalism and U.S. power, as well as presumptive whiteness even in the face of Third World activism. The final section traces evangelicals after the Cold War, looking at how they radically transformed the global frameworks by which they understood their own (neoliberal) subjectivity and how they mapped the world. In the remainder of this introduction, we discuss each of these moments in U.S. evangelical history, analyzing the historiography on evangelicalism as we also trace the framework of a broad international narrative of the global faith and worldly power of U.S. evangelicals.

America's Missionary Impulse

Scholarship on U.S. evangelical internationalism is not new, but the focus has changed over the last several decades. Missionary work in particular has long captured a good deal of attention, and the thinking about the impact and import of missionaries' global reach has evolved considerably. Scholars have examined both the ways missionaries shaped the various contexts in which they operated (as evangelists, medical practitioners, and teachers) and the influence they had on the global imaginaries of parishioners at home. For some decades, however, scholarship on missionaries was of the church history variety, telling the brave tales of those who died in the jungles of the Amazon or faced down the Boxer Rebellion in China. Then, starting in the 1970s, there was a turn toward examining the complex role of missionaries in laying the groundwork for empire: the expansive push westward and outward, the imperial imagination, the intersecting racial logics embodied and furthered by both U.S. and European missionaries.[12]

That research has been crucial in accounting for how thoroughly U.S. Protestants, including the supposedly inward-looking conservative wing, crossed borders. Indeed, scholarship on empire and expansion (U.S. and European) has often made missionaries central, as have the history and literature of decolonization. Chinua Achebe's masterful 1958 novel *Things Fall Apart*, for example, was an early and brilliant brief in the case against British missionaries in Nigeria as agents and allies of empire. Some twenty-five years later, Emily Rosenberg's *Spreading the American Dream* carefully unpacked the relationship between missionaries, the civilizing mission, and capitalist expansion. "Protestant missionaries became some of the most zealous and conspicuous overseas carriers of the American Dream," Rosenberg wrote, echoing a consensus reached earlier by anthropologists and historians of European empire.[13]

This fact—the reality of missions as the forward advance of an imperial project, or perhaps (and also) its retrospective justification—is crucial to understanding the role that missionaries have played in the global expansion of European and U.S. power. The "civilizing mission" was not the only task of missions, but it has been the soft edge of a great deal of hard power starting with the settler colonialism of the first European settlers in the Americas, and that fact must be central to any truly global story of American evangelicalism. The long arc of missionary work is one of the places where racist assumptions have been most overt and where the alliance of Christianity and capitalism has been most naked. And yet missionary and humanitarian work was also one of the sites where altogether different sentiments were sometimes cultivated. As a broad range of scholars writing on missions would soon elaborate, the racial politics of this expansion were complicated. American missionaries were representatives of the settler-colonial society from which they emerged, but they also imagined themselves as patriarchal caretakers, focused on literacy education and the voluntary conversion of people loved by God.

On the one hand, racism and belief in Anglo-Saxon superiority saturated almost all Protestant missionary writings in the nineteenth century and well into the twentieth. Such racism was clear in both Catholic and Protestant reports about the Indigenous peoples of the Americas from the arrival of Europeans centuries earlier. A British colonist in New England in the seventeenth century, for example, had little success proselytizing Native Americans, whom he described as "the dregs of mankind" who could never be converted to Christianity "whilst they live so unfixed, confused, and ungoverned a life, uncivilized and unsubdued to labor and order."[14] Indeed, a great deal of scholarship has shown how quickly and with what dispatch white U.S. Christians were able to justify their belief in the fundamental and enduring inequality of Africans, Native peoples, and Mexicans, despite Bible verses and Sunday school songs that averred otherwise.[15] A masculinist and imperialist logic of racial supremacy often undergirded Protestant support for U.S. expansion, military occupation, and colonial conquest. Even in situations where missionary motivations were perhaps more complicated, or where, as Amy Kaplan has shown, the project of empire was linked to domesticity and the home, there was often a close alliance between evangelization projects and the expansion of state power.[16] For example, as Tom Smith shows in this volume, U.S. missionaries in the Philippines in the early twentieth century promoted processes of indigenization and "found an antidote to interwar America's theological turmoil" in indigenous forms of belief. At the same time, the missionaries remained tied to a colonialist gaze. This gaze included concepts of their own muscular Christianity as opposed to the "effeminacy" and "superstition" of local beliefs, an emphasis on co-opting local elites largely supportive of U.S. influence, and exoticizing the inherent religiosity of local people.[17]

On the other hand, missions and missionaries could and did challenge the racial politics and imperial logic of white U.S. and European society. In the late nineteenth and early twentieth centuries, for example, African Americans were an important component of the U.S. missionary force. The theologically conservative African Methodist Episcopal (AME) Church was institutionally distant from the denominations of white evangelicalism, but it shared many theological propositions and a deep commitment to evangelization. AME leaders took important stances against the systems of racist segregation and discrimination in both the United States and, later, South Africa. Although the response to racism among AME leaders often focused more on racial uplift than on direct political agitation against injustice, some important AME members were outspoken about the right to challenge racist structures head-on. (Those members included, for a time, anti-lynching activist Ida B. Wells, before she moved to a Presbyterian congregation.) Whatever they believed about strategy, AME churches overall were clear about their commitment to supporting rights for Black peoples in the United States and internationally.[18] AME churches were also deeply invested in missions and had established congregations across the Caribbean and parts of Africa that were integrated into the U.S.-based denomination. Christina Cecelia Davidson analyzes the work of Black missionaries from the AME and other denominations in Hispaniola in the nineteenth century, where African American missionaries helped to create vibrant, cosmopolitan communities in Haiti and the Dominican Republic. The AME Church in particular had a large footprint, teaching lessons of freedom, self-help, and moral uplift.

Likewise, at the turn of the twentieth century, white and Black Protestant missionaries played a key role in contesting colonial policies in the Congo. At the time, King Leopold II of Belgium ruled the area as his own personal fiefdom, and the collection of rubber was at the heart of the territory's vast wealth. As the "rubber frontier" rolled forward in the 1890s, Congolese were forced into the labor of harvesting rubber and building roads, living close to the edge of starvation. Those who failed to harvest their assigned allotment of rubber were mutilated—their hands were cut off—or simply killed.[19]

Soon a powerful social movement began to challenge the practices in the Congo, built from the activism of missionaries and others in Britain and the United States. William H. Sheppard was not only the first African American missionary to Africa but also one of the early and best-known reformers in the Congo. After spending almost a decade in the field, Sheppard penned a vivid report about a massacre carried out at the behest of King Leopold's Force Publique. He soon became one of the most important figures in the burgeoning Congo reform movement, embraced and idealized by reformers on both sides of the Atlantic.[20]

One might argue that Protestant missionaries were particularly willing to challenge Belgian Catholic rule in the Congo, that this was simply anti-Catholicism combined with the rivalries among expansionist powers. But there are numerous other examples, from the U.S. West to Mount Lebanon, where missionaries were willing to take positions that challenged—sometimes vigorously, sometimes only partially—the dominant imperial and racial logics of their time. Of course, there are also many examples where missionaries did no such thing. The general response of Protestant writers to the Boxer Rebellion in China in 1900, for example, was a martyrological lament for the loss of Christian lives, absent an effort to appreciate the profound social and cultural tensions in China that had been prompted by imperialism.[21]

In short, there was Orientalism and racial condescension, but also a direct encounter with the complexities of teaching universal salvation and individual knowledge of the Bible, which led Protestants to see themselves as distinctly unlike either secular frontier settlers or Catholic missionaries. Amid the harsh and unswerving racial typologies that circulated broadly in the United States in the nineteenth and early twentieth centuries, there was a kind of culturalist cast to the thinking of many missionaries, who believed that Christianization would transform cultures and create reformed peoples. The theology of conversion carried a seemingly egalitarian logic, albeit one with many caveats.

Conversations about the concrete ramifications of the theoretical equality of all souls before God were not just arcane discussions among erudite theologians. The encounters with foreign people in the context of the massive expansion of evangelical overseas missions, institution building, and Bible tourism had a distinct impact on the movement in the United States. Missionaries were often the source of information about the rest of the world, and they were also central to an ongoing conversation about the relationship between evangelism and other social or humanitarian goals.

The role of missionaries in educating supporters at home and encouraging their donations and prayers was crucial to the way that evangelicals' work abroad was translated to ordinary people in the pews. As Emily Conroy-Krutz shows in this volume, evangelicals were taken by the increasingly available information from missionary fields: magazines and missionary reports, radio shows, and lectures and visitors from foreign lands told not just of evangelization successes but of the political and cultural realities in places far from Chattanooga or Chicago.[22]

The clearest indication of this "domestic cosmopolitanism" was that missionary reports frequently promoted funding for humanitarian projects as well as direct proselytizing; indeed, the two were often impossible to separate. In times of crisis—be it natural disasters or political conflict—missionaries encouraged American believers to see material aid to far-away peoples as part of their mandate. If those who were under threat were Christians, the impetus was strong, as in the case of the persecution of the Armenian population by the Ottoman Empire in the mid-1890s, which inspired both the activists of the Woman's Christian Temperance Union and the readers of the *Missionary Herald* to give generously. And just a few years later, evangelicals mobilized to send grain to respond to the famine in India, hoping to support the starving and, once the source of the food was advertised to the local population, to "give a great impetus to mission work in India."[23]

The growing entanglement of mission work with humanitarian aid paved the way for a new divide between evangelical and mainline Protestantism that would eventually be a significant mark of difference between the two wings of the faith tradition. The question of how much evangelization was central to Protestant identity would soon become one of the defining features of the split between modernists and fundamentalists in the 1910s and 1920s. The agenda-setting Edinburgh Missionary Conference of 1910, which included Protestants from a broad variety of denominations, had established the lofty goal of "evangelism of the world in this generation." In reality, the Edinburgh generation was soon deeply divided on the very question of whether conversion should be a goal. As David Hollinger has shown, in China— long the prized field for Protestant evangelization projects (and European and American imperialist adventuring)—missionaries began to have early doubts about the entire enterprise. The Southern Baptist missionary Frank Rowlinson was dismissed in 1921 for his provocative and public doubts; he then moved his sponsorship to the more liberal American Board of Foreign Missions and wrote a 1925 book that asked how Americans would feel "if 8,000 Buddhist missionaries backed up by hundreds of societies" were to mount in Christian America a missionary enterprise "equal in economic and propagandic strength to that carried out by us in China."[24]

A few years later, several Protestant denominations and the Rockefeller Foundation sponsored publication of *Re-thinking Missions: A Layman's Inquiry after 100 Years*—colloquially known as the Hocking Report. This report was so influential in part because it was so shocking to the people it was aimed to convince, as Hocking argued that it was time for the churches to stop trying to convert other people and instead to focus on humanitarian aid and practical assistance—"educational and other philanthropic projects." Christians must "cooperate with non-Christian agencies for social improvement" and indeed should step out of the way, allowing indigenous communities to lead, "defining the ways in which we shall be invited to help." Christians, Hocking believed, should respect other religions and cultures as having deep and profound validity.[25] This was distressing enough for many of the ecumenical Protestants who were the report's primary audience, but it left evangelicals apoplectic.

This changing view of missions on the part of ecumenical Protestants left the mission field far more open to evangelicals, whose missionary work exploded, particularly after World War II, when travel became easier, funds were more available, and interdenominational missionary organizations flowered. The initial face of that outward reach was the celebrity preacher Billy Graham, whose crusading trips to Europe (and later behind the Iron Curtain and around the globe) inspired a missionary workforce that grew steadily larger and whose agencies eventually claimed a majority role in the mission field. Alongside other global initiatives, such as Francis Schaeffer's work in Switzerland, and entrepreneurial missionary movements, such as Operation Mobilization (founded by a nineteen-year-old Tennessee college student), Graham's celebrated trips to Europe and beyond built momentum for evangelical hopes overseas.[26]

Powerhouse organizations like China Inland Mission and Africa Inland Mission had been around since the late nineteenth century, but now added to their numbers were Unevangelized Fields Mission (founded in 1931), Wycliffe Bible Translators (1942), New Tribes Mission (1942), and Evangelical Alliance Mission (1890/1949). Denominational missions also grew rapidly, as the Assemblies of God, the Southern Baptist Convention, and others sent out more missionaries to the field as their own congregations grew. Among Protestant missionaries worldwide, Americans were replacing Europeans, and evangelicals were replacing ecumenical Protestants. Evangelicals made up about 50 percent of U.S. missionaries in 1952; they would be 72 percent in

1969.[27] By then, U.S. evangelical foreign missions were by far the dominant missions force in the world. Much of this expansion of missions happened during the height of the U.S. civil rights movement, and some evangelicals soon began to criticize certain racial and cultural attitudes that their own missionaries displayed. But they never challenged the fundamental notion that their international focus should be conversion; proselytism was the baseline logic of evangelical global visions. That fact undergirded a broad range of additional political and cultural investments.

Of course, as missionaries had long realized, people in "receiving" countries never responded in a single or uniform fashion to the arrival of outsiders bringing "good news." Some portions of the population might be receptive to missionaries, but at other times there was indifference, or resistance, or rebellion. And even in cases where conversion was successful over time—and it often was, whether in various sections of what would become the United States, or in the Caribbean, Africa, Asia, or Latin America—the fact of Christian conversion meant a broad range of different realities on the ground. The indigenization of Protestant Christianity produced distinct versions of evangelicalism in local contexts, often drifting—even if temporarily — into a liberal or mainline direction, particularly in the context of state-building, nationalism, and modernization. As Dana L. Robert shows in her contribution, what for American evangelical missions organizers meant a sense of identity rooted in a vaunted transnational mission enterprise was for Japanese a means to a nationalist end, namely, the definition of a modern state. The YMCA, which often served as an institutional platform for urban missionizing in overseas contexts, for the Japanese was a mechanism for appropriating a U.S. model of education, baseball, and, ironically, the modernist practice of higher criticism.

Global Christianity and the Cold War

The military and economic footprint of the U.S. abroad expanded rapidly after World War II. The growth of evangelical mission and humanitarian aid activities needs to be viewed in this context. The neo-evangelical movement—networked through organizations such as *Christianity Today*, Fuller Theological Seminary, and the National Association of Evangelicals—came to believe that evangelicals must have a different, more cosmopolitan profile. These evangelicals remained deeply conservative on many issues but saw themselves as a vanguard of the believers who would challenge the presumption that theological conservatives were uninterested in the world.

One of the first international agenda items for the neo-evangelical movement was a quick and enthusiastic embrace of anti-communism, which evangelicals saw as linked not only to American nationalism but also to support for Christianity abroad. After Mao Zedong's 1949 victory in the Chinese civil war, China had forced missionaries out. The "loss" of China shaped a great deal of how Americans viewed the likely fate of Christianity under communist rule. After North Korea invaded South Korea in 1950, white evangelicals strongly supported Harry Truman's decision to send troops to the Korean Peninsula (although some criticized the president for not being tough enough on communism overall).[28] As Billy Graham put it in 1953, "Either Communism must die, or Christianity must die, because it is actually a battle between Christ and the anti-Christ."[29] Those to the right of the neo-evangelicals, such as Christian Crusade founder Billy James Hargis, went even further. Hargis was known to open his fundraising letters with "Dear Patriots Whose Children and Grandchildren Are Being Threatened by Communism."[30] As Gene Zubovich analyzes in his essay, U.S. evangelicals were deeply invested in forms of Christian nationalism, developed both in opposition to the ecumenical movement's investment in Christian globalism and in concert with a vision of the United States as having a special role to play in forwarding Christ's kingdom. This nationalism, Zubovich writes, built on a "long tradition of conceiving of nation-states as sanctified entities, with the United States standing above all others." All of this put evangelicals and fundamentalists generally in line with the mainstream of U.S. foreign policy in this era, as U.S. policy makers' statements—and Voice of America broadcasts—promoted religious freedom as being at the heart of the American way of life, and communism as its antithesis.[31]

World War II not only paved the way for U.S. global supremacy and the Cold War standoff but also ushered in the end of European empires. Americans in general were clear beneficiaries of this process of decolonization. This was true at the broad level of American state power: the United States expanded its political, economic, and cultural reach in tandem with the pullback of European empires and the rise of national independence in Asia, Africa, and the Middle East. Indeed, American policy makers often justified the expansion of U.S. political and economic power on the basis of the nation's supposedly non-colonial history. (Of course, that self-image strategically ignored the history of U.S. destruction of Native peoples, westward expansion, appropriation of Mexican territory, and the multiple extra-continental expansions and colonial occupation of the Philippines, Puerto Rico, and other territories.)[32] U.S. policy makers' methods of nationalist expansion during the Cold War did not (for the most part) involve occupying vast territories or growing a territorial empire along the lines of Europe. Instead, U.S. strategies included a far-reaching network of military bases, a close alliance between corporations and U.S. state politics, a willingness to intervene militarily and install friendly governments, and the promotion of American popular culture as a form of soft power.[33]

U.S. evangelicals also specifically benefited from decolonization. They correctly believed that people in newly independent nations might be more open to their missionary efforts than to those of European missionaries because, as Americans, they were not generally identified with European colonial powers. Thus, in a number of cases, U.S. evangelicals triumphantly argued that the end of empire was ultimately good for the cause of Christ. The authors of *Missions in Crisis*—a book by two former missionaries that was handed out to every attendee at the 1961 conference of InterVarsity Christian Fellowship—argued that "the pent-up frustrations and resentments of the past that have been locked up in the breasts of the exploited, underprivileged masses of mankind have at last reached a boiling point."[34] But the crisis brought opportunity; if Americans would heed the clarion call of anti-colonial foment, they might reach the world with the gospel.

Evangelicals also benefited in another sense: as the United States developed its international reach after World War II, the power of the U.S. state was apparent in the globe-spanning ring of military bases, the large footprint of U.S. corporations, and the massive influence of U.S. culture, all of which shaped how American missionaries were perceived.[35] In the most direct sense, as Sarah Miller-Davenport makes clear, American military occupation in places such as the Philippines and Japan provided a material basis of support for evangelical projects. U.S. power shaped missionary opportunity precisely because that power was different from, but certainly as fearsome as, direct colonialization.

An additional advantage was the prestige and power that accrued to evangelical leaders and their organizations as those actors forayed more ambitiously into global waters. The evangelical mission project has never been a one-way enterprise. The efforts expended abroad historically have rebounded—as they were expected to—in salutary effects on the social standing of the evangelical churches back home. Billy Graham's Cold War–era globe-trotting tours, for example, not only resulted in reports of converted persons overseas but also raised the profile of Graham as a national leader and bolstered the reputation of his organization and of evangelicals as a whole. That recursive benefit of evangelical missionizing, which had been an important part of missions since the nineteenth century and was acknowledged as such by contemporaries, increasingly became part of the calculus of evangelical missions. Successful missions overseas were a means to evangelicalism's enhanced social position, greater visibility, and political authority domestically, which in turn primed the fundraising operations of mission societies and enabled them to extend their global reach.

The expanded U.S. political and religious footprint also meant that evangelicals' global agendas broadened considerably. By the early 1960s, a wide range of evangelical organizations and publications were providing detailed analyses of political issues. These often focused on domestic topics, from Catholic-Protestant relations to civil rights. But foreign policy was also on the table. Spokespersons such as writer Francis Schaeffer, Boston pastor Harold Ockenga, Campus Crusade founder Bill Bright, Harlem-based evangelist Tom Skinner, broadcaster Oral Roberts, and evangelist Billy Graham, along with such outlets as *Christianity Today* and the *Pentecostal Evangel*, offered opinions on international issues ranging from the Guatemalan coup of the mid-1950s to the early days of U.S. action in Vietnam. Although their positions varied, these observers generally mobilized their constituencies to join U.S. state agendas, first and foremost the Cold War struggle against communism. In fact, opposition to communism also meant that American evangelicals' notational support for an end to European empires was deeply compromised in practice, since so many national liberation movements were influenced by socialist ideas or backed by the Soviet Union. In Congo, Kenya, Korea, Vietnam, Indonesia, and elsewhere, American missionaries and their sponsors often claimed to uphold the idea of independence from European empires but in practice expressed deep doubts about the ability of local people to rule themselves and, in particular, to resist the sway of communism.

Decolonization also reinforced the racial divide within U.S. evangelicalism. Theologically conservative Black churches were equally anti-communist overall but were wary of the ways that anti-communism was used as a brief against liberation movements. The Reverend Smallwood Williams of Bible Way Church of Washington, DC, for example, wrote to the *Pittsburgh Courier* in 1961 to complain about the U.S. government's response to the nationalist government of Patrice Lumumba in Congo. Williams noted that the U.S. administration had seemed unable to distinguish nationalism from communism and that anti-communist rhetoric used against Lumumba was the same kind of smear used against civil rights activists at home.[36]

Indeed, on civil rights, the position of most of the predominantly white evangelical churches ranged from seemingly grudging acquiescence to vicious hostility. Although the Southern Baptist Convention, for example, had hotly debated whether to embrace *Brown v. Board of Education* in 1954, with a moderate faction strongly in favor, the anti–civil rights contingent had the preponderance of power. In 1956, the famously eloquent Southern Baptist minister W. A. Criswell was the featured speaker at a South Carolina Baptist evangelism conference. Preaching to an overflowing crowd, many of them preachers themselves, Criswell railed against *Brown v. Board of Education,* calling the decision "idiocy"—designed to force integration and set against the entire culture and values of the South. Criswell admitted that it was possible to have cross-racial fellowship on the mission field. He had seen that. And he knew that "in heaven, we'll all be together." Until then, however, the white South had the right to maintain its boundaries. "Let them integrate," he said of the Supreme Court and the supporters of its decision. "Let them sit up there in their dirty shirts and make all their fine speeches. But they are a bunch of infidels, dying from the neck up."[37] With this kind of hostility, and the thundering silence of most white evangelicals in the face of the upswing in civil rights activism in the 1960s, it was not surprising that Black and white churches that shared many theological views had little to do with each other institutionally.

There is a serious and important debate about exactly how intransigent theologically conservative white churches were on racial politics, since domestic issues and international issues were closely intertwined. A lively conversation among white evangelicals of several stripes argued for "moderation" on civil rights for the simple reason that American racism was making missions more difficult, and several scholars have traced the genuinely robust struggles around civil rights in Southern-based white churches during the Cold War.[38] Other scholars have argued that, at the fundamental level, the presumptions of white supremacy have infused white evangelicalism from root to branch, impacting relations not only with African Americans but also with Latinos, Indigenous peoples, Asian Americans, and Muslims of all races. In Anthea Butler's words, "Racist evangelicals shielded cross burners, protected church burners, and participated in lynchings. Racism is a feature, not a bug, of American evangelicalism."[39] While we believe this project highlights the diversity of white evangelical views and also brings in people of color as actors essential to a larger story, thus complicating this picture of racism as inexorable, it remains the case that evangelical history cannot be told without recognizing race and racism as a central component.

For many theologically conservative Christians of color in the Cold War era, then, the question of when or how to engage with the political or social worlds of white evangelicalism was often fraught. A few joined forces with white-led evangelical institutions: Howard Jones of the Billy Graham Evangelistic Association, William Bentley of the National Black Evangelical Association, and Ruth Lewis, who became a staffer at InterVarsity Christian Fellowship, were among the important examples in the 1960s and 1970s. But, more often, Black churches in the United States were likely to ally themselves institutionally with the liberal Protestant churches, which had taken increasingly affirmative anti-racist stances, culminating in the 1968 Uppsala meeting of the World Council of Churches, where Martin Luther King Jr. was scheduled to deliver the opening address. (He was assassinated three months before the meeting.)[40] This meant that, before the 1980s—when denominational identities began to fracture and interracial megachurches and parachurch organizations grew in strength—most U.S. Black Protestants, no matter how theologically conservative, operated separately from white evangelical institutions.

As the reality of decolonization continued to shape U.S. evangelical missionary work into the 1960s and beyond, and the news of white American militarism abroad and racism at home dominated headlines around the world, the relationship between U.S. evangelicals and the U.S. state was increasingly fraught. Americans in general often hotly debated the expansion of U.S. military power in what was then called the Third World, and evangelicals were no exception. From the 1950s onward, Asia and the Middle East became the sites of a series of particularly deadly military struggles. In Korea, Vietnam, Indonesia, Cambodia, Bangladesh, India-Pakistan, Lebanon, Iran, Afghanistan, and Palestine/Israel, battles between local parties over nationalism, minority rights, communism, and the nature of liberation from colonialism were structured deeply by the conflict between the superpowers. Some 70 percent of the people killed in violent conflicts between 1945 and 1990—14 million people—died along Asia's southern rim. Those areas were, in Paul Chamberlain's succinct summary, the "Cold War's Killing Fields."[41]

As Helen Jin Kim shows in her chapter on World Vision in Korea, evangelical humanitarianism as well as missionary work thrived in part because of the role of the U.S. state in the Global South: "The geopolitics of the emerging Cold War in Asia restricted access to China but also paved new routes into South Korea," and in so doing laid the groundwork for "the business of evangelical humanitarian care" at mid-twentieth century. The rise of the most powerful engine for evangelical giving was deeply implicated in the power of the U.S. state. At the same time, a proper recounting of the story also highlights the central role of Asian Christians in emergent global humanitarianism. The origin stories about World Vision often focus on U.S. missionary Bob Pierce, ignoring the centrality of the Korean minister who cofounded it, Kyung Chik Han.[42] A properly transnational and multiracial account must consider both U.S. power and Global South agency in the making of evangelical worlds.

The war in Vietnam was a turning point for evangelicals, as it was for U.S. society at large. As the conflict escalated in the early and mid-1960s, opposition among ecumenical Protestants and some Catholics was increasingly common, but white evangelicals generally supported the war. Billy Graham was outspoken in promoting his friend Richard Nixon's foreign policy, and *Christianity Today* backed U.S. action in Vietnam, increasingly so after the Southern Baptist conservative Harold Lindsell took over its editorship in 1968. Some younger evangelical liberals, however, strongly opposed the war: the young white activists who founded the organization Sojourners and the magazine by the same name (first called the People's Christian Coalition, and its publication the *Post-American*) were strongly critical, as were a large number of leading Black Christians, including those identified with evangelical organizations, such as the National Black Evangelical Association, and a number of Latin American thinkers, including Samuel Escobar, René Padilla, and Orlando Costas.[43] Indeed, as David C. Kirkpatrick argues in this volume, Latin Americans were at the leading edge of evangelical movements toward social justice, as a generation influenced by the civil rights and antiwar movements in the United States and by the rise of liberation theology in Latin America forged a distinct model for charting an evangelical course toward what they described as "social concern." That small but significant global evangelical left got a decisive push from Latin American believers with an international platform and strong ties to—and criticisms of—U.S. evangelicalism.

The Middle East was an arena of passionate evangelical investment. Starting with the founding of Israel in 1947, white evangelicals, in particular, were increasingly focused on the U.S. relationship with a state that many believed was the fulfillment of scripture. After the 1967 Arab-Israeli War, one long-standing apocalyptic strain in U.S. evangelical life moved rapidly to center stage. Since the nineteenth century, fundamentalist and evangelical believers had been fascinated by the prophetic chapters of the Bible and had frequently interpreted those as having direct relevance to contemporary events. With the dramatic events of the 1967 war, which gave Israel control over territories that had been controlled by Egypt, Syria, and Jordan, many Protestant prophecy-watchers saw a set of biblical promises fulfilled. One reader of *Christianity Today* praised the magazine's extensive coverage of the war, saying that "the prophetic clock of God is ticking while history moves inexorably toward the final climax. And as that clock ticks, the Christian believer lifts his head high, for he knows that a glorious redemption draws near."[44] American Christians from a broad variety of backgrounds had long seen the "Holy Land" as a site for pilgrimage and a symbol of their faith. Now, evangelicals argued, it was also a place of God's action in bringing about the ever-more-near second coming of Jesus.

Throughout the late 1960s and 1970s, evangelical and fundamentalist anti-communism was thus complicated by the realities of U.S. power on the ground. During what Odd Arne Westad has memorably described as the "global Cold War," the politics of evangelical anti-communism was muddled by the ongoing tensions between the goals of evangelization and the problems with being associated with an expansionist global power. As U.S. power played out on the ground in Vietnam and Cambodia, showed its hand in Latin America, and was increasingly invested in ongoing conflicts in the Middle East, the U.S. record on human rights, civil rights, and respect for the independence of the Global South came under greater scrutiny.

In the context of revolutionary fervor or enlivened movements for social justice in the Global South, there were real problems for U.S. evangelicals in being associated with the United States as the ascendant world power. This reality became a matter of intense public controversy in 1974, when two former intelligence officials published *The CIA and the Cult of Intelligence*.[45] The authors described how both Catholic and Protestant missionaries had been approached by the CIA for information about local conditions. In one case, a Protestant missionary in Bolivia reported on the Communist Party, labor unions, and farmers' cooperatives.[46] Soon, the *Washington Post* made its own allegations, reporting that missionaries themselves were upset about the CIA's activities, since it was "not uncommon" to be contacted for information.[47] Stanley Mooneyham, president of the evangelical aid organization World Vision, went beyond the practical problem of risk. When missionaries were identified as working with the CIA, he said, "the discredit is total—of the missionary, his message, and his God."[48] In 1975, Republican senator Mark Hatfield introduced a bill to ban any CIA communication with missionaries. The bill did not pass, although the CIA did agree to stop making contact with missionaries while they were still in the field.[49] The damage was done, however. Or, to put it more exactly, the fact that many people around the world already identified missionaries as likely spies was now public knowledge in the United States.

Even as Christian missionaries were receiving unfavorable coverage for their international activities, evangelical Christians within the United States were in political ascendance. Just weeks before the Southern Baptist Jimmy Carter was elected president in 1976, *Newsweek* declared the "Year of the Evangelicals." Most of its readers might have "overlooked" the fact, the magazine explained, but evangelical Christianity now had "a position of respect and power." Carter had been outspoken about his Christian faith during the campaign, and he promised to make "human rights" a signature focus of his presidency. This was an issue that carried real weight for evangelicals, who, in the late 1960s and early 1970s, had been deeply involved in the activism on behalf of Soviet Jews that led to the Jackson-Vanik amendment of 1974, which denied the status of most favored nation to the Soviet Union and many of its allies for restricting the freedom of emigration and human rights.[50]

By the time of Ronald Reagan's election in 1980, however, those politics had moved noticeably to the right. In the 1970s and 1980s, neo-fundamentalists, including Jerry Falwell and Pat Robertson, organized in broad-based, trans-denominational groups, such as Christian Voice, the Moral Majority, the National Religious Broadcasters, and the Religious Roundtable, which focused on conservative activism on both domestic and international issues. In turn, the large-scale political mobilization of evangelicals, which had been a key aspiration of the National Association of Evangelicals but had also generated mixed feelings within the organization, finally came to pass under the auspices of neo-fundamentalists, who built a militant, broadly Christian, anti-secularist political movement. Domestically, neo-fundamentalists cooperated with Catholics and others in campaigns against abortion, gay rights, pornography, and other alleged moral ills. In terms of foreign policy, many of the groups considered both anti-communism and support for Israel as cornerstones of their politics. Various campaigns for religious liberty fostered a new sense of cooperation among conservatives in all three main Judeo-Christian traditions.[51]

President Reagan's speech before the National Association of Evangelicals in 1983 perfectly exemplified the religious nationalism that brought together a more socially focused segment of the Republican Party with a more politically savvy group of conservative evangelicals. "I'm pleased to be here today with you who are keeping America great by keeping her good," Reagan told the group. "Only through your work and prayers and those of millions of others can we hope to survive this perilous century and keep alive this experiment in liberty, this last, best hope of man."[52]

During the 1980s, evangelicals became deeply embroiled in debates about the political turmoil in Latin America. Evangelicals had established themselves as interested not only in opposing communism in Latin America but also in supporting "human rights," particularly the right to religious freedom. Evangelicals had spoken out for Jews in the USSR in the early 1970s, but their most energetic activism was generally reserved for cases of Protestant believers under threat. In Guatemala, Argentina, Honduras, and Nicaragua, local conflicts with varied motivations—conservative anti-communist forces were often arrayed against left-wing guerrillas—frequently included Latin American Protestants primarily on one side. For example, as Lauren F. Turek argues in this volume, evangelicals collaborated with the Reagan White House to support the Nicaraguan Contras against the Marxist Sandinista government. Since the Sandinistas were accused of violating the human rights of their political opponents and of persecuting conservative Christians in the country, the Reagan White House argued—and many major Christian right organizations agreed—that U.S. support for the Contras was a human rights imperative. For an administration facing strong pushback for its policy of endorsing clear human rights violators in Guatemala and El Salvador, as well as South Africa, Namibia, Saudi Arabia, and elsewhere, this rhetorical position carried great symbolic weight.[53]

Reagan's approach toward South Africa was among the most controversial of his foreign policy positions. After the Soweto uprising in South Africa in 1976, U.S. and European social movements had become increasingly outspoken in opposition to apartheid. Several of the ecumenical Protestant churches were taking major roles in the anti-apartheid movement, pushing for boycotts in Europe and divestment and sanctions in the United States.[54] Reverend Leon Sullivan, pastor of Zion Baptist Church in Philadelphia and a member of the Board of General Motors, proposed the Sullivan Principles, a series of ethics requirements for corporations that wanted to do business in South Africa. The principles soon became controversial, because corporations rushed to sign them as a way to continue to do business under apartheid.[55] By the time Reagan took office in 1981, major evangelical organizations were split on how to respond to the increasingly visible anti-apartheid movement. Some well-known members of the Christian right, including Jerry Falwell, claimed to condemn apartheid but were strongly supportive of the white South African government. Many U.S. evangelical and Pentecostal churches, from the largely white Southern Baptist Convention to the Pentecostal Apostolic Faith Mission to the historically Black AME Church, had churches and missionaries in South Africa and so cultivated ties there.

They almost all took positions that opposed apartheid, but they focused on "reconciliation" and moral influence rather than pushing for real change. As the anti-apartheid movement reached its height in the United States in the 1980s, evangelicals such as Falwell were visible and active on the right; others made connections that focused primarily on evangelism; and a few, such as the Christian Life Commission of the Southern Baptist Convention, spoke out in favor of divestment and sanctions.[56]

All of these foreign policy debates among evangelicals happened in conjunction with the other great mandate of the movement: evangelization of the world. Throughout the 1970s and 1980s, U.S. evangelicals became an ever-larger proportion of U.S. Protestant missionaries in the field, as the ecumenical churches became increasingly concerned about the imperial thrust of missionary work. They were not alone. In 1971, the Reverend John Gatu, secretary general of the Presbyterian Church of East Africa, had proposed a "missionary moratorium" in Africa. Highlighting the rise of the church in the Global South, Gatu and others argued that African churches could and should develop without Western missionaries' involvement.[57] Gatu was active in both the ecumenical World Council of Churches and the global evangelical movement, and his arguments were a galvanizing part of a much larger reality that was becoming apparent: by the late twentieth century, the global Christian church was shifting. Its demographic and political heart was increasingly in Asia, Africa, Latin America, and the Middle East.[58] This meant that American evangelicals, powerful as they were both financially and politically, were also on their way to becoming a global minority.

One of the most important factors in this process was the dramatic rise in Pentecostalism. Pentecostalism was known for its distinctive focus on "gifts of the spirit," such as speaking in tongues or faith healing, and with its emergence in the early twentieth century came renewed faith in modern miracles and new forms of affective worship. At the same time, the rise of Pentecostalism globally saw a rapid ascent of the prosperity gospel—a vision of faith that argued that spiritual commitment would be reflected in material wealth. This was not the Calvinist ethos of an elect few chosen by God. Instead, the prosperity gospel merged components of Pentecostal practices of spiritual gifts (faith was a "gift" that would be materially rewarded) with strands of American "New Thought" from the nineteenth and twentieth centuries (the idea that the mind could control events in the world).

As with evangelicalism overall, the prosperity gospel has sometimes been described as an American export. There is no doubt that, within the United States, a striking number of the most popular televangelists, such as Oral

Roberts, Kenneth Copeland, and Jim and Tammy Bakker, were based in charismatic and Pentecostal traditions and promoted versions of the prosperity gospel—ministries that promised riches for those who believed . . . and donated.[59] Their impact can be seen, at least in part, as a classic example of U.S. cultural imperialism, a version of missionary work that carried enormous weight globally. Sociologist Paul Gifford has argued, therefore, that American Pentecostal pastors who promoted the prosperity gospel were responsible for fundamentally reshaping African Protestantism. They created a language, a set of affective models, and a performative style that, starting in the 1980s, transformed Christianity in Ghana, Nigeria, Kenya, and South Africa, among other places.[60] Other observers, however, have advanced different interpretations. Historian Ogbu Kalu, for example, insists that Pentecostalism in Africa had its own indigenous orientations—that it was neither dependent on an American model nor necessarily oriented toward the prosperity gospel variant.[61]

As the Cold War drew to a close in the late 1980s, American believers were becoming less central to the global faith, while the foreign policy positions of American evangelicals were all over the map. Human rights politics had shaped a generation, but what those rights were remained a matter of contention. In practice, were evangelicals interested in human rights only when it was a matter of opposing communism or supporting religious freedom for Protestants? The language of rights, after all, was as slippery as it was robust.[62] And, although no one was fully aware of it when the Berlin Wall came down in 1989, U.S. power was about to shift dramatically, and American evangelicals would find both new opportunities and new enemies.

Evangelicals in the Neoliberal Order

With the fall of the Berlin Wall in 1989 and the disintegration of the USSR in 1990–91, the Cold War came to a rapid but not unanticipated end. For most U.S. evangelicals, the narratives were of liberation and victory. For them, the impact of the end of the Cold War was not only about political transformation but also about missionary opportunity. Most of the nations of the Soviet bloc—including the new nations formed out of the old USSR—became the site of an unprecedented wave of evangelism, as Christians from all around the world began pouring into the region as missionaries.[63] Many of these missionaries were from the Global South regions where Christianity had been growing rapidly since the 1970s. Nigeria, for example, had seen an explosion of Pentecostalism, with megachurches springing up all over the country in the 1980s. (By the early years of the twenty-first century, two of Nigeria's Pentecostal congregations would be among the top five largest churches in the world.) Nigerian evangelists made their way into the Soviet bloc after 1989. Within fifteen years, Kiev, Ukraine, would boast not one but two megachurches pastored by African Pentecostals. One, the Embassy of God, was founded in 1994 by Nigerian pastor Sunday Adelaja, who, preaching in Russian, built a membership of 20,000 over the next ten years.[64]

The dramatic transformations that were remapping the global media landscape meant new opportunities and challenges for evangelicals, both in the United States and internationally. Overall, evangelical networks of the post–Cold War era did particularly well with neoliberal models of privatization, flexibility, and border-crossing connectivity. At the end of the twentieth century, there emerged what Gregorio Bettiza diagnoses as a "religious foreign policy regime" in the United States—alongside the "religionization" of global politics. Even without the threat of communism to organize foreign policy concerns, U.S. policy makers transferred significant public resources to religious leaders, institutions, and communities at home and around the world.[65] After 1989, evangelicals actually intensified their focus on religious freedom issues, now highlighting not the struggle for faith under communism but claims of the persecution of Christians more broadly, particularly in Muslim-majority contexts. In other words, by the beginning of the new millennium, U.S. evangelicals were linked to global issues through ties of faith with Christians around the world; were distinctly interested in international affairs, particularly as it related to religious conflict; and were increasingly able to articulate those concerns in universalist language of human rights and humanitarian concern.

As Axel R. Schäfer shows in his essay, scholarly attention to evangelicals' border-spanning investments has become far more central to both religious studies and diplomatic history over the last few decades. Historians' own transnational turn has allowed for a great deal of scholarship, represented by many of the contributors in this volume, that attends to "networks, ecologies, diasporas, and subaltern groups." Writing evangelical history means exploring travel, activism, military deployment, media, and education as activities that have reshaped U.S. evangelical lives in a globalizing register.

Several issues were central to the globalizing realities and the foreign policy views of American evangelicals in the post–Cold War era. First was the series of conflicts in the Middle East and beyond that eventually were branded by U.S. policy makers as the "war on terror." Beginning with the Gulf War of 1990–91, the United States expanded its post–Cold War influence in the Middle East, Africa, and South Asia. At the same time, evangelicals globally had been focused on evangelizing the Muslim world. Such evangelization efforts were not new, but they intensified after 1989, when a series of enthusiastic missionary endeavors (campaigns such as the Unreached Peoples movement, the 10/40 Window, and the Year 2000) all targeted Muslims (and others) for new forms of evangelism. The new initiatives concentrating on Muslims took shape as extensions of the growing concern about the mistreatment of Christians in Muslim-majority nations. Inventorying state-sponsored persecution of Christians as well as broader culturally grounded intolerance, evangelical groups became increasingly vocal about Muslim-Christian relations. Indeed, the supposed dangers of Islam to Christianity became an intellectual and affective heart of a great deal of evangelical activity. The movement on behalf of "persecuted Christians" was one of the most energized forms of evangelical foreign affairs activism in the 1990s and the following decade, and it played a key role in supporting the International Religious Freedom Act of 1998, which made support for religious minorities into a key plank of U.S. foreign policy.[66]

After September 11, 2001, the persecuted Christians movement grew in visibility, as Candace Lukasik discusses in this volume, organizing new campaigns and new forms of affective ties, ultimately creating various forms of alliance between evangelicals, Catholics, and orthodox Christians, in the United States and globally. It would frame (and misrepresent) a wide range of global conflicts, including those in southern Sudan, Nigeria, Egypt, Syria, and Lebanon. It also would shape U.S. evangelicals' thinking about their seeming predicament at home. They concluded that American believers, also, were systematically persecuted by a secularist liberal culture, a belief that prompted evangelicals to identify ever more closely with persecuted Christians overseas and to redouble efforts to support them.

The Trump administration also courted conservative evangelicals with its selection of Senator Sam Brownback to be the U.S. Ambassador-at-Large for International Religious Freedom—a position created after the International Religious Freedom Act twenty years earlier. As governor of Kansas, Brownback had signed one of the anti-sharia laws that, in the first years of the twenty-first century, were key to the strategy of anti-Muslim activists in the United States. He also joined other Republican governors in trying to bar Syrian refugees from being resettled in his state.[67] Brownback was soon joined by Secretary of State Mike Pompeo in promoting support for (very specific forms of) religious freedom as a hallmark of the Trump administration. The issue had particularly powerful resonance for a range of American evangelicals who were energized by the issue of religious freedom both domestically (since they argued religious freedom protected discrimination against LGBTQ+ people) and internationally, particularly the freedom of Christians in Muslim-majority contexts. (It would not be fair, however, to argue that religious freedom activism overall was motivated solely or even primarily by either of these issues.)[68]

The second key post–Cold War issue for U.S. evangelicals has been immigration. The end of the Cold War saw the full triumph of neoliberal economics globally, and the profound economic dislocations that resulted from that triumph led to changing patterns of migration and immigration globally. That, in turn, significantly changed the makeup of the U.S. Protestant community, affecting its politics as well as its demographics. The U.S. Latinx population, for example, increased from 6.5 percent of the U.S. population in 1980 to 18 percent in 2020, due to both migration and natural increase. This demographic change was accompanied by a religious one. Since the 1980s, Latin America has been a major center of growth for the charismatic and Pentecostal churches. In Latin America overall, a population that was 92 percent Catholic in 1970 was, by 2020, 19 percent Protestant. Most of those Protestants were Pentecostal.[69] This paralleled changes within the United States overall as Protestantism, like the rest of the country, became increasingly Latinx.[70] Latinx evangelicals are more conservative politically than Latinos overall and vote more conservatively than Latinx Catholics, although they are less conservative than white evangelicals (or, indeed, than white people overall).[71]

Asian American immigration to the United States had already begun to increase noticeably after the 1965 Hart-Celler Immigration Act and with the end of the Vietnam War. Overall, Asians rose from 2 percent of the U.S. population in 1980 to 5.9 percent in 2020. The U.S. census category of "Asian" is remarkably diverse, including people whose heritage ranges from Indonesian to Japanese to Indian. Not surprisingly, then, Asians are perhaps the most religiously diverse community in the United States, including Buddhists, Hindus, Muslims, and mainline Protestants and Catholics. Only 13 percent of Asian Americans are evangelical. But evangelicals have an outsized impact in certain subsets of the Asian community, particularly among people with Korean or Filipino heritage.[72] Asian Americans are important players in U.S. evangelical movements—as members of organizations such as InterVarsity Christian Fellowship and as authors, speakers, and pastors.[73]

Latinx and Asian American evangelicals have both been outspoken on issues of immigration policy in the twenty-first century. Their views are not uniform: Asian American evangelicals tend to have liberal views on immigration, but Latinos are divided, as Cuban evangelicals in Miami, for example, are more critical of liberal borders (and are more conservative overall) than Puerto Ricans, Central Americans, and Mexican Americans. At the same time, white evangelicals overall have retained a strongly conservative stance on immigration, but they also increasingly recognize the significance of immigrants (and their children and grandchildren) to U.S. evangelical life. These lines became clearer, and the stakes significantly increased, when President Trump launched his major immigration policies. First in 2017, the Trump administration announced that it would phase out the DACA (Deferred Action for Childhood Arrivals) program, which had protected approximately 800,000 undocumented people who had been brought to the United States as children. Then in 2018, the Trump administration began enacting its "zero tolerance" policy of separating migrant families at the U.S.-Mexico border. The Evangelical Immigration Table issued a letter of protest asking Trump to reverse the policy. Even Franklin Graham, a staunch Trump defender, said he found the policy "disgraceful"—although, notably, he failed to blame the president for it.[74]

The upshot of these developments regarding immigration was that evangelicalism in the United States became more diverse. But as so many of the new arrivals were persons of color and in general less conservative than white evangelicals, fissures that had been present in the evangelical community widened. America-first evangelicals who favored strict limitations on immigration from Muslim nations and who were anxious about the race and ethnicity of immigrants in general became more assertive in their voicing of support for immigration restrictions. The reality of diversity at home and broadening visions of connection abroad were diffused and challenged by a reemergent nativist/isolationist ideology.

An additional factor in U.S. evangelicals' internationalism was the ever-expanding impact of mass media. Mass media had been central to U.S. evangelical life throughout the twentieth century, as a number of scholars have described.[75] And organizations such as CARE and the Southern Baptist International Mission Board had long used media outreach to promote a particular vision of Christian benevolence, enacted via donations to abject "others" who needed American Christian help. As John Corrigan points out in his contribution, even as people in faraway places were orientalized, reduced and judged as they stood before the imperializing Protestant gaze, they also were constructed as humans who lived, worked, played, loved, and mourned like Americans. The egalitarian perspective embedded in

Protestant theology (although unevenly deployed) enabled that feat of interpretation, even demanded it. Protestant missionaries' empathy for the foreign populations to which they tended was grounded in a habit of recognizing a common humanity, even if that humanity had to be reformed, that is, brought to Jesus by the preaching of the gospel. Accordingly, the humanitarian efforts of Protestants arose from Protestant cultivation of a sense of likeness between missionary and missionized, and that process in turn led recursively to missionaries' certainty that they were authorized, as the enlightened party among putative equals, to impose upon their hosts what they believed was best for them. Humanitarian aid not only abetted the survival of suffering populations. As a continuous performance of a certain kind of empathy, it embedded the project of conversion more securely in a trust that the Protestant responsibility was to make people who already were "like" Americans even more like them—in terms of not only religious piety but also social and political ideology.

At the same time, the end of the Cold War coincided with new vectors for information sharing, particularly about global humanitarian needs. With the rapid rise of the evangelical humanitarian organization World Vision (and its magazine) in the 1970s, and with the growing prevalence of short-term missions, which sent Americans abroad for anywhere from two weeks to two months (starting in the 1960s, but taking off in the 1980s and 1990s), information from abroad increasingly described a world shaped by inequality—one that needed repair as well as humanitarian aid. Young people returned from their trips, for example, and presented slide shows for their home churches about the needs of the people they had met. As such information was decentralized and in some sense democratized, the content of humanitarianism —both within and outside evangelical communities— also became more politicized.

The end of the twentieth century also saw the remarkable growth in the impact of U.S. Christian broadcasting abroad. Previous generations of pastors and preachers had certainly possessed a border-crossing capacity—via their traveling crusades and revivals or circulated cassette tapes or rebroadcasts of radio sermons. With the rise of satellite television, an ever-larger number of ministries developed global reach. The Pentecostal-oriented Trinity Broadcasting Network (TBN) was quickly a dominant player, distributing Christian programs though local stations, cable networks, satellite, and ultimately the Internet. Its lineup of U.S.-based evangelists (from Jim and Tammy Bakker in the early 1980s to Benny Hinn in the 1990s and Paula White in the 2010s) was, if anything, more popular outside than inside the United States. By

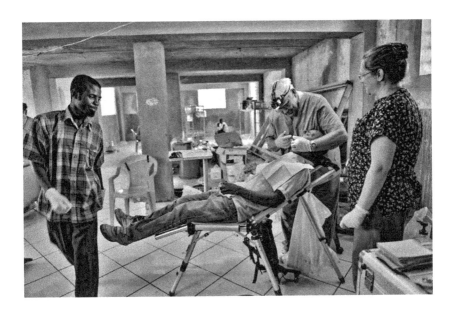

Modern missionaries often focused on humanitarian aid, which included a complex politics of empathy and assumptions about American benevolence. Here, Dr. James Jenkins, a dentist and member of the Florida Baptist Convention, works on a patient in a police station that was converted into a clinic by Rescue Mission, a Christian missionary group. Port-au-Prince, Haiti, February 9, 2010. *Lynsey Addario/Getty Images Reportage.*

2010, TBN had 6,000 stations worldwide, airing programs twenty-four hours a day.[76] Similarly, Pat Robertson's Christian Broadcasting Network made a global push in the 1990s and had broadcasts in eighty-nine languages by the turn of the century.[77] The preachers and teachers who had the most success in this new environment were not necessarily the white men who had dominated earlier generations. Instead, Black men and women such as T. D. Jakes, Carlton Pearson, and Juanita Bynum; white women such as Paula White and Joyce Meyer; and Latinx pastors such as Luis Palau have large audiences globally, representing both Americanized images of "success" and (in the case of African American or Latinx evangelists) a model of people of color as Christian leaders.[78]

It would be a misreading, however, to suggest any kind of unidirectional Americanization model for the global flows of evangelical media. A number of scholars have explored the complex ways that televangelism in the Global South in the twenty-first century is an assemblage, combining U.S.-produced content with content that is more distinctly local in its orientation. Much of the media is "glocal"—a mix of local or regional productions but American-derived grammars. (One scholar of televangelism in India describes the "Masala McGospel.")[79] Even if we consider the U.S.-based TBN, for example, the realities of a global network have long meant an international stable of on-air personalities, speaking in multiple languages and to audiences around the world.[80] By the turn of the twenty-first century, TBN faced serious competition from upstarts such as God TV and Daystar in English, Esperanza and Nación in Spanish, and scores of channels in Arabic, Russian, Vietnamese, and so on.

The rise of the Internet (and eventually Internet access via cell phone) democratized an already democratizing media environment. Pastors who were already helming megachurches in their own countries now could reach audiences across borders with nothing more than a YouTube channel: David Oyedepo of Winners' Chapel in Nigeria; Mensa Otabil, head of the International Central Gospel Church in Ghana; David Yonggi Cho, based in Seoul and pastor of the world's largest church (Yoido Full Gospel Church); Guatemala's Cash Luna (Casa de Dios); Brazil's Bishop Edir Macedo (Universal Church of the Kingdom of Good).[81] These changes in the media landscape meant that the message got out from a wide variety of evangelical actors, operating across borders and in ways that challenged any notion of cultural diffusion from the Global North to the Global South. Evangelicals in many parts of the world, including the United States, increasingly understood themselves as part of a global community with many centers.

Evangelicals also came to see the media value that emerged from projects to collect and deploy statistics about the waxing and waning of religious communities around the world. The "mediality" of statistics was grasped by evangelicals such as Ed Stetzer, the executive director of the Billy Graham Center for Evangelism. Stetzer beseeched evangelicals to recognize that "statistics help teach people," that "statistics help leaders make strategic decisions," and, most importantly, that "statistics help define reality."[82] Evangelicals since the 1930s, and with great energy during and after the Cold War, had been systematically constructing statistical profiles of Christian communities overseas. That effort was an extension of the project of linking information and media production.

The *World Christian Encyclopedia*, published in 1982, the creation of David B. Barrett, who eventually held the title of Research Professor of Missiometrics at Pat Robertson's Regent University in Virginia, gathered 1,000 pages of numbers bearing on Christian denominations worldwide.[83] The encyclopedia served as a resource for researchers interested in global religious demography, but additionally it modeled a certain kind of census taking for other aspiring religious demographers and, most importantly, prompted a reassessment of the value of censuses to the promotion of Christian missions worldwide. Gordon-Conwell Theological Seminary in Massachusetts subsequently invested in producing new iterations of the encyclopedia, publishing updated figures, offering fresh demographic categories, and developing informants through the World Christian Database. The database became a full-blown global census not only of Christianity but of other religions as well (and subsequently was known as the World Religion Database, or WRD).[84] It was a powerful tool for evangelical radio and television hosts and a go-to source for journalists who advocated for evangelical missions. It gave the appearance of muscle in evangelical reporting and advocating.

The new world order of media also mattered to evangelical politics and identity because of the ways it shaped evangelical affective orientations and identities, within and across national borders. The broad diffusion of media outlets and social media connectedness intensified long-standing trends toward nondenominationalism among evangelicals. The significance of parachurch organizations such as InterVarsity Christian Fellowship and multidenominational media like *Christianity Today* had long been a factor in blurring theological boundaries among evangelicals. Mass media only increased this trend. A given believer, whether in the United States or Nicaragua or Korea, might listen to a sermon by African American evangelist Juanita Bynum online, listen to a musical recording by the Australian-based Hillsong worship band, read one of the best-selling *Left Behind* novels written by U.S.-based apocalyptic authors Tim LaHaye and Jerry Jenkins, and turn to the Twitter feed of Nigerian pastor T. B. Joshua, all without paying much attention to theological distinctions among them. Recognizing in all of these cultural texts a kind of affective "rightness"—something that reads as faith in a familiar and satisfying register—audiences construct forms of believing that are emotionally rich and theologically thin. This is not an entirely new practice for evangelicals. Three decades ago the scholar Mark Noll complained about the "scandal of the evangelical mind" as being one of affect over theology.[85] The point here is that changes in the media landscape have created border crossings of all sorts, helping to construct an evangelical community that is both transnational and transdenominational.

The war on terror, immigration debates, new media technologies—all of these issues highlight the ways U.S. evangelicals after the Cold War wielded measurable political and ideological power. In addition, the period saw a dramatic increase in U.S. evangelical humanitarianism that emerged alongside and was tied to changes in the global economy. Evangelicals had long been willing to donate generously to support both evangelism and aid for those in need. Often, the two goals were understood to go hand-in-hand, with aid for the needy seen as either secondary, or as a precursor, to evangelism. But in the 1990s and into the twenty-first century, humanitarian aid became an ever more central part of evangelical action in the world, enabled in part by larger changes in the climate for development and humanitarian aid. Neoliberal models of aid meant that development and humanitarian assistance was increasingly handled by nongovernmental organizations rather than directly by governments. In 1990, for example, only 10 percent of the projects supported by the World Bank were run by NGOs. Most of the rest were run by governments. By 2001, NGOs received 40 percent of the World Bank's funds. The profusion of NGOs was nowhere more evident than in Christian humanitarian and development organizations. Samaritan's Purse, run by Billy Graham's son Franklin Graham, was a relatively small organization in the early 1990s. By 2015, it had a budget of $520 million, making it the twenty-fifth largest charity in the United States.[86]

Of the evangelical groups, World Vision was by far the largest and most influential and the most dramatically changed by the NGO surge. It had begun as a missionary organization and until the 1970s basically operated through "adopt-a-child" fundraising programs that primarily supported missionary orphanages. Beginning in 1970, World Vision began to develop new ways of drawing attention to world hunger, and as a result, its income increased dramatically over the decade, from $4 million to $94 million. After the 1984 Ethiopian famine, donations poured into World Vision and other relief organizations. By then, World Vision had begun to invest more in programs that not only offered temporary assistance but also built local capacity—drilling wells and introducing new agricultural techniques, for example. The organization did not stop providing relief or humanitarian aid, but it combined those programs with a larger development agenda. In the first decades of the twenty-first century, World Vision expanded even more rapidly. In 2000, it was already an impressively large organization, with a budget of $886 million. In 2014, the organization's expenditures were $2.8 billion, 48 percent of which was spent in Africa. It had offices in 100 countries, with 40,000 employees. In addition, its new microfinance arm, Vision Fund, provided 1.5 million small loans totaling $900 million. This made World Vision a behemoth in the world of international NGOs, an economic powerhouse whose projects and perspectives would shape both humanitarianism and development globally.[87]

Evangelicals also were deeply involved in global U.S. policy on HIV/ AIDS. When President George W. Bush launched the President's Emergency Plan for AIDS Relief (PEPFAR) in 2004, he did so with significant U.S. evangelical support. This was a change. When HIV/AIDS originally emerged in the 1980s, U.S. evangelicals (like many other Americans) had largely blamed the victims.[88] As late as 2001, an internal World Vision survey found that most of the organization's supporters did not want to donate to AIDS programs in Africa. But starting in the early 2000s, California pastor Rick Warren spearheaded a campaign to encourage American evangelicals to respond compassionately to HIV/AIDS, and particularly to support treatment programs in Africa, where the disease was killing millions of people. Under President Bush, and with strong support from both U.S. and some African evangelical leaders, the PEPFAR program provided generous funding for treatment, but its funding for prevention programs was deeply skewed: because of the mandates tied to the program, approximately two-thirds of HIV/AIDS education programs aimed at preventing sexual transmission in Africa were focused on teaching abstinence, rather than on condom use, as the safest way of preventing HIV/AIDS.[89]

This policy allowed American evangelicals, most of whom held quite conservative views on gender and sexuality, to shape a key apparatus of U.S. foreign aid. It also meant that U.S. policy was implicitly and explicitly linked to the anti-LGBTQ+ activism that was on the rise in many parts of Africa. The irony, perhaps, was that this position carried a patina of internationalist racial liberalism: American evangelicals and the U.S. state both could claim to be supporting policies that African leaders wanted, particularly in states that were hard-hit by HIV/AIDS, such as Uganda, Nigeria, Kenya, and Rwanda. (South Africa, equally hard-hit, had liberal state policies on LGBTQ+ acceptance, although those policies were controversial among South African Pentecostals and evangelicals.)[90] As Lydia Boyd describes in this volume, U.S. evangelical support for HIV/AIDS funding in places such as Uganda also linked American visions of evangelical "compassion" with specific rhetorics and ideologies of "personal responsibility." Ugandan Christians often found the expectations associated with such humanitarianism to be controversial, in conflict with locally meaningful expectations about moral obligations and reciprocity.

Finally, but perhaps most fundamentally, post–Cold War evangelicalism tied itself ever more closely to capitalist modernity. American Protestantism had of course long been linked to capitalism. Well before Max Weber offered his famous analysis in *The Protestant Ethic and the Spirit of Capitalism* (1905),

American Protestants had affixed their particular forms of faith practice to the twin engines of self-discipline and entrepreneurialism. In the nineteenth century, Protestants often narrated their own austerity. As one woman described her elementary school years, she was "penetrated through every fibre of thought with the idea that idleness is a disgrace. It was taught with the alphabet and the spelling book; it was enforced by precept and example, at home and abroad; and it is to be confessed that it did sometimes haunt the childish imagination almost mercilessly."[91] In the Calvinist model that undergirded a significant component of this culture, wealth was seen as a sign of God's grace (Calvinists spoke of being the "elect"), but spending and display were morally suspect.

However, Calvinism was not the only strand of Protestantism, nor the only tendency of capitalism. American Christians were equally able to wield their enthusiasm for the emerging consumer culture of the twentieth century in the context of their faith. By the 1920s, American Protestantism was as much about emotional experience, affective satisfaction, and self-fashioning as it was about discipline and the accumulation of wealth. This was the opposite of Weber's notion of the Calvinist "spirit" of modern capitalism, but, then again, capitalism was changing, too, and the rise of a consumer economy meant a different kind of modern subject. Protestantism in the United States had a strong strain of small-scale entrepreneurialism, with Methodist revivalism, nondenominationalism, and Baptist anti-creedalism playing an outsized role in the construction of a sense of consumer choice in matters of religion. Then too there emerged increasingly personalized narratives of faith—a sense of Jesus as one's friend, a manly and handsome ally, as promoted in popular literature, sermons, and music.[92]

This sense of choosing affective experiences meant that, by the 1970s, there was a great deal more movement among denominations—more church shopping—and a progressively media-saturated set of Protestant options. The "spiritual marketplace" was now fully acknowledged, if frequently decried. To some, the rise of megachurches in the 1980s seemed to be about the success of a certain consumer-oriented model of church formation. To others, it was a recognition that, given the option, many people would choose passionate, charismatic, and dynamic forms of faith practice. But this too was part of the capitalist ethos: the industrial economy produced products, and products needed both producers and consumers.[93]

The capitalist ethos applied particularly well to Pentecostalism and the brand of prosperity-oriented preaching that was increasingly associated with it. In the twenty-first century, Pentecostal churches in the Global South were growing faster than any other subset of Christianity. Globally, some of the most important megachurches were prosperity churches, and their names sometimes suggested that: the Winners' Chapel in Lagos, Nigeria; the Church of Signs and Wonders in India's Punjab region; Faith World in Orlando (now defunct). Often, they operated in the hybrid model that combined some American-style grammars with distinctively local values and beliefs.

As a number of scholars of Pentecostalism and the prosperity gospel have pointed out, these churches are often *not* associated with the highly wealthy or privileged but with the poor or those who are racially oppressed. The historically Black Church of God in Christ is one of the two largest Pentecostal churches in the United States (the other is the Assemblies of God), and, globally, the prosperity gospel is by far the largest variant of Pentecostalism, thriving in slums and middle-class communities alike. The sometimes ostentatious wealth of the church leadership is understood by the parishioners to model their aspirations rather than their reality. In the lives of ordinary believers, prosperity and health are often contextual: enough money to make rent, healing from an illness. Marla Frederick has described this form of prosperity preaching as a kind of theology of racial uplift. And it makes sense that it would proliferate in a context of rapidly increasing global inequality. As it became clear that the twenty-first century would be marked by a great division in wealth, health, and safety—with the global rich absorbing ever more of the capital, consumer goods, health care, and environmental resources—surely, the prosperity gospel seemed to say, God would not want his people to be on the starving end of a globally bifurcated economy.[94]

The growing embrace of the prosperity gospel was not the only indication of the increasing merger of mission and markets. When the Cold War ended, evangelicals in the United States and globally were well positioned to take advantage of the neoliberal economic program of privatization, devolution, and retrenchment that progressively informed government policy. There *were* challenges to the linkage between new forms of consumer capitalism and evangelism—a sly ad in U.S. evangelical magazines in the 1990s promised to explain "why the devil takes Visa." But the larger sense among American evangelicals was that the Cold War victory was also a victory for the faith—an opportunity for a great missionary outreach and the proof that capitalism in some form was to be the soil in which global Christianity flowered. Capitalism no longer had competition as a global model, and the evangelical nexus of faith-culture-economics was a great beneficiary.

The encounter with foreign people in the context of decolonization, mission work, or humanitarian aid thus frequently translated into a reinforcement of norms and values aligned with capitalism. As John Corrigan maintains, the gospel of Christianity could ultimately not be disaggregated from the gospel of capitalism. As much as religious narratives emphasized kinship with "unreached peoples" and the cultivation of feeling for people abroad, these sentiments were ultimately generated within a particular cultural setting infused with liberal and neoliberal affective concepts. These centered on heteronormative marriage, romantic individualism, and Christian views of proper sexuality that, in turn, were regarded as apposite for maximizing accumulation, productivity, and entrepreneurialism.

Conclusion

In the United States, media and scholarly commentators alike often talk about "white American evangelicalism" as if its parameters were obvious and static, with national borders and political boundaries both equally solidified. And, in a certain way, that is precisely how some of the leaders of today's religious right would like to be defined. The supporters of "Evangelicals for Trump"—enthusiastic, angry, refusing to admit their candidate's defeat— embody precisely the religious nationalism that evangelicals writ large are assumed to support.

But evangelicalism, as this collection shows, encompasses a broad range of people who do not always even recognize each other as fellow travelers. In developing this project, the three editors discussed the vexed question of whether "U.S. evangelicalism" is any longer even a viable category of analysis. Scholars and pundits have defined evangelicals variously as those who claim to be "born again" or as Protestants who affirm a set of beliefs about the authority of the Bible, the need for salvation through Jesus alone, and a focus on conversion. Other observers have expanded or altered that theological focus to define evangelicals through sociological categories (often focusing on white conservatives) or experientially, with attention to activist, energetic, sometimes charismatic forms of faith expression. As a term of self-identification, "evangelical" has waxed and waned across the decades—from periods in the nineteenth century when most Protestants could comfortably have been grouped under its theological rubric, to sharp divisions at midcentury, to the more capacious situation today, where the term covers a broad range of theologies and terms of self-identification. White U.S. evangelicals today might describe themselves as Baptist or nondenominational or even just "Christian." Asian Americans or Latinos are more likely to use the term "evangelical" than African Americans, and people in nondenominational churches might have more ties to the broader evangelical world than Southern Baptists or members of the Church of God in Christ. And any boundaries that denominations aim to uphold are increasingly breached by the role of the media, where Pentecostals, Southern Baptists, and conservative Presbyterians all draw audiences who may not recognize—or care—that they have distinctly different theologies. The same is true of parachurch organizations, such as InterVarsity Christian Fellowship or Campus Crusade (now Cru), which have increased the networked and nondenominational character of evangelical life.

Our contributors do not all share the same assumptions about what defines their subject. But all of us recognize that, whatever else U.S.-based evangelicals are, they are not entirely bounded by the nation-state. In the chapters that follow, we see Coptic Christians from Egypt engaging white conservatives in Washington; Black Americans from the AME Church missionizing in the Caribbean; Latin Americans leading the way for an American evangelical left; and conservative white evangelicals trying to overthrow the government of Nicaragua. Our goal is not to staff the borders of who should be included in studies of evangelicals but to show the complexity that comes when global contexts are taken fully into account.

The U.S. empire has taken a number of forms over its 250-year history: from formal control of territory to economic power to cultural dominance and institutional control. In a similar way, U.S. evangelicals have long dominated an empire of faith, crossing borders and shaping a broad range of institutions. Indeed, as we have discussed here, these two forms of empire have not infrequently operated in concert. As Axel Schäfer suggests in his contribution, the substance of both evangelicalism and U.S. foreign policy is, to a certain extent, located in their interrelationship, and both the nation-state and evangelical religion were highly unstable political forms that required complex and sustained negotiations. In the twenty-first century, however, both the U.S. state and U.S. evangelicals are waning as global forces, in decline relative to emerging powers and a reshaped global system. This shift in the location of evangelicalism is significant, even as the power of U.S. money and resources, as well as the long arm of the U.S. state, still fundamentally shapes the global evangelical community. The question that emerges now is how the long history of evangelicals' global faith and worldly power can help us understand the role of religion and politics on the global stage in the coming decades.

Notes

1. The boomerang effect of missions is discussed in David A. Hollinger, *Protestants Abroad: How Missionaries Tried to Change the World but Changed America* (Princeton, NJ: Princeton University Press, 2017).

2. Nicholas D. Kristof, "Opinion | Following God Abroad," *New York Times*, May 21, 2002, www.nytimes.com/2002/05/21/opinion/following-god-abroad.html.

3. Yeganeh Torbati, "How Mike Pence's Office Meddled in Foreign Aid to Reroute Money to Favored Christian Groups," ProPublica, November 6, 2019, www.propublica.org/article/how-mike-pences-office-meddled-in-foreign-aid-to-reroute-money-to-favored-christian-groups; Melani McAlister, "Evangelical Populist Internationalism and the Politics of Persecution," *Review of Faith and International Affairs* (September 2019): 105–17.

4. Heather D. Curtis, *Holy Humanitarians: American Evangelicals and Global Aid* (Cambridge, MA: Harvard University Press, 2018), 58.

5. Thomas S. Kidd and Barry G. Hankins, *Baptists in America: A History* (New York: Oxford University Press, 2018), 179.

6. Jonathan P. Herzog, *The Spiritual-Industrial Complex: America's Religious Battle against Communism in the Early Cold War* (New York: Oxford University Press, 2011).

7. This often very fine scholarship is too vast to do justice to here but includes Frances Fitzgerald, *The Evangelicals: The Struggle to Shape America* (New York: Simon and Schuster, 2017); Susan Friend Harding, *The Book of Jerry Falwell: Fundamentalist Language and Politics* (Princeton, NJ: Princeton University Press, 2001); Angela M. Lahr, *Millennial Dreams and Apocalyptic Nightmares: The Cold War Origins of Political Evangelicalism* (New York: Oxford University Press, 2007); Michael Lienesch, *Redeeming America: Piety and Politics in the New Christian Right* (Chapel Hill: University of North Carolina Press, 1993); William C. Martin, *With God on Our Side: The Rise of the Religious Right in America* (New York: Broadway Books, 1996); and Daniel K. Williams, *God's Own Party: The Making of the Christian Right* (New York: Oxford University Press, 2010).

8. Michael Lienesch, *In the Beginning: Fundamentalism, the Scopes Trial, and the Making of the Antievolution Movement* (Chapel Hill: University of North Carolina Press, 2009).

9. Axel R. Schäfer, *Countercultural Conservatives: American Evangelicalism from the Postwar Revival to the New Christian Right* (Madison: University of Wisconsin Press, 2011); Molly Worthen, *Apostles of Reason: The Crisis of Authority in American Evangelicalism* (New York: Oxford University Press, 2013); William Martin, *A Prophet with Honor: The Billy Graham Story* (New York: W. Morrow, 1991).

10. Daniel Cox and Robert P. Jones, "America's Changing Religious Identity," PRRI, September 6, 2017, www.prri.org/research/american-religious-landscape-christian-religiously-unaffiliated/.

11. On the transnational turn in scholarship on evangelicals—in addition to the work cited in the rest of this introduction, see Andrew Preston, "Evangelical Internationalism: A Conservative Worldview for the Age of Globalization," in *The Right Side of the Sixties: Reexamining Conservatism's Decade of Transformation*, ed. Laura Jane Gifford and Daniel K. Williams (New York: Palgrave Macmillan, 2012), 221–42; Christopher Gehrz, "The Global Reflex: Toward a Transnational Turn in Evangelical Historiography,"

Fides et Historia 47, no. 1 (2015): 107; Kendrick Oliver, Uta A. Balbier, Hans Krabben-dam, and Axel R. Schäfer, "Special Issue: Exploring the Global History of American Evangelicalism Introduction," *Journal of American Studies* 51, no. 4 (2017): 1019–42; and Robert Wuthnow, *Boundless Faith: The Global Outreach of American Churches* (Berkeley: University of California Press, 2009).

12. There is a great deal of important work in missionaries and empire, including Allan Anderson, *Spreading Fires: The Missionary Nature of Early Pentecostalism* (Marynoll, NY: Orbis Books, 2007); James T. Campbell, *Songs of Zion: The African Methodist Episcopal Church in the United States and South Africa* (New York: Oxford University Press, 1995); Jay Riley Case, *An Unpredictable Gospel: American Evangelicals and World Christianity, 1812–1920* (New York: Oxford University Press, 2012); Jean Comaroff and John L. Comaroff, *Of Revelation and Revolution*, Volume 1: *Christianity, Colonialism, and Consciousness in South Africa*, and Volume 2: *The Dialectics of Modernity on a South African Frontier* (Chicago: University of Chicago Press, 1991); Emily Conroy-Krutz, *Christian Imperialism: Converting the World in the Early American Republic* (Ithaca, NY: Cornell University Press, 2015); Elisabeth Engel, *Encountering Empire: African American Missionaries in Colonial Africa, 1900–1939* (Stuttgart: Franz Steiner Verlag, 2015); Norman Etherington, ed., *Missions and Empire* (New York: Oxford University Press, 2008); Kevin Grant, *A Civilised Savagery: Britain and the New Slaveries in Africa, 1884–1926* (New York: Routledge, 2004); Patricia R. Hill, *The World Their Household: The American Woman's Foreign Mission Movement and Cultural Transformation, 1870–1920* (Ann Arbor: University of Michigan Press, 1984); Jane Hunter, *The Gospel of Gentility: American Women Missionaries in Turn-of-the-Century China* (New Haven, CT: Yale University Press, 1984); William R. Hutchison, *Errand to the World: American Protestant Thought and Foreign Missions* (Chicago: University of Chicago Press, 1987); Sylvia Jacobs, ed., *Black Americans and the Missionary Movement in Africa* (Westport, CT: Greenwood Press, 1982); Paul S. Landau, *The Realm of the Word: Language, Gender, and Christianity in a Southern African Kingdom* (London: J. Currey, 1995); Ussama Makdisi, *Artillery of Heaven: American Missionaries and the Failed Conversion of the Middle East* (Ithaca, NY: Cornell University Press, 2008); Lamin Sanneh, *Abolitionists Abroad: American Blacks and the Making of Modern West Africa* (Cambridge, MA: Harvard University Press, 1999); Heather J. Sharkey, *Living with Colonialism: Nationalism and Culture in the Anglo-Egyptian Sudan* (Berkeley: University of California Press, 2003); and Dana L. Robert, ed., *Converting Colonialism: Visions and Realities in Mission History, 1706–1914* (Grand Rapids, MI: Eerdmans, 2008).

13. Emily S. Rosenberg, *Spreading the American Dream: American Economic and Cultural Expansion, 1890–1945* (New York: Hill and Wang, 1982), 28; Chinua Achebe, *Things Fall Apart* (1958; repr., New York: Anchor, 1994).

14. Quoted in Makdisi, *Artillery of Heaven*, 24.

15. See, in particular, Katherine D. Moran, *The Imperial Church: Catholic Founding Fathers and United States Empire* (Ithaca, NY: Cornell University Press, 2020); Conroy-Krutz, *Christian Imperialism*; Case, *Unpredictable Gospel*; Makdisi, *Artillery of Heaven*; and Peggy Pascoe, *Relations of Rescue: The Search for Female Moral Authority in the American West, 1874–1939* (New York: Oxford University Press, 1990).

16. Amy Kaplan, *The Anarchy of Empire in the Making of U.S. Culture* (Cambridge, MA: Harvard University Press, 2002).

17. On the Philippines, see also Paul A. Kramer, *The Blood of Government: Race, Empire, the United States, and the Philippines* (Chapel Hill: University of North Carolina Press, 2006).

18. Dennis C. Dickerson, *The African Methodist Episcopal Church: A History* (Cambridge: Cambridge University Press, 2020); Campbell, *Songs of Zion*.

19. Grant, *Civilised Savagery*, 39–78; David Lagergren, *Mission and State in the Congo: A Study of the Relations between Protestant Missions and the Congo Independent State Authorities with Special Reference to the Equator District, 1885–1903*, Studia Missionalia Upsaliensia 13 (Lund, Swed.: Gleerup, 1970). This discussion of Congo is drawn from Melani McAlister, *The Kingdom of God Has No Borders: A Global History of American Evangelicals* (New York: Oxford University Press, 2018), 33–37.

20. James T. Campbell, *Middle Passages: African American Journeys to Africa, 1787–2005* (New York: Penguin Press, 2006), 136–87. On the larger role of African Americans in the Congo reform movement, see the discussion of Booker T. Washington's involvement in Ira Dworkin, *Congo Love Song: African American Culture and the Crisis of the Colonial State* (Chapel Hill: University of North Carolina Press, 2017). See also Adam Hochschild, *King Leopold's Ghost: A Story of Greed, Terror, and Heroism in Colonial Africa* (Boston: Houghton Mifflin, 1999), 185–308.

21. Raffaella Perin, "Protestant Missionaries and the Concept of Martyrdom during the Boxer Rebellion," *Studi e Materiali di Storia delle Religioni* 84 (2018): 377–92.

22. See also Curtis, *Holy Humanitarians*. These investments were part of a larger cultural fascination with other places and their mysteries at the turn of the twentieth century. See Kristin L. Hoganson, *Consumers' Imperium: The Global Production of American Domesticity, 1865–1920* (Chapel Hill: University of North Carolina Press, 2007); Mari Yoshihara, *Embracing the East: White Women and American Orientalism* (New York: Oxford University Press, 2002); and Marianna Torgovnick, *Gone Primitive: Savage Intellects, Modern Lives* (Chicago: University of Chicago Press, 1991).

23. See also Curtis, *Holy Humanitarians*. On "domestic cosmopolitanism," see Hoganson, *Consumers' Imperium*.

24. Quoted in Hollinger, *Protestants Abroad*, 62.

25. Hollinger, 69.

26. Uta A. Balbier, *Altar Call in Europe: Billy Graham, Mass Evangelism, and the Cold-War West* (New York: Oxford University Press, 2021); Martin, *Prophet with Honor*; Grant Wacker, *America's Pastor: Billy Graham and the Shaping of a Nation* (Cambridge, MA: Belknap Press of Harvard University Press, 2014).

27. Gerald H. Anderson, "American Protestants in Pursuit of Mission: 1886–1986," *International Bulletin of Missionary Research* 12, no. 3 (July 1988): 108–10; Joel A. Carpenter, *Revive Us Again: The Reawakening of American Fundamentalism* (New York: Oxford University Press, 1997), 185.

28. Andrew Preston, *Sword of the Spirit, Shield of Faith: Religion in American War and Diplomacy* (New York: Knopf, 2012), 479–81.

29. "Christianity or Communism," *Hour of Decision*, 1953, quoted in Martin, *Prophet with Honor*, chap. 10.

30. Heather Hendershot, *What's Fair on the Air? Cold War Right-Wing Broadcasting and the Public Interest* (Chicago: University of Chicago Press, 2011), 185.

31. Laura A. Belmonte, *Selling the American Way: U.S. Propaganda and the Cold War*, illustrated ed. (Philadelphia: University of Pennsylvania Press, 2010).

32. Scholarship on U.S. extra-continental empire before World War II is extensive and growing. Recent work includes Jason M. Colby, *The Business of Empire: United Fruit, Race, and U.S. Expansion in Central America* (Ithaca, NY: Cornell University Press, 2011); Greg Grandin, *Fordlandia: The Rise and Fall of Henry Ford's Forgotten Jungle City* (London: Picador, 2010); A. G. Hopkins, *American Empire: A Global History* (Princeton, NJ: Princeton University Press, 2018); and Daniel Immerwahr, *How to Hide an Empire: A History of the Greater United States* (New York: Farrar, Straus and Giroux, 2019).

33. Immerwahr, *How to Hide an Empire*. Of course, this did not preclude massive military intervention and violence, including in Vietnam and Southeast Asia, Central America, and the Middle East.

34. Eric S. Fife and Arthur Glasser, *Missions in Crisis: Rethinking Missionary Strategy* (London: InterVarsity Press, 1961), 18.

35. Axel R. Schäfer, "Evangelical Global Engagement and the American State after World War II," *Journal of American Studies* 51, no. 4 (2017): 1069–94.

36. Williams, letter to the editor, *Pittsburgh Courier*, March 19, 1961, sec. 2, 26, quoted in James H. Meriwether, *Proudly We Can Be Africans: Black Americans and Africa, 1935–1961* (Chapel Hill: University of North Carolina Press, 2002), 232. See also McAlister, *Kingdom of God Has No Borders*, 42.

37. Curtis Freeman, "'Never Had I Been So Blind': W. A. Criswell's 'Change' on Racial Segregation," *Journal of Southern Religion* 10 (2007): 1–2. Freeman is quoting from the transcript of Criswell's speech the next day before the South Carolina assembly, when he repeated his sermon, minus the biblical references. See also David Christopher Roach, "The Southern Baptist Convention and Civil Rights, 1954–1995" (PhD diss., Southern Baptist Theological Seminary, 2009), 33–40.

38. David L. Chappell, *A Stone of Hope: Prophetic Religion and the Death of Jim Crow* (Chapel Hill: University of North Carolina Press, 2005); Alan Scot Willis, *All According to God's Plan: Southern Baptist Missions and Race, 1945–1970* (Lexington: University Press of Kentucky, 2004); Mark Newman, *Getting Right with God: Southern Baptists and Desegregation, 1945–1995* (Tuscaloosa: University of Alabama Press, 2001); McAlister, *Kingdom of God Has No Borders*, 17–29.

39. Anthea D. Butler, *White Evangelical Racism: The Politics of Morality in America* (Chapel Hill: University of North Carolina Press, 2021), 2. See also Jemar Tisby and Lecrae Moore, *The Color of Compromise: The Truth about the American Church's Complicity in Racism* (Grand Rapids, MI: Zondervan, 2019).

40. Claude E. Welch, "Mobilizing Morality: The World Council of Churches and Its Program to Combat Racism, 1969–1994," *Human Rights Quarterly* 23, no. 4 (November 2001): 863–910; Thomas A. Mulhall, "Making All Things New: Martin Luther King Jr., the 1968 Civil Rights Movement, and the World Council of Churches," *Ecumenical Review* 70, no. 2 (2018): 247; Annegreth Schilling, "The Ecumenical Movement and 1968: The Uppsala Assembly as the Beginning of a New Era?," *Ecumenical Review* 70, no. 2 (2018): 194–215.

41. Paul Thomas Chamberlin, *The Cold War's Killing Fields: Rethinking the Long Peace* (New York: Harper, 2018), 1. See also Odd Arne Westad, *The Global Cold War:*

Third World Interventions and the Making of Our Times (Cambridge: Cambridge University Press, 2007).

42. This point is also made by David R. Swartz, *Facing West: American Evangelicals in an Age of World Christianity* (New York: Oxford University Press, 2020).

43. Brantley W. Gasaway, *Progressive Evangelicals and the Pursuit of Social Justice* (Chapel Hill: University of North Carolina Press, 2014); David C. Kirkpatrick, *A Gospel for the Poor: Global Social Christianity and the Latin American Evangelical Left* (Philadelphia: University of Pennsylvania Press, 2019); David R. Swartz, *Moral Minority: The Evangelical Left in an Age of Conservatism* (Philadelphia: University of Pennsylvania Press, 2012).

44. Quoted in Lahr, *Millennial Dreams*, 157.

45. Victor Marchetti and John D. Marks, *The CIA and the Cult of Intelligence* (New York: Knopf, 1974).

46. James Robison, "Spy Role of Missionaries Told," *Chicago Tribune*, August 2, 1975.

47. Marjorie Hyer, "Clergy Wary of CIA Approaches," *Washington Post*, August 5, 1975.

48. Open letter, Stanley Mooneyham to Gerald Ford, published in *World Vision*, March 1976, 3.

49. Wesley Granberg-Michaelson, "CIA and Missionaries: Half a Loaf," *Sojourners*, May–June 1976, https://sojo.net/magazine/may-june-1976/cia-and-missionaries-half-loaf; "CIA Reverses Policy in Relation to Missionaries," *Christian Leaders*, July 20, 1976, 14.

50. Preston, *Sword of the Spirit*, 565–80; Lauren Frances Turek, *To Bring the Good News to All Nations: Evangelical Influence on Human Rights and U.S. Foreign Relations* (Ithaca, NY: Cornell University Press, 2020), 107–16.

51. Schäfer, *Countercultural Conservatives*, esp. chap. 4.

52. Ronald Reagan, remarks at annual National Association of Evangelicals convention, quoted in Angela Lahr, "American Evangelical Politics during the Cold War," *Oxford Research Encyclopedia of Religion*, 2020.

53. See also Turek, *To Bring the Good News*.

54. Tal Zalmanovich, "'What Is Needed Is an Ecumenical Act of Solidarity': The World Council of Churches, the 1969 Notting Hill Consultation on Racism, and the Anti-Apartheid Struggle," *Safundi* 20, no. 2 (2019): 174–92; Ian Macqueen, "Ecumenism and the Global Anti-Apartheid Struggle: The World Council of Churches' Special Fund in South Africa and Botswana, 1970–75," *Historia* 62, no. 2 (2017): 87–111; Tristan Anne Borer, *Challenging the State: Churches as Political Actors in South Africa, 1980–1994* (Notre Dame, IN: University of Notre Dame Press, 1998).

55. Robert Kinloch Massie, *Loosing the Bonds: The United States and South Africa in the Apartheid Years* (New York: Nan A. Talese, 1997).

56. Turek, *To Bring the Good News*; McAlister, *Kingdom of God Has No Borders*.

57. Robert Reese, "John Gatu and the Moratorium on Missionaries," *Missiology: An International Review* 42, no. 3 (July 1, 2014): 245–56. See also Swartz, *Facing West*.

58. Philip Jenkins, *The New Faces of Christianity: Believing the Bible in the Global South* (New York: Oxford University Press, 2006).

59. Kate Bowler, *Blessed: A History of the American Prosperity Gospel* (New York: Oxford University Press, 2013).

60. Paul Gifford, *Ghana's New Christianity: Pentecostalism in a Globalizing African Economy* (Bloomington: Indiana University Press, 2004); Steve Brouwer, Paul Gifford, and Susan D. Rose, *Exporting the American Gospel: Global Christian Fundamentalism* (New York: Routledge, 2013).

61. Ogbu Kalu, *African Pentecostalism: An Introduction* (New York: Oxford University Press, 2008), 87–167.

62. Mark Philip Bradley, *The World Reimagined: Americans and Human Rights in the Twentieth Century* (New York: Cambridge University Press, 2016); Sarah B. Snyder, *From Selma to Moscow: How Human Rights Activists Transformed U.S. Foreign Policy* (New York: Columbia University Press, 2018); Barbara Keys, *Reclaiming American Virtue: The Human Rights Revolution of the 1970s* (Cambridge, MA: Harvard University Press, 2014).

63. See Hannah Waits, "Missionary-Minded: American Evangelicals and Power in a Postcolonial World, 1945–2000" (PhD diss., University of California Berkeley, 2019), https://escholarship.org/uc/item/8s33m84t.

64. J. Kwabena Asamoah-Gyadu, "An African Pentecostal on Mission in Eastern Europe: The Church of the 'Embassy of God' in the Ukraine," *Pneuma* 27, no. 2 (Fall 2005): 297–321.

65. Gregorio Bettiza, *Finding Faith in Foreign Policy: Religion and American Diplomacy in a Postsecular World* (New York: Oxford University Press, 2020).

66. McAlister, *Kingdom of God Has No Borders*, 144–74; Allen Hertzke, *Freeing God's Children: The Unlikely Alliance for Global Human Rights* (Lanham, MD: Rowman and Littlefield, 2004); Elizabeth Castelli, "Praying for the Persecuted Church: US Christian Activism in the Global Arena," *Journal of Human Rights* 4, no. 3 (September 2005): 321–51; John Corrigan, *Religious Intolerance, America, and the World: A History of Forgetting and Remembering* (Chicago: University of Chicago Press, 2020).

67. Nahal Toosi, "Brownback, No Longer in Kansas, Has 'Big' Plans as Religious Freedom Envoy," Politico, May 28, 2018, https://politi.co/2kxfCvN.

68. McAlister, "Evangelical Populist Internationalism and the Politics of Persecution."

69. Pew Research Center, "Religion in Latin America," *Pew Research Center's Religion & Public Life Project* (blog), November 13, 2014, www.pewforum.org/2014/11/13/religion -in-latin-america.

70. Pew Research Center, "The Shifting Religious Identity of Latinos in the United States," May 7, 2014, www.pewforum.org/2014/05/07/the-shifting-religious-identity-of -latinos-in-the-united-states; Pew Research Center, "Religion in Latin America"; Larry L. Hunt, "Hispanic Protestantism in the United States: Trends by Decade and Generation," *Social Forces* 77, no. 4 (1999): 1601–24; Mark T. Mulder, Aida I. Ramos, and Gerardo Martí, *Latino Protestants in America: Growing and Diverse* (Lanham, MD: Rowman and Littlefield, 2017).

71. Janelle Wong, "The Evangelical Vote and Race in the 2016 Presidential Election," *Journal of Race, Ethnicity and Politics* 3, no. 1 (March 2018): 81–106; Janelle Wong, Kathy Rim, and Haven Perez, "Protestant Churches and Conservative Politics: Latinos and Asians in the United States," in *Civic Hopes and Political Realities: Immigrants,*

Community Organizations, and Political Engagement, ed. S. Karthick Ramakrishnan and
Irene Bloemraad (New York: Russell Sage Foundation, 2008), 271–99.

72. Some 61 percent of Koreans in the United States are evangelical. Pew Research
Center, "Asian Americans: A Mosaic of Faiths," July 19, 2012, www.pewforum.org/2012
/07/19/asian-americans-a-mosaic-of-faiths-overview/.

73. Jane H. Hong, "In Search of a History of Asian American Evangelicals,"
Religion Compass 13, no. 11 (2019): e12347; Tim Stafford, "The Tiger in the Academy,"
ChristianityToday.com, April 1, 2006, www.christianitytoday.com/ct/2006/april/33.70
.html; Melani McAlister, "A Kind of Homelessness: Evangelicals of Color in the Trump
Era," Religion and Politics, August 7, 2018, https://religionandpolitics.org/2018/08/07
/a-kind-of-homelessness-evangelicals-of-color-in-the-trump-era.

74. Evangelical Immigration Table, "Evangelical Leaders Urge Trump to
Keep Families Together," Evangelical Immigration Table, June 1, 2018, https://
evangelicalimmigrationtable.com/evangelical-leaders-urge-president-trump-to-keep
-families-together; Elizabeth Dias, "Evangelical Leaders Lament Border Separations,
but Stand behind Trump," New York Times, June 20, 2018, sec. U.S., www.nytimes.com
/2018/06/20/us/politics/evangelicals-immigration-trump.html.

75. Heather Hendershot, Shaking the World for Jesus: Media and Conservative
Evangelical Culture (Chicago: University of Chicago Press, 2004); Curtis, Holy Human-
itarians; Marla F. Frederick, Between Sundays: Black Women and Everyday Struggles of
Faith (Berkeley: University of California Press, 2003); Matthew Avery Sutton, Aimee
Semple McPherson and the Resurrection of Christian America (Cambridge, MA: Harvard
University Press, 2009); Linda Kintz, Between Jesus and the Market: The Emotions That
Matter in Right-Wing America (Durham, NC: Duke University Press, 1997); Jonathan
L. Walton, Watch This! The Ethics and Aesthetics of Black Televangelism (New York: New
York University Press, 2009); Harding, Book of Jerry Falwell; Eileen Luhr, Witnessing
Suburbia: Conservatives and Christian Youth Culture (Berkeley: University of Califor-
nia Press, 2009); Amy Johnson Frykholm, Rapture Culture: Left Behind in Evangelical
America (New York: Oxford University Press, 2007); David W. Stowe, No Sympathy for
the Devil: Christian Pop Music and the Transformation of American Evangelicalism (Chapel
Hill: University of North Carolina Press, 2011); Lerone A. Martin, Preaching on Wax: The
Phonograph and the Shaping of Modern African American Religion (New York: New York
University Press, 2014).

76. Justin Wilford, "Televangelical Publics: Secularized Publicity and Privacy in the
Trinity Broadcasting Network," Cultural Geographies 16, no. 4 (2009): 505–24.

77. Michael Serazio, "Geopolitical Proselytizing in the Marketplace for Loyalties:
Rethinking the Global Gospel of American Christian Broadcasting," Journal of Media
and Religion 8, no. 1 (January 2009): 40–54.

78. Marla Frederick, Colored Television: American Religion Gone Global (Stanford, CA:
Stanford University Press, 2016).

79. Jonathan D. James, McDonaldisation, Masala McGospel and Om Economics: Televangelism in Contemporary India (New Delhi: Sage Publications, 2010).

80. Victoria Meng, "Everyday a Miracle: History according to Trinity Broadcasting
Network (TBN)," Journal of Religion and Popular Culture 21, no. 3 (Fall 2009): 1–29.

81. See the multiple articles on Christian televangelism and outreach in Pradip
Ninan Thomas and Philip Lee, eds., Global and Local Televangelism (London: Palgrave

Macmillan, 2012). On Oyedepo: Paul Gifford, "Healing in African Pentecostalism: The 'Victorious Living' of David Oyedepo," in *Global Pentecostal and Charismatic Healing*, ed. Candy Gunther Brown (New York: Oxford University Press, 2011), 251–66. On Cho: Sean Kim, "Reenchanted: Divine Healing in Korean Protestantism," in *Global Pentecostal and Charismatic Healing*, ed. Candy Gunther Brown (New York: Oxford University Press, 2011), 267–85.

82. Ed Stetzer, "Why You Should Use Stats in Ministry," *The Exchange*, July 27, 2016, www.christianitytoday.com/edstetzer/2016/july/how-to-use-stats.html; and Ed Stetzer, "Defining Evangelicals in Research," National Association of Evangelicals, Winter 2017/18, www.nae.net/defining-evangelicals-research (accessed December 4, 2020). On "mediality": a census, a table of statistics, an encyclopedia of demographics, a ranked order—all are "medial formats." See Liam Cole Young, "'What's in a List?' Cultural Techniques, Logistics, Poesis" (PhD diss., University of Western Ontario, 2014), 31.

83. David B. Barrett, *World Christian Encyclopedia: A Comparative Study of Churches and Religions in the Modern World, 1900–2000* (New York: Oxford University Press, 1982). The fact that the historical coverage advertised in the title of the encyclopedia reached eighteen years beyond the publication date suggests the prescriptive agenda of "Great Commission" evangelizing that informed the project.

84. World Religion Database, https://worldreligiondatabase.org/wrd/#/homepage/wrd-main-page (accessed February 15, 2020). The site is not free, although access is possible through institutions of higher education that subscribe to the site.

85. Mark Noll, *The Scandal of the Evangelical Mind* (Grand Rapids, MI: Eerdmans, 1994).

86. McAlister, *Kingdom of God Has No Borders*, 237–38.

87. David P. King, *God's Internationalists: World Vision and the Age of Evangelical Humanitarianism* (Philadelphia: University of Pennsylvania Press, 2019). World Vision's budget numbers are from World Vision International Annual Review 2000 (Monrovia, CA: World Vision, 2001), and World Vision International Annual Review 2014 (Monrovia, CA: World Vision, 2015).

88. Christine J. Gardner, *Making Chastity Sexy: The Rhetoric of Evangelical Abstinence Campaigns* (Berkeley: University of California Press, 2011), 145.

89. John W. Dietrich, "The Politics of PEPFAR: The President's Emergency Plan for AIDS Relief," *Ethics and International Affairs* 21, no. 3 (2007): 277–92. On the impact of PEPFAR in Uganda, see Lydia Boyd, *Preaching Prevention: Born-Again Christianity and the Moral Politics of AIDS in Uganda* (Athens: Ohio University Press, 2015).

90. An excellent collection that covers the debates across the continent is Adriaan van Klinken and Ezra Chitando, eds., *Public Religion and the Politics of Homosexuality in Africa* (New York: Routledge, 2016).

91. Quoted in Daniel T. Rodgers, *The Work Ethic in Industrial America, 1850–1920* (Chicago: University of Chicago Press, 1979), 11.

92. Stephen R. Prothero, *American Jesus: How the Son of God Became a National Icon* (New York: Farrar, Straus and Giroux, 2003); Richard W. Fox, *Jesus in America: Personal Savior, Cultural Hero, National Obsession* (San Francisco: HarperOne, 2005); R. Marie Griffith, *Born Again Bodies: Flesh and Spirit in American Christianity* (Berkeley: University of California Press, 2004); Kristen Kobes Du Mez, *Jesus and John Wayne: How White Evangelicals Corrupted a Faith and Fractured a Nation* (New York: Liveright Publishing, 2021).

93. The broad and useful literature on Christianity and consumption includes Wade Clark Roof, *Spiritual Marketplace: Baby Boomers and the Remaking of American Religion* (Princeton, NJ: Princeton University Press, 1999); Leigh Eric Schmidt, *Consumer Rites: The Buying and Selling of American Holidays* (Princeton, NJ: Princeton University Press, 1995); Robert Wuthnow, *After Heaven: Spirituality in America since the 1950s*, new ed. (Berkeley: University of California Press, 1998); Vincent J. Miller, *Consuming Religion: Christian Faith and Practice in a Consumer Culture* (New York: Continuum, 2005); and Kathryn Lofton, *Consuming Religion* (Chicago: University of Chicago Press, 2017).

94. Frederick, *Colored Television*, 11; Bowler, *Blessed*; Candy Gunther Brown, ed., *Global Pentecostal and Charismatic Healing* (New York: Oxford University Press, 2011); Simon Coleman, *The Globalisation of Charismatic Christianity: Spreading the Gospel of Prosperity* (Cambridge: Cambridge University Press, 2000).

PART ONE

America's Missionary Impulse

CHAPTER ONE

The Meaning of Missionary Labor

Evaluating Nineteenth-Century Global
Missions in the Early Twentieth Century

Emily Conroy-Krutz

When Daniel Bradley arrived in Singapore, one of the first things he did was open a medical dispensary at his mission station. Bradley had received medical training before he had left the United States. Singapore, like the other foreign mission stations of the American Board of Commissioners for Foreign Missions (ABCFM), needed to have some staff available with medical training. The missionaries themselves required access to reliable care, after all. But, over the past two decades, some missionaries had discovered that medical care could be a tool for evangelism as well. Dispensaries and eventually hospitals soon became central missionary institutions alongside schools. But not all missionary supporters were enthusiastic about this development. Some worried that it took too much of the missionaries' time—time that would be better spent tending to people's souls and not their physical bodies.

Bradley himself was conflicted. In a letter to board secretary Rufus Anderson, he described the crowds that would gather to seek medical treatment at the mission building. Bradley ultimately had to set a time limit for the dispensary in order to have time for what he called his "work." Two and a half hours in the morning would have to be enough. Translation and evangelization had motivated his trip to Singapore, not medical care. Anderson worried that dispensaries seemed to occupy "so much of the time of some of our missionary physicians," and he was not at all sure that they were a good use of that time. Anderson reached out to friends at the London Missionary Society for their thoughts. Yet Bradley was convinced that medical work was rewarding and, ultimately, of great help in bringing souls to Christ. Bradley would treat physical ailments and then discuss "diseases of the soul." Every patient received a tract and, he hoped, returned home with good feelings about the missionaries. Singapore was home to a bustling port and streets filled with sailors and traders from throughout Asia. Bradley's dispensary, then, saw a particularly mobile group of patients. He hoped that they would spread news to China about the good works of American missionaries, leading to a further willingness to accept missionary work. Bradley would soon leave Singapore for Bangkok, and there too he combined medical care with evangelization.[1]

Bradley's and Anderson's questions came down to a debate about why missionaries were really in Asia and what sort of work they should be doing. They talked about method and prioritization and how evangelism should relate to institution building. As they did so, they asked which behaviors were essential to spreading the Christian faith and which were not. These questions resonated with early twentieth-century debate about how evangelical Protestants ought to respond to the modern age, most notably between modernists and fundamentalists. The modernist-fundamentalist controversy has long been important in the study of American evangelicalism. This debate of the 1910s and 1920s focused on theology and the role of the church in the modern world. Changes in politics, education, popular culture, and industry challenged many Christians. While liberal Protestants responded with new interpretations of the Bible and an embrace of a social gospel that called Christians to social action as part of their lived faith, those who would come to be known as fundamentalists critiqued what they saw as a rejection of orthodoxy.

Among other things, the modernist-fundamentalist controversy was a debate over what types of actions and activities were essential to the life of faith and what were not. The question of whether to prioritize institution

Evaluating Nineteenth-Century Global Missions

building (including hospitals) or evangelism, discussed by Bradley and Anderson, was one of the many facets of this debate. Both sides of the controversy were motivated by the sense that they (and they alone) had a proper and faithful interpretation of Christianity. Though this division would have profound effects on the future of American evangelicalism and American politics, it was hardly new in American religious history. As Kathryn Lofton expressed it, this was part of the "familiar fracturing template in U.S. religious history." By the time of the fundamentalist-modernist controversy, American evangelicals had been engaging in nearly a century of discussion—sometimes friendly, sometimes quite contentious—about the ways that the church ought to respond to the needs of the world.[2]

After all, Bradley and Anderson's discussion about hospitals in Singapore took place in 1835, many decades before the rise of fundamentalism and its attendant appeals to focus on evangelization over institution building. Examining evangelicalism in a global context forces us to recognize important continuities across the nineteenth and twentieth centuries. In both eras, evangelicals argued about what should be categorized as "religious" and, accordingly, what methods ought to be used in evangelism. Bradley's experience, and that of countless other missionaries of the mid- to late nineteenth century, reveals important discussions within evangelical circles about the meaning of Christianity, the ways in which it could and should be spread, and the role of the United States in such projects. The nineteenth-century foreign mission movement shifts our periodization of some of the central defining questions of evangelicalism. Nineteenth-century missionaries help to remind us that the modernist-fundamentalist split was the culmination of a long-term debate that often came out in discussions of missionary methods and theory.

The early twentieth century did provide a turning point for the American mission movement in a number of ways. Between the missionary movement itself becoming more diverse, American religious culture going through its own transitions and conflicts over the relationship of religion to public life, and the professionalization of the American diplomatic corps, conflicts over the role of missions in foreign relations were inevitable.[3] These early twentieth-century debates concerned a number of issues, but a central one was what missionaries ought to be doing and what counted as evangelism. Out of the many things that nineteenth-century missionaries did—preaching, teaching, writing, providing medical care, assisting the American government, and more—what was "religious" and what was not? The nineteenth-century foreign mission movement was an evangelical project that cast a wide net. Then, as in the twentieth century, the dividing line between religious and secular activities was fuzzy and contested.

This nineteenth-century history is essential for a proper understanding of the ways that later conflicts fit into the broader story of American evangelicalism—and, indeed, into a broader history of American public life and politics. The global framework of foreign missions made these earlier cleavages in American Protestantism more evident, largely due to concerns about expense. Foreign missions were costly, both in financial terms and, by the end of the nineteenth century, in other ways as well. With the Boxer Uprising in China, some observers began wondering more vocally about the cost of missions in terms of American foreign relations and even human life.

The Boxer Uprising and its aftermath became a moment for reflection on what, exactly, missionaries ought to be doing overseas. Emerging as it did in a period of religious and political transformation in the United States and abroad, it could hardly be otherwise. As Americans debated the role of the United States in China, they found themselves arguing about the place of missionaries and their potential benefits or risks for broader American goals. As one writer explained, the question on everyone's lips had become, "What is a missionary good for, anyway?"[4] The answers to this question reveal debates within and outside of evangelical circles that spanned the nineteenth and twentieth centuries concerning missionary methods, the links between global missions and the U.S. government, and the place of the United States in the world.

Nineteenth-Century Missionary Models

Nineteenth-century American Protestantism tore itself apart time and time again. The first half of the century alone saw strident debates over Unitarianism, fervent arguments in the Old School–New School controversy, and the institutionalization and later schism of multiple denominations. Yet those were also the years of the so-called benevolent empire, when Protestants of multiple denominations could come together around a number of reform issues, including temperance, moral reform, and missions. "Civilization" was at the center of these various projects and so became an important framework for understanding nineteenth-century evangelicalism more generally. When these evangelicals thought about what a Christian society looked like, they thought not only of worship, churches, and sacraments but of gender relations, educational systems, cultural institutions, and government structures. Their emphasis on civilization made "religion" a capacious category.

Evaluating Nineteenth-Century Global Missions

Accordingly, the first generations of American missionaries understood that they could not rely on preaching alone to bring souls to the gospel. When they looked out to the world, they had many ways of thinking about difference. On the one hand, there was the Christian world and the "heathen world," a distinctly bifurcated way of perceiving humanity.[5] But they also saw much more subtle gradations between cultures and communities that corresponded with how civilized (or not) any given place was. The Christian world and the civilized world overlapped. Though missionaries and their supporters debated the precise ways that it worked, many of the early nineteenth-century missionaries, particularly from the ABCFM and Presbyterian Board of Foreign Missions, understood that while one could gain civilization without becoming Christian, one could not become a true Christian without also being civilized. Thus, their Christianization project worked alongside a civilization project. Yet the perceived risks of civilizing—that international commerce, in particular, could lead not to Christianity but to debauchery and worldliness—made this a contested project over the coming decades.

Education was one of their first priorities. Mission schools appeared wherever American missionaries went, sometimes staffed by missionaries and their American assistants, sometimes staffed by native teachers hired by the mission. They established schools for boys and for girls, with the latter being an especially important statement about the ways that Christian and civilized cultures ought to uplift women and provide them with opportunities to support themselves and their families. At grammar schools, academies, trade schools, and colleges, missionaries joined their work of evangelism with the work of education.

Their interest in education was twofold. On the one hand, they shared a genuine belief in the importance of education to the Protestant faith (to read the Bible, one must first be able to read) and to civilized society. On the other hand, though, they knew that parents wanted schools for their children, and those who might not have visited a chapel would happily enroll their children in a mission school. These schools seemed to offer the promise of economic and social advancement, particularly in the colonial spaces in which nineteenth-century missions operated. These material benefits gave missionaries a captive audience for their spiritual message. Scripture reading, chapel attendance, and prayer could all be required of students in the mission schools alongside the practical and academic subjects that brought them to the schoolhouse.[6]

That these institutions could become sites of power struggle is unsurprising. Missionaries in Bombay, for example, were dependent on Indian teachers to staff their day schools and constantly worked to ensure that these teachers would not hinder their efforts to evangelize through school texts and mandated prayer. This, and the suspicion that students came to the schools in order to gain worldly, and not spiritual, benefits, made some evangelical supporters wonder about the value of mission schools. Missionary schools in this period did not often lead to baptism, even as missionaries insisted that the schools were an essential part of their work.[7]

Medical institutions served a similar double purpose. They, too, met a real need while attracting people who might otherwise have avoided missionaries. As Bradley and Anderson's discussions in the 1830s reveal, it was not immediately obvious that hospitals and dispensaries would be a good use of missionary energies. From the very beginning, mission supporters wondered about cost, time, and effectiveness for conversion. But once the mission movement embraced medical work, medical missionaries were an important group of American missionaries overseas.[8] By the end of the century, one observer counted some 450 American medical missionaries operating throughout the world, assisted by local doctors and nurses whom they had trained at the hospitals and mission schools that other missionaries had built.

Supporters of medical missions argued that this method had multiple benefits. In the first place, they relieved suffering by providing superior care to that which would have otherwise been available. Missionary descriptions of indigenous health care were deeply critical, often emphasizing that it was unscientific and "cruel in the extreme." The benefits of Western medicine seemed, to these missionaries, an obvious improvement in the lives of the people they hoped to serve. Modeling themselves on Jesus as the divine healer, medical missionaries were confident that relieving suffering in itself had important Christian value. As Dr. William Wanless, a medical missionary in India, would explain, medical missionaries were called by "our humanity, as well as our Christianity."[9]

But this was not all. Medical missionaries also, like missionary teachers, believed that their work was critical for opening the way for later evangelization. The physical healing that medical missionaries performed worked in conjunction with spiritual benefits. Like schools, missionary hospitals and dispensaries brought a new captive audience to the missionaries. Part of the spiritual work that the hospitals did was practical: the hospitals provided space in which evangelization could happen. Doctors distributed religious tracts. Bible women, Chinese Christian women who were employed by the missionaries, prayed and addressed those waiting for care. But missionaries and their supporters also understood that medical work would have a longer and more subtle spiritual effect as well.

Through their good works, medical missionaries hoped, they would provide living examples of the Christian life. They aimed to show that Christians were people who would travel great distances to help others with little expectation of benefit to themselves. They hoped that this example would move the people with whom they interacted and inspire them to embrace the faith that had prompted such actions. All missionaries desired to model this kind of selflessness, but the particular type of labor that medical missionaries provided had the potential to make this dynamic particularly effective. As one supporter explained at the end of the century, the medical missionaries were important "in disarming anti-foreign prejudice, in breaking down caste barriers, and, in general, in preparing the way for the preaching of the gospel" wherever they went. While mass conversions did not generally accompany the creation of missionary hospitals, medical missionaries and their supporters trusted in more gradual effects among their patients and those who witnessed the patients' healing.[10]

In addition to schools and hospitals, missionaries established publishing houses in the nineteenth century. From the very beginning of the 1800s, the press sprouted into the third branch of mission methods. Scriptural translation and publication were important goals for these printers and writers. But the missionary press did not publish scripture and religious tracts only. They also wrote in a number of other genres. In China, for example, missionaries believed that an important part of their success depended upon the ability of the Chinese to reach a better understanding of Western history and culture. To accomplish this, missionaries there joined with Western merchants to publish the *Chinese Repository* as well as texts like the first Chinese-language history of the United States.[11]

Missionaries also wrote for American audiences, and here the full scope of their interests and activities could be seen clearly. In addition to discussions of their evangelistic work, they became prolific writers of history, geography, and ethnography. In all of these genres, they endeavored to establish themselves as the American experts on the places where they lived and worked. Merchants and diplomats were geographically limited, with stays of shorter duration than those of their missionary peers. They often remained in port cities and capitals and did not share the missionaries' expectation of life-long residence among a foreign people. On the strength of their writings and demonstration of expertise, some missionaries became members of

American scientific organizations such as the American Oriental Society and the American Ethnological Society.[12]

Schools, hospitals, and the press were all essential to the missions in this era but often had a limited effect on actual conversions or baptisms. Missionaries worried about this. Many, such as those in Bombay, liked to use a metaphor of seeds being planted to explain the need to continue on in spite of an apparent lack of success. Though for now the seeds were "buried and apparently fruitless," they would eventually "spring up at some future period and bring forth an abundant harvest." In time, they were sure, the full effects would be felt. For now, missionaries would "continue to labor and pray and hope."[13]

Indeed, not everyone was pleased with these non-evangelistic efforts on the parts of missionaries. Some, like the critic of fundraising efforts that shared geographic and ethnographic information from the missionaries, felt that it was an inappropriate distraction from evangelism. She complained to the directors of the ABCFM that too much time, energy, and money had been put into the tasks of exploring "heathen" countries and distributing information about them within the United States.[14]

To these critics, the ABCFM was clear that spreading the gospel would require a range of projects. The geographic and ethnographic writing brought in new American audiences; just as schools and hospitals could draw people abroad to the missions who might not otherwise be interested, Americans who were not normally excited about global missions might pick up a book or attend a meeting to learn about exotic lands and find themselves changed. Later in the century, Wanless would address these concerns directly for the medical field, parsing the distinction between "secular" hospitals and missionary ones. Missionaries came to their medical work with an interest in saving not only bodies but souls. This, he trusted, suffused the entire project, making it a type of evangelism that should be valued, even if it did not result in baptisms.[15]

What this response did not address, however, was cost. This remained a subject of concern throughout the nineteenth century. Institutions were expensive to build and maintain. Whenever possible, they were funded by people in the countries where missionaries were working, but American donors were essential. Institutions also kept missionaries in place for a long time. For those who hoped that missionaries might come in, create a Christian community, and then leave it to run itself, the institution-building missionary model was a challenge. One of the most prominent voices expressing this critique was, perhaps ironically, also one of the most powerful leaders of the institution-building ABCFM in the nineteenth century: Rufus Anderson.

Anderson was a leader of the ABCFM for over three decades: as a member of the Prudential Committee, as corresponding secretary from 1832 to 1866, and as a historian of the board and its missions in the 1860s and 1870s. During these years, he developed a theory of missions that has come to be known as the "three-self" model. Missions, he argued, should aim to create native churches that would be self-supporting, self-governing, and self-propagating. Though this model had theological grounding, it was also deeply concerned with expense. After the Panic of 1837, missionary organizations struggled with fundraising to support their work around the world. In 1827, the annual budget of the ABCFM had grown to over $100,000. By 1850, it had more than doubled again to $254,329. In the middle of the century, Anderson had a hard time justifying that kind of a budget to support missionary projects that were not successful in leading to baptisms or the training of native ministers.[16]

Education was a particularly fraught topic for Anderson. In 1833, he had written in the *American Quarterly Observer* about the importance of scientific education as part of the mission project. The sciences, he wrote, were "the natural allies of religion" in preparing the mind for religious truth. To those who had found the institution-building model of the early foreign mission movement too far away from apostolic example, Anderson had then articulated the importance of civilization. The apostles had worked among "the most enlightened portions of the then civilized world," while the board's missionaries instead worked among uncivilized people. Schools and the press were thus an important part of their work, preparing the way for evangelistic success.[17] Within a decade, however, Anderson had changed his mind about schools and the press. He was particularly critical of English-language missionary education that he believed drew students away from their communities and made them unable to function as preachers to them. Anderson repeatedly encouraged missionaries throughout the board's global missions to reduce their educational programs in favor of preaching.

Missionaries regularly pushed back against Anderson's proposals. His theories, they argued, did not reflect the reality that they experienced in the field. An emphasis on preaching could do little if there was no one to preach to; schools, missionaries argued, were essential for drawing people in to hear the message of the gospel at all. Many missionaries were able to largely ignore Anderson's directions. Due to the slow nature of correspondence in this period, debates between the board's headquarters in Boston and the mission stations around the world could take years to resolve. In the meantime, missionaries with on-the-ground knowledge and experience did what they felt was best. Even at the height of Anderson's three-self program, missionaries embraced institution building.[18]

By the 1860s, these debates over missionary methods were further complicated by the emergence of women's mission boards. The women's boards ushered in a huge influx of single women in the mission field and, with them, an increased emphasis on institution building. Because the various denominations denied ordination to women in this generation, women missionaries mainly served as teachers and nurses. Under their leadership, mission schools and hospitals grew to an even larger scale than the missionaries of the antebellum era could have imagined. Historian Carol Chin has described the attitude of these female missionaries at the end of the century as one of "beneficent imperialism," emphasizing the ways that American women worked to change the culture that they encountered overseas. Because the missionaries were convinced of the superiority of their own cultural norms, they openly sought to use institutions like mission schools to create significant cultural transformations.[19]

Throughout the nineteenth century, then, missionary work embraced a number of forms that emphasized evangelism to a greater or lesser extent. Historian William Hutchison has referred to this as the tension between Christ and culture, and it has been an important dynamic in the American missionary movement throughout its history.[20] It concerned both praxis and theory. It asked what missionaries should be doing with their time and efforts. At the same time, though, it spoke to deep questions about the purpose of missions and the way that conversion worked. To truly become Christian, how much civilization was required? Where and how was God acting through missionaries and their preaching, teaching, healing, and publications? Much like the conflict that would divide denominations and other religious institutions over slavery, these discussions of civilization in the mission movement revealed deep issues within nineteenth-century American Protestantism that were, at their center, about what it really meant to be a Christian: Which parts of Christian faith and practice were essential, and which were just a part of culture?

In the nineteenth century, these debates occurred within denominations and within missionary societies. As yet, it was not an issue that would cause formal division. That would happen only after decades of internal tensions came to bear on the theological debates of the early twentieth century that

Evaluating Nineteenth-Century Global Missions

would split evangelical Protestants into two camps. But tensions strained the bonds of unity long before they snapped.

The Missionary Diplomats

These tensions are particularly stark in another branch of nineteenth-century missionary efforts: diplomacy. Missionaries did not travel overseas as official representatives of their government, but they could not help having their Americanness perceived as an important part of their identity by those whom they sought to convert. Indeed, some missionaries welcomed this. Once they were in the field, and especially once they had a facility with the local language, they could shift from being an unofficial representative of the United States to a participant in America's emerging diplomatic infrastructure. Missionaries served as translators and consuls, valued by their government for their local expertise in the same way that they were by many of their supporters at home. How they combined their duties as missionaries with their duties as "patriots," as one missionary put it, could at times be tense but mostly presented little conflict. After all, many of these missionaries understood the work of evangelical missions and the work of U.S. diplomacy to have many important goals in common.

Divie Bethune McCartee presents a helpful example of this model. A graduate of Princeton and a lifelong supporter of the foreign mission movement, McCartee was approached by the Presbyterian Board of Foreign Missions in 1842 when the Treaty of Nanjing made it possible for Americans to access new port cities in China. This had long been a goal of American foreign missionaries, and the Presbyterians were anxious to jump on the opportunity. McCartee was not an ordained minister. Instead, he would serve as a medical missionary. Within months, McCartee was the pioneer Protestant missionary at Ningpo. He was not only the first missionary but also the first American there, which immediately put him in place to represent both his faith and his country. He would serve as acting consul for eleven years and, in time, would work for the American diplomatic corps in a number of different ways.[21]

Over a sixty-year career, McCartee served as a medical missionary, acting consul, American representative to the Mixed Court in China, and professor of international law at the University of Tokyo (among other work for the American, Chinese, and Japanese governments). In his diplomatic work, he joined other missionaries in similar roles in focusing American attention on the rights and liberties of missionaries and Christian converts. His proximity to and cooperation with the American government, in other words, allowed him to smooth the way for further missionary presence abroad. Anson Burlingame celebrated McCartee as a man of "rare qualities as a Christian, patriot, and a scholar."[22]

At times, McCartee wondered about what tasks he should be prioritizing. Since he understood that his primary calling was to serve as a missionary, how and when was it appropriate to spend his time working in more political capacities? Could these two roles really be combined? By the end of the century, he was well aware of ongoing debates within some denominations about the merging of evangelism with other sorts of work—not only the explicit political work that he had been doing but also the medical work that had brought him to China in the first place seemed, to some groups, potentially inappropriate. Why spend money on establishing medical institutions if they didn't seem to lead directly to conversions? The government work he took part in was, understandably, even more controversial and involved multiple leaves of absence from the Presbyterian board—even as McCartee himself considered the roles to be reconcilable.

For McCartee and missionary diplomats like him, it was possible to serve both God and country because the goals were linked: both the mission movement and, he hoped, American diplomacy sought to bring about the improvement of the world—the spread of "civilization" and stability, of peace and goodwill—and, of course, the kingdom of God.

McCartee died in San Francisco in 1900, just as news was coming to the United States about a nationalist and anti-Christian uprising that would cast doubt on the role of missionaries there and around the world. Following so quickly on the heels of the wars of 1898 and the rise of a vocal anti-imperialist movement in the United States, the Boxer Uprising became yet another moment for considering both the role of the United States in the world and the role of the mission movement in American diplomacy.

It was McCartee's nephew Henry Rankin who, when trying to defend what he saw as his uncle's legacy of combining patriotism and piety, claimed that "everyone" was now asking, "What is a missionary good for, anyway?"[23] To that question, Rankin had an answer based on more than a half century of missionary activity that had combined evangelism with other related pursuits. But the first decade of the twentieth century saw a vigorous debate about the role of missionaries, one that drew attention to many long-standing differences of opinion about missionary strategy and foreign relations.

The Boxer Uprising and the Debate over Missionary Methods

In the decades since McCartee had first arrived as a medical missionary in China, the Protestant missionary presence in the country had grown significantly, as had the Western presence in China more generally. Localized societies known as "Boxers" began forming in the Shandong region of northern China in the mid-1890s in response to this growth. Long-term shifts in the regional economy, China's defeat in the Sino-Japanese War, economic depression, and drought together created a context of political anxiety and unrest. The presence of foreign powers continually attempting to extend their economic and religious reach into China was not helping.[24] Away from the port cities, the most palpable embodiment of these foreign powers was Christian missionaries. And missionaries, of course, had long been active participants in the imperialism that the Boxers would come to challenge. Most objectionable, from the Boxers' perspective, were the ways in which missionaries could use the extraterritoriality guaranteed by Western treaties (and encouraged by missionary diplomats) to aggressively defend the legal rights of their Chinese converts and interfere in legal proceedings on their behalf.[25]

Over the summer of 1899, the Boxer Uprising escalated attacks against the foreign community and Christian converts. Americans joined forces with other foreign powers in opposition to the Boxers and, when the Chinese government embraced the uprising, the Chinese more generally.[26] For months, Americans at home did not have direct information about what was going on. Newspapers and the evangelical press alike feared the worst and pushed for intervention to protect missionaries from harm. By its end, the Boxer Uprising claimed the lives of over 200 foreigners and many thousands of Chinese Christians and set off a series of debates about the role of the United States in China generally and the work of missionaries specifically.[27]

When resolutions were finally reached in September 1901, there were still many lingering questions. The press had reported the echoing of the chant "Support the Qing, destroy the foreign!" through the streets during the uprising, and American observers nervously noted the seeming equation of this problematic foreignness with Christian evangelism.[28] Missionaries were recognized as victims of the uprising. Memorials, such as that at Oberlin College, celebrated those who had fallen. But the debates over indemnities in China—how much the Chinese would have to pay for damages suffered— once again uncomfortably blurred the lines between the goals of the mission movement and of American diplomacy. Missionary demands seemed too high, even greedy, to many observers. The government understood, too, that it would be far more important to secure America's long-term trade relations with China and not ask for more than the Chinese could pay.[29]

These critiques of missionaries after the Boxer Uprising raised a number of questions about what, exactly, the missionaries were up to. If the Boxers were, at heart, anti-Christian, was this an example of foreign missionaries dragging American foreign relations into unnecessary and dangerous crises? Was the identification of mission work with Western imperialism the ultimate effect of missionary institution building? Were missionaries setting aside their proper work of evangelization and taking on inappropriate secular work? Stories about missionary prejudice, intolerance, and narrow-mindedness became common in those years. The American press roundly criticized them over the indemnities: missionaries were looting in northern China, the charges went.[30] American diplomats in China, further, could be quite critical of the missionaries. Some, such as Anson Burlingame Johnson, American consul at Amoy, seemed to blame the Boxers' anti-foreign stance entirely on the missionaries. Missionaries had been stepping beyond their evangelistic roles and inappropriately "meddling" in "secular matters." To avoid another situation like the Boxer Rebellion, missionaries needed to be restricted to purely spiritual work.[31]

Johnson was trying to draw a clear line between what missionaries could properly consider their work abroad (evangelism) and that which was outside of their proper interests (secular activities). Similar concerns had been voiced by others in the U.S. government who, looking at other situations around the world, believed that any problems that missionaries faced were the result of their own inappropriate behavior. In Turkey, for example, missionary attempts to print and distribute texts (correctly understood as part of their evangelism) had led to problems since at least the 1880s. Senator John Sherman had argued that the U.S. government should not act to protect American missionaries in Turkey just because they were U.S. citizens. "If our citizens go to a far distant country, semi-civilized and bitterly opposed to their movements, we cannot follow them there and protect them," he stated.[32] American missionaries in Turkey, like those in China a few years later, faced physical violence that seemed to have government complicity. Sherman's suggestion that, in going where they were not wanted, they had, therefore, voided any promise of protection from the U.S. government spoke to the same sorts of concerns that Johnson voiced. Missionaries were meddling and causing problems.

Evaluating Nineteenth-Century Global Missions

But missionaries had their defenders, too. These supporters found missionaries to be, on average, beneficial to the goals of the United States in the world precisely because they combined secular and spiritual labors. One of the most passionate of these defenders was Henry Rankin, who would spend the first decade of the twentieth century defending missionaries and their position in American diplomacy. As Rankin watched these events and the ensuing debates unfold, he was sure that the observers who blamed the missionaries had it all wrong. "It is not the western creed but the western greed which has made most of the trouble between China and the Occident," he would write.[33] To those who argued that missionaries destabilized the places where they worked, Rankin argued that, on the contrary, missionaries were essential to the stability of any Western presence in Asia. Rankin, for his part, would make a particularly strong claim in his defense of missionaries—that missionaries were, in fact, the key to U.S. relations with China and the rest of Asia.

In these claims, Rankin echoed missionary supporters earlier in the century who had praised the beneficial effects of schools and hospitals in creating goodwill. To make this point, Rankin returned to the stories of his uncle Divie Bethune McCartee and other missionary-diplomat colleagues of the mid- to late nineteenth century—men like Peter Parker, Elijah Bridgman, and Samuel Williams who had identified as, and indeed served as, both Christian missionaries and agents of the American government. Looking at these men, Rankin insisted that the nineteenth century had key lessons for the twentieth. Most importantly, he wanted this new generation to understand the impossibility of differentiating a religious role and a secular role for missionaries.[34] The correct understanding of the relationship between these roles became Rankin's new goal, one that seemed particularly vital in the aftermath of the Boxer Uprising.

Rankin overstated his uncle's significance, giving McCartee credit for all the "good relations" between China and Japan during his tenure, but important in this claim is Rankin's reasoning behind it. McCartee's effectiveness as a diplomat, Rankin argued, was all due to his missionary character.[35] These partnerships were so essential to American foreign relations, Rankin argued, because missionaries and diplomats shared a common vision for American relations with East Asia. At a time when missionaries were being accused of working against American interests abroad, creating ill will and destabilizing colonial spaces, Rankin insisted just the opposite.[36] To all those who found missionaries' institution building to be imperialistic or distracting from the proper attentions of evangelists, Rankin and his fellow supporters disagreed.

It was the unity of the American missionary and political visions—a unity that was based, he believed, in the Golden Rule—that made missionaries such ideal partners for American diplomacy.

Rankin was part of a small flurry of missionary defenses in the first decades of the century, all responding to similar critiques of missionary interference in world politics. Some of these came from missionaries and their supporters, of course, such as the several volumes by secretary of the Presbyterian Board of Foreign Missions Arthur Judson Brown, or the special issue of the *Missionary Herald* in October 1900 that sought to answer through interviews with sympathetic diplomats the "many flippant utterances" blaming missionaries for the Boxer Uprising.[37] Far from getting in the way of America's global interests, these defenders all argued, missionaries had in fact been important in making the United States appear benevolent and attractive to foreign countries.

These writers insisted that the Boxer Uprising was misunderstood by Americans who wanted to blame missionaries. Anti-Western sentiment in Asia was not simple opposition to missionaries, as former U.S. minister to Siam John Barrett argued. Rather, it had emerged out of economic and political contexts in which the missionaries played only one small part.[38] Barrett's easy defense of the missionaries emerged in part out of his understanding of the United States as "a Christian as well as a commercial nation." Though he, too, had come to Asia with "a slight prejudice against missionaries," his experience in the field had totally changed his mind, he informed his readers at home. In the fields of medicine and education, missionaries had done much to relieve suffering and advance American interests in China, Japan, Korea, and elsewhere in Asia (and, indeed, around the world). Now in this moment of tension, Americans could not "think of withdrawing the messengers of Christianity from Asia until we are ready to withdraw the merchants of commerce and the ministers of diplomacy." If the United States was to have any relations with Asia, in other words, Barrett felt that it needed to send missionaries. They were an essential part of American foreign relations.[39] In this evaluation, Barrett insisted that he did not stand alone: "Nearly every Minister or Consul of the United States who has lived many years in Asia" would agree.[40]

Rankin agreed. To those who argued that missionaries destabilized the places where they worked, Rankin argued that, on the contrary, missionaries were essential to the stability of any Western presence in Asia. Through the schools and hospitals they built, they fostered goodwill and thus (he claimed) could stabilize colonized populations and prepare them for eventual independence and self-government.[41] Only after "Christian ideals of the social order" spread in colonial spaces could imperial powers safely withdraw, Rankin believed. Missionaries were needed to help "make a new moral climate" to transform the world.[42]

This transformation was at once moral, religious, and political. The overarching goal of missions was to transform the world into God's kingdom, and Rankin suggested that evangelism was not the only way that missionaries could accomplish this. The consular and diplomatic work that some missionaries did for their governments was also essential.[43] So, too, were their educational, medical, and literary efforts.

Long-standing internal arguments over missionary methods were becoming more public by the time of Rankin's writing. At the same time that politicians debated the role of missionaries in diplomacy, missionaries themselves were examining how they ought to relate to what some increasingly considered secular matters. The nineteenth-century conviction that missionary work would inevitably and appropriately aid in the spread of "civilization" was now contested among some groups. The growth of missionary hospitals and universities had led to more questioning regarding what kinds of work missionaries really ought to be doing.[44] For some, medical missions, schools, and diplomatic efforts seemed too separate from the central evangelistic goals of mission work. Yet to Rankin and some other commentators at the time, the earlier linkages between missions and diplomacy continued to make sense, if in slightly different terms that reflected their new era.

By the turn of the twentieth century, American missionaries around the world had been experimenting with a range of methods for spreading the gospel. They had translated scriptures and built schools; they had written tracts and trained doctors; they had created colleges and served as consuls; they had supported native preachers and advised American diplomats. All of this, in the eyes of generations of missionaries, could be the work of spreading the gospel just as much as preaching was. How to balance the various emphases within mission work was an ongoing topic of discussion for mission boards, their supporters at home, and the missionaries abroad. Developments at the turn of the century, particularly the Boxer Uprising in China, led to increased volatility in these conversations about missionary methods and the potential problems that missionaries could create for American diplomacy.

The global context of evangelicalism in this period highlights the ongoing debates about what types of activities could and should be categorized as "religious" and what the connection between religious groups and the state ought to be. Decades of missionary experience and the growing strength of the U.S. government challenged the casual association of Christianity and civilization that characterized nineteenth-century evangelicalism at home and abroad. As they juggled evangelical and political roles, missionaries and those who observed them came to ask what to make of the compatibility of missionaries' religious, political, and—it's worth also adding—humanitarian roles. These types of questions have been at the heart of American evangelicalism throughout its history. A global framework for studying that history helps us to remember how early those debates began.

Notes

1. Daniel Bradley to Rufus Anderson, Singapore, April 25, 1835; Daniel Bradley to Rufus Anderson, Bangkok, April 17, 1836, American Board of Commissioners for Foreign Missions Archives, Houghton Library, Harvard University, Cambridge, MA (ABC) Reel 225; Rufus Anderson to William Ellis, Boston, January 19, 1835, ABC 2.1.1, vol. 01.

2. On the modernist-fundamentalist controversy, see George Marsden, *Fundamentalism and American Culture* (New York: Oxford University Press, 1980); William Hutchison, *The Modernist Impulse in American Protestantism* (New York: Oxford University Press, 1976); Matthew Avery Sutton, *American Apocalypse: A History of Modern Evangelicalism* (Cambridge, MA: Belknap Press of Harvard University Press, 2014), chap. 3; and Kathryn Lofton, "Commonly Modern: Rethinking the Modernist-Fundamentalist Controversies," *Church History* 83, no. 1 (March 2014): 137–44.

3. On turn-of-the-century missions, see Patricia R. Hill, *The World Their Household: The American Woman's Foreign Mission Movement and Cultural Transformation, 1870–1920* (Ann Arbor: University of Michigan Press, 1984); Jane Hunter, *The Gospel of Gentility: American Women Missionaries in Turn-of-the-Century China* (New Haven, CT: Yale University Press, 1984); William R. Hutchison, *Errand to the World: American Protestant Thought and Foreign Missions* (Chicago: University of Chicago Press, 1987); and Ian Tyrrell, *Reforming the World: The Creation of America's Moral Empire* (Princeton, NJ: Princeton University Press, 2010).

4. Henry W. Rankin to Peter McCartee, E. Northfield, MA, December 16, 1901, Rankin Family Papers, box 1, folder 22, Presbyterian Historical Society, Philadelphia, PA.

5. Kathryn Gin Lum, "The Historyless Heathen and the Stagnating Pagan: History as a Non-native Category?," *Religion and American Culture* 28, no. 1 (2018): 52–91.

6. On missionary education projects in the early nineteenth century, see Jon Butler, *The Heathen School: A Story of Hope and Betrayal in the Age of the Early Republic* (New York: Knopf, 2014); Emily Conroy-Krutz, *Christian Imperialism: Converting the World in the Early American Republic* (Ithaca, NY: Cornell University Press, 2015), chap. 3; and Amanda Porterfield, *Mary Lyon and the Mount Holyoke Missionaries* (New York: Oxford University Press, 1997), chap. 4.

7. Conroy-Krutz, *Christian Imperialism*, chap. 3.

8. On nineteenth-century medical missions, see Kristin L. Gleeson, "The Stethoscope and the Gospel: Presbyterian Foreign Medical Missions, 1840–1900," *American Presbyterians* 71, no. 2 (Summer 1993): 127–38; and John R. Haddad, *America's First Adventure in China: Trade, Treaties, Opium, and Salvation* (Philadelphia: Temple University Press, 2013), chap. 4.

9. William Wanless, *The Medical Mission: Its Place, Power, and Appeal* (Philadelphia: Westminster Press, 1898), 18.

10. Wanless, 47.

11. Elizabeth L. Malcolm, "The *Chinese Repository* and Western Literature on China, 1800 to 1850," *Modern Asian Studies* 7, no. 2 (March 1973): 165–78; Murray A. Rubinstein, "The Wars They Wanted: American Missionaries' Use of 'The Chinese Repository' before the Opium War," *American Neptune* 48, no. 4 (1988): 271–82.

12. On missionary contributions to scientific knowledge, see Thomas Laurie, ed., *The Ely Volume: or, The Contributions of Our Missions to Science and Human Well-Being* (Boston: American Board of Commissioners for Foreign Missions, 1881).

13. Samuel Newell, Horatio Bardwell, and Gordon Hall to Samuel Worcester, Bombay, February 4, 1817; Newell, Bardwell, and Hall to Worcester, Bombay, April 1817, 1817, ABC 16.1.1, vol. 1.

14. David Greene, corresponding secretary of the ABCFM, responded to one such letter from a Mrs. Lydia Pratt. (I have not found Pratt's initial letter yet, though the reply gives a good sense of the substance of her critique.) David Greene to Mrs. Lydia Pratt, September [1838] ABC 1.1, vol. 10.

15. Wanless, *Medical Mission*, 77.

16. Paul William Harris, *Nothing but Christ: Rufus Anderson and the Ideology of Protestant Foreign Missions* (New York: Oxford University Press, 2000); American Board of Commissioners for Foreign Missions, *Report of the American Board of Commissioners for Foreign Missions* (Boston: American Board of Commissioners for Foreign Missions, 1850), 39:202–9.

17. Anderson, quoted in Harris, *Nothing but Christ*, 56.

18. On Anderson's policy and its effect on girls' education in the Ottoman Empire, see Barbara Reeves-Ellington, *Domestic Frontiers: Gender, Reform, and American Interventions in the Ottoman Balkans and the Near East* (Amherst: University of Massachusetts Press, 2013), 142–50.

19. Carol C. Chin, "Beneficent Imperialists: American Women Missionaries in China at the Turn of the Twentieth Century," *Diplomatic History* 27, no. 3 (June 2003): 327–52.

20. Hutchison, *Errand to the World*.

21. Robert E. Speer, ed., *A Missionary Pioneer in the Far East: A Memorial of Divie Bethune McCartee, for More Than Fifty Years a Missionary of the Board of Foreign Missions of the Presbyterian Church in the USA* (New York: Fleming H. Revell, 1922).

22. Anson Burlingame to D. B. McCartee, Peking, February 20, 1865, copy enclosed with No. 100 Legation of the United States, Peking, March 7, 1865; and Anson Burlingame to William H. Seward, McCartee Family Papers, folder 3, Presbyterian Historical Society, Philadelphia, PA.

23. Rankin to McCartee, December 16, 1901.

24. On the uprising itself, see Paul A. Cohen, *History in Three Keys: The Boxers as Event, Experience, and Myth*, rev. ed. (New York: Columbia University Press, 1998); Joseph W. Esherick, *The Origins of the Boxer Uprising* (Berkeley: University of California Press, 1987); and David J. Silbey, *The Boxer Rebellion and the Great Game in China* (New York: Hill and Wang, 2012). On American connections and missionary roles, see Carol C. Chin, *Modernity and National Identity in the U.S. and East Asia, 1895–1919* (Kent, OH: Kent State University Press, 2010); Heather D. Curtis, *Holy Humanitarians: American Evangelicals and Global Aid* (Cambridge, MA: Harvard University Press, 2018); and Stuart Creighton Miller, "Ends and Means: Missionary Justifications of Force in Nineteenth Century China," in *The Missionary Enterprise in China and America*, ed. John K. Fairbank (Cambridge, MA: Harvard University Press, 1974).

25. This legal category made it possible for Westerners to avoid coming under the jurisdiction of local Chinese powers. Instead, if they faced legal troubles, they could be tried by people of their own country. While German Catholic missionaries were more aggressive than some of the other groups (and received criticism from Americans, missionary and otherwise, for the practice), all to a greater or lesser degree made use of this benefit, not only for themselves but also for the Chinese Christians who worked and worshipped with them. In the words of U.S. minister Frederick F. Low in 1871, this practice "practically remov[ed] this class [Chinese Christians] from the jurisdiction of their own rulers." Quoted in Arthur Judson Brown, *New Forces in Old China: An Inevitable Awakening*, 2nd ed. (New York: Fleming H. Revell, 1904), 256.

26. Conger to Hay, June 4–10, Papers Relating to the Foreign Relations of the United States, with the Annual Message of the President Transmitted to Congress December 3, 1900 (Washington, DC: Government Printing Office, 1902), 139–50.

27. Cohen, *History in Three Keys*, 51.

28. Cohen, 26.

29. "Report on Questions Relating to Chinese Taxation, Indemnity, and Proposed Conventional Provisions," in William W. Rockhill, *Appendix. Foreign Relations of the United States, 1901. Affairs in China* (Washington, DC: Government Printing Office, 1902), 210.

30. "Looting by Missionaries," *Missionary Herald*, February 1901, 46; "The Collection of Indemnities in China," *Missionary Herald*, August 1901, 312. In Mark Twain's anti-imperialist writings as well, missionaries emerged as greedy, callous figures in China, demanding retribution from a peasantry that could hardly afford to pay the exaggerated claims of Western powers. Mark Twain, "To the Person Sitting in Darkness," *North American Review*, February 1901, 161–76.

31. "It is well-known here that the ill-feeling toward the foreigners in this province is entirely confined to the missionaries," he reported in August 1900. Johnson was joined in this analysis by Consuls McWade and Wilcox. Anson Burlingame Johnson to Assistant Secretary of State, August 24, 1900, U.S. Department of State, Consular Despatches, U.S. Consulate, Amoy, quoted in Linda Madson Papageorge, "The United States Diplomats' Response to Rising Chinese Nationalism, 1900-1912" (PhD diss., Michigan State University, 1973, 49.

32. John Sherman, quoted in Cyrus Hamlin, "America's Duty to Americans in Turkey: An Open Letter to the Hon. John Sherman, United States Senator from Ohio," *North American Review*, September 1896, 276.

33. Henry Williams Rankin, "Political Values of the American Missionary," *American Journal of Sociology* 13, no. 2 (September 1907): 172.

34. David Murray, "Divie Bethune McCartee MD: Pioneer Missionary in China and Japan," *New York Observer and Chronicle*, July 17, 1902, 73; Henry W. Rankin, E. Northfield, MA, to Dr. David Murray, November 12, 1901, Rankin Family Papers, box 1, folder 22.

35. Rankin to Murray, November 12, 1901, Rankin Family Papers.

36. Rankin, "Political Values," 145–46.

37. Arthur Judson Brown, *The Foreign Missionary: An Incarnation of a World Movement* (New York: Fleming H. Revell, 1907); Brown, *New Forces in Old China*; "The Diplomatists concerning Missionaries in China," *Missionary Herald*, October 1900, 395–98. The *Missionary Herald* piece interviewed John Foster, a former secretary of state; former U.S. ministers to China James Angell, Charles Denby, George Seward; and a former minister to Siam, John Barrett.

38. John Barrett, "Some Truths about the Missionaries," *Outlook*, October 20, 1900, 462–65.

39. Barrett quoted in "The Diplomatists concerning Missionaries in China."

40. Barrett, "Some Truths about the Missionaries."

41. Rankin, "Political Values," 165.

42. Rankin, 164–65.

43. Rankin, 151.

44. McCartee in Speer, *Missionary Pioneer in the Far East*, 178–79.

CHAPTER TWO

Mission, Migration, and Contested Authority

Building an AME Presence in Haiti in the Nineteenth Century

Christina Cecelia Davidson

In 1877, a dispute arose in the Methodist chapel in Port-au-Prince, Haiti. The African American minister Charles W. Mossell had arrived from the United States to take charge of the congregation of Black U.S. immigrants who had settled in Haiti between 1824 and 1825. Representing the African Methodist Episcopal (AME) Church, Mossell at first "found an open door to preach the gospel" among the immigrants and their descendants.[1] However, within nine months, his relationship with the Methodist congregation soured. Mossell insisted that his parishioners adhere to the laws of the church, according to the AME discipline. Leaders of the Haitian congregation, however, retorted, "We are not members of the A.M.E. Church. Our church is independent and has been for forty years."[2] The title and deed to the church property proved their point. St. Peter's Haitian Union Methodist Episcopal Church was not bound to the rules and regulations of the AME Church of the United States despite the fact that its members had petitioned the AME Church for a minister. Charles Mossell promptly took his leave. The AME Church would have to construct a new church building if it were to establish a permanent missionary presence in the Black republic.

The spat between Mossell and leaders of the Union Methodist Church underscores the divide that existed between African American missionaries and their would-be congregants in foreign lands. After the U.S. Civil War (1861–65), northern African Americans sought to evangelize newly freed southerners, and many Black Protestants hoped to spread the gospel message to Black people around the world. The AME Church, as the era's most prominent Black religious institution, led in this early Pan-Africanist evangelical movement. As church membership ballooned in the U.S. South, AME leaders planned to expand the denomination to Haiti, the independent Black republic and a perennial symbol of Black achievement. Yet, Protestantism had already reached the Catholic island of Hispaniola decades before 1877, as thousands of African Americans had immigrated to Haiti in the 1820s. Leaders of the AME Church like Mossell expected that their "kinfolk" would assent to U.S. leadership and remain faithful African Methodists. This U.S.-based vision of missionary work, however, did not square with realities on the ground. Eventually, even Charles Mossell came to understand that Protestant missionary work in Port-au-Prince at times required a more ecumenical (or *union*) ethos.

This chapter analyzes the history of Protestantism in Haiti and the formation of the AME Church's missionary station in Port-au-Prince at the end of the nineteenth century. Beginning with the Haitian emigration movement of the 1820s, the chapter shows how the AME Church's relationship to Haiti changed over time. As other scholars have discussed, African Americans' participation in the United States' missionary impulse at the end of the nineteenth century was both distinct from and similar to that of the broader white majority.[3] Black church leaders distinguished themselves from whites in that they proudly used both Christian theology and foreign missions to fight for Black liberation at home and abroad. However, like white Americans, most African American clergy also believed in Protestant Christian supremacy. Consequently, AME leaders' demands for the "racial uplift" of Black people across the world advanced the colonial project inherent in white Americans' Christian missionary enterprise. In this way, the "white man's burden" and the "Black man's burden" were one and the same.[4]

Changes within the AME denomination of the United States, however, tell only half the story. Once missionaries arrived on the island, they had to interact with various people groups: African American immigrants who were now Haitian citizens, other Protestant missionaries, and Catholic Haitian officials. In Port-au-Prince, Mossell confronted a congregation that no longer considered itself part of the AME fold but instead existed as an independent church. The AME Church's efforts to erect a new AME chapel in Port-au-Prince in the early 1880s evidences these dynamics. The same history also reveals that, in the absence of a robust AME presence in Haiti, Mossell's congregation forged local ecumenical ties in Port-au-Prince. Relationships with other Protestant denominations and Catholic officials provided a sense of Christian unity and religious tolerance for Protestantism in Haiti's capital despite stark denominational differences. The short glimpses of ecumenical cooperation that appear in missionaries' letters to the United States suggest that a distinct story about AME foreign missions might be told if events that took place in Haiti were to form the center of analysis.

New Nodes along the Black Protestant Atlantic Littoral

The history of African Methodism in Haiti is intricately tied to the history of circum-Caribbean migration, specifically the 1824–26 Haitian emigration movement, and to the broader history of Protestant evangelization of the island. As African Americans and Afro-Caribbean émigrés relocated to Hispaniola throughout the nineteenth century, they maintained their faith and sacred practices by forming Protestant religious societies. These societies later affiliated with larger Protestant bodies such as the British Wesleyan Methodist Church, the American Baptists, the United Foreign Missionary Society, the Episcopal Church, and the African Methodist Episcopal Church, which all sent missionaries to migrant communities living in the island's port towns in the 1800s. The relationship between Black Protestant societies and their missionary affiliations linked Hispaniola (conceptually) to the history of Protestantism in the Atlantic world and (physically) to a broader network of Protestant missionary activity on the island and in the circum-Caribbean. It also reinforced a cosmopolitan ethos in ports like Port-au-Prince, Gonaives, Cap-Haïtien, Monte Cristi, Puerto Plata, and Samaná, where Protestants banded together in supporting the fight for freedom. The history of African Methodism in Haiti begins here.

Founded two decades after the Haitian Revolution, immigrant African American communities on Hispaniola created new nodes along the Black evangelical Atlantic littoral. Since the late seventeenth century, white missionaries had traveled across the Protestant Atlantic to convert enslaved people

Building an AME Presence in Haiti

to Christianity. The first groups of converted Blacks in the Anglophone and Dutch Caribbean helped develop new notions of Christian slavery whereby a person of African descent could be both enslaved and a Christian; previously, masters prohibited slave conversion for fear that it would lead to freedom.[5] As Black Christians grew in faith and numbers, they challenged white Christians' beliefs and practices regarding slavery, albeit without toppling the slave system. By the end of the eighteenth century, however, a growing Black evangelical network in the Caribbean and North America "used the white missionary infrastructure that was then developing as a way to reach out to other like-minded people of color, connect to international humanitarian organizations, and fight for freedom."[6] Black evangelists from the British Caribbean traveled to the North American mainland, bringing with them Christian ideas influenced by African-derived religions that emphasized benefits in this world and not the next. Some Black preachers began to speak of "deliverance and earthly liberation."[7] These traveling preachers carried a freedom message first in whispers and then in shouts as the abolitionist movement gained steam across the British Atlantic.

The age of revolution brought additional hope for Black converts to Protestant Christianity. The American Revolution (1765–83) expanded Black Protestant networks as escaped bondspeople and free Blacks joined the British army and later immigrated to Canada, Africa, and the Caribbean. A few migrants, like Baptists George Liele and David George and Calvinist John Marrant, became prominent evangelists and ministers of Black churches in British Caribbean territories and Africa, even while most African descendants in the Americas remained in bondage.[8] Rumors of slave rebellion in Saint-Domingue soon set a new tone across the Atlantic world and inspired some Black evangelicals in North America to resist slavery and other forms of racial oppression. Galvanized by the Haitian Revolution (1791–1804), for example, both Denmark Vesey and Nat Turner used Christianity and Black Protestant networks to incite rebellions in South Carolina (1822) and Virginia (1832). The same channels of information and faith that tied Haiti to the United States also inspired the independent church movement that spread across the U.S. Northeast at the end of the eighteenth century. Around 1787, Richard Allen led Black members of Philadelphia's St. George Methodist Episcopal Church out of the sanctuary, and founded the independent Black congregation from which the African Methodist Episcopal denomination would emerge in 1816.[9] Drawing the connection between the Haitian Revolution and the AME Church, AME bishop Daniel Alexander Payne avowed decades later, "As the Haytians have completely thrown off the white man's yoke in their national affairs, so have the leaders and members of the AME Church in ecclesiastical affairs."[10] This declaration implicitly signaled the long history of Protestant networks that made possible the hereditary relationship Payne claimed. Historical Afro-Atlantic Protestantism had enabled and propagated a revolutionary theological imagination.[11]

This revolutionary imagination, as well as a growing network of independent Black churches in New England, likewise facilitated the massive emigration movement of free Blacks and escaped slaves from the United States to Haiti throughout the nineteenth century. At the invitation of Haitian president Jean-Pierre Boyer, the first large wave of emigration took place between 1824 and 1826, when Haiti governed both sides of the island. Hoping for U.S. recognition and aiming to populate the eastern side of the island, Boyer sent his agent Jonathas Granville to the United States to seek willing emigrants. Granville arrived first in Philadelphia, where he met Richard Allen (then the bishop of the AME Church) and other leaders of Philadelphia's African Methodist congregation. At first, Allen and others expressed skepticism about emigration. In 1816, white Americans had founded the American Colonization Society, which aimed to deny Black Americans citizenship by removing them from the United States and relocating them to Liberia. African Methodists questioned whether Haitian emigration equated to much of the same. They ultimately decided to support the Haitian movement, however, since the initiative remained Black-led and they could set their own terms. Thus, the AME denomination helped arrange the migration of between 6,000 to 13,000 Black people to the island.[12] They did so by organizing groups of emigrants within Black church congregations and by discursively tying Black freedom and the promise of citizenship to independent Haiti.[13] Thus, Haitian emigration also took on a religious character as thousands of African Americans left the United States not only in response to slavery but also because they believed that God had divinely ordained Haiti as a Black "promised land."[14]

Throughout the nineteenth century, African descendants in the United States would seek other such "promised lands" as a source of spiritual and physical freedom and racial uplift, even while emigration remained a contentious subject among African Americans. For example, while many Black Americans (including Richard Allen and Frederick Douglass) opposed schemes to send African Americans to Africa, thousands of people still immigrated to Liberia and Sierra Leone. Some viewed their new home as a haven, while others longed to return to the United States.[15] Other Black North Americans made their way to Canada, Mexico, Jamaica, and Central and South America.[16] Although scholars have yet to develop an extensive literature on migration to these other places, the religious convictions of Black emigrants remained a common theme. In each place, emigrants saw divine purpose in their migration, and they drew from Christian scripture to give meaning to their resettlement in new lands. Moreover, many emigrants, along with the congregations that sent them, believed that Black American colonies would foster Christianity in supposedly "heathen" lands. Consequently, ordained Black ministers and preachers of the Methodist, Baptist, Presbyterian, and Episcopal persuasions became prominent members among the groups of migrants leaving the United States for Africa, Canada, Hispaniola, and elsewhere.

In the case of African Methodists on Hispaniola, Black Protestant preachers who immigrated to the island established Protestant societies as an act of faith and to sustain cohesion among African American colonists. Their labor—as described in the limited documentation of the religious institutions that sponsored them—provides glimpses into immigrants' religious lives. Representing the AME Church, for example, immigrant missionaries Scipio Beans, Richard Robinson, Isaac Miller, and Jacob Roberts established Methodist societies in Port-au-Prince, Samaná, and Santo Domingo.[17] Within these small congregations, African American communities on Hispaniola recreated the social structure and hierarchy of the AME Church. While the preacher in charge led the societies, local class leaders mentored smaller groups, or "classes," in the Methodist tradition. The first congregations also had a board of trustees that worked alongside the preacher and aided in decisions on various community issues. By 1830 the Santo Domingo and Samaná societies had organized well enough to hold an annual conference, a yearly meeting of two or more AME congregations. At the conference, the congregations voted to send their preachers Miller and Roberts to the AME Church's Baltimore annual conference, where the city's African Methodist leaders received them into the AME connection by vote. Leaders of the AME Baltimore conference also approved Miller's and Roberts's respective ordinations as deacon and elder and subsequently charged them to return to the island to continue their work.[18] The mention of these men and their work in Payne's famous history of the AME Church suggests that many immigrants to Hispaniola remained on the island, despite scholarship that has interpreted the Haitian emigration movement as a failure.[19]

African Methodists, however, were not the only Protestants on Hispaniola, nor were they the first to bring Protestantism to the island in the post-colonial era.[20] The Society of Friends (Quakers), the American Baptist Church, and the British Wesleyan Methodist Church all sent missionaries to Haiti prior to the mass emigration of African Americans in 1824–26. In these cases, the missionaries aimed to convert Catholic Haitians. Quaker missionaries Stephen Grellet and John Hancock, for example, preached in French and distributed Bibles while touring the island in 1816. The first Wesleyans, John Brown and James Catts, arrived in Port-au-Prince a year later, where they established the first permanent Protestant mission and started a school. Within two years, however, Catholic opposition drove them out of the country, and they left their young church in the hands of two local Haitian preachers, Jean-Claude Pressoir and John-Baptiste Evariste.[21] Mme. Antoine Victor Bauduy, a woman of color and a class leader for the Wesleyans, and her son Victor St. Denis Bauduy also assisted Pressoir and Evariste. The Baptist ministry on Haiti likewise faced a rough start when Thomas Paul, the founder and minister of the First African Baptist Church in Boston (established 1806) traveled to Port-au-Prince in 1823. Paul preached to Haitians at Le Cap but returned to the United States after only eight months. These early missionary efforts paved the way for later Wesleyan, Baptist, AME, Anglican, and other missionaries working in the nineteenth century.[22]

Of the denominations represented in the early decades of the nineteenth century, only the Wesleyans sustained missionaries on the island for a prolonged period. When British Wesleyans returned to Hispaniola in the 1830s, they met distinct circumstances. Boyer still served as president of Haiti, but the presence of African American emigrants changed religious demographics in Port-au-Prince and along the northern coast. Black Protestants in these areas, who were mostly African Americans, began to petition the Wesleyans for aid. In 1832, for example, twenty-four African American emigrants in Puerto Plata, representing themselves and a community of thirty women and sixty children, informed the British society that they had met its missionary Theophilus Pugh, who worked on Grand Turk Island to the north, and requested the institution to send another missionary to Puerto Plata.[23] The London-based society sent John Tindall to Puerto Plata in 1834, and the following year he became the chairman of the Haiti district, which included Puerto Plata, Cap-Haïtien, and Port-au-Prince, where St. Denis Bauduy still labored. Two years later, African American emigrants in Samaná followed suit and received British missionary William Cardy, who brought the former AME society into the Wesleyan fold in 1838.[24] Around this time, Tindall attempted to respond to yet another request from the AME American emigrants in Santo Domingo city, but the military commandant prohibited him from preaching there.[25] Still, by Dominican independence from Haiti in 1844, the British Wesleyans had instituted a missionary circuit that linked western and eastern port cities to each other despite the new political division of the island. Hispaniola's Wesleyan missionary stations also linked to Wesleyan activity on other Caribbean islands, although in the early years this connection remained largely figurative for Black parishioners, since only the church's appointed missionaries traveled these circuits on official church business. Still, the new nodes in the historic Atlantic evangelical littoral created ties between islands that lasted throughout the nineteenth century and into the early decades of the twentieth. Such ties strengthened as Wesleyan congregations on Hispaniola produced local Black preachers who, like their predecessors in the broader Protestant Atlantic world, traveled to the United States and other Caribbean islands.

Unlike the Wesleyan Church, the AME Church did not sustain early ties to Hispaniola, despite attempts to establish societies in Port-au-Prince, Samaná, and Santo Domingo in 1827 and 1830. In fact, by 1841, the Baltimore conference of the AME Church declared its branches on Hispaniola to be lost.[26] A few factors precipitated this rupture. The existence of slavery in the southern United States made it extremely difficult and dangerous for Black clergy to travel between the two locales, especially after the Fugitive Slave Act passed in 1850. Furthermore, poverty prohibited the AME denomination from sending material aid to the emigrants, and the correspondence over the waterways was slow. Added to these hinderances, African Americans' attitudes regarding emigration began to change. While hundreds of U.S. Blacks continued to immigrate to Haiti in the 1830s, African American leaders' fears of forced deportation increased. Abolition, they resolved, would occur only if they stayed in the United States and carried on the fight against slavery. Thus, at the first Colored Convention held at Bethel AME Church in Philadelphia in 1830, Black leaders dismissed Haiti and Liberia as viable locations for emigration.[27] Three years later, the "Colored Convention" denounced all emigration schemes, and by 1835 "anyone who merely mentioned emigration or colonization would be branded a race traitor."[28] The change in attitude reflected new strategies in the fight for freedom in the United States, if not a change in the spirit of racial solidarity that African Americans felt toward Haiti. Yet consumed by the struggle in the United States and facing multiple constraints, AME leaders turned away from Haitian emigration and thereby reinforced their efforts to fight for Black liberation stateside.

The AME Church did not reestablish formal religious ties with African American immigrants in Haiti until after the U.S. Civil War and the Dominican War of Restoration (1863–65). By then, a generation had passed away, and the fight for Black freedom for both African Americans in the United States and Black people on Hispaniola had transformed. The United States had abolished slavery in 1863, while rumors spread that Spain, which had annexed the Dominican Republic in 1861, would reinstitute plantation slavery in eastern Hispaniola.[29] Then, between 1863 and 1865, Dominicans with the aid of Haitians and other Antillean peoples ousted the white Spanish colonizers in a war to restore Dominican independence; people of all colors had fought and died, blood spilling into the streets. Black survivors on the island and the mainland laid claim to an ephemeral, shape-shifting liberty—freedom denied, won, lost, reclaimed, and redefined across time and space. Soon it became clear that war had transformed the fight for Black freedom both for African Americans in the United States and for Black people on Hispaniola.

AME Expansion to Haiti Post-1865

In the aftermath of the two wars, the ways that AME Church leaders perceived and discussed their relationship to Hispaniola shifted. In the antebellum period, African Americans viewed Haiti as a haven for Black people. Yet wars across the island in the later part of the century placed the symbolic significance of the Haitian Revolution in perpetual jeopardy. White Americans asserted that political disfunction in Haiti and the Dominican Republic proved Black inferiority.[30] AME leaders reacted to whites' criticism by calling for Hispaniola's "redemption" via Western education and Protestant evangelization.[31] Fusing the theological concept of redemption with the contemporary idea of racial uplift, they perceived African Methodism to be both a natural and an urgent solution to the island's problems.[32]

On the surface, it seemed that racial and religious solidarities that had existed during the earlier decades of the century would sustain the AME Church's new missionary efforts in Haiti in the postwar period. Most AME leaders, however, did not consider the financial cost of missions or how their "gospel of freedom" message would translate in the Haitian and Dominican context—especially as U.S. imperialism grew in the Caribbean, the United States' supposed "natural zone of influence."[33] AME missionaries carried a new freedom message that "exhorted 'middle-class' values, self-help, moral reform, and racial pride."[34] This message had evolved from a long tradition of Black Protestantism in the Atlantic world.[35] But it now carried the additional weight of U.S. empire and the financial responsibilities that came with it. Such ideological conflicts and monetary obligations, however, did not much concern the AME Church's male leadership in the early 1870s, when hopes for foreign missions ran high.

Stoking AME leaders' enthusiasm, the denomination's growth in membership and infrastructure since the Civil War made foreign expansion seem more feasible than ever before. During and after the war, dozens of AME missionaries had traveled south to evangelize newly freed Black people.[36] By 1876, the denomination reported 206,730 members, a substantial increase from the 50,000 members reported in 1866.[37] The AME Church's institutional organization and financial policies also shifted during these years. Prior to 1860, the church's regional conferences sanctioned missionaries and appointed them to specific towns or locations abroad.[38] That year, however, the General Conference voted to make the missionary department a distinct entity with its own leadership board, which consisted of the bishops (then numbering only seven) and the secretary of missions. The first mission secretary, John M. Brown, was elected in 1864.[39] At the following General Conference in 1868, the denomination enacted the "Dollar Money" law, a rule that required every church member to offer one dollar to the institution; the dollar money would later constitute the missionary department's yearly budget.[40] Prior to using this money to finance missions, however, the General Conference instituted a finance department in 1872, which received and disbursed the dollar money to the church's auxiliary departments and seven episcopal districts.[41] Female church leaders also organized the Women's Parent Mite Missionary Society on May 18, 1874, which aided the missionary department in raising and disbursing funds for foreign missions.[42] This consolidated organizational system provided infrastructure and a primary source of income (at least, theoretically) for the AME Church's missionary department throughout the 1870s.

Facing a new day in the United States and in the AME Church's institutional history, many AME leaders believed that the denomination should continue its progress by advancing toward foreign lands. "Our Church is fast rising up to the full conception of her duty in the premises," the *Christian Recorder* trumpeted months before the 1872 General Conference. "Already has she no little zeal for the salvation of her heathen kindred."[43] This statement tapped into the growing sense that African Americans had a special role to play abroad as the harbingers of Western civilization.[44] With the hope of Reconstruction still ignited in 1872, many African Methodists perceived foreign missionary work as a complement to white-led American missions abroad, and they presumed that the AME Church was the only Black-led denomination mature enough to organize such an endeavor. Such early traces of U.S. chauvinism within AME foreign missionary thought would soon transform into a more urgent—and arguably more ominous—"Black man's burden" ideology directed toward Africa at the end of the century.[45] Yet in 1872, AME leaders still imagined activating the "latent missionary power of the Church," and their collective gaze fell steadily upon Hispaniola.[46]

During Reconstruction, Hispaniola represented the natural progression of the denomination's missionary efforts in the U.S. South. Besides African Americans' sustained historical and political interest in the progress of the island's two nations, the timing seemed especially providential in the early 1870s due to the contemporary debate over U.S. annexation of the Dominican Republic. Furthermore, the AME Church received petitions from immigrant communities on the island who wished the denomination to send missionaries.[47] Dominican annexation failed in 1871, but the denomination responded to the petitions by sending the missionary secretary Theophilus Gould Steward to Port-au-Prince in 1873.

The Haitian missionary station met a slow start. Steward's short trip to Haiti did not establish a permanent station on the island as AME leaders had hoped, and years passed before the denomination could send another representative to Port-au-Prince in the person of Charles W. Mossell. The problems were both organizational and financial. AME bishop James A. Shorter, who became the chairman of the missionary board in 1876, explained that Steward had refused to return to the island after his initial trip, and his successor as missionary secretary, Richard H. Cain, had neglected his duties after becoming a U.S. congressman.[48] Since many African Americans lived in poverty and did not have much money to donate to missions, it was the missionary secretary's duty to inspire congregants to give what they could. Thus, raising funds for Haiti at a denominational level was nearly impossible without the missionary secretary's leadership, and the process of establishing a missionary station in Port-au-Prince stalled between 1873 and 1877, the year Charles and Mary Ella Mossell went to Haiti.[49]

These problems shifted slightly in 1878 when James M. Townsend became missionary secretary. Under Townsend, the missionary department raised over $2,000 for Haiti within two years. The denomination used this money to fund the Mossells' mission in Port-au-Prince, where Charles had met resistance from the independent St. Peter's Union Methodist Episcopal congregation. Despite this initial setback, Mossell became the AME Church's first missionary to operate under a new regime in which he received a regular salary from the denomination.[50] For the next few years, the AME Church sent the majority of its missionary funds to Port-au-Prince, signaling the

Building an AME Presence in Haiti

denomination's commitment to the Mossells and to developing missions on Hispaniola despite the many hardships—disease, war, and natural disasters—that the Mossells faced. In the late nineteenth century, Protestant missionaries across Hispaniola frequently wrote home about these challenges. However, not everyone had the ear of the denomination's most powerful leaders. Charles and Mary Ella did.

As Townsend and Shorter read the Mossells' letters from Port-au-Prince, they began to lobby the AME Church for greater missionary support. Between 1878 and 1880, Townsend and Shorter—with the aid of the Women's Parent Mite Missionary Society and senior bishops Daniel Alexander Payne, Jabez P. Campbell, and John M. Brown and their respective districts—raised over $3,500 to cover Mossell's salary. Convincing church members to donate to the Haitian cause was not easy due to the impoverished state of the people, yet the clergymen and missionary-minded women did their best. "I am here simply to say by hook and crook, we have raised enough to give [Mossell] up until today," Shorter reported before the 1880 General Conference.[51] Supporters of Haitian missions found additional satisfaction when the conference pledged to send another salaried missionary to Haiti to assist Mossell. The bishops and episcopal officers renewed this pledge in June 1881, when they also vowed to construct a church building in Port-au-Prince. This answer to a specific petition from the Mossells indicated that the AME Church would not back down from its commitment, and it likely filled the Mossells and their friends on the island and in the United States with hope of more aid to come.

Funding a Church for Haiti

For AME leaders in the United States, the promise to construct a new AME chapel in Port-au-Prince was easier said than done. AME leaders continued to face an uphill battle when it came to fundraising, and soon AME leaders' pursuit of foreign expansion in Africa eclipsed their financial commitment to Haitian missions. These developments indicated that the struggles, mindsets, and fates of African Americans in the United States and their immigrant counterparts on Hispaniola no longer fully aligned.

Leaders of the AME Church faced a huge financial challenge in June 1881 when they pledged to build a church for the Haitian mission. To fulfill their commitment, the board of bishops promptly initiated a capital campaign to raise $10,000 for the missionary department, $5,500 of which they promised to the Haitian building fund.[52] According to the bishops' agreement, the nine bishops were to raise $660 each for the Haitian fund, and each AME member was to give five cents toward missions. "Give us this amount and we can this year build our church, pay our salaries, double the force both in Africa and Haiti, and assist our home missionaries as well," an optimistic Townsend declared in 1881 and 1882.[53] The missionary secretary also gave practical advice for pastors by suggesting that each congregation organize a women's missionary society, and he incentivized the membership by promising to print in the *Christian Recorder* the names of the congregations that raised the most money. African Methodists across the United States responded positively to the fundraising campaign. Within a year, pledges for future monetary donations covered the total amount requested to erect the church in Port-au-Prince. Based on these pledges, Townsend signed a contract with an English company that would construct the church's iron frame and ship it from London to Haiti.[54] By the end of 1882, the *Christian Recorder* reported that Townsend was "in the home stretch in the race for a church to be sent out to Haiti."[55] Good feelings ran high.

Yet, as Townsend pursued various fundraising methods and accumulated myriad pledges of financial support, it became increasingly clear that raising substantial funds for Haiti would not be easy. Much of the work for fundraising lay in the hands of women who labored in the AME Church's Women's Parent Mite Missionary Society. The women had raised most of the funds that supported the Mossells in Haiti, but even with the new capital campaign, AME coffers were never full enough. A letter from Sarah E. Tanner, president of the Women's Parent Mite Missionary Society in December 1880 (and wife of the *Christian Recorder* editor), underscored this point. According to Mrs. Tanner, Mossell's "pressing obligations make it necessary for him to urge us to send him his money; and we feel it a duty to do so, but we have [nothing] sufficient in the treasury. . . . We have paid out nearly every dollar."[56] In her call for all local women's societies to send financial support, Mrs. Tanner encouraged other members to "awaken more fully to our duty" and to "renew our covenant for the new year to work more effectually in our Mite Societies."[57] She believed that such work would enable the society to build the church and support additional missionaries in Haiti. Yet, the larger question of how to develop the work so that missionaries in Haiti were not wholly dependent upon monthly donations from the AME Church in the United States was not addressed.

Despite the great effort put forth by the women's missionary society, by the end of 1882 Townsend began to worry that the denomination's members would not follow through on their pledges. The will to support Haiti seemed constant; however, the lack of follow-through caused Townsend

Building an AME Presence in Haiti

considerable stress and put the campaign in jeopardy. Between September and November of that year, Townsend raised $1283.50 in pledges during his visits to various AME regional conferences, but by November 30 he had collected only $261.58.[58] Articles in the *Christian Recorder* called on the church's members to send their money to Townsend. "The Secretary has no wish to have the church appear in a bad light," one article pleaded. "Don't desert him now."[59] This exhortation appeared again months later in January 1883 and was repeated throughout the year.[60] Anxious to receive the promised money, Townsend boosted the incentives. Members who contributed over $100 would have their names inscribed in a window of the Haitian church, and those who donated $5 would be included on the Haitian congregation's memorial list.[61] He moreover promised to publish a list of congregations that had already sent money. These positive reinforcements, however, did not augment the missionary department's treasury, and by January 1884 Townsend feared that the AME Church would lose the down payment it had made on the Haitian church's iron frame. The London-based contractors had already sent measurements to Mossell for the foundation, and they projected that the frame would ship to the island in March 1884, but Townsend lacked $1,500 to complete the deal.[62] With only two months to fulfill the contract and over $6,000 in outstanding pledges overall, Townsend could do nothing more but pray for a miracle.

Just how the missionary department fulfilled its contract for the iron church remains unknown, but a general sense of triumph pervaded the spring air as clergy and lay delegates headed to Baltimore for the AME Church's 1884 General Conference. Townsend had just returned from England from whence he had shipped the iron frame to Haiti. The Mossells' Haitian congregation had begun construction in Port-au-Prince.[63] Keen to demonstrate the AME Church's strength, the Haitian mission became a boasting point for many clergy. Famed minister of New York's Sullivan Street church and Caribbean immigrant William B. Derrick extolled the iron frame as "the greatest [step] that has ever transpired in the history of our beloved Zion in the mission department." He reveled, "Even our enemies, who have questioned our ability in managing so gigantic an undertaking as mission fields in foreign lands, acknowledge our capability as a church."[64] Bishop John M. Brown also listed the iron frame as one among many of the AME Church's accomplishments. "Few people realize the strength of the African Methodist Church in the United States. . . . We purchased and sent to Port-au-Prince, Haiti, in March last, an iron church," he boasted.[65] In reciting accolades, AME leaders ignored the church's financial trouble, which evoked pessimism and doubt in God and Black people's abilities. Thus, in this moment, elation and faith in the AME Church's continual progress superseded concerns over the sustainability of church growth abroad.

Fervidly optimistic, such cursory summaries of the denomination's achievements led many church members to miss the warning signs. The obvious ones loomed large. The campaign for the Haitian church had nearly failed. The missionary department had fallen far short of its $10,000 mark. Townsend's trip to London had depleted the Women's Parent Mite Missionary Society's funds, and not a single pastor had attended that group's party to wish Townsend farewell for the journey.[66] A less obvious caveat had also come to light during the campaign. As Townsend faced increased scrutiny over his fundraising, church members began to question why Port-au-Prince had become the denomination's primary missionary station. A few members suggested that missions in the Anglophone Caribbean would cost the church much less money and grief.[67] Many other parishioners called for missions in Africa. "Haiti, first tilled and watered by the illustrious [Richard] Robinson, now leads on the triumph under the noble Mossell, while Africa, long slumbering, wakes from the sleep of ages," admonished a *Christian Recorder* editorialist.[68] For many AME members, it was high time to move on from Haiti toward other lands.

This shift in perspective reflected the expansionist goals of a new generation of AME leadership in the United States. In 1880, the ousted missionary secretary Richard H. Cain triumphed in an election to the AME bishopric along with two other prominent ministers, Henry McNeal Turner and William F. Dickerson. Representing the southern AME districts, a region of growing power in the AME Church, both Cain and Turner championed missions in Africa over the Mossells' work in Haiti.[69] Cain even had reason to resent Haitian missions, since the cost of constructing the church in Port-au-Prince had actually inhibited his intended missionary trip to West Africa in 1883. Together, these energetic bishops pushed the denomination toward the African continent at Haiti's expense. As Cain explained in 1883, "After surveying the financial condition of the Church Treasury, and the pressing demands of the Haytian work, namely, the immediate erection of the iron church there . . . it is deemed wise to wait [on African missions] until that is accomplished. The missionary society will then declare the Haytian work self-supporting and will turn the future efforts to Africa."[70] The declaration of the Haitian station as "self-supporting" was an arbitrary decision fashioned to make room for African missions. In the following years, the denomination dedicated more resources to its Liberian missions

Building an AME Presence in Haiti

and moved into Sierra Leone.[71] By 1891, these stations had become official AME conferences under Turner.

Not all African Methodists felt satisfied by the abrupt shift in missionary focus from Hispaniola to Africa. The transition not only directly threatened the Mossells' work but also put in jeopardy concurrent efforts to spread the AME denomination to the Dominican Republic and the British Caribbean.[72] Recognizing that the Mossells' mission and other nascent AME missionary stations in the Caribbean depended upon monetary donations, senior bishop Daniel Alexander Payne chastised his more junior peers (Cain, Turner, and others), reminding them that the struggle to fund Haitian missions did not end with the building campaign.[73] Perhaps because of Payne's objections, Bishop Brown published a notice to the Women's Parent Mite Missionary Society in the *Christian Recorder*, burdening the women's organization with the repercussions of the younger clergymen's decision. "Your mites must come in as before, full and plenty," Brown directed. "Our expense goes on. Brother Mossell, wife and child must be succored, must be fed, must be cared for."[74] This exhortation may have seemed supercilious, even hypocritical, to the women who had labored so hard to raise funds for the Haitian church. It was even more alarming to Mossell and other AME missionaries working in the Caribbean region.[75] Yet in this strange moment in which U.S.-based AME leaders touted a chauvinistic vision of Pan-Africanist expansion, the drive for foreign expansion overshadowed alternative visions of AME missions and Protestantism on the island of Hispaniola more generally.

Ecumenical Cooperation in Haiti

While AME leaders in the United States declared Africa the new missionary field, the Mossells and members of their congregation celebrated the construction of the new AME chapel in Port-au-Prince. The few reports detailing their celebrations suggest a radically different vision of missions from that which AME leaders in the United States promoted. Rather than seeing the AME Church as a harbinger of Western civilization and Pan-African Christian unity, members of the Haitian congregation experienced a form of ecumenical cooperation in Port-au-Prince. AME missionaries like the Mossells served the AME denomination, but they did not isolate themselves from Catholic authorities or other Protestant groups for the sake of AME orthodoxy. In other words, in the absence of robust AME denominational investment, AME missionaries on Hispaniola built networks of survival with other Protestants as well as Catholic officials, despite the Catholic Church's

denunciation of Protestantism. Such intersections did not go without critique—even among African Methodists on the island—but they did enable
underfunded AME missionaries to see themselves as part of a local Protestant culture that had little to do with the AME bishops' expansionist goals.
When taking this perspective into account, the 1884 construction of a new
AME chapel in Port-au-Prince epitomized the frictions between U.S. actors'
plans for foreign evangelization and the sometimes unexpected results their
actions produced on the ground in Haiti.

The building project provides a clear example of the quotidian collaboration between local African Methodists, other Protestants, and Catholic
Haitians. To celebrate the new church, the AME congregation in Port-au-
Prince hosted a cornerstone-laying service in April 1884. On the day of the
ceremony, a dense crowd of Protestants and Catholics gathered in the market
square. Mrs. Mossell, likely with the aid of Haitian women who had formed
a local branch of the Women's Parent Mite Missionary Society, had adorned
the enclosed grounds of the church property with evergreens. The women
had additionally covered the area from the sun, laid out seats for the city's
inhabitants, and raised a platform for the event's distinguished male orators.
As city residents found their seats, they would have recognized these men,
including three of the city's Protestant ministers: Mossell of the AME Church;
Thomas Richard Picot, the superintendent of the Wesleyan Church's Haitian
mission; and John Robert Love, a minister who had formerly worked closely
with the African American bishop of the Haitian Episcopal Church James
Theodore Holly. Several government officers also graced the stage. Among
them sat the judge of the Court of Instructions, a Haitian general, and a
congressman.[76] The presence of these men demonstrated that the AME
Church had friends in high places of Haitian society. Such friendships legitimized the event in the eyes of the public, imbuing it with significance and
making it easier for residents to ignore the local Catholic priests' warnings
against the Protestants.[77] As one observer opined, "A strong manifestation
of sympathy with the cause seemed to pervade the whole assembly, everyone appearing determined to do his part in this important work."[78] The
cornerstone-laying ceremony was indeed a collaboration among various
sectors of Haitian society.

The religious service also reflected an ecumenical spirit, as the three
Protestant ministers led the ceremony. After Mary Ella Mossell sang a hymn
and Charles Mossell prayed, the Wesleyan missionary Thomas Picot and
Mossell offered comments. Next, the property's Haitian trustee, Mr. I. Day,
read the congregation's confessions of faith, and together the three Protestant

missionaries—Mossell, Picot, and Love—descended from the platform and laid the building's cornerstone on the northwest edge of the grounds. The men buried the stone with the confession of faith and several contemporary Haitian, British, and American newspapers, symbolizing the inclusive nature of the service. When the ministers returned to the platform, Picot prayed, and Love, Picot, and Mossell all offered speeches before taking up a collection and dismissing the participants. The cooperation displayed at the ceremony indicated that the Protestant leaders and congregations in Port-au-Prince often worked side by side and saw themselves as part of the same team despite representing distinct denominations and ethnicities.[79]

General cooperation among Port-au-Prince's foreign missionaries, however, did not eliminate white missionaries' racial prejudice or occasional conflict between denominations. Haitian African Methodist James Tucker's critique of the cornerstone-laying ceremony provides a clear example. In a letter to AME leaders in the United States, he related a dramatic tragedy of events. First, Mossell had originally invited the minister of justice to speak, but when this government representative could not attend the event, Mossell gave Picot the honor of speaking first. Tucker took umbrage with this move since Picot "holds the opinion that the Negro is unfit for the ministry," and Mossell could have invited another Haitian official instead.[80] According to Tucker, Mossell knew that Picot habitually refused to ordain Black preachers and yet still allowed him to preach. Second, and more offensive still, Picot's sermon had undermined Mossell's authority since Picot had disavowed the AME Church and spoke only of the Wesleyan mission, "taking this grand opportunity of profiting, so to speak, from the sweat of our brow."[81] Third, Mossell had erred in including John Robert Love of the Haitian Episcopal Church. Although Love was a man of color and spoke eloquently about African Methodism, James T. Holly had recently deposed him from office.[82] Tucker wondered why Mossell had not invited a local Haitian preacher instead of Love. "Are we as an independent body, in full communion with churches throughout the universe, to open our arms to receive a degraded priest in our pulpit [whom] the Protestant Episcopal Church has thrown out as unfit for the ministry?" he deadpanned.[83] Tucker's critique indicated that ecumenical cooperation, politicking, or what Tucker called "over-politeness" sometimes weakened the AME Church's institutional integrity in Port-au-Prince. It also suggests that ethnocentrism, Anglophone chauvinism, classism, or even colorism may have biased Mossell against local Haitian preachers. Such political jockeying and displays of favoritism not only injured the denomination's reputation but also could discourage the ministerial development of Haitians. Thus, ecumenical cooperation sometimes undercut the AME Church's racial uplift message and praxis.

Tucker's negative report moreover suggests that ecumenical cooperation acted as a check upon foreign missionaries whose congregations could complain to higher ecclesiastical figures, involve governmental authorities, or simply defect to another Protestant denomination in the case of any disputes. In Tucker's case, it seems that Mossell heeded the warning, despite the fact that ecumenism prevailed. At the subsequent July 13 inauguration of the AME Church building in Port-au-Prince, both Haitian officials and local Haitian preachers spoke about African Methodism before the nearly 400 people assembled in the newly constructed chapel. First, Mossell introduced a Haitian official, the deputy of the south coast of Haiti, who was a Protestant and often held Protestant services in Port-au-Prince.[84] According to Tucker, this man "made a beautiful discourse on Protestantism."[85] Two Haitian preachers, Paul Oashard of the Wesleyan mission and one Monsieur Lilaias (likely of the AME Church) extolled the Mossells' work, celebrated the new temple, and curried "the sympathy of all Protestant and Catholics to aid [the Mossells] in the noble work of carrying on the gospel throughout the Island of Haiti."[86] U.S. Minister to Haiti John Mercer Langston also lauded the Mossells. "Many a time, after the burning of the city in the last revolution, [Mossell] came to [me] without garments for himself and family," Tucker reported Langston as saying, "and what has he given [the Haitian people]? This very same temple which he inaugurates today."[87] Elevated six feet above the street and adorned with a gilded cross at the top of its steeple, the AME church must have captivated the audience as Langston and the other orators spoke. While listening to their speeches, some members of the public likely marveled at the sanctuary draped in red and blue bunting and a canopy of white lace that enhanced the varnished wood panels and pews. Others perhaps gazed out the large windows that let in the ocean breeze. The building, the speeches, the Mossells, and the people present stood as testaments to the AME Church's increasing entrenchment within Port-au-Prince's social milieu.[88]

Glimpses of AME Church life in Port-au-Prince in the late nineteenth century and early twentieth century remain few and far between in AME Church literature. Yet as one reads between the lines of the few letters and reports on Caribbean-based congregations, it becomes clear that AME missionaries on Hispaniola depended upon other Protestants and Catholics for support. Counting Wesleyan missionaries, Episcopal priests, and Catholic government officials among their "friends and well-wishers," AME missionaries in Haiti forged local partnerships out of convenience, social obligation, and necessity.[89] In the early 1880s, the salience of such local relationships accentuated the distinctions between U.S.-based AME leaders' expansionist goals and the reality of Protestant missionary work in Haiti. While AME missionaries like the Mossells and AME-trained Haitian ministers held fast to their AME affiliation, their local version of "the gospel of freedom" necessarily took on a different form.[90]

Conclusion

The events leading up to the founding of the AME Church in Haiti—and specifically the construction of a new AME chapel in Port-au-Prince—not only evidence that African Americans' ideas about Haiti changed over time but also underscore the fact that Americans' expansionist ideologies often led to unexpected results. African Americans participated in U.S. global evangelism under their own terms. Persecuted and marginalized in the United States, Black Protestant denominations did not possess the institutional wealth or mainstream white support to raise funds for foreign missions. The AME Church pushed forward in Haiti anyway, believing that the conversion of supposedly heathen lands would uplift Black people across the world and combat global white supremacist ideology. Infused with this sense of divine purpose, U.S.-based AME leaders initiated a fundraising campaign to erect a new AME church building in Haiti. Yet when fundraising for the Port-au-Prince mission inhibited certain bishops' missionary efforts in Africa, AME leaders declared the Haitian field self-supporting and directed their attention and financial resources to Liberia, Sierra Leone, and eventually South Africa. In response, AME missionaries in Port-au-Prince turned to ecumenical networks of survival.

Glimpses of African Methodists' participation in ecumenical networks in Port-au-Prince appear in missionaries' letters back to AME leaders in the United States. Such relationships can be detected in the broader history of Protestantism in Haiti and the Dominican Republic. On Hispaniola, the absence of a robust AME missionary presence produced a culture of cooperation between AME congregations and other Protestant denominations. Catholic politicians also aided the cause by guaranteeing religious tolerance. Such relationships with local non-AME Protestants and Catholics reinforced solidarities that sometimes undermined the cross-border ties between AME leaders in the United States and those based in the Caribbean. These dynamics remind us that a long view of Protestant history on Hispaniola remains significant to the study of African American missions in the Caribbean. At the end of the nineteenth century, the AME Church's post-1865 "gospel of freedom" message ran up against a long history of interracial, interdenominational ecumenical cooperation on the island that originated when the first groups of U.S. Black émigrés sought freedom in the Black republic. They and their descendants came to know Haiti as home. Their experiences and viewpoints provide a distinct vision of U.S. global evangelicalism and the expanding Black church in the nineteenth century.

Notes

1. Charles W. Mossell, *Toussaint L'Ouverture, the Hero of Saint Domingo, Soldier, Statesman, Martyr; or, Hayti's Struggle, Triumph, Independence, and Achievements* (Lockport, NY: Ward and Cobb, 1896), 407.

2. Mossell, 408.

3. See, for example, Sylvester A. Johnson, *The Myth of Ham in Nineteenth-Century American Christianity: Race, Heathens, and the People of God* (New York: Palgrave Macmillan, 2004), 73–74.

4. For "Black man's burden," see Michele Mitchell, *Righteous Propagation: African Americans and the Politics of Racial Destiny after Reconstruction* (Chapel Hill: University of North Carolina Press, 2004), 51–75.

5. Katherine Gerbner, *Christian Slavery: Conversion and Race in the Protestant Atlantic World* (Philadelphia: University of Pennsylvania Press, 2018); Jon F. Sensbach, *Rebecca's Revival: Creating Black Christianity in the Atlantic World* (Cambridge, MA: Harvard University Press, 2006), 51–52; Albert J. Raboteau, *Slave Religion: The "Invisible Institution" in the Antebellum South* (Oxford: Oxford University Press, 2004), 98–103.

6. Catron, *Embracing Protestantism: Black Identities in the Atlantic World (Gainesville: University of Florida Press, 2016)*, 151.

7. Catron, 196.

8. For descriptions of these men, see Catron, 200–209.

9. The exact date of the walkout is disputed, but the denomination was formally incorporated in 1816. Dennis C. Dickerson, *The African Methodist Episcopal Church: A History* (Cambridge: Cambridge University Press, 2020), 31–32.

10. Daniel Alexander Payne, *History of the African Methodist Episcopal Church* (Nashville, TN: Publishing House of the AME Sunday School Union, 1891), 477. Also quoted in Léon Dénius Pamphile, *Haitians and African Americans: A Heritage of Tragedy and Hope* (Gainesville: University Press of Florida, 2001), 12.

11. For an overview of these events, see Claude Clegg, "African Americans and the Making of Evangelical Christianities, 1760–1860," in *The Cambridge History of Religions in America*, ed. Stephen J. Stein (Cambridge: Cambridge University Press, 2012), 2:178–202. For specific topics, see the following. For Vesey, see Douglas R. Egerton and Robert L. Paquette, eds., *The Denmark Vesey Affair: A Documentary History* (Gainesville: University Press of Florida, 2017); Edward A. Pearson, *Designs against Charleston: The Trial Record of the Denmark Vesey Slave Conspiracy of 1822* (Chapel Hill: University of

North Carolina Press, 1999); John Lofton, *Denmark Vesey's Revolt: The Slave Plot That Lit a Fuse to Fort Sumter* (Kent, OH: Kent State University Press, 1983); and Robert S. Starobin, *Denmark Vesey: The Slave Conspiracy of 1822* (Englewood Cliffs, NJ: Prentice-Hall, 1970). For Turner, see Kenneth Greenberg, ed., *The Confessions of Nat Turner with Related Documents*, 2nd ed. (Boston: Bedford/St. Martin's, 2017); Kenneth S. Greenberg, *Nat Turner: A Slave Rebellion in History and Memory* (Oxford: Oxford University Press, 2003); and James Thomas Baker, *Nat Turner: Cry Freedom in America* (Fort Worth, TX: Harcourt Brace, 1998). For Richard Allen and the independent Black church movement, see Dickerson, *African Methodist Episcopal Church*, 17–55; Richard S. Newman, *Freedom's Prophet: Bishop Richard Allen, the AME Church, and the Black Founding Fathers* (New York: New York University Press, 2008); and Carol V. R. George, *Segregated Sabbaths: Richard Allen and the Emergence of Independent Black Churches, 1760–1840* (New York: Oxford University Press, 1973).

12. Estimates range drastically. In 1860, Benjamin Hunt claimed the higher number. Benjamin Hunt, *Remarks on Hayti as a Place of Settlement for Afric-Americans; and on the Mulatto as a Race for the Tropics* (Philadelphia: T. B. Pugh, 1860), 11, cited in Sara Fanning, *Caribbean Crossing: African Americans and the Haitian Emigration Movement* (New York: New York University Press, 2014), 125.

13. Laurie Maffly-Kipp, *Setting Down the Sacred Past: African American Race Histories* (Cambridge, MA: Belknap Press of Harvard University Press, 2010), 109–53.

14. African American immigration to Haiti took place over the course of the nineteenth century. For "promised land" see Laurie Maffly-Kipp, *Setting Down the Sacred Past: African American Race Histories* (Cambridge, MA: Belknap Press of Harvard University Press, 2010), 111. For a general overview, see Chris Dixon, *African America and Haiti: Emigration and Black Nationalism in the Nineteenth Century* (Westport, CT: Greenwood Press, 2000). For the 1824–26 movement, see Sara Fanning, *Caribbean Crossing*; Dennis Hidalgo, *La primera inmigración de negros libertos norteamericanos y su asentamiento en la Española (1824–1826)* (Santo Domingo: Academia Dominicana de la Historia, 2016); Julie Winch, "American Free Blacks and Emigration to Haiti" (San Juan: Centro de Investigaciones del Caribe y América Latina, 1988); James O'Dell Jackson, "The Origins of Pan-African Nationalism: Afro-American and Haytian Relations, 1800–1862" (PhD diss., Northwestern University, 1976); Jean Stephens, "La inmigración de negros norteamericanos en Haití en 1824," *Eme Eme* 3, no. 14 (1974): 40–71; and Rayford Logan, *Diplomatic Relations of the United States with Haiti, 1776–1891* (Chapel Hill: University of North Carolina Press, 1941), 216–17.

15. For immigration to Liberia, see Claude Clegg, *The Prince of Liberty: African Americans and the Making of Liberia* (Chapel Hill: University of North Carolina Press, 2004). David Kazanjian has shown that African American migrants' uneasy settlement in Liberia provides insights on their speculative notions of freedom. David Kazanjian, *The Brink of Freedom: Improvising Life in the Nineteenth-Century Atlantic World* (Durham, NC: Duke University Press, 2017), 66–76.

16. For Canada, see William H. Pease, *Black Utopia: Negro Communal Experiments in America* (Madison: State Historical Society of Wisconsin, 1963). For Jamaica, see Gale Kenny, "Manliness and Manifest Racial Destiny: Jamaica and African American Emigration in the 1850s," *Journal of the Civil War Era* 2 (2012): 151–78. For Mexico, Central America, and South America, see Alice L. Baumgartner, *South to Freedom: Runaway*

Slaves to Mexico and the Road to the Civil War (New York: Basic Books, 2020); Thomas Shoonover, "Misconstrued Mission: Expansionism and Black Colonization in Mexico and Central America during the Civil War," *Pacific Historical Review* 49, no. 4 (1980): 607–20; Nicolas Guyatt, "'The Future Empire of Our Freedmen': Republican Colonization Schemes in Texas and Mexico, 1861–1865," in *Civil War Wests: Testing the Limits of the United States*, ed. Adam Arenson and Andrew R. Graybill (Berkeley: University of California Press, 2015), 95–117; and Phillip W. Magness and Sebastian N. Page, *Colonization after Emancipation: Lincoln and the Movement for Black Resettlement* (Columbia: University of Missouri Press, 2011), 13–23. See also Samantha Seeley, "Beyond the American Colonization Society," *History Compass* 14, no. 3 (2016): 93–104; and essays by Thomas Mareite and Dexter J. Gabriel in *In Search of Liberty: African American Internationalism in the Nineteenth-Century Atlantic World*, ed. Ronald Angelo Johnson and Ousame K. Power-Greene (Athens: University of Georgia Press, 2021).

17. The denomination recognizes Scipio Beans, who immigrated to Haiti in 1827, as its first missionary in Port-au-Prince. Robinson was appointed in 1830 in absentia. Miller and Roberts were sent to Santo Domingo and Samaná, respectively. Payne, *History of the African Methodist Episcopal Church*, 66; Stephen W. Angell, "'The Shadows of the Evening Stretched Out': Richard Robinson and the Shaping of African Methodist Identity, 1823–1862," *Journal of Africana Religions* 3, no. 3 (2015): 231–32.

18. Payne, *History of the African Methodist Episcopal Church*, 66.

19. In response to the hardships, many immigrants (about one-third) returned to the United States. For return, see Fanning, *Caribbean Crossing*, 99–118; and Winch, "American Free Blacks and Emigration to Haiti," 13. Dismissing the two-thirds who remained, scholars have generally portrayed the Haitian emigration movement as a failure. See, for example, H. Hoetink, "'Americans' in Samaná," *Caribbean Studies* 2, no. 1 (April 1962): 7; and José Gabriel García, *Compendio de la historia de Santo Domingo*, 3rd ed. (Santo Domingo: Imprenta de García Hermanos, 1894), 2:122. Recently, scholars have critiqued this assessment. See Brandon R. Byrd, "A Reinterpretation of African Americans and Haitian Emigration," in Johnson and Power-Greene, *In Search of Liberty*, 197–223.

20. Protestant presence on the island has a longer colonial history as well, beginning with Sir Francis Drake's attack in 1583. A letter from Archbishop Nicolas Ramos also attested to Protestant presence in 1594. The presence of Protestant Dutch and English traders who participated in the contraband trade served as a principal reason for the Devastaciones de Osorio in 1605–6. See Bienvenido Alvarez Vega, "Movimiento Pentecostal Dominicano," in *El campo religioso dominicano en la década de los 90's: Diversidad y expansión* (Santo Domingo: Departamento de Estudios de Sociedad y Religión, [1996]), 102n5.

21. Two other Wesleyan missionaries, Elliot Jones and William Woodis Harvey, also began missionary stations at Cap-Haïtien, but they had to leave within a few months due to illness. G. G. Findlay and W. W. Holdsworth, *The History of the Wesleyan Methodist Missionary Society*, vol. 2 (London: Epworth Press, 1921), 266.

22. For a general history of these events, see Catts Pressoir, *Le Protestantisme Haitien* (Port-au-Prince: Imprimerie de la Société Biblique et des Livres Religieux d'Haïti, 1945), 51–145. For Methodist histories, see Findlay and Holdsworth, *History of the Wesleyan Methodist Missionary Society*, 264–66; Leslie Griffiths, *A History of Methodism in Haiti* (Port-au-Prince: Méthodiste-D.E.L., 1991), 13–106. For early Baptist missionaries, see

Philip Everhard, *History of the American Baptist African and Haytien Missions* (Boston: T. R. Marvin, 1831), 56–67; Ivah T. Heneise, *Pioneers of Light: Stories of the Baptist Witness in Haiti, 1823–1998* (Penney Farms, FL: International Christian Education Fund, 1999), 21–29; John Saillant, "'This Week Black Paul Preach'd': Fragment and Method in Early African American Studies," *Early American Studies* 14 (2016): 60.

23. Findlay and Holdsworth, *History of the Wesleyan Methodist Missionary Society*, 491–92.

24. Rev. William Cardy arrived in the community in the fall of 1837. For accounts of Cardy, see Findlay and Holdsworth, *History of the Wesleyan Methodist Missionary Society*, 493–99; George A. Lockward, *Cartas de Cardy: Primer misionero metodista en Samaná* (Santo Domingo: Educativa Dominicana, 1988); and Hidalgo, *La primera inmigración de negros libertos norteamericanos*, 163–95.

25. Findlay and Holdsworth, *History of the Wesleyan Methodist Missionary Society*, 493.

26. James A. Handy, *Scraps of African Methodist Episcopal History* (Philadelphia: AME Book Concern, 1902), 135; Payne, *History of the African Methodist Episcopal Church*, 478. This declaration specifies Haiti but refers to branches established on both sides of the island.

27. Leslie M. Alexander, "A Land of Promise: Emigration and Pennsylvania's Black Elite in the Era of Haitian Revolution," in *The Civil War in Pennsylvania: The African American Experience*, ed. Samuel W. Black (Pittsburgh: Pennsylvania Heritage Foundation, 2013), 113–14.

28. Alexander, 117–18.

29. Anne Eller, "Rumors of Slavery: Defending Emancipation in a Hostile Caribbean," *American Historical Review* 122, no. 3 (2017): 653–79.

30. George M. Fredrickson, *The Black Image in the White Mind: The Debate on Afro-American Character and Destiny, 1817–1914* (Middletown, CT: Wesleyan University Press, 1987), 259; Brandon R. Byrd, *The Black Republic: African Americans and the Fate of Haiti* (Philadelphia: University of Pennsylvania Press, 2019), 7.

31. Byrd, *Black Republic*, 7. See also Brandon Byrd, "Black Republicans, Black Republic: African-Americans, Haiti, and the Promise of Reconstruction," *Journal of Slave and Post-Slave Studies* 36, no. 4 (2015): 546–47.

32. A. Nevell Owens, *Formation of the African Methodist Episcopal Church in the Nineteenth Century: Rhetoric of Identification* (New York: Palgrave Macmillan, 2014), 48.

33. For "gospel of freedom," see Reginald F. Hildebrand, *The Times Were Strange and Stirring: Methodist Preachers and the Crisis of Emancipation* (Durham, NC: Duke University Press, 1995), 51.

34. Hildebrand, 51.

35. Dickerson, *African Methodist Episcopal Church*, 3.

36. William E. Montgomery, *Under Their Own Vine and Fig Tree: The African-American Church in the South, 1865–1900* (Baton Rouge: Louisiana State University Press, 1993), 98–99; Hildebrand, *Times Were Strange and Stirring*, 31–49.

37. "AME Church Statistics, 1875," *Christian Recorder*, March 9, 1876; "Statistics of the AME Church," *Christian Recorder*, April 7, 1866. See also Payne, *History of the African Methodist Episcopal Church*, 465. As Hildebrand has stated, "Statistics are notoriously unreliable"; however, the reported statistics reflect the dramatic growth that took place. Hildebrand, *Times Were Strange and Stirring*, 48.

38. This process took place when, as discussed above, AME missionaries left the United States as emigrants. In fact, the AME Church's missionary department, the Parent Home and Foreign Missionary Society (established 1844), actually fell under the Baltimore conference's jurisdiction during the antebellum period.

39. Llewellyn L. Berry, *Century of Missions of the African Methodist Episcopal Church* (New York: Gutenberg, 1942), ix and 91.

40. From 1844 to 1868, all members paid two cents monthly to the denomination, but in 1868 the General Conference voted to raise dues to one dollar per year. This money was to support the operation of the whole denomination. I use the word "law" here because this rule was voted upon and written into the AME Church's book of discipline. C. S. Smith, *A History of the African Methodist Episcopal Church: Being a Volume Supplemental to "A History of the African Methodist Episcopal Church," by Daniel Alexander Payne* (Philadelphia: AME Book Concern, 1922), 79.

41. J. H. W Burley was the first financial secretary. He served from 1872 to 1879. Smith, 344.

42. Clara E. Harris, *The Women's Parent Mite Missionary Society of the African Methodist Episcopal Church* (Baltimore: African Methodist Episcopal Church, 1935), 9–11.

43. "The Mission Work," *Christian Recorder*, March 30, 1872.

44. Sylvester A. Johnson, *African American Religions, 1500–2000: Colonialism, Democracy, and Freedom* (Cambridge: Cambridge University Press, 2015), 251–53.

45. For African missions, see Walter L. Williams, *Black Americans and the Evangelization of Africa, 1877–1900* (Madison: University of Wisconsin Press, 1982); James T. Campbell, *Songs of Zion: The African Methodist Episcopal Church in the United States and South Africa* (Chapel Hill: University of North Carolina Press, 1995); and Elisabeth Engel, *Encountering Empire: African American Missionaries in Colonial Africa, 1900–1939* (Stuttgart: Franz Steiner Verlag, 2015).

46. "Mission Work."

47. Christina C. Davidson, "Converting Spanish Hispaniola: Race, Nation, and the AME Church in Santo Domingo, 1872–1904" (PhD diss., Duke University, 2017), 53–54.

48. "Bishop Shorter's Testimony," *Christian Recorder*, May 13, 1880.

49. For further details on AME leaders' perspectives on Haitian missions during these years, see Dickerson, *African Methodist Episcopal Church*, 147–48.

50. B. W. Arnett, *The Budget for 1881* (Xenia, OH: Torchlight Printing Company, 1881), 58, 86–87. See also Dickerson, *African Methodist Episcopal Church*, 151.

51. "Saturday, May 22, 1880," *Christian Recorder*, May 24, 1880.

52. "Office of the Corresponding Secretary," *Christian Recorder*, December 1, 1881; Townsend, "Last Appeal."

53. "Office of the Corresponding Secretary." This article repeated throughout the spring of 1882.

54. The contract was with Kent and W. Finley of London, England. See "Glimpses and Gleanings," *Christian Recorder*, May 10, 1883; and "Early Attention," *Christian Recorder*, January 14, 1884.

55. "The Corresponding Secretary of Our Church Missionary Society," *Christian Recorder*, November 30, 1882.

56. "To the Mite Societies," *Christian Recorder*, December 23, 1880.

57. "To the Mite Societies."

58. "Glimpses and Gleanings," *Christian Recorder*, November 30, 1882.

59. "Corresponding Secretary of Our Church Missionary Society."

60. Jas. M. Townsend, "Notice," *Christian Recorder*, January 18, 1883.

61. Townsend, "Notice."

62. J. M. Townsend, "A Last Appeal," *Christian Recorder*, January 10, 1884.

63. The church's foundation was laid in Port-au-Prince on April 27, 1884. "African Methodist Episcopal Church in Haiti," *Christian Recorder*, June 19, 1884.

64. "Complimentary," *Christian Recorder*, May 15, 1884. Born in Antigua, W. B. Derrick came to the United States in 1860. He was ordained a deacon in 1868 and later became the missionary secretary and then bishop in the AME Church. See William J. Simmons, *Men of Mark: Eminent, Progressive and Rising* (Cleveland, OH: G. M. Rewell, 1887), 88–96.

65. "Bishop John M. Brown," *Christian Recorder*, August 28, 1884. Brown listed several other achievements, including a membership of over 500,000, multiple educational institutions, and nascent missionary stations in the Dominican Republic, the British Caribbean, and Africa.

66. Two days before his departure, on Monday, March 3, 1884, Townsend attended a farewell party at T. G. Steward's Union AME Church of Philadelphia. During the reception, the honored guest and Bishops Campbell and Brown offered remarks to the Women's Parent Mite Missionary Society, but it was "regretted that not a single pastor in the city was present." Their absence may have indicated waning support for Haitian missions among AME clergy. See "The Farewell Reception Tendered to Rev. Dr. J. M. Townsend," *Christian Recorder*, March 6, 1884.

67. "Our Mission Abroad," *Christian Recorder*, September 30, 1880.

68. "Not to Ruin but to Victory," *Christian Recorder*, January 19, 1882.

69. Stephen Ward Angell, *Bishop Henry McNeal Turner and African-American Religion in the South* (Knoxville: University of Tennessee Press, 1992), 119–22.

70. Richard H. Cain, "The African Missionary Work," *Christian Recorder*, September 27, 1883.

71. Christina Cecelia Davidson, "'What Hinders?': African Methodist Expansion from the U.S. South to Hispaniola, 1865–1885," in *Reconstruction and Empire*, ed. David M. Prior (New York: Fordham University Press, 2022), 70.

72. For further information on conflict surrounding the British Caribbean these years, see Christina Cecelia Davidson, "An Organic Union: Theorizing Race, Nation, and Imperialism in the Black Church," *Journal of African American History* 106, no. 4 (2021): 577–600.

73. Daniel A. Payne, "The Past, Present, and Future of the AME Church," *AME Church Review* 1 (April 1885): 315–16.

74. J. M. Brown, "To All the Ladies of the Mite Missionary Society," *Christian Recorder*, May 1, 1884.

75. See, for example, Davidson, "'What Hinders?,'" 70.

76. "African Methodist Episcopal Church in Haiti." This article lists many other prominent government officials and merchants.

77. In his version of the story, Tucker states that people "were seen wending their way to assist in performing the ceremony, in spite of all the Romish priest's excommunicants [*sic*]." James Tucker, "A Voice from Port-au-Prince, Haiti," *Christian Recorder*, August 7, 1884.

78. "African Methodist Episcopal Church in Haiti."

79. "African Methodist Episcopal Church in Haiti."

80. Tucker, "Voice from Port-au-Prince."

81. Tucker, "Voice from Port-au-Prince."

82. In 1884, Love no longer worked for the Episcopal Church. Deposed from the ministry on September 5, 1882, Love remained at odds with Holly, his former bishop and mentor. For details of their dispute and Love's accusations against Holly, see David M. Dean, *Defender of the Race: James Theodore Holly, Black Nationalist Bishop* (Boston: Lambeth Press, 1979), 74–78; and "Rev. Dr. J. Robert Love, Priest," *Christian Recorder*, November 8, 1883. For Love's charges against Holly, see J. Robert Love, *Is Bishop Holly Innocent* (Port-au-Prince: T. E. F. de T-M Brown, 1883); and J. Robert Love, *Proofs of Bishop Holly's Guilt: Supplement to "Is Bishop Holly Innocent"* (Port-au-Prince: T. E. F. de T-M Brown, 1883). The *Christian Recorder* reported on the two Episcopalian ministers' dispute but declined to choose sides. "Rev. J. Robert Love," *Christian Recorder*, July 12, 1883.

83. Tucker, "Voice from Port-au-Prince."

84. In a speech that Mossell reprinted, the U.S. minister to Haiti, John Mercer Langston, stated that the congregation had prepared a special seat for the president of Haiti, Lysius Salomon, who sent this officer to represent him. Mossell, *Toussaint L'Ouverture*, 427.

85. Tucker faulted the deputy only for failing "to open the eyes of the Roman Catholics that are still in spiritual bondage." Tucker, "Voice from Port-au-Prince."

86. Tucker, "Voice from Port-au-Prince."

87. Tucker, "Voice from Port-au-Prince." The fire burned down the Mossells' home and caused the death of their daughter. Mossell, *Toussaint L'Ouverture*, 427–32. See this work as well, for a reprint of the speech in full.

88. On African Americans' early incorporation into Haiti's social milieu, see Byrd, "A Reinterpretation of African Americans and Haitian Emigration," 206–10.

89. Rev. S. G. Dorce, "Home Again," *Christian Recorder*, November 27, 1884.

90. Two AME-trained and ordained Haitian ministers at the time were Samuel G. Dorce and Adolphus H. Mevs. For more information on Dorce and Mevs, see Davidson, "'What Hinders?,'" 68–71.

CHAPTER THREE

American Missionaries and the Boundaries of Evangelicalism in the Philippines

Tom Smith

In the early twentieth century, American evangelicalism was in transition. The nineteenth century's "loose, transatlantic alliance of Protestant believers who prioritized conversion, warmhearted piety, revivalism, and the reform of society" was under strain from evangelicals' varying responses to modern intellectual currents and competing visions of the American nation.[1] Nonetheless, before World War I, certain common interests allowed "liberals" and "conservatives" to share the "evangelical" label, including support for foreign missions.[2] Theologically diverse leaders had placed a commitment to missions at the heart of evangelical identity in the late nineteenth century, and their shared confidence in the superiority of Western culture smoothed over finer philosophical differences.[3] American missionary numbers had swelled, making the United States the world's leading exporter of Protestant evangelists by 1910.[4]

For American evangelicals, their nation's colonization of the Philippines in 1898 had presented a particularly special opportunity. While the missionary movement of the era was generally collaborative and transnational rather than nationalistic, American missionaries embraced a national mood that understood the United States' decisive victory in the Spanish-American War as providential and its resultant new empire as having evangelistic purpose.[5] A number of American mission boards enthusiastically responded to the God-given opportunity to evangelize the Philippines, previously closed off by centuries of Spanish Catholic rule.[6] Yet, this chapter argues, even in this atmosphere of confidence, as a burgeoning missionary movement hitched its wagon to an assertive "formal" U.S. empire, American evangelicalism proved unstable as it crossed borders. In the Philippines in the early twentieth century, some American missionaries who self-defined as evangelicals revised their expectations that U.S. imperialism would lead to evangelical Protestantism's triumph over Catholicism and instead proposed that historical indigenous expressions of Christianity had "evangelical" potential.

For these missionaries, looking to claim success in an enterprise for which they harbored high expectations, the boundaries of evangelical faith became more porous. Their project became less contingent on conspicuous conversion—a key pillar of evangelicalism according to David Bebbington's influential definition—and more about an ability to orient Filipinos' existing spiritual sensibilities toward identification with a loosely defined "evangelical" purpose.[7] At times, this meant questioning fundamental American Protestant assumptions about evangelicalism, for example by assessing whether even Catholicism, which missionaries supposedly went to the Philippines to displace, could be a vehicle for evangelical faith.[8] Such an approach was not by any means accepted by all missionaries, but its presence indicates how evangelicalism renegotiated its meaning as it crossed borders.

Underpinning missionaries' adaptation was a sense of insecurity relative to American colonial rule. They were haunted by waning enthusiasm in the United States for the colonial project, fearing that their entire enterprise would be threatened if America were to leave the Philippines. Decolonization was not completed until 1946, but missionaries were preparing for it decades before, trying to find a basis upon which their work could generate a legacy. Their response, like that of the AME missionaries in Haiti analyzed by Christina Cecelia Davidson elsewhere in this volume, was to pursue a "Christian cosmopolitanism" in order to survive. To an extent, they handed over evangelicalism's definition to Filipinos, particularly to elites who rejected Spanish forms of Catholicism and embraced spiritual renewal but affirmed the inherent religiosity of Filipinos rather than valuing wholesale conversion to an American faith. Therefore, the Philippines, even as a U.S. territory, exemplifies where evangelicalism and Protestant mission were not wholly synonymous with American hegemony, but rather "indigenous actors either seized the initiative for themselves or subverted . . . American dominance into a genuinely transactional exchange."[9]

As missionaries pragmatically toyed with expanded conceptions of evangelicalism, some also looked to the Philippines to conceive of alternative futures at a time of uncertainty. If the American evangelical coalition was strained as the twentieth century opened, it was torn apart by World War I. From that point, historians have identified evangelicalism with a "radical" or "conservative" viewpoint, set against "liberal" or "ecumenical" Christians turning toward "internationalism."[10] Indeed, Gene Zubovich's essay in this volume shows how fundamentalists in the 1940s consciously adopted both Christian nationalism and the label "evangelical" as a direct counterpoint to ecumenical globalism. Through the crisis years between the world wars, however, some "liberal" missionaries with internationalist leanings still thought of themselves as evangelicals and found possibilities for evangelicalism in a nascent Filipino faith. Indigenous elites, coopting evangelicalism in an age of Filipino nationalism, emphasized ecumenism and inclusivity, conceiving of a nondenominational movement uniting historical Philippine religious traditions. In this Filipino definition of evangelicalism, some missionaries found an antidote to interwar America's theological turmoil. By considering the ways in which missionaries responded to Filipino religion, the chapter argues for greater attention to what American evangelicalism was, or might have become, when engaging with the world in a period between the consensus-based evangelicalism of the late nineteenth and early twentieth centuries and the more divisive neo-evangelicalism of the post–World War II years. Looking to a decolonizing archipelago in an uncertain moment, some Americans hoped evangelicalism might become the ecumenical faith that it ended up defined against.

While this story of fluidity and possibility resonates with arguments that "liberal" missionaries were unusually sensitive to foreign peoples' contributions and needs, some caveats are necessary.[11] Only certain Filipinos were celebrated as displaying "evangelical" sensibility—they were men, educated urban elites, and collaborators with the colonial regime who thanked America even as they stressed Filipinos' readiness for independence.[12] In other words, they were Filipinos who allowed Americans to feel that their colonial duty to conquer effeminacy and superstition with rational masculinity had been fulfilled and to forget the colonial violence and racism that defined the American project.[13] Even as their perspectives shifted, missionaries trod paths forged by colonial epistemologies.[14]

The chapter's argument rests upon two case studies. The first is of the Manila Young Men's Christian Association (YMCA), which, motivated by the United States' failure to break through Catholic dominance and an ever-increasing sense that decolonization was imminent, questioned American assumptions about the association's evangelical and Protestant nature. The Manila Y turned away from viewing the Philippines through the lens of U.S. imperialism, instead engaging with a transnational debate about whether Catholics could be considered "evangelical." Other studies show how foreign populations selectively responded to the YMCA. Cubans, for example, adopted sport without Protestantism, while Japanese Christian leaders, as Dana L. Robert emphasizes in this volume, used the platform provided by the Y to engage with the latest scientific and comparative thought.[15] This chapter, however, reveals how Filipino resistance to wholesale conversion actually destabilized the YMCA's own religious assumptions.

The second case is of Frank Laubach of the American Board of Commissioners for Foreign Missions (ABCFM), who in the 1920s wrote "the story of Evangelical Christianity" in the Philippines.[16] Against the backdrop of promised decolonization and World War I, Laubach narrated this history as one of fulfillment—the joining together of multiple spiritual strands that had prepared Filipinos for global evangelical leadership. The languages deployed by the YMCA and Laubach were somewhat different—the YMCA emphasized pragmatism in reaching out to Catholic elites, while Laubach was more effusive about the genuine spiritual opportunities inherent in Philippine evangelicalism. In both cases, however, the outcome was similar: self-proclaimed American evangelicals deemphasized U.S. Protestant definitions of "evangelicalism" and yielded to the foreign.

Evangelicalism and the Challenges of Filipino YMCA Work

The American YMCA's overseas work was emblematic of U.S. Protestants' fervent drive to evangelize the world from the late nineteenth century. Out of YMCA-sponsored student conferences at Northfield, Massachusetts, led by the revivalist Dwight L. Moody, emerged the Student Volunteer Movement, which sent thousands of college-educated American missionaries across the globe between the late 1880s and the 1920s.[17] The Student Volunteer Movement in turn invigorated the American YMCA to become a more explicit missionary force, and historians have pointed to the Y's aggressive overseas evangelism and uncompromising theology in the late nineteenth century, tied to American nationalism.[18] Around the turn of the twentieth century, however, the Y overseas increasingly found itself challenged both by fellow Protestants and by foreign nationalists.[19] Consequently, guided by John R. Mott's moderate evangelical voice, it reinvented itself as a modernizing urban youth association tolerant of foreign philosophical traditions.[20]

In the early twentieth-century Philippines, the YMCA partnered with U.S. colonialism's "civilizing" mission yet retained an explicitly "evangelical" identity. It was tied to the American colonial project from the start—YMCA chaplains worked among U.S. troops during the Spanish-American War and led the first Protestant services in the islands.[21] Subsequently, as the Manila YMCA was incorporated in 1907 and opened its buildings for Americans and Europeans in October 1909, it was celebrated by key figures within the colonial administration who saw it as aiding the American conquest of the enervating tropics.[22] Yet while the Manila Y's first general secretary, William A. Tener, underscored this practical benefit to the colonial project, he also emphasized that "there was no attempt to disguise the religious motive": to create a positively evangelical outpost.[23] The Manila branch retained the American "Portland Basis" for Y membership, devised in 1869 and diverging from European principles, which stated that any "active" Y member, eligible to vote or hold office, had to be a member of a recognized evangelical church.[24] J. M. Groves, the associate general secretary of the branch, clarified one particular assumption underpinning this basis: "Roman Catholics have been held not to be evangelical in the meaning of our constitution."[25]

Such candid evangelicalism was significant in the context of what was, as far as Protestant missionaries were concerned, American empire's failure to fulfill its Protestant potential.[26] Asserting a clean break with Spain's intertwinement of religion and politics, the colonial government committed to the strict separation of church and state, offered an exclusively secular education, and even welcomed the participation of American Catholics— Jeremiah Harty became the first American archbishop of Manila in 1903.[27] Missionaries were convinced that this secular atmosphere, combined with the tropical climate, encouraged licentiousness in American soldiers and businesspeople, hampering them in their duty to raise moral standards.[28] The Y's work for Americans and Europeans in the Philippines, therefore, was one expression of a broader missionary idea that the United States had not done enough to export American evangelical religiosity alongside colonial bureaucracy.

From the first half of 1909, YMCA leaders in the Philippines considered extending their work to Manila's 6,000 Filipino students. The colonial government, an April 1909 memorandum noted, had neglected the "physical, social and moral and religious needs" of young Filipino men. Students received secular education but existed in "an atmosphere of agnosticism, materialism, and immorality," rooming in crowded and unsanitary boardinghouses, spending their evenings at "moving-picture shows" and dance halls, and graduating without "the fundamentals of religious truth." The idea of opening a YMCA dormitory for these students seemed practical and nonsectarian enough for colonial officials to lend their vocal support, yet also Protestant enough for other missionaries to laud the potential benefits to their work of conversion.[29]

The extension of Y work to Manila's Filipinos was motivated in part by the increasing indigenization of Philippine politics, especially following the first elections in July 1907 for the Philippine Assembly. The assembly was designed by the colonial government in the 1902 Philippine Organic Act as the lower house in a bicameral legislature, to be composed entirely of Filipinos, under the authority of an upper house, which continued to be populated by American colonial administrators.[30] As the creation of a Filipino governing class through the American public school system proceeded apace, a YMCA dormitory for students would ensure that the "future teachers and leaders of the entire race . . . could be touched with the message of the Bible" and that some could be drawn into Christian ministry.[31]

The Y's plan sought to make the best of a situation with which most missionaries were uncomfortable. Despite frustrations with the colonial government, there was still a consensus among missionaries that the triumph of Protestant "civilization" in the Philippines was contingent upon the United States' guiding hand being in place for the foreseeable future. However, with indigenization proceeding rapidly, and against the backdrop of ongoing partisan debates in Washington over imperialism's propriety, America could not be relied upon to uphold its responsibility indefinitely— the "premature" creation of the Philippine Assembly was one sign of this.[32] Colonial impermanence was on the minds of YMCA leaders as they planned work among Filipinos: "The big question of the future still remains," wrote Tener in October 1911, "as to how long Uncle Sam will maintain sovereignty."[33] If the American colonial project would not protect Protestant mission

American Missionaries in the Philippines

indefinitely, there was a pressing need to ensure that Christianity became rooted among Filipino leaders themselves.

From early in discussions about work among Filipinos, however, there was a conviction that the Y could not simply replicate its work for Americans. Tener underscored the need for a segregated enterprise: there were "tastes and customs distinctly American as there are tastes and customs distinctly Filipino. . . . Filipino students are clannish and conceited, . . . and are very pleased if they can be in an institution by themselves."[34] This approach diverged from that in Puerto Rico, where the Y envisioned a single association for all, perhaps reflecting an awareness that while Puerto Rico was to remain a U.S. territory, the Philippines was headed for independence.[35] Setting up a separate Filipino organization, however, presented challenges. Commissioned by Mott to report on the prospects for a Filipino YMCA, Presbyterian missionary James B. Rodgers expressed theoretical support but also anxieties about raising money among Filipinos, given that "the wealthy are almost all of the Roman church, and our Evangelical people are almost all poor."[36]

Work for Filipinos was not incorporated until November 1911, well over two years after discussions began, as the Manila Y puzzled over how it could secure the patronage of Filipino elites, whom Rodgers suggested sat outside the borders of evangelicalism because of their Catholicism. In April 1911, the YMCA secretary for Asia, renowned evangelist G. Sherwood Eddy, visited the Philippines and opened the door to a potential solution by enquiring "whether it would be wise to ask for the approval of the Foreign Department of electing a small number of high class Catholics on our Board."[37] J. M. Groves in turn sought the advice of the Episcopal bishop of Manila, Charles Henry Brent, the most prominent missionary in the islands and one of the most sympathetic to the idea of partnering with Catholics.[38] Brent recognized that beneath the question as to whether Filipino Catholics could be included in the YMCA was one about whether they were "evangelical." He said, reported Groves, that although "he certainly did not consider the Roman Catholic Church evangelical in the Philippine Islands, . . . he did consider it so in certain places." He moreover "thought it would be fair, as well as generous, to give [the church in the Philippines] the credit for its good intentions and efforts in recent years . . . in the direction of eliminating the abuses that crept in under Spanish control."[39] This willingness to seek "evangelical" potential among Catholics indicates how forces in the Philippines—colonial uncertainty and Filipino elites' religious adherence—challenged fundamental American assumptions about evangelicalism's boundaries.

Despite missionaries' initial confidence that U.S. empire in the Philippines presaged Protestant triumph, the Y in its discussions about how to reach Filipinos turned away from viewing its work within the frame of colonialism and engaged instead with a transnational debate. Groves noted that co-opting Catholics would offset the risk of repeating the situation the Y had faced in Cuba, when "opposition by the ultra-montane priests and members of the church" had caused "defeat."[40] There was also precedent in Mexico City, whose YMCA became the first to modify the Portland Basis in 1907 in order to include Catholics among its directors.[41] By 1919, an enquiry showed that the majority of Y branches across the Americas had either modified or rejected the Portland Basis to accommodate Catholics.[42] In this sense, Manila was treated by the Y not as an American outpost that presented a unique opportunity for Protestant mission work among an "Oriental" people but as characterized by its heritage of Spanish Catholicism. It required treatment like the other "Latin" nations in which the YMCA was having to compromise.

After the incorporation of the Filipino YMCA, Groves outlined the decision ultimately taken: up to a third of the Manila Y's board of directors would be Catholics, and, while the American and European department would maintain the Portland Basis, Filipinos would be drawn in on the "Paris Basis."[43] Established in 1855, the Paris Basis proffered active YMCA membership to those who, "regarding Christ as their God and Saviour, according to the Holy Scriptures, desire to be his disciples," thus putting the onus on an individual's faith rather than on membership in an evangelical church.[44] This shift was deemed important by Groves in securing "the permanent confidence and sympathy of the community." He argued that it was a providential solution that did not compromise an "aggressively evangelistic policy" but "invoked the liberty exercised by other branches of the same movement in new fields."[45]

Thereafter, despite the Catholic hierarchy's ongoing opposition, elite Filipinos who professed Catholicism offered the YMCA their support. A campaign for donations yielded 100,000 pesos in five days, exceeding a target of 80,000 pesos in ten days, and big donors included the chief justice of the Supreme Court and "Catholic laym[a]n" Cayetano Arellano and businessman, philanthropist, and "liberal Catholic" Teodoro R. Yangco, who became the first president of the Filipino Y, with Catholic judge Manuel Camus as vice president.[46] Groves celebrated "the greatest single stroke for religious liberty since American occupation," and the construction of two YMCA buildings for Filipinos in Manila was underway by July 1912.[47]

American Missionaries in the Philippines

Promotional material promised that the Manila Y would "transcend the tragic differences of Churches and . . . lead young men into the community of their traditional or chosen Church."[48]

The Manila YMCA's directors in fact took a step beyond recognizing individual Catholics' professions of faith, and a step beyond other Y branches in Latin America, by modifying the Paris Basis to state that "members in good standing in the Roman Catholic Church or in any other Christian Church, who are eighteen years of age or over, may become active members."[49] There were two innovations here: first, ensuring that individual professions of faith were still underpinned by some institutional affiliation; and second, naming the Catholic Church as a church from which active Y members could be drawn. Tener stated to Mott that this "unusual" move was made "at the request of one of our Filipino Directors, a staunch Roman Catholic," in order to "absolutely bar any criticism."[50]

In allowing local actors and circumstances to influence policy to the extent that the Catholic Church was named in a YMCA constitution, the Manila Y's leaders opened themselves to the charge that they were redefining evangelicalism. An April 1913 letter from Groves to L. Wilbur Messer, general secretary of the Chicago YMCA, defended the branch against criticism that Messer had made in a Y publication. Messer had expressed anxiety that the Manila YMCA was making a statement about "what are evangelical churches" that threatened the American Y's integrity: "With the adoption of this alternative definition it will be entirely possible for Roman Catholics to vote or hold office in any of our North American Associations if the local organization so desires." Groves wrote to quell Messer's fears, insisting that the Manila Y had no intention of redefining evangelicalism: "The Paris Basis itself is a purely personal statement of Christian faith. . . . We in the Philippines have made . . . no contribution to the oft-discussed question as to what is an 'evangelical Church.'"[51]

Yet the attitudes of those shaping Manila YMCA policy suggest that Messer's fears were not without foundation. In his earlier memorandum, Groves had lamented that "neither Catholics nor Protestants went beneath the surface of the word 'evangelical' but a large majority of both understood it to be synonymous with Protestant." Referring to Brent's analysis, he maintained that there was "good authority for including the Roman Catholic Church as evangelical" and stated that the removal of the word "evangelical" from the Filipino membership basis was more out of expediency than principle.[52] In other words, Groves knew that the assumptions underpinning the Portland Basis's evangelical test were such that it could not be applied in the

Philippines but was also moved toward a sincere contemplation of whether evangelicalism really had to exclude Catholics.

After the Manila Y finally opened work for Filipinos in 1915, it continued to attract opposition from the Catholic hierarchy, including American clergy, who deemed it a "secret [promoter] of Protestant beliefs." It was also criticized by Protestant missionaries, the majority of whom never questioned the need to convert Catholics.[53] YMCA leaders themselves meanwhile expressed divergent opinions about whether their ultimate goal was still to lead Catholics to Protestantism.[54] Yet despite these tensions, the Manila Y on the whole reaffirmed its membership basis and continued to imply that Filipino Catholics had evangelical potential. A 1918 memorandum restated that the local YMCA's "principal objection to the basis of the American Association was the fact that Catholics were not considered to be Evangelical. . . . Such a basis in the Philippines would make our work very weak and of little influence. . . . We have not the right to assume that all members of the Catholic Church cannot meet the personal test."[55]

Indeed, if the ultimate goal of creating a Filipino YMCA and modifying the membership basis had been to protect evangelicalism in the event that Philippine politics and religion would no longer be subject to America's guiding hand, the urgency of this need only intensified across the 1910s. Woodrow Wilson's election as U.S. president in 1912 marked the first time since the Philippines' annexation that a Democrat had been in office, breaking the dominance of a Republican Party that had championed overseas imperialism. After Wilson appointed Francis Burton Harrison as Philippine governor-general, who accelerated the process of "Filipinization," YMCA leaders soon sensed that the wind was blowing in a new direction.[56] Tener in October 1914 wrote that for Filipino nationalists, "every horizon looked clear and favorable for the realization of their fondest dreams."[57] Groves meanwhile noted the increasingly fraught nature of political discussion and the potential detriment to mission work of "the least appearance of . . . partisanship."[58] In 1916, the Jones Law passed the U.S. Congress, marking America's first formal commitment to Philippine decolonization, and in September 1918, Groves, continuing to offer advice even after his time as a branch official had ended, noted the need for the Y to keep up with the times: "The present Government policy of thorough going Filipinization . . . is an added reason for the early application in the Philippines of the general policy of putting native leaders forward as soon as they can be discovered and trained. . . . If we lag behind in this matter, it will naturally put us in a bad light." World War I, Groves further suggested, had heightened the urgency of such a shift, undermining European and American claims to moral authority.[59] By 1920, H. W. Love, the Manila YMCA's general secretary, remarked upon heightened "unrest": "The political leaders insist that independence must be granted at once."[60]

Against this backdrop, another extended discussion emerged about the YMCA's boundaries, specifically about the propriety of promoting Manuel Camus, the Catholic judge and vice president of the Filipino Y, to executive secretary for Filipino work. Groves earmarked Camus as "outstandingly the man to head our movement among the Filipinos."[61] Arguments favoring Camus's appointment hinged on the notion that he was "a nominal Catholic . . . alive to the dangers of Catholic influence."[62] Such a statement echoed a frequent line of reasoning taken by YMCA leaders justifying the inclusion of educated Filipino Catholics: although these men retained allegiance to the church for historical and social reasons, they were no longer subservient to it and were making individual spiritual decisions.[63] Their conversion may not have been "conspicuous" but was real—"a 'new man' may continue in his former Church with his new experience."[64] There is indeed evidence that Filipino Catholics did not see allegiance to the church and criticism of its particular manifestations in the Philippines as incompatible—in a letter to Mott in January 1918, Camus lambasted the vestigial "Catholic absolutism" that he perceived to motivate opposition to the YMCA.[65] The decoupling of personal adherence from what was stereotyped as Catholic "thinking" smoothed the path to conceiving of individual Filipino Catholics as somewhat "evangelical."

Yet, regardless of the Manila Y's need to respond to a heightening sense of colonial impermanence and of the opportunities represented by Camus, the calculations made by the Y's International Committee in America were rather different. In late 1918, Elwood S. Brown, a pioneering sports organizer and general secretary of the Manila Y, warned that "if the word went forth in Manila that the International Committee hesitated to appoint Judge Camus . . . because he was a Catholic, it would wreck the native work."[66] Nevertheless, E. C. Jenkins, on behalf of the International Committee, reminded Brown that the postwar atmosphere in America, far from indicating better Protestant-Catholic ties, had in fact soured interconfessional relations.[67] As a result, "there would be in the Association Brotherhood a very decided opposition to the radical step of appointing a Roman Catholic."[68] Repeated pleas from Manila across 1919 to consider "the wishes of the local field" and to help remove the impression "that the Association is a 'wolf in sheep's clothing'" fell on deaf ears.[69] By April 1920, Camus was still only the vice president of the Filipino Y.[70] Indigenization took more time: a national board with Filipino secretaries was created in 1925, the first Filipino national secretary was appointed in 1940, and the Philippine YMCA became the first in Asia with a completely indigenous staff.[71] In America, meanwhile, the YMCA moved away from the Portland Basis and its "evangelical test" in 1931.[72]

In 1920, H. W. Love wrote of the growth of the Filipino YMCA since 1915 as a "miracle." It claimed a membership of 1,200 in the student branch and an additional 1,300 in the city branch. Its dormitories accommodated nearly 300 men, with many more being turned away.[73] Such growth was undoubtedly facilitated by drawing in Catholics. However, Y leaders' readiness to even entertain the possibility that Catholicism could be a vehicle for evangelical faith indicates the instability of U.S. evangelicalism as it moved across borders. Even in a setting seemingly defined by America's colonial presence, and in an organization that had historically used specific Protestant definitions of evangelicalism to separate those included from those excluded, local contingencies opened up challenging questions for missionaries. It was unclear that the U.S. colonial state had either the will or the longevity to protect Protestant work among Filipinos, and as such YMCA leaders had to think beyond the colonial project, partaking instead in a transnational conversation about how the boundaries of YMCA "evangelicalism" could be stretched in order to ensure its survival in particular climes. In so doing, they put themselves at odds with religious orthodoxies in America, particularly as Protestant-Catholic tensions flared after World War I, and moved away from the earlier missionary assumption that U.S. colonialism would open the door for a transformative Protestantism in the Philippines. Heading into the 1920s, the drawing of elite Filipinos into an "evangelical" fold increasingly allowed Filipino actors to define evangelicalism for themselves, in turn shaping the ways in which American missionaries thought and wrote about it.

Frank Laubach and the "Story of Evangelical Christianity"

Arriving in 1915, Frank Laubach of the ABCFM spearheaded a new generation of American missionaries to the Philippines who embraced fresh ideas.[74] Against the backdrop of both World War I and U.S. commitment to decolonization, Laubach by the early 1920s identified as an "internationalist," arguing that the world's future was dependent upon America befriending the people of Asia and embracing their capacity for global spiritual leadership.[75] Episodes from Laubach's career across the first half of the 1920s, culminating in the publication of his book *The People of the Philippines*—an attempt to tell the "story of Evangelical Christianity" in the islands—furnish evidence that Filipinos were taking control of the evangelical movement in the archipelago, influencing the ways in which American missionaries described evangelicalism.[76] In a moment of uncertainty, as the broad church of American evangelicalism fragmented, Laubach looked to the Philippines to reorient himself, to articulate his impatience with "meaningless divisions" in the church, and to posit more expansive ideas about what it meant to be an evangelical.[77]

Laubach became best known for promoting literacy among the Muslims of the Philippines' southern islands after 1930, but in the early 1920s he was stationed at Union Theological Seminary in Manila.[78] His letters to the ABCFM from the Philippine capital, reprinted in the *Missionary Herald* for an American Christian audience, described how, as Filipinos were given more spiritual authority, they claimed the "evangelical" label as a marker of unity and openness. The union of evangelical Protestant denominations in the Philippines was not in itself a new idea. It dated back to the formation of an Evangelical Union in April 1901 by seven American mission boards in the islands who sought to cast aside denominational distinctions and to divide the mission field such that work could be conducted efficiently rather than competitively.[79] Nonetheless, Laubach was struck by the fresh impetus given to the ideal of unity after Filipinos were invited to join the union in 1920. It had previously been an organization only of American missionaries, but the prevailing mood of Filipino nationalism and colonial uncertainty after World War I prompted the inclusion of Filipino Christian leaders from across the archipelago.[80] In a January 1923 meeting, Jorge Bocobo, dean of the College of Law at the University of the Philippines, was elected as the union's first Filipino president, and, at the same time, delegates agreed to redouble efforts to "make the Evangelical Union a real union enterprise" by appointing secretaries to travel throughout the islands, visit churches, and tie them to the union "in a real effective way." In particular, all churches would be asked to drop their denominational names in favor of the label "Evangelical Church"—again, this was not a new idea, having been part of the plans of the Evangelical Union since its inception, but it had been only partly fulfilled. The new developments led Laubach to identify "greater optimism and belief in the triumph of . . . Evangelical Christianity now than there ever was before."[81] As ruptures took place in America that would see U.S. evangelicalism increasingly define itself *against* ecumenism, Christians in the Philippines were assertively adopting the word "evangelical" to identify themselves as members of a broad union.[82]

In the *Missionary Herald* for March 1924, Laubach celebrated the leadership of "educated Christian young men" in another ambitious ecumenical enterprise. One of the member missions of the Evangelical Union, the Church of the United Brethren in Christ, proposed to transform its church in the heart of Manila into a "United Church," inviting all the city's congregations to participate. A constitution had been adopted in September 1923, and Laubach stressed that "the leadership is Filipino. Only two Americans besides myself have had any part in the organization or conduct of the church." The constitution's roster of signatories made Laubach's "head swim. . . . It includes nearly all the greatest men of Manila." The "grand old man" of the Philippines, Teodoro Yangco, president of the Filipino YMCA (1911–25) and former resident commissioner of the Philippines to the U.S. Congress (1917–20), was the first to affix his name—his involvement suggests continuity between the inclusive membership basis of the Filipino Y and Filipinos' ecumenical experiments.[83] Two younger men educated in America also signed: Camilo Osías, president of the National University and future senator; and Jorge Bocobo, the "Prophet of the Philippines."[84] This local success was followed in 1929 by the formation of the United Evangelical Church, which harbored national ambitions.[85]

Laubach observed that the signatories to the constitution of Manila's United Church represented not only a variety of Protestant denominations but also Catholics and Aglipayanos—adherents of the Iglesia Filipina Independiente, established by Filipino Catholic priest Gregorio Aglipay in 1902 as an expression of Filipinos' spiritual independence from Spain and Rome. Laubach made sense of this inclusivity in much the same way that YMCA leaders had justified their support of Camus, by asserting that elite Filipino Catholics were not really Catholics at all: "The leading people of this city who are still nominally Roman Catholic are Protestants in everything excepting name, and have never joined any Protestant denomination simply because of their unwillingness to submit to religious denominations." The establishment of a nondenominational evangelical church, therefore, was "the thing for which they have been waiting."[86] Nevertheless, building on the inclusive definition suggested by the YMCA and on the structures created by the Evangelical Union, Filipinos were conceiving of an evangelical church that did not assume that its members professed Protestantism and thus pushed past American orthodoxies.

The lives and writings of some of the "greatest men of Manila" whom Laubach lauded further indicate this unwillingness to limit the constituency of the Filipino church. Yangco, for example, was repeatedly described by

YMCA leaders as a liberal or nominal Catholic, despite his long involvement with the Y and the assertions of his straightforward Protestantism in later scholarship.[87] Writing in August 1917 to celebrate the impact of the YMCA in the Philippines, Yangco emphasized Filipinos' "innate and devoted belief to the teachings of Christ," which had provided fertile ground for YMCA work—even before America's arrival, they were "the only homogeneous group of Christian people in Asia." In other words, it was not U.S. Protestantism that had created true Christianity in the Philippines—in fact, according to Yangco, while "America's material contribution to the Filipino people is unparalleled in the history of countries controlled by outside agencies, . . . of her spiritual contribution . . . so much cannot yet be said." Rather, it was the historical Christian unity of the Filipino people, which Yangco did not pigeonhole under any single confessional identity, that led them to embrace the YMCA.[88]

That such a way of thinking about Filipino Christianity underpinned Filipino definitions of evangelicalism is evident in a 1931 book by another of the elite Filipino men mentioned by Laubach, Camilo Osías, and his wife, Avelina Lorenzana. *Evangelical Christianity in the Philippines* was published in Ohio by the United Brethren, and a short introduction by Bishop A. R. Clippinger suggested that American evangelicals could learn from their colonized counterparts—"continental America has been cursed with too much denominationalism," whereas in the Philippines, a union movement had been a key fruit of evangelicalism.[89] Strikingly, the book presented evangelical Christianity not as a transformative, totalizing faith to which Filipinos had converted but as the natural fulfillment of centuries of Philippine religious history. Clippinger introduced the book as "a veritable history of civilization in the Philippines with its culmination in Evangelical Christianity," emphasizing that Protestants had simply built upon Catholic foundations.[90] Osías and Lorenzana themselves invoked Filipino creation myths, precolonial ancestor worship, and the historical influence of Hinduism, Buddhism, Islam, and Spanish Catholicism, while presenting Protestantism, Catholicism, and Aglipayanism as distinct strands that had all contributed to evangelical life.[91] The book's prevailing themes were unity, mutual tolerance, historical fulfillment, and the specificity of Filipino evangelicalism, portrayed as defying the assumptions of American missionaries who had sought "to transplant institutions and practices, dogmas and creeds which may have been perfectly good and useful elsewhere but were not quite so effective" in the Philippines.[92] In other words, "evangelical Christianity" provided Osías and Lorenzana with a framework for discussing the Philippines' specific, deep-rooted, and multifaceted spiritual culture.

Osías and Lorenzana articulated their vision of evangelicalism in the context of Philippine independence having long been promised, but not yet delivered, and conveyed a belief that an unambiguous end to U.S. colonialism would allow Philippine evangelicalism to fulfill its divine purpose—their expression of evangelicalism, therefore, like that of the Manila YMCA's leaders, was tied to a sense of colonial impermanence.[93] Laubach too was conscious of this impermanence and, unlike earlier missionaries, was at peace from early in his work with the idea that he might soon be working in an independent Philippines. He wrote in 1917 that "rapidly Filipinos are taking the place of Americans in all positions of responsibility. . . . The way in which the positions have been filled proves that the Filipinos are equal to the tasks of government."[94] He was also aware, however, that Protestantism, or evangelicalism—he used the two words interchangeably, differentiated from "corrupted and corrupting" Philippine Catholicism—seemed to be losing the battle for Filipino hearts and minds in this decolonizing world.[95] For example, also in 1917, he wrote that he had befriended an Aglipayan priest at Cagayan and "entertained some real hope of making a Protestant minister out of him," only to hear him deliver "a fiery anti-foreign sermon, urging the people to cling to the Aglipiano Church in the name of Patriotism."[96] By 1925, therefore, when he published *The People of the Philippines*, Laubach had embraced the idea that for evangelicalism to survive in the archipelago, it needed to demonstrably connect to the ideal of a politically and spiritually autonomous Philippines: "Many persons are prevented from giving the claims of Evangelical Christianity a fair hearing because they regard missionaries as retentionists. . . . The mistake is natural in light of the silence maintained by the missionary group."[97] However, having witnessed the desire for unity and openness among Filipinos in the Evangelical Union, which he again celebrated in the book, Laubach's advocacy of Filipino leadership was more than pragmatic—it helped him frame his own evangelical faith at a time in which he saw Europeans and Americans leading Christianity "into a slough of theological despond."[98]

Like Osías and Lorenzana's volume, Laubach's book purported to narrate "the story of Evangelical Christianity" in the archipelago.[99] It was published by major New York press George H. Doran and so, again like Osías and Lorenzana's book, spoke to American Christian audiences. Throughout, Laubach upheld a basic equation of evangelicalism with Protestantism and a distinction from Catholicism. Spanish Catholicism in the islands, he argued, may have started out with noble intentions but had descended into corruption and abuse, ultimately driving Filipinos to revolt in the late nineteenth century.[100] Laubach furthermore identified a generational divide between Catholic parents and educated young people who believed that the "call of their country as well as of Christ" was to Protestantism, or "out-and-out" evangelicalism.[101] He identified an ongoing, oppressive "spirit of inquisition" among Catholics that hindered the evangelical movement and demonstrated the difference between Protestant and Catholic ideals.[102]

However, the more striking characteristic of Laubach's work was that it framed "the story of Evangelical Christianity" not as one of radical spiritual transformation initiated by American actors but as a narrative of fulfillment. This focus seems to have surprised Laubach himself: "The study has revealed many facts which were wholly unexpected. The greatest of these facts becomes the theme of the book: The preparation of the Filipino people for the spiritual leadership of the Far East and perhaps of the whole world."[103] Like Osías and Lorenzana, he suggested that in order to tell the story of evangelicalism in the islands, it was necessary to go back to Philippine religion before the year 1000 and then to examine the influence of India and China between 1000 and 1521.[104] It was also important to appreciate the contribution of Spanish priests and laymen—"heroes" who chose to work for "the cross of Christ" across "the boundless Pacific."[105] As these "fanatically zealous" missionaries came into contact with a people with "readiness and capacity for a higher conception of religion, . . . the result was the conversion of an entire branch of the Malay race."[106] With regard to contemporary Catholicism, moreover, Laubach repeated the argument that thousands of Filipinos had "remained members of the Roman Catholic Church" but "become earnest students of the Bible."[107] They joined Protestants in the National Civic League to champion temperance, became YMCA officials, and constituted around half of the delegates at the Y's annual student conference in Baguio, defying their church's leadership.[108]

Laubach also identified indigenous origins for a Philippine "Protestant movement," pointing to the theology that had underpinned the campaign for Filipino independence from Spain in the late nineteenth century. Leading revolutionary thinkers, notably Apolinario Mabini and Isabelo de los Reyes, had laid the philosophical groundwork for a Filipino church that could assert spiritual independence alongside political independence, ultimately manifesting itself in the Aglipayan movement.[109] Thereafter, Laubach suggested, there were respects in which Aglipay became a "thoroughgoing Protestant," supposedly kept apart from American Protestant missionaries only by the "political situation."[110] Laubach's assertion of a distinction between "the Independent movement and the *orthodox* Evangelical churches" indicated that even if Aglipay's church was not evangelical in the sense that Americans might recognize it, there was scope to consider it as an *unorthodox* form of evangelicalism.[111] Laubach similarly discussed the various schisms from Protestant missionary churches that had taken place in the decades since the mission began—even though these churches had broken from American control in a climate of nationalistic fervor, they had organized themselves on "strictly evangelical lines" and could be called "independent Evangelical churches."[112] Moreover, Laubach praised the YMCA's eschewal of a "narrow outlook" and enunciation of "the broad, general principles of the Christian faith." This was vital "in the upbuilding of a race of men characterized by deep religious feeling and the presence of the spirit of charity, helpfulness and social service" and in allowing Protestants and Catholics to discover that "they have the same Bible and the same God."[113]

If it was indeed "the story of Evangelical Christianity" Laubach wished to tell, then he left his readers with the impression that it was in large part about how different streams of indigenous spiritual thought, and Filipinos' experiences of different colonialisms, had converged. It was in this hybridity that the strength of Filipino evangelicalism was found. The endpoint would be "the ultimate true Filipino National Christian Church," which would not represent a Protestantism transplanted from America but would, in its doc-trines, ethics, organization, and forms of worship, meet local needs. While there were dangers, "the potentialities of Filipinos are such that they will, one may hope, work out a finer type of Christian church and Christian nation than the world has yet seen."[114] In a bombastic conclusion, Laubach argued that Filipinos' history marked them as a "Chosen People" who would provide "some of the great international prophets of the future" and "be able to do what the Occident has so signally failed to accomplish" for Christianity.[115]

Like YMCA leaders a decade before, Laubach suggested that what Amer-icans recognized as evangelicalism had to be defined anew by Filipinos for it to survive in the Philippines. Disappointed by the "extreme hands-off" approach of the American government regarding religious education, faced with fewer converts than missionaries had initially hoped for, and sensing the time was ripe for Philippine independence, Laubach's book articulated a breakdown of the earlier missionary certitude that U.S. colonialism and Protestantism would together transform Philippine religion.[116] While some of Laubach's grandiosity might be attributed to a desire to secure ongoing support for evangelistic work in the Philippines, there was also a genuine sense that, against the backdrop of religious turmoil in interwar America, a turn away from U.S. colonialism and toward Filipino Christianity offered hope—Laubach showed that outside American borders, evangelicalism represented the fulfillment and unity of multiple traditions, rather than something exclusive and uncompromising. The fact that the historian David Hollinger places Laubach within a mainline ecumenical tradition distinct from evangelicalism indicates that this vision failed to win out.[117] However, at a moment of fluidity in the 1920s, Laubach sought ways of holding onto the evangelical label by looking to the Philippines. He pointed American audiences toward the Philippine example, rather than vice versa.

Conclusion

The cases examined here demonstrate that although American evangelicalism proved unstable as it crossed borders, and although in the turmoil of the interwar years it became increasingly associated with a "conservative" faction, the word "evangelical" retained currency for more "liberal" missionaries in the 1910s and 1920s. It described something that they wanted themselves and their proselytes to be and a brand of Christianity that they wanted to secure against the likelihood of a decolonized future in the Philippines. The Evangelical Union, the YMCA's debates over the boundaries of "evangelical" faith, and Laubach's "story of Evangelical Christianity" all demonstrated impulses toward claiming the evangelical label in the Philippines as a vital, nondenominational Christianity suited to the religious history and needs of the archipelago while leaving behind the theological turmoil that wracked the American evangelical coalition. As Filipino Christian leaders increasingly used the label "evangelical" themselves, asserting spiritual and political independence, Laubach viewed their faith as a model for evangelicalism's future worldwide. In the process, the notion that an American colonial project provided the best opportunity for transplanting American evangelical Protestantism abroad was turned on its head—decolonization of the Philippines would provide the best opportunity for evangelicalism's global triumph. As Sarah Miller-Davenport shows in her chapter in this volume, indifference to formal colonialism would also characterize the attitude of evangelical missionaries to the Philippines after World War II, though they would deepen their ties to the U.S. state by other means.

In reality, the picture in the islands was not as rosy as Laubach suggested, perhaps indicating the extent to which he, like later evangelicals, exoticized indigenous spirituality and sought "enchantment" within it rather than examining its complex contours.[118] First, interdenominational unity always faced opposition and was implemented only fitfully.[119] Second, the Philippines was indeed affected by the theological controversies of the interwar years—the 1920s saw schisms among the Disciples of Christ and the Baptists and also the arrival of "fundamentalist" missionaries of the Assemblies of God.[120] Moreover, the Evangelical Union, having renamed itself several times in the intervening decades, finally became the National Council of Churches in the Philippines in 1963—a looser confederation drawing in independent Filipino Catholics.[121] In the process, it yielded the evangelical label to churches more recognizably evangelical in the midcentury American sense of the word, who formed the Philippine Council of Evangelical Churches in 1965. In these senses, the Philippines was not insulated from broader global currents, often driven from America.

Still, the story of self-proclaimed American evangelicals in the Philippines in the 1910s and 1920s invites us to think more carefully about the history and meaning of U.S. evangelicalism. At the very point in time when it seemed that evangelicalism and ecumenism were emerging as two distinct and diametrically opposed strands of American Christianity, some American missionaries from their vantage point in the Philippines articulated possibilities for transcending this dichotomy. While on the one hand it might appear that they lost their battle, on the other they exemplify the fact that across the twentieth century, the direction and definition of American evangelicalism was contested—we need only look at how Billy Graham reached out across denominational and confessional lines on his crusades to understand that there was always a nuanced relationship between evangelicalism and ecumenism. Axel R. Schäfer argues elsewhere in this volume that attention to the transnational sheds particular light on the contingencies and conflicts that shaped evangelicalism, and indeed it was in the mission field that the Manila YMCA and Frank Laubach partook in early conversations about the nature of twentieth-century evangelicalism that would echo across the years.

Notes

1. Heather D. Curtis, *Holy Humanitarians: American Evangelicals and Global Aid* (Cambridge, MA: Harvard University Press, 2018), 9–10.

2. On foreign missions as a shared interest of theologically diverse evangelicals, see William R. Hutchison, *Errand to the World: American Protestant Thought and Foreign Missions* (Chicago: University of Chicago Press, 1987), 95; Kendrick Oliver, Uta A. Balbier, Hans Krabbendam, and Axel R. Schäfer, "Special Issue: Exploring the Global History of American Evangelicalism Introduction," *Journal of American Studies* 51, no. 4 (November 2017): 1025–26; and Andrew Preston, *Sword of the Spirit, Shield of Faith: Religion in American War and Diplomacy* (New York: Knopf, 2012), 178. On other factors holding

together an evangelical coalition in this period, see Curtis, *Holy Humanitarians*, 10; and Grant Wacker, "The Holy Spirit and the Spirit of the Age in American Protestantism, 1880–1910," *Journal of American History* 72, no. 1 (June 1985): 45–62.

3. Hutchison, *Errand to the World*, 103, 112–23.

4. Hutchison, 91–94.

5. On the collaborative, transnational nature of the late nineteenth- and early twentieth-century missionary movement, see Oliver et al., "Special Issue," 1026; Preston, *Sword of the Spirit*, 184–85; and Ian Tyrrell, *Reforming the World: The Creation of America's Moral Empire* (Princeton, NJ: Princeton University Press, 2010), 59–60. On the Protestant nationalism underpinning American empire and mission work in the Philippines, see Kenton J. Clymer, *Protestant Missionaries in the Philippines, 1898–1916: An Inquiry into the American Colonial Mentality* (Urbana: University of Illinois Press, 1986), 153–54; Susan K. Harris, *God's Arbiters: Americans and the Philippines, 1898–1902* (New York: Oxford University Press, 2011), 13–14; Matthew McCullough, *The Cross of War: Christian Nationalism and U.S. Expansion in the Spanish-American War* (Madison: University of Wisconsin Press, 2014); and Tisa Wenger, *Religious Freedom: The Contested History of an American Ideal* (Chapel Hill: University of North Carolina Press, 2017), 23.

6. Clymer, *Protestant Missionaries*, 4–7.

7. David W. Bebbington, *Evangelicalism in Modern Britain: A History from the 1730s to the 1980s* (London: Unwin Hyman, 1989), 2–17.

8. On missionary attitudes toward Philippine Catholicism, see Clymer, *Protestant Missionaries*, 94–99.

9. Oliver et al., "Special Issue," 1029.

10. David A. Hollinger, *Protestants Abroad: How Missionaries Tried to Change the World but Changed America* (Princeton, NJ: Princeton University Press, 2017), 10–11; Melani McAlister, *The Kingdom of God Has No Borders: A Global History of American Evangelicals* (New York: Oxford University Press, 2018), 8–9; Oliver et al., "Special Issue," 1027–28; Matthew Avery Sutton, *American Apocalypse: A History of Modern Evangelicalism* (Cambridge, MA: Belknap Press of Harvard University Press, 2014); Michael G. Thompson, *For God and Globe: Christian Internationalism in the United States between the Great War and the Cold War* (Ithaca, NY: Cornell University Press, 2015); Wacker, "Holy Spirit," 47.

11. Hollinger, *Protestants Abroad*, 2; Preston, *Sword of the Spirit*, 183–84.

12. On indigenous collaboration with U.S. colonial and Protestant projects in the Philippines and Puerto Rico, see Julian Go, *American Empire and the Politics of Meaning: Elite Political Cultures in the Philippines and Puerto Rico during U.S. Colonialism* (Durham, NC: Duke University Press, 2008), chap. 3; Paul A. Kramer, *The Blood of Government: Race, Empire, the United States, and the Philippines* (Chapel Hill: University of North Carolina Press, 2006), chap. 3; and Antonio Sotomayor, "The Triangle of Empire: Sport, Religion and Imperialism in Puerto Rico's YMCA, 1898–1926," *The Americas* 74, no. 4 (October 2017): 484, 497–98.

13. On masculinity and U.S. empire, see Kristin L. Hoganson, *Fighting for American Manhood: How Gender Politics Provoked the Spanish-American and Philippine-American Wars* (New Haven, CT: Yale University Press, 1997); and Sotomayor, "Triangle," 481. On racial violence in the Philippines, see Kramer, *Blood of Government*, chap. 2.

14. On the importance of this theme in scholarship on American missionaries, see Clymer, *Protestant Missionaries*, 173; and Oliver et al., "Special Issue," 1032.

15. Sotomayor, "Triangle," 483.

16. Frank Charles Laubach, *The People of the Philippines: Their Religious Progress and Preparation for Spiritual Leadership in the Far East* (New York: George H. Doran, 1925), viii.

17. Tyrrell, *Reforming the World*, 50, 67.

18. Jon Thares Davidann, *A World of Crisis and Progress: The American YMCA in Japan, 1890–1930* (Bethlehem, PA: Lehigh University Press, 1998), 10; Tyrrell, *Reforming the World*, 68, 89.

19. Davidann, *World of Crisis and Progress*, 11; Tyrrell, *Reforming the World*, 90–92.

20. Davidann, *World of Crisis and Progress*, 31, 42–43, 109; Hutchison, *Errand to the World*, 119–20; Tyrrell, *Reforming the World*, 64, 93.

21. Clymer, *Protestant Missionaries*, 5.

22. John W. Beardsley in the *Manila Times*, March 16, 1907, Kautz Family YMCA archives, Elmer L. Andersen Library, University of Minnesota, Minneapolis (hereafter Y.USA).9-2-10, box 1, Correspondence 1906–1907; John J. Pershing, "[Laying the cornerstone of the YMCA gymnasium]," October 1908, Y.USA.9-2-10, box 1, Correspondence and Reports 1908; YMCA of Manila, *Dedicatory Address by Honorable Charles W. Fairbanks; The Strong Young Man, A Sermon by the Rt. Rev. Charles H. Brent, D.D., Opening Week, October 20–24, 1909* [Manila, 1909], 4–7.

23. Tener to Woodward, April 17, 1907, Y.USA.9-2-10, box 1, Correspondence 1906–1907.

24. J. M. Groves, "The Basis of Membership in the Young Men's Christian Association in the Philippine Islands," [1911], Y.USA.9-2-10, box 1, Correspondence 1910–1911. On the distinction between "active" and "associate" membership, see Leo A. Cullum, "The Religion of the YMCA," *Philippine Studies* 1, no. 3/4 (December 1953): 251.

25. Groves to Mott, June 28, 1911, Y.USA.9-2-10, box 1, Correspondence 1910–1911.

26. Clymer, *Protestant Missionaries*, 160–63.

27. Clymer, 163; Wenger, *Religious Freedom*, 16–17, 34–44.

28. Clymer, *Protestant Missionaries*, 166–67, 175; Tyrrell, *Reforming the World*, 124–30.

29. "Memorandum concerning YMCA Building for Filipino Students in Manila," 1909, Y.USA.9-2-10, box 1, Correspondence and Reports 1909.

30. Kramer, *Blood of Government*, 244.

31. "Memorandum concerning YMCA Building for Filipino Students in Manila," 1909, Y.USA.9-2-10.

32. Clymer, *Protestant Missionaries*, 134–44.

33. Tener to Christy, October 24, 1911, Y.USA.9-2-10, box 1, Correspondence 1910–1911.

34. Brent to Mott [postscript by Tener], April 30, 1909, Y.USA.9-2-10, box 1, Correspondence and Reports 1909.

35. Sotomayor, "Triangle," 498, 505.

36. "Memorandum concerning YMCA Building for Filipino Students in Manila," 1909, Y.USA.9-2-10.

37. On Eddy's visit to the Philippines see Rick Nutt, *The Whole Gospel for the Whole World: Sherwood Eddy and the American Protestant Mission* (Macon, GA: Mercer University Press, 1997), 92. The quote, which paraphrases Eddy's proposal, is found in Groves to Mott, June 28, 1911, Y.USA.9-2-10.

38. Clymer, *Protestant Missionaries*, 51.

39. Groves to Mott, June 28, 1911, Y.USA.9-2-10.

40. Groves to Mott.

41. Sotomayor, "Triangle," 501.

42. "Summary of the Results of the Inquiry as to the Membership Basis of Various Latin American Associations," 1919, Y.USA.9-3, box 10, Membership Base 1891–1935 (1).

43. Groves, "Basis of Membership in the Young Men's Christian Association in the Philippine Islands."

44. See "Paris Basis—1855," World YMCA, www.ymca.int/about-us/ymca-history /paris-basis-1855 (accessed February 16, 2022).

45. Groves, "Basis of Membership in the Young Men's Christian Association in the Philippine Islands."

46. Groves.

47. Groves to Mott, February 15, 1912, Y.USA.9-2-10, box 1, Correspondence and Reports 1912; Groves to Eddy, July 9, 1912, Y.USA.9-2-10, box 1, Correspondence and Reports 1912.

48. *The Religious Policy of the YMCA* [Manila, undated].

49. Groves, "Basis of Membership in the Young Men's Christian Association in the Philippine Islands"; "Summary of the Results of the Inquiry as to the Membership Basis of Various Latin American Associations," 1919, Y.USA.9-3.

50. Tener to Mott, April 5, 1912, Y.USA.9-2-10, box 1, Correspondence and Reports 1912.

51. Groves to Messer, April 14, 1913, Y.USA.9-2-10, box 1, Correspondence and Reports 1913.

52. Groves, "Basis of Membership in the Young Men's Christian Association in the Philippine Islands."

53. Elwood S. Brown, "Annual Report for the Year Ending September 30, 1917," Y.USA.9-2-10, box 5, Administrative Reports 1917–1919.

54. E. S. Turner, "Report for Quarter Ending December 31st, 1915," Y.USA.9-2-10, box 1, Correspondence and Reports 1915; A. T. Morrill, "Report to the International Committee of Young Men's Christian Association by City Department, Manila," 1916, Y.USA.9-2-10, box 5, Administrative Reports 1914–1916; H. A. Wilbur, "Report of Association Work in Manila, P.I., February, 1918," Y.USA.9-2-10, box 1, Correspondence and Reports 1918.

55. [Elwood S. Brown], "Answers to Questions regarding the Basis of Membership of the Young Men's Christian Association in Manila," [1918], Y.USA.9-2-10, box 1, Correspondence and Reports 1918.

56. Kramer, *Blood of Government*, 352–53.

57. Tener to Colton, October 3, 1914, Y.USA.9-2-10, box 1, Correspondence and Reports 1914.

58. Groves to Eddy, June 29, 1914, Y.USA.9-2-10, box 1, Correspondence and Reports 1914.

59. Groves to Jenkins, September 3, 1918, Y.USA.9-2-10, box 1, Correspondence and Reports 1919.

60. H. W. Love, "Replies to General Questionnaire," 1920, Y.USA.9-2-10, box 1, Correspondence and Reports 1920.

61. Groves to Jenkins, September 3, 1918, Y.USA.9-2-10.

62. Brown to Jenkins, December 23, 1918, Y.USA.9-2-10, box 1, Correspondence and Reports 1918.

63. Barrows to Mott, June 14, 1909, Y.USA.9-2-10, box 1, Correspondence and Reports 1909.

64. Love, "Replies to General Questionnaire," 1920, Y.USA.9-2-10.

65. Camus to Mott, January 26, 1918, Y.USA.9-3, box 6, Catholic Church 1910–1929.

66. Brown to Jenkins, December 23, 1918, Y.USA.9-2-10. On Brown, see Stefan Hübner, "Muscular Christianity and the Western Civilizing Mission: Elwood S. Brown, the YMCA, and the Idea of the Far Eastern Championship Games," *Diplomatic History* 39, no. 3 (June 2015): 532–57.

67. Jenkins to Brown, February 6, 1919, Y.USA.9-2-10, box 1, Correspondence and Reports 1919. On anti-Catholic nativism after World War I, see Jay P. Dolan, *In Search of an American Catholicism: A History of Religion and Culture in Tension* (New York: Oxford University Press, 2003), 134–36.

68. Jenkins to Brown, February 6, 1919, Y.USA.9-2-10.

69. Mazurkiewicz to Jenkins, August 14, 1919, Y.USA.9-2-10, box 1, Correspondence and Reports 1919; "Recommendations to the International Committee," [1919], Y.USA.9-2-10, box 1, Correspondence and Reports 1919.

70. E. S. Turner, "Special Report for the Year Ending April 17, 1920," Y.USA.9-2-10, box 1, Correspondence and Reports 1920.

71. See "Records of YMCA International Work in the Philippines," University of Minnesota Libraries, https://archives.lib.umn.edu/repositories/7/resources/940 (accessed May 8, 2020).

72. Davidann, *World of Crisis and Progress*, 43.

73. Love to "Friends," September 10, 1920, Y.USA.9-2-10, box 1, Correspondence and Reports 1920.

74. Clymer, *Protestant Missionaries*, 8.

75. *Missionary Herald*, August 1921, 268–69; *Missionary Herald*, January 1922, 13.

76. Laubach, *People of the Philippines*, viii.

77. Laubach, Woodward, Woodward, and Fox to Brethren, October 1, 1919, American Board of Commissioners for Foreign Missions archives, Houghton Library, Harvard University, Cambridge, MA (hereafter ABC) 19.7, vol. 2, no. 24.

78. Hollinger, *Protestants Abroad*, 253–54; *Missionary Herald*, July 1922, 283.

79. Clymer, *Protestant Missionaries*, 32–36.

80. Laubach, *People of the Philippines*, 209.

81. *Missionary Herald*, July 1923, 304.

82. Hollinger, *Protestants Abroad*, 10–11.

83. *Missionary Herald*, March 1924, 115.

84. *Missionary Herald*, March 1924, 115; Laubach, *People of the Philippines*, 273.

85. Raymundo Go, *The Philippine Council of Evangelical Churches: Its Background, Context, and Formation among Post–World War II Churches* (Carlisle, UK: Langham Monographs, 2019), 77–78.

86. *Missionary Herald*, March 1924, 116.

87. Groves, "Basis of Membership in the Young Men's Christian Association in the Philippine Islands"; Brown to Jenkins, December 23, 1918, Y.USA.9-2-10; Love, "Replies to General Questionnaire," 1920, Y.USA.9-2-10; Cullum, "Religion of the YMCA," 262.

88. Teodoro R. Yangco, "Contributions of the Young Men's Christian Association to the Filipino People," 1917, Y.USA.9-2-10, box 1, Correspondence and Reports 1917.

89. A. R. Clippinger, foreword to *Evangelical Christianity in the Philippines*, by Camilo Osías and Avelina Lorenzana (Dayton, OH: United Brethren Publishing House, 1931), viii–ix.

90. Clippinger, v–vi.

91. Osías and Lorenzana, *Evangelical Christianity*, 7–9, 61–62, 137–39, 201–2, chaps. iii, ix.

92. Osías and Lorenzana, 94–95.

93. Osías and Lorenzana, 20–21.

94. Frank Charles Laubach, "Report for 1917," ABC 19.7, vol. 2, no. 12.

95. Frank Charles Laubach, "Exhibits," undated, ABC 19.7, vol. 2, no. 236.

96. Laubach to Barton, March 15, 1917, ABC 19.7, vol. 2, no. 273.

97. Laubach, *People of the Philippines*, 444–45.

98. Laubach, 208–16, 461.

99. Laubach, viii.

100. Laubach, 89–97.

101. Laubach, 275.

102. Laubach, 281, 286.

103. Laubach, vii.

104. Laubach, chaps. 1–2.

105. Laubach, 78.

106. Laubach, 81. On the broader idea among missionaries and colonial administrators that Catholicism had served a historical function in the Philippines, see Katherine D. Moran, *The Imperial Church: Catholic Founding Fathers and United States Empire* (Ithaca, NY: Cornell University Press, 2020), chaps. 5–6.

107. Laubach, *People of the Philippines*, 454.

108. Laubach, 230–31, 401, 454.

109. Laubach, 126–29, 137.

110. Laubach, 140–41.

111. Laubach, 152 (emphasis mine).

112. Laubach, 301, 308.

113. Laubach, 179, 380.

114. Laubach, 218.

115. Laubach, 458–61.

116. Laubach, 331. On the relatively low numbers of converts, see Clymer, *Protestant Missionaries*, 194.

117. Hollinger, *Protestants Abroad*, 10–11, 64, 253–57.

118. On "enchanted internationalism," see McAlister, *Kingdom of God Has No Borders*.

119. David E. Gardinier, "Ecumenism among Philippine Protestants, 1945–1963," *Philippine Studies* 50, no. 1 (First Quarter 2002): 3–22.

120. Go, *Philippine Council*, 82–85.

121. Go, 78–82; Gardinier, "Ecumenism," 17–18.

CHAPTER FOUR

"Make Jesus King" and the Evangelical Missionary Imagination, 1889–1896

Dana L. Robert

In 1889, two student conferences on opposite sides of the world captivated a generation. Japanese college students meeting in Kyoto, Japan, sent a telegram to college students meeting in Northfield, Massachusetts. The simple message was "Make Jesus King." By staking a claim to world evangelization, Japanese Christian students signaled the dawning of a new age—one in which young evangelical Asians, Europeans, and Americans could unite worldwide for a common cause.

The excitement of transnational collaboration culminated in the International Students' Missionary Conference in Liverpool, England, in January 1896. Called "Make Jesus King," after the inspirational telegram, the conference brought together over 900 Christian students from twenty nations, determined to become missionaries. Forty-four mission societies sent representatives to recruit the students, then meeting at the Liverpool YMCA.[1]

Medical student John Rutter Williamson of Edinburgh University captured the thrill of the historical moment:

> We see how Japan set a light blazing in Scandinavia amongst the students; we realise how it was a Swede that really began the very first Student Volunteer Movement in this country. . . . The first missionaries to our great Indian Empire were Germans. For generations no Englishmen could be found to go out as missionaries. Englishmen supplied the money and Germans went, sent out by a Danish king. And thus the co-relation and co-operation of these various nations have been established, and our oneness in Christ Jesus has been realized. God has decreed that no nationality should have the unique opportunity of publishing the Gospel, but that in our independence we are also to be inter-dependent.[2]

During the final decade of the nineteenth century, the mythmaking power of the telegram rippled along missionary communication networks, from Europe to Asia to Africa.[3]

"Make Jesus King" had become a touchstone for the global evangelical imagination and a mantra for the fin de siècle generation of college students. More than the story of a few student conferences, the slogan "Make Jesus King" fueled a rapidly expanding networked conversation among American, British, Scandinavian, East Asian, and other Christian college students who hitched their national identities to a shared project of missionary internationalism. It also energized an emerging global infrastructure of conferences, personal pledges, and study groups for missionary recruitment known as the Student Volunteer Movement for Foreign Missions.[4]

Placed in historical perspective, the events of 1889 do not align precisely with the legend. In this chapter, I deconstruct the defining moment of "Make Jesus King" and show that its significance for Western students of the 1890s lay in shaping evangelical identity through commitment to "foreign" transnational mission. What mythology characterized as a spontaneous telegram sent by Japanese students appears on closer examination to have been orchestrated by American YMCA leaders. "Make Jesus King" signaled the calculated exportation of an American version of putatively "global" evangelicalism. Yet for the Japanese Christians, who were religious minorities in their own country, "Make Jesus King" signified their networking with Western Christians as a tool for building a modern nation-state.

The lens of entangled history demonstrates that American and Japanese experiences of the moment were mirror images: as they encountered each other, they defined themselves.[5] For both Japanese and Americans, the inspired internationalism of "Make Jesus King" exploited national pride. Christian students in both countries found themselves potential protagonists on the cusp of empire: in 1898, the United States fought the Spanish-American War and then seized the Philippines, Cuba, and Puerto Rico as colonies. Engaged in rapid modernization, in 1905 Japan defeated Russia and by 1910 had seized Korea as its colony. Even for the European students who embraced the vision, shared generational euphoria was no match for the juggernaut of competing nationalisms and rapid militarization. Less than twenty years later, the Great War revealed the limitations of the global evangelical imagination launched by "Make Jesus King." John Rutter Williamson, for example, after a distinguished career as missionary physician in India, served six grueling years in the Royal Army Medical Corps. Although the Student Volunteer Movement fragmented after World War I, its founding narratives provided an enduring vision of world evangelization—a "global" identity that continued to inspire later generations of American evangelicals.

Northfield, Massachusetts, 1889

Late June marked the onset of summer in the rolling green hills of northwestern Massachusetts—and in 1889 the hamlet of Northfield hosted the third annual conference of the intercollegiate Young Men's Christian Association (YMCA). Trains delivered nearly 500 registered delegates from 126 North American colleges and universities, from Ontario to North Carolina, Wisconsin to Maine. Twenty-two delegates were Japanese students studying in the United States. Fourteen British students, plus a scattering of Europeans, arrived by steamship and train. Reporting the entire conference in detail, the *Springfield Daily Union* noted the presence of hundreds of interested observers over the course of the two-week conference.

For delegates and visitors alike, a central attraction of the conference was the dynamic leadership of revivalist Dwight L. Moody, YMCA stalwart and founder of the Northfield Seminary and its companion, the Mount Hermon School for Boys. While YMCA leaders held seminars on such topics as how to organize meetings and lead small groups, a rotating cast of distinguished divines offered lectures and Bible studies.[6] Especially enjoyable was the seamless intersection of moral reflection, spiritual inspiration, and afternoon sports. Men moved straight from Bible lessons to the baseball diamond and from meals to prayer groups. Overflow crowds prayed outside the conference halls, heads bowed and tennis rackets in hand. "Muscular Christianity" was front and center.[7] Conference sports chairman was the great Yale baseball pitcher Amos Alonzo Stagg, soon to be selected to the first collegiate All-American football team.[8] No doubt the Japanese exposure to baseball was formative for Japan's adoption of it as a national passion. William Blaikie, a father of the physical fitness movement and weight training, lectured on the poor physical condition of college students.[9] The most visible demonstration of "muscular Christianity" at the conference was a game of football, whose seething mass of bodies elicited the question from a ministry student, "Isn't this rather a rough game?"[10]

The conference delegates were officers of their respective college branches of the YMCA, the largest interconnected movement among North American colleges. Born after the Civil War, members of their generation experienced a rapid rise in literacy and expansion of educational institutions. They lived through the consolidation of capitalist economic systems, worldwide regularization of time zones and currency standards, and other features characteristic of what is now called globalization.[11] They experienced the escalating race for raw materials and markets that represented growing economic competition among nation-states in the age of imperialism.

The two weeks of Bible studies and sports led the young men from their parochial worldviews into global concerns. The vantage point of the small midwestern town or college club shifted to passionate excitement about the communication and travel possibilities of the modern age—though neither economic nor political critiques were at the forefront of student interests at Northfield. Rather, the emotional energy of the conference moved inexorably toward commitment to "missions"—the responsibility to carry Christianity from Europe and North America to Asia. The visibility of international students worked magic. Speaker after speaker shared his hopes: as no generation before, this special generation would follow Jesus's command to go into the world! Empire obliterated barriers to trade and travel. With better organization and deeper spiritual consecration, could not this generation of students evangelize the world before the end of the century?

In evening prayer meetings and woodland walks, each participant wrestled individually with God's call upon his life. By the end of the conference on July 10, approximately forty young men had signed a pledge committing themselves, God willing, to be missionaries. Joined with the sixty who had already signed the Student Volunteer pledge before attending the conference, about one-fourth of the official delegates publicly indicated their intentions to enter the ministry or to become a foreign missionary.

"Make Jesus King"

The Northfield conference of 1889 was on one level a stunningly successful youth leadership training event. Its innovative combination of intellectual, spiritual, and physical activity among young men in the great outdoors created a powerful model soon copied by other youth movements such as the Boy Scouts of America—with the help of YMCA leaders who had attended Northfield conferences.[12] But to limit the historical interpretation of the conference to a North American production is complicated by the presence of the international students. Why did international students from Japan and from top British universities spend their time crossing the ocean to go camping in the middle of nowhere? Why did seminary presidents, university lecturers, missionaries on furlough, and famous preachers donate their vacation days speaking to a few hundred student leaders?

In historical perspective, Dwight Moody's Northfield conferences were liminal spaces carefully crafted to internationalize the consciousness of evangelical youth. The high point of the 1889 conference occurred at the evening missionary meeting on Saturday, July 6. The secretary of the YMCA international committee, Richard C. Morse, read aloud a cablegram that had just arrived from Japan. It simply said, "Make Jesus King." The message came in the name of over 500 Japanese students then meeting in Kyoto at Doshisha College, the largest Christian school in Japan. This first intercollegiate student conference ever held in Japan was a twin to that of Northfield. It gathered Christian students from colleges around the country, leading Japanese pastors, businessmen, and a hundred interested female observers. Like at Northfield, the Kyoto Summer Conference was organized by YMCA leaders who employed a conference format as a new strategy for connecting Christian students with each other. The momentum built from Bible study toward missions, with the goal of converting and commissioning Japanese students for the evangelization of Japan. Upon its adjournment, Japanese students scattered in every direction for evangelism campaigns.

Back at Northfield, the reading of the "Make Jesus King" cablegram concretized abstract speeches about world evangelization. At that point, the presence of the twenty-two Japanese students, who had been holding daily morning prayers of their own, moved from the sidelines to center stage. Japanese students sang the first verse of the familiar hymn "The Morning Light Is Breaking." Although they sang in Japanese, it was an inspiring choice for delegates from the "sunrise kingdom."[13] After prayers in Japanese, the foreign delegates began giving speeches. One student pleaded for Western missionaries with the intellectual and cultural capacities to navigate the complexities of an ancient civilization undergoing rapid modernization. In February, the Japanese emperor had announced the Meiji Constitution. Although the document retained the powerful monarchy, it technically allowed freedom of religion. Japanese Christians hoped it would be the beginning of modern government for Japan.[14] The student noted that 1889 would be remembered both as the year that Japanese people gained equal rights and the year the YMCA was founded in Japan.

The Reverend J. T. Isé stood to speak. No doubt his reputation had preceded him. Isé (also known as Tokio Yokoi, or John T. Yokoi) was a second generation Christian and influential pastor in Japan. He also carried the authoritative genealogy of a martyr: his father had been beheaded for supporting Christianity, democratization, and modernization.[15] Isé recounted his own story of becoming a Christian under the mentorship of Captain L. L. Janes, a West Point man and military officer who was hired by the daimyo of Kumamoto to introduce Western learning to boys of his clan.[16] After several years of mentoring the young samurai and instilling into them strict personal discipline, Janes began meeting with about forty boys for Wednesday evening Bible studies. From this group came the "Kumamoto Band," one of the earliest groups of Protestant converts and future leaders of Japanese Christianity. From Janes they imbibed the idea that the Christian religion and modern education were the chief means of building character and developing their country.[17] Isé described how in 1876 thirty of Janes's students gathered on a hillside and pledged themselves to spend their lives spreading the new religion among their fellow countrymen.[18] Within a few years, Isé had assembled the largest church in Japan. He concluded his Northfield speech by speaking of the needs of Japan's youth and affirming their openness to the gospel.

The passion generated by the telegram and by the evening's speeches carried into the next day. American students were seized by the conviction that they composed the vanguard of a movement to take the best of the West to the East. Following Sunday worship, the evening missionary meeting whipped student fervor to fever pitch, with a series of testimonies by men who had either gone to Japan already as missionaries or were preparing to go. Leland, Yale class of 1885, was on his way in a few months. He asked his fellow students, "Will you go and put forth your power where it will count for the most?"[19] Price of Hampton-Sidney College admonished his fellow students to remember that "the field is the world and there is as much call to go to Japan as to Dakota."[20] John T. Swift of Yale, who had already spent two years in Japan trying to launch the YMCA, spoke of the 80,000 students in Tokyo alone, with no "Christian work" established among them except his own and that of Luther Wishard, the senior YMCA worker simultaneously leading the parallel Kyoto Summer Conference.

In efforts to channel the energy of the eager crowd into a constructive direction, Moody suggested that those present donate money for the building of Reverend Isé's church. Hats passed among the students quickly collected $400. With additional pledges by observers, the group raised $1,000. "Rev. Mr. Isé was almost overwhelmed, and could hardly express his gratitude," the *Daily Union* noted.[21] To cap off the excitement, on Monday morning the Northfield conference returned a message to the Kyoto Conference: "Students hundred twenty-six colleges greeting."[22] The Kyoto Conference adjourned on July 9, no doubt without having received the American telegram. Since a Pacific submarine cable was not laid until 1902, the message had to travel across the Atlantic Ocean to London, down to India, and up through Hong Kong to the southern island of Japan. The Northfield conference adjourned on July 10.

The excitement generated by the Northfield-Kyoto connection in 1889 can be understood only in light of the dawning consciousness of "simultaneity"—the expanding interconnective possibilities of the present age. Rather than events happening far away, in the past or the future, global connections gave people the consciousness of simultaneous happenings worldwide, at the same time in the present.[23] One could argue that the stronger impact of the Northfield meeting was on the Western participants rather than the Japanese students. Being foreigners, the Japanese students had already crossed cultural boundaries prior to arriving at Northfield. On the other hand, the experience of warm Christian fellowship was striking for the Japanese, who typically experienced prejudice against Asians in America. Thus, the convergence was powerful for all students, though likely for different reasons.

After the Northfield Conference, "Make Jesus King" validated the global imagination of European and North American students eager to move outward on the convenient ships and railroads of Western empire. The inspiration of the telegram also stimulated the organizational capacity to promote it. Karl Fries recalled being a student at the University of Uppsala in 1888. He went to a meeting arranged by Luther Wishard, then en route to Japan and China to establish student YMCAs in Asia. Swedish students objected to the difficulties in the way of launching a student movement. But the next year, Fries received a letter telling the story of the "Make Jesus King" telegram.

Empowered by the simultaneous gatherings at Northfield and Kyoto, in 1890 he and a Norwegian friend, K. M. Eckhoff, organized the first meeting of what became the Scandinavian Student Movement.[24] Fries went on to become the chairman of the World's Student Christian Federation, founded in 1895 as the overarching global entity of national Student Christian Movements.

After several years of working to organize a national student missionary movement parallel to that of the North Americans, in 1892 British students led by Donald Fraser of Glasgow University founded the Student Volunteer Missionary Union of Great Britain and Ireland. In 1896, it held its first international student conference and of course named it "Make Jesus King." The impact of the conference was astounding. Students heard inspirational addresses on "the evangelization of the world in this generation," the official watchword of the American student mission movement. By the end of the conference, the British students had adopted the motto as their own. Response to a prayerful collection for conference expenses was so great that an extra 200 pounds was collected and sent to American student leader John R. Mott, then on an organizing tour in Asia, with instructions to expand the movement to Australia and New Zealand. Students from Africa and Europe stood and testified to the recent outburst of mission activism in their own countries and shared the Lord's Prayer in their own languages. Conference leaders noted with almost military zeal,

> With unfeignedly thankful hearts, we look back over the wonderful
> way in which God has led us during these past few years. He has
> brought hundreds of men and women to a new obedience to His
> Royal Commission. . . . We wait to see our Continental brothers clasp
> hands with us, and form one strong Union to make Jesus King. We
> wait to see the students of the East bow down before Christ Jesus,
> and become with us the messengers to their nations. As those that
> look for His appearing, let us press forward with a deeper fervency
> of prayer and effort, that before another generation shall have passed
> away, the Gospel may be preached as a witness to all nations.[25]

As British participants cheered the presence of foreign delegates from Germany, Holland, Scandinavia, France, Japan, and China, the conference chairman declared, "We ask you whether you will not join hands with us in making a world-wide brotherhood to crown Jesus Christ King."[26] By the end of the year, 212 British student missionary volunteers had departed for foreign "mission fields."

The Kyoto Conference, 1889

The Kyoto Conference of 1889 represented the confluence of Western-style higher education with the internationalist vision of the intercollegiate YMCA. It met not in a bucolic setting like that of Northfield but at a premier symbol of modernization, Doshisha College. As part of an emerging global network of Christian colleges supported by Americans, Doshisha was a huge point of pride for both American Congregationalists and Japanese Christians. Starting in the mid-nineteenth century, international students from Asia had begun studying in the United States. In 1864, a young Japanese named Joseph Hardy Neesima (Niijima Shimeta) stowed away on an American ship and arrived in Massachusetts. With the sponsorship of a couple from Old South Church in Boston, Neesima attended prep school and graduated from Amherst College. In 1866 he was baptized and then attended Andover Theological Seminary. After being ordained in 1874, Neesima raised money from American Congregationalists to begin what became Doshisha College in Kyoto. It soon became the largest Christian school in Japan and sent out its graduates both to plant churches in Japan and to modernize Japanese society. Although Neesima and his college were visible objects of Western benevolence, at a deeper level Neesima was an entrepreneur who harnessed Western partnerships for his own purposes.[27]

As Neesima's example showed, the initial founding of Western institutions of higher education in Japan was accompanied by the conversion to Christianity of Japanese students, typically young samurai displaced by the end of the feudal system. These young men seized upon Western resources, including the English language, mathematics, science, and Christianity, to chart a new future for themselves—and they hoped, for Japan. The inspiration behind the 1889 "Make Jesus King" telegram was a remarkable letter written in 1878 by Japanese students at Sapporo Agricultural College to Christian students at the Massachusetts Agricultural College (the future University of Massachusetts at Amherst). The two schools shared the same president, the scientist Colonel William S. Clark, who in 1876 went from his own institution at the request of Japanese officials to found an agricultural college in Sapporo, Japan. The readiness of the students to embrace Christianity and Western learning became legendary. Along with the Kumamoto and Yokohama Bands, the "Sapporo Band" was one of the three nodes from which Christianity radiated into Meiji Japan.

Upon learning from Clark of a Christian student group at Massachusetts Agricultural College, students calling themselves "Believers in Jesus" wrote to their counterparts in Massachusetts:

> Though we are living in this side of the world, separated from you by the broad water of the Pacific, yet we are united with you in the chain of love, because we know that you are our brothers, living under the grace of the same heavenly Father. We have learned also that "we are one Body in Christ and every one members one of another," and we wish to work together with you for our Lord, to promote his Glory. . . . While we are working for Jesus in the Eastern side of the world, we hope you will advance His Kingdom in the Western side.[28]

Meanwhile, the World Alliance of Young Men's Christian Associations had already claimed the terrain of internationalism when in 1855 it defined its goals as working for Christian unity and toward the reign of God.[29] A diasporic culture of movement that assumed young men would leave their traditional communities to find work was a decisive factor in the success of the YMCA model, as opposed to the traditional church with its fixed location and family-centered constituency. The simultaneous expansion of higher education also created a growing leadership class of educated students. Old urban YMCA working-class organizers like Dwight Moody shifted their attention to students, as the next frontier for youth work. Dislocated rural Asian youth migrated to urban hubs for trade and educational opportunities, such as Tokyo, Manila, Singapore, and Chinese coastal cities. Thus by the late 1800s, the YMCA model of outreach to workers was ripe for expansion both to student groups in Europe and North America and to urban nodes in Asia.

Luther Wishard and "Foreign" YMCA Student Work

In North America, the opening of public universities and the secularization of curricula meant that religious formation needed to evolve separately from the educational structures themselves. The idea of an intercollegiate YMCA began with Princeton graduate Luther M. Wishard. Inspired by the 1878 letter from Sapporo students, Wishard was hired the same year to organize the intercollegiate YMCA. With a strong personal call to be a missionary, he toured American colleges for the purpose of setting up student Associations, often by linking preexisting student missionary clubs together.[30] After the Tokyo YMCA was established in 1880, the movement was poised to spread to Japanese students. The intercollegiate movement quickly formed a global network: in 1881 American YMCA members opened correspondence with students in missionary colleges abroad.[31] Recent college graduates who took teaching assignments overseas also introduced the YMCA. As a fresh graduate and new teacher from Ripon College in Wisconsin, Frank K. Sanders in 1884 started an Association at the Congregationalist-founded Jaffna College in Ceylon—supposedly the first such collegiate organization in Asia.[32]

As Wishard's strategic vision for students bore fruit, he conceived the idea of holding summer Bible and leadership training for leaders of the new collegiate YMCAs. He convinced Dwight L. Moody to host them at his summer home in Northfield, Massachusetts. Beginning in the summer of 1886, Wishard recruited delegations of male student leaders to attend Moody's Bible conferences. In his effort to impart a missionary vision to the collegiate YMCAs, he deliberately included the sons of missionaries in the conference delegates. Career missionaries typically sent their children back to Europe or to the United States for their higher education. Missionary children often joined whatever mission club existed at their educational institution. As cultural bridges between their classmates and the distant non-Western world, they sometimes succeeded in influencing their peers toward careers as missionaries, especially when combined with excitement about the modern technology and trade networks that were opening previously "closed" Asian countries to Western infiltration. To Wishard and his YMCA partners, the expansion of God's kingdom lay in the unprecedented opportunities provided by the infrastructures of empire. By the time of the 1889 "Make Jesus King" interchange between Northfield and Kyoto, the annual summer training program for college leaders had become a proven recruitment ground for student missionary activists.[33]

The global expansion of the collegiate YMCA took place because of a strategic alliance between the evangelical parachurch and established missionary networks. To launch the expansion, the indefatigable Luther Wishard undertook a four-year tour of Britain, western Europe, and Asia. He visited 216 mission stations in twenty countries, including the major mission colleges.[34] On his trip he personally met over 1,000 missionaries. Everywhere he went, they proved to be his most valuable allies and founded collegiate YMCAs in his wake.[35] In a continued link with the YMCA's roots in urban industrialization, Wishard started placing enterprising young YMCA secretaries—basically new college graduates with a mandate to organize Associations—in major Asian cities with preexisting Protestant missionary infrastructures.[36]

June 1889 found Wishard at Doshisho College in Kyoto, Japan. He organized the Kyoto student conference to coincide with the Northfield meeting back in Massachusetts. In retrospect, "Make Jesus King" was not as spontaneous a happening as it seemed but rather emerged from a brilliant strategy to build momentum for the simultaneous global expansion of the intercollegiate YMCA, via world evangelization by college graduates of all lands.[37] Just as Japanese delegates transformed the Northfield conference of 1889 into a transnational moment, the presence of Americans—missionaries and YMCA representatives—shaped the Kyoto conference. For example, the young missionary Harlan Page Beach traveled from North China to the Kyoto conference. A teacher and founder of one of the first YMCAs in China, Beach was a role model for the Japanese students.[38] As at Northfield, in Kyoto the self-consciously global parachurch organization—the YMCA—linked Christian college students with denominational missionaries to promote world evangelization as identity marker of a transnational evangelicalism, American style.

For Wishard, sending the telegram "Make Jesus King" from the 500 Japanese students gathered at Neesima's Doshisha College must have been the high point of a decade of planning and anticipation. What could be more expressive of global Christian unity than to send a telegram from Japanese students hosting Americans to American students hosting Japanese? The activism of the telegram invited its participants to show, through missions, patriotic loyalty to Christ's kingdom above and beyond that of their own national identities.

Mirror Images or "Through the Looking Glass"?

By the 1890s, global consciousness had become the driving force for an entire generation of American evangelical young adults. Students and pastors gathered at Northfield in 1889 saw in the Kyoto conference a mirror of their own dreams of global evangelical unity. But just as Asian students who traveled to the United States because they thought it was a Christian country were disillusioned by the racism they encountered, Westerners who went abroad to "do good" soon realized that Japanese, Chinese, and Indian Christians were not theological soulmates waiting with open arms for American leadership. Rather than a cheerful reflection in the mirror, "Make Jesus King" could play out like Alice's experiences in *Through the Looking Glass*. Instead of seeing her own face, Alice found herself in a strange upside-down world of rules that made no sense and of creatures who seemed familiar but differed from English society in unexpected and bizarre ways.

Postcolonial perspectives and communication theory underscore that common discourse is not the same thing as shared meaning. A case in point was the predictable tension between the Western and Japanese interpretations of the 1889 Kyoto conference. Luther Wishard tried to mobilize Asian students for "aggressive Christian work." In his book *A New Programme of Missions*, he shared hopeful stories of missionary commitment by Asian Christian students, including one of poor Chinese students who went without food to support a Zulu student in South Africa who was preparing for the ministry.[39] To senior YMCA leaders and Western missionaries, the true meaning of the Kyoto conference of 1889 was its role in creating a self-motivated Japanese movement for world evangelization. Wishard opined that the interdenominational basis of the Japanese student movement made it "the forward movement of the one united Christian army for the evangelization of the world."[40]

In his autobiography published many years later, the Reverend Hiromichi Kozaki remembered the meaning of the conference rather differently. A member of the famous "Kumamoto Band," Kozaki was a graduate and later president of Doshisha College, founder and first president of the Tokyo YMCA, the founding pastor of major Japanese congregations, an architect of unity between Congregationalists and Presbyterians in Japan, and one of the most public representatives of Japanese Christianity in the first third of the twentieth century. Kozaki gave Bible lectures at the 1889 conference. Relying upon recent research by biblical scholars at Yale and Harvard, Kozaki both affirmed the basic reliability of the Bible and accepted the new "higher criticism" that placed it in historical and literary context. His primary concern was to equip Japanese church leaders for the challenges of modernization and public-spirited citizenship, including sharing with them the latest in scientific and comparative thought. Yet for his violation of evangelical norms of biblical inspiration—the perspectives so vigorously propagated by Moody and senior speakers at the twin Northfield conference—Kozaki's lectures were omitted from the Kyoto conference report.[41] In his autobiography, Kozaki recounted the years of tension with Congregational missionaries that followed the conference, including bitter fights over the control of Doshisha College. Was Doshisha a mission institution whose primary role was to inculcate biblical orthodoxy and send out Japanese evangelists and pastors? Or was Doshisha College like Amherst, Yale, Williams, and other New England colleges that had been founded by Christians but whose purpose was the preparation of young men for public leadership?[42]

Ultimately, American and Japanese purposes were different. Graduates of Doshisha were minority Christians in an increasingly militarized country. Their attempts to hold open a space for Christianity in a hostile context made urgent the task of crafting a public Japanese Christian identity entirely separate from Western paternalism or control. As Kozaki succinctly stated in 1938 in an English-language article published posthumously in the *International Review of Missions*, "It is quite natural that a seed when planted in foreign soil produces a somewhat different crop from the product of the same kind of seed when sown in its original soil, because of the climatic and geological characteristics of the foreign soil. This same natural law applies to the spiritual world as well, and Christian churches developed in different lands will inevitably differ from each other, in order that together they may contribute to the wealth of Christian truth."[43]

The Japanese YMCA was a similar site of contested meanings in the decades following the 1889 conference. Historian Jon Davidann argues that just as North American YMCA leaders took to Japan their own cultural assumptions about the positive role of evangelization in spreading progress, so Japanese Christian leaders developed their own nationalistic form of Christianity whose purpose was to craft a moral center for a modern Japanese identity.[44] The unique character of Japanese Christianity would both reject American attempts at control and later impose its own form of Christianity on Korea and other nations under Japanese colonialism. In 1890, Japanese collegiate YMCA leaders insisted on organizing their own summer conference. They rejected the evangelical framework that had been imposed on them in the "Make Jesus King" conference of 1889.

For the American and Japanese participants, "Make Jesus King" symbolized a common discourse for the convergence of expanding global Protestant networks. Nevertheless, beneath it lay different cultures, theologies, social locations, and political priorities. The specters of imminent competing empires and national resistance continually haunted the shared project.

The future paths of two participants at the Northfield conference illustrate the ephemeral nature of the common global evangelical discourse. Yale graduate and YMCA missionary John Swift attended the 1889 Northfield conference to appeal for missionary volunteers. Returning to Japan to organize YMCAs there, he quickly found himself caught between the theological conservatism of the international YMCA and the liberal "New Theology" of Japanese Christian leaders. The international YMCA supported principles both of self-support and of evangelical orthodoxy. But the implication of Japanese self-support would entail the acceptance of liberal theology and

Japanese nationalism on the part of Western sponsors. As Swift wrote to another missionary, "We have to constantly remind ourselves that we are working for a people very different from ourselves, and the trouble may be often in our not being able to understand them."[45]

Over time, Swift became fluent in Japanese and increasingly close to his Japanese friends and partners. Despite a successful decade of founding Japanese YMCAs for urban workers and students and erecting the Tokyo YMCA building, Swift's navigation of multiple networks grew increasingly untenable. Finally, he resigned from the YMCA to stay in Japan. Like many empathetic missionaries, his ultimate sympathy shifted to the Japanese Christians. He became a professor of English at Imperial University in Tokyo. After he died in 1928, he was buried in Yokohama. Davidann reports that Swift became a "folk hero" to leaders of the Japanese YMCA and that they still bring flowers to his grave once a week.[46]

Another example of "through the looking glass" involved Reverend Isé, aka Tokio Yokoi, who in 1889 gratefully collected money for his church building from the Northfield participants and who appealed for missionaries to come to Japan. The next year, when the Meiji emperor issued the Imperial Rescript on Education, it became clear that the era of Western tutelage was over, including in theology. From now on, the people of Japan were required to bow to portraits of the emperor as the symbol of the sacred Japanese nation. Rather than adhering to the evangelistic theology he appeared to espouse the year before, Yokoi wrote an article and then a book that signaled the alliance of liberal theology with Japanese nationalism. Yokoi argued that just as Western theology was based on Greek and Roman traditions, so Japanese theology should be based on traditional Japanese culture and rituals. Missionary theology must give way to an independent Japanese theology, and Christianity should become a resource to serve the Japanese nation.[47] Ultimately Yokoi went into politics.

Conclusion: The Entangled Empire of the American Evangelical Imagination

At the end of the day, the idea of "Make Jesus King" was an extension of the American evangelical imagination, configured to mobilize the 1890s generation of college and university students toward world evangelization. In this goal, it was highly successful. It linked an expanding parachurch organization, the YMCA, with older missionary networks for education and evangelism to craft a global evangelical identity shared by fin de siècle North American students with counterparts in other countries. The mythic

The Evangelical Missionary Imagination

power of "Make Jesus King" resonated across a globalizing generation. By 1915, over 9,000 American student mission volunteers had reached the "mission field."[48] Yet underneath the common discourse lay the realities of nationalism. Student delegations at Northfield were organized according to their national identities. Competition among nations overlapped the new "muscular Christianity" that excited athletic competition between the colleges and universities that fed the movement.[49] The photos of Japanese delegates at the Northfield conferences of the late 1880s show some of them wearing their American college colors, no doubt fresh off the field of the baseball games in which they participated.[50]

Hard on the heels of intercollegiate student movements organized for world evangelization, empire came calling. During the 1890s, the subtext of patriotic nationalism permeated evangelicalism. Joining Europe in its colonial ambitions, both Japanese and American Christian students girded themselves for wars of conquest. Yet by seeing Japanese Christian students as mirror images of themselves, the American enthusiasts of "Make Jesus King" both embraced a nationalistic evangelical identity and contested it in the name of a shared transnational imaginary.

Notes

1. Tissington Tatlow, *The Story of the Student Christian Movement of Great Britain and Ireland* (London: Student Christian Movement Press, 1933), 72.

2. John Rutter Williamson, "The World's Student Christian Federation," in *"Make Jesus King": The Report of the International Students' Missionary Conference, Liverpool, January 1–5, 1896*, 2nd ed. (New York: Fleming H. Revell, 1896), 119. This chapter is adapted from a draft chapter of Dana L. Robert, *Fractured Fellowship: Transnational Imagination and the Politics of World Christian Community, 1919–1939*. Many thanks to Allison Kach for assisting with the endnotes.

3. For example, in January 1899, the legendary French missionary François Coillard preached on the importance of "Make Jesus King" to assembled African chiefs in Lesotho. W. John Young, *The Quiet Wise Spirit: Edwin W Smith 1867–1957 and Africa* (Peterborough, UK: Epworth Press, 2002), 24–25.

4. The Student Volunteer Movement was founded in 1888. On its history, see Dana L. Robert, "The Origin of the Student Volunteer Watchword: 'The Evangelization of the World in This Generation,'" *International Bulletin of Missionary Research* 10, no. 4 (1986): 146–49; Michael Parker, *The Kingdom of Character: The Student Volunteer Movement for Foreign Missions (1886–1926)* (Lanham, MD: University Press of America, 1998); William Henry Morgan, *Student Religion during Fifty Years: Programs and Policies of the Intercollegiate Y.M.C.A.* (New York: Association Press, 1935); and Nathan D. Showalter, *The End of a Crusade: The Student Volunteer Movement for Foreign Missions and the Great War* (Lanham, MD: Scarecrow Press, 1998).

5. Entanglement is a postcolonial stance by which the historian assumes that categories of human organization are not static. Not only do they impact each other, but they change in response to each other. Unlike comparative history, which privileges static binaries, entanglement assumes interdependent and therefore unexpected consequences on multiple fronts. For a fine overview of entangled history, see Sönke Bauck and Thomas Maier, "Entangled History," InterAmerican Wiki: Terms—Concepts—Critical Perspectives, 2015, www.uni-bielefeld.de/cias/wiki/e_Entangled_History.html.

6. Biblical scholar William Rainey Harper of Yale; A. T. Pierson, editor of the *Missionary Review of the World*; and Oregonian pulpiteer and Christian apologist I. D. Driver were just a few of the big names who attracted pastoral observers from up and down the Eastern Seaboard. Apparently the older generation was worried about the inroads that liberal "New Theology" was making on the university-educated theology students of the late 1800s, for Moody's concern to defend traditional evangelical orthodoxy was apparent in the large number of presentations on the reliability of the Bible.

7. On muscular Christianity, see Clifford Putney, *Muscular Christianity: Manhood and Sports in Protestant America, 1880–1920* (Cambridge, MA: Harvard University Press, 2001).

8. At Northfield, Stagg supervised eighteen tennis courts, two baseball diamonds, cricket, swimming, and races. He played in the first basketball game and was the great founding coach in American football. See Dominic Bertinetti Jr., "Biography—Amos Alonzo Stagg," www.liskahaas.org/stagg/biography.htm (accessed January 1, 2019).

9. The author of *How to Get Strong and How to Stay So* emphasized the beneficial effects of running and the need to incorporate exercise of different muscle groups into student life. Doug Bryant, "William Blaikie and Physical Fitness in Late Nineteenth Century America," *Iron Game History* 2, no. 3 (July 1992): 3–6.

10. "Talks on Missions—Interspersed with Hints on Physical Culture by Qualified Instructors," *Springfield* (MA) *Daily Union*, July 8, 1889, 8.

11. Jürgen Osterhammel and Niels P. Petersson, *Globalization: A Short History* (Princeton, NJ: Princeton University Press, 2005), esp. chap. 5.

12. Native American physician Charles Alexander Eastman, then a medical student at Boston University, was present at the conference, winning the steeplechase and pitching baseball. He was later an important leader of the Boy Scouts. As traveling secretary for the YMCA in the 1890s, he founded Native American branches. See his autobiography: Charles A. Eastman, *From the Deep Woods to Civilization: Chapters in the Autobiography of an Indian* (Boston: Little, Brown, 1916).

13. "The morning light is breaking; / The darkness disappears; / The sons of earth are waking / To penitential tears; / Each breeze that sweeps the ocean / Brings tidings from afar / Of nations in commotion, / Prepared for Sion's war."

14. These hopes were in vain, as the new constitution solidified the emperor as sacred head of the state. In 1890 followed the Imperial Rescript on Education and the end of the "seven wonderful years" of Christian expansion in Japan. Sandra C. Taylor, *Advocate of Understanding: Sidney Gulick and the Search for Peace with Japan* (Kent, OH: Kent State University Press, 1985), 30–32.

15. When Commodore Matthew Perry steamed into Edo Bay in 1853 and forcibly opened Japanese ports to Western trade, Isé's father, Yokoi Héishiro, counseled the nobles to open relationships with the West. Yokoi read the Constitution of the United

The Evangelical Missionary Imagination

States and the Bible in Chinese. A modernizer, he advised the establishment of a parliament. Yokoi was beheaded by a hit squad in 1869. Wrote his missionary biographer, the Reverend William Elliot Griffis, "The blood of this martyr was the seed of New Japan. Shall it be the seed of the holy Church of Christ also?" William E. Griffis, "Editorial Notes," *Our Day: A Record and View of Current Reform* 4, no. 22 (1889): 394.

16. The newspaper account of Isé's speech incorrectly names Captain Jenks rather than Janes. "Talks on Missions—Interspersed with Hints on Physical Culture by Qualified Instructors," 8. I am correcting and supplementing the account of the events through reliance on other sources, notably Hiromichi Kozaki, *Reminiscences of Seventy Years: The Autobiography of a Japanese Pastor* (Tokyo: Christian Literature Society of Japan, 1933), 10–30.

17. Kozaki, *Reminiscences*, 29.

18. What Isé did not mention was that his own mother threatened to commit suicide when she learned of her son's conversion and had to be physically restrained. Kozaki, 22.

19. "A Great Day—No Preaching to Empty Air but Enthusiastic Men," *Springfield Daily Union*, July 8, 1889, 4.

20. "Great Day," 4.

21. "Great Day," 8.

22. Charles Kellogg Ober, *Luther D. Wishard, Projector of World Movements* (New York: Association Press, 1927), 139.

23. Osterhammel and Petersson indicate that a key feature of the period from 1880 to 1945 was the "mastery of space and distance" through a redefinition of the present. Osterhammel and Petersson, *Globalization*, 84.

24. Karl Fries, "Vadstena Memories," *Student World*, July 1915, 81–84.

25. *"Make Jesus King,"* 117.

26. *"Make Jesus King,"* 121.

27. J. D. Davis, *A Sketch of the Life of Joseph Hardy Neesima* (New York: Fleming H. Revell, 1894).

28. Quoted in Ober, *Luther D. Wishard*, 98–99.

29. C. Howard Hopkins, *History of the Y.M.C.A. in North America* (New York: Association Press, 1951), 77.

30. The growth in the number and quality of American institutions of higher education was instrumental in the expansion of the YMCA in the last quarter of the nineteenth century. Some 350 colleges in 1878 had increased to 500 by the twentieth century.

31. Morgan, *Student Religion*, 25.

32. The importance of missionary networks is apparent in the travel literature of parachurch movement leaders in the 1890s. For example, see the memoir of the founder of Christian Endeavor, Francis E. Clark, *Fellow Travellers: A Personally Conducted Journey in Three Continents, with Impressions of Men, Things and Events* (New York: Fleming H. Revell, 1898). Prominent missionary families such as the Murrays in South Africa sponsored multiple organizations. For example, the spiritual writer Andrew Murray Jr. founded the first South African YMCA in Cape Town, and his sister introduced Christian Endeavor into girls' schools.

33. In 1886, Princeton seminary student Robert Wilder was a missionary kid "planted" at Moody's summer conference, with the hope of putting the cause of missions

before the student leaders. By the end of the summer conference, exactly 100 of the collegiate YMCA leaders had volunteered to become foreign missionaries—the famous "Mt. Hermon 100." Over the next academic year, Robert Wilder and John Forman, another son of Presbyterian India missionaries, visited 162 colleges and recruited over 2,000 students who signed a pledge to become foreign missionaries. At the Northfield summer conference of 1887, students, YMCA secretaries, sons of missionaries, missionary speakers, delegates from Cambridge University, and church-sponsored international students created a potent mix. The India missionary Jacob Chamberlain appealed for a missionary YMCA that would give to India "the life, the fire, the method" it was giving to Americans. Jacob Chamberlain, quoted in Hopkins, *History of the Y.M.C.A.*, 300, 294–99. On the Mt. Hermon 100, see Dana L. Robert, *"Occupy until I Come": A. T. Pierson and the Evangelization of the World* (Grand Rapids, MI: Eerdmans, 2003), 145–50; Robert, "Origin of the Student Volunteer Watchword," 146–49; and James Findlay Jr., *Dwight L. Moody* (Chicago: University of Chicago Press, 1969).

34. Sherwood Eddy, *A Century with Youth: A History of the Y.M.C.A. from 1844 to 1944* (New York: Association Press, 1944), 90.

35. Hopkins, *History of the Y.M.C.A.*, 146. See chap. 8 of Hopkins on Wishard's world tour. Tension between British and American ways of organizing things emerged in the organization of YMCAs in India.

36. For a classic study of the sending of YMCA secretaries from North America to the non-Western world, see Kenneth Scott Latourette, *World Service: A History of the Foreign Work and World Service of the YMCAs of the United States and Canada* (New York: Association Press, 1957). For a study of female YWCA secretaries abroad, see Nancy Boyd, *Emissaries: The Overseas Work of the American YWCA, 1895–1970* (New York: Woman's Press, 1986); and Elizabeth Wilson, *Fifty Years of Association Work among Young Women, 1866–1916* (New York: Garland, 1987). The YWCA sent its first foreign secretary in 1894.

37. Luther Deloraine Wishard, *A New Programme of Missions: A Movement to Make the Colleges in All Lands Centers of Evangelization* (New York: Fleming H. Revell, 1895).

38. Later as analyst and professor of missions at Yale, Beach became the leading statistician of the early twentieth-century missionary movement, and he assembled the preeminent American collection of Asian missionary documentation. On his involvement in the 1889 Kyoto conference, see Hopkins, *History of the Y.M.C.A.*, 330. For a brief biography and linked publications of Harlan Page Beach, see "Beach, Harlan Page (1854–1933)," www.bu.edu/missiology/missionary-biography/a-c/beach-harlan-page -1854-1933 (accessed January 1, 2019).

39. Wishard, *New Programme*, 67.

40. Wishard, 85.

41. Kozaki, *Reminiscences*, 92. Unfortunately, I am unable to access Japanese-language sources for this paper.

42. Kozaki, 93–95.

43. See Hiromichi Kozaki, "Christianity in Japan," *International Review of Missions* 27 (July 1938): 355–58. Despite his ardent Japanese nationalism and his vehement disagreements with Congregational missionaries, Hiromichi Kozaki continued to appreciate his relationships with Western Christian partners throughout his life.

The Evangelical Missionary Imagination

44. Jon Thares Davidann, *A World of Crisis and Progress: The American YMCA in Japan, 1890–1930* (Bethlehem, PA: Lehigh University Press, 1998).

45. Swift quoted in Davidann, 45. On John Trumbull Swift, see Richard Cary Morse, *History of the North American Young Men's Christian Associations* (New York: Association Press, 1913), 198–99; Ian Tyrrell, *Reforming the World: The Creation of America's Moral Empire* (Princeton, NJ: Princeton University Press, 2010), 86; Young Men's Christian Associations, *YMCA Year Book and Official Rosters* (New York: Association Press, 1896), 34; and Jon Thares Davidann, "The American YMCA in Meiji Japan: God's Work Gone Awry," *Journal of World History* 6, no. 1 (1995): 107–25.

46. Davidann, *World of Crisis and Progress*, 46–49.

47. In 1890, he published an article arguing that Japanese theology should be based on Japanese traditions, including rites and ceremonies, rather than just be a "pale imitation" of Western Christianity. Taylor, *Advocate of Understanding*, 33; Emily Anderson, *Christianity and Imperialism in Modern Japan: Empire for God* (London: Bloomsbury Academic, 2014), 35–36, 47, 61.

48. Charles W. Forman, "II. The Americans," *International Bulletin of Missionary Research* 6, no. 2 (1982): 54–56.

49. The year 1896 was also the year of the first modern Olympics, held in Athens. The YMCA was instrumental in facilitating the early Olympic games through training athletes, providing facilities, organizing the competitions, and inventing the sports of basketball, volleyball, and weight-lifting.

50. Random photographs exist of student delegations to Northfield conferences in the Northfield Mount Hermon Archives, Mount Hermon, MA. The Japanese delegation of 1887, for example, posed together, but no photo exists of the Japanese delegation of 1889. Email from archivist Peter Weis to author, January 4, 2020. The solidarity of national identity was also expressed in the Japanese-language Bible signed by twenty-one Japanese and presented to Dwight L. Moody at Northfield in 1890. Among the signatories were both men and women who later became distinguished educators, businesspeople, and church leaders in Japan. The intriguing connection to Japanese sports provided by the Northfield conferences includes a signature by Gompei Kuwada, previously a student at Worcester Polytechnic Institute, quarterback of the football team, and later considered the "father of Japanese football." The Worcester Polytechnic Institute mascot was named "Gompei" after him. David Sneade, "Gompei Revealed," October 10, 2014, WPI, www.wpi.edu/news/gompei-revealed.

PART TWO

Global Christianity and the Cold War

Christian Globalism, Christian Nationalism, and the Ecumenical-Evangelical Rivalry

Gene Zubovich

Buell Gordon Gallagher is best remembered, if he is remembered at all, as the president of City University of New York whose career was ended by the "open enrollment" crisis in 1969. He resigned amid violence surrounding an occupation of buildings by student demonstrators, whose demands for the restructuring of the university Gallagher for the most part supported. It was a sudden and dramatic end to a long career that saw him running for Congress, working for the Truman administration, serving the National Association for the Advancement of Colored People (NAACP), ministering at an interracial church, and working as a professor of social ethics at a Protestant seminary.[1] Like many mid-twentieth-century elites, Gallagher was a product of the ecumenical Protestant milieu. Ecumenical Protestants, sometimes called "liberal" or "mainline" Protestants, were a major force in U.S. and international politics. From local battles against segregation to global debates about human rights, ecumenical Protestants like Gallagher were at the center of religious politics in the middle decades of the twentieth century.

When the modern evangelical movement came into being in the 1940s, it defined itself against the example of ecumenical Protestants like Buell Gallagher. In the 1940s a group of fundamentalists adopted the label "evangelical" partly to distinguish themselves from ecumenical Protestants. In that decade, "'evangelical' and 'fundamentalist' were not then separate entities," writes George Marsden.[2] Both were part of a long-standing effort to distinguish "true" Christian faith from the "false" theology and politics of ecumenical Protestants. Earlier in the twentieth century, fundamentalists and ecumenicals often shared denominations, missionary organizations, journals, and seminaries. In the 1920s, some fundamentalists moved to create their own organizations, especially new seminaries and Bible colleges. After World War II, evangelicals continued to pull away from ecumenical institutions and formed their own—but always with an eye toward their most intimate religious opponents.

This chapter uses the example of Gallagher to highlight key characteristics of the ecumenical-evangelical rivalry. In doing so, it helps us better understand how the modern evangelical movement defined itself against its perceived enemies and the ways this oppositional relationship shaped the politics of evangelicals from the 1940s to the present day. Beginning in the 1940s, fundamentalists, now calling themselves evangelicals, modeled their new institutions on those of their ecumenical opponents. The National Association of Evangelicals, founded in 1942, was modeled on the ecumenical Federal Council of Churches. The pathbreaking evangelical magazine *Christianity Today* was modeled on the ecumenical *Christian Century*. And it was not only institutions that were shaped by the ecumenical-evangelical rivalry. Ideas also flowed from ecumenicals to evangelicals. Evangelicals selectively adopted some aspects of ecumenism—that is, boundary crossing among Protestant denominations—to create a united front against their opponents. They would also adopt the language of Judeo-Christianity, racial liberalism, and human rights that were initially pioneered by ecumenical Protestants.[3] In each case, evangelicals adopted these rhetorics and practices selectively, often decades after they were first promoted by ecumenical Protestants, and they did so in a markedly different political and ideological context. Nonetheless, the modern evangelical movement was deeply influenced by competition with ecumenical Protestants. One cannot understand evangelicals today without a historical account of their rivalry with ecumenical Protestants and of the way they selectively appropriated ideas and practices from their rivals.

At the heart of the ecumenical-evangelical rivalry were two strikingly different orientations toward the world beyond America's borders: Christian globalism and Christian nationalism. Between the 1930s and 1960s, a broad swath of ecumenical Protestants, like Gallagher, subscribed to Christian globalism. It was a new way of conceiving space. Protestant intellectuals came to argue by the 1930s that the lines between nation-states we see on maps do not accurately represent the interconnectedness of peoples across the world, the religiously based transnational solidarity of the international ecumenical movement, or the ultimate source of authority that sits over and above all nation-states from which all rights are derived. It was also a new way of thinking about governance, with religious leaders like Gallagher calling for a world government.[4] As Michael Thompson points out, Protestant globalism was deeply anti-nationalist, opposed to the Christian nationalism that predominated among evangelicals. And as Or Rosenboim argues, by the 1940s this way of imagining space was not confined to religious figures but was broadly shared by intellectuals throughout the North Atlantic West. Indeed, as Susan Schulten and Samuel Zipp point out, the notion of a shrinking, interconnected globe was popular among Americans in the 1940s and pregnant with political possibilities. Historians have largely downplayed the enthusiasm that many Americans, especially American ecumenical Protestants, felt for world government in the era of World War II and emphasized instead the coming Cold War. Nevertheless, Christian globalism was a politically vibrant ideology that shaped the ecumenical Protestant community and also elicited a backlash from evangelical Protestants.[5]

Partly in reaction to ecumenical Protestants' promotion of Christian globalism, evangelicals largely devoted themselves to Christian nationalism. The term is difficult to define because it is so widely used in both academic and popular discourse. Sociologists Andrew L. Whitehead and Samuel L. Perry define Christian nationalism as an ideology that fuses "American civic life with a particular type of Christian identity and culture," which includes the blurred boundaries of "religious identity (Christian, preferably Protestant) with race (white), nativity (born in the United States), citizenship (American), and political ideology (social and fiscal conservative)."[6] More historically minded analysts have traced the association between Christianity and nation-state, and especially the exceptional "mission" of the United States to the world, from the Puritans to the end of the Cold War.[7] The Christian nationalism of evangelicals in the middle decades of the twentieth century built upon this long tradition of conceiving of nation-states as sanctified entities, with the United States standing above all others.

This chapter makes three arguments about Christian nationalism as it was practiced by evangelicals in the mid-twentieth century. First, Christian nationalism was not solely centered on domestic questions, like church-state relations and economic policy.[8] Rather, Christian nationalism was partly a response to the Christian globalism of ecumenical Protestants and their support for international organizations. Evangelicals intertwined their antipathy for ecumenical theology and politics, their insistence that the United States was founded as a Christian nation, and their fear of supranational institutions like the United Nations.

Second, this chapter emphasizes how evangelicals grafted a series of political initiatives—like libertarian economics and segregation—onto Christian nationalism. As Gallagher backed world government and called for the observance of human rights in the United States, evangelicals moved in the opposite direction by rejecting both.

Finally, this chapter examines the oppositional nature of Christian nationalism. Although rooted in a long tradition of associating their nation with their religious tradition and suspicion of international institutions, evangelicals who subscribed to Christian nationalism in the mid-twentieth century were more consistent in their opposition to their rivals than they were in advocating for a coherent ideological program.[9] Their political commitments, some of which were long-standing, became more rigid as they responded to the activism of their religious opponents. Evangelicals were already hostile to the United Nations, the New Deal, and racial liberalism, and when ecumenical Protestants backed these initiatives, it made evangelicals only more fervent in their resistance. Initially united in their opposition to their enemies, only in the late 1950s did evangelicals begin forming a clear and consistent political identity as conservatives.

This is not to say that evangelicals were "isolationists" or disengaged from international affairs. On the contrary, evangelicals created missionary and humanitarian organizations that would dwarf those of ecumenical Protestants by the end of the twentieth century. The label "Christian nationalist" invites us not to debate whether American evangelicals engaged the world but to consider on what terms they did so—and how different those terms were from the Christian globalism of ecumenical Protestants.

Buell Gallagher's career exemplifies the political possibilities Christian globalism presented to Americans at midcentury. But his political ambitions and ethical commitments would collide with the Christian nationalism of

Christian Globalism and the Ecumenical-Evangelical Rivalry

the evangelical movement. His career and the attacks against him reveal how Christian globalism and Christian nationalism shaped the intertwined trajectories of ecumenical and evangelical Protestantism.

When the historically Black Talladega College in Alabama was looking for a new president in 1933, the twenty-nine-year-old Buell Gallagher was an unlikely choice. Talladega College was governed by the American Missionary Association, an arm of the mostly white and predominantly northern Congregationalist denomination, which had been active in Black education since Reconstruction. Gallagher was ambitious and smart and had experience in an interracial church organization in New Jersey. But he also was young, did not have a doctorate, and had very little teaching experience.[10] While there were many talented African American educators at Talladega and beyond, Gallagher did meet one basic requirement of most university heads of that era: he was white.

Gallagher grew up in a Congregationalist family in a small town in Illinois. His father was a pastor, his mother worked in the missionary movement, and his sister would later become a missionary in China. After attending a small denominational college in Minnesota, he received a degree at Union Theological Seminary in New York, which had strong ties to the Social Gospel tradition.[11] It was at Union that Gallagher drifted toward socialism and wrote an undergraduate thesis on the class struggle in ancient Greece.[12]

Gallagher was part of an ecumenical Protestant generation that drew inspiration from the international ecumenical movement. With roots stretching back into the nineteenth century, the ecumenical movement was inaugurated in 1910 at a meeting in Edinburgh, Scotland.[13] Americans, Canadians, and Europeans, along with some participants from the Global South, launched institutions that would later become the International Missionary Council and the World Council of Churches. Putting aside some of their denominational differences, the leaders of the ecumenical movement inspired Gallagher's generation with promises of global Christian unity as well as social reform across the world. Idealistic Protestant youths like Gallagher understood their local activism as part of a broader effort to transform the world. Evangelicals, on the other hand, rejected this international movement. As Melani McAlister explains, "The World Council of Churches was maligned and feared by evangelicals because it had successfully positioned itself as the voice of a united Christian community" while excluding evangelicals. They complained that the organization was becoming a superchurch—a Protestant version of the Vatican—and was promoting politics that evangelicals found reprehensible.[14]

Thinking globally but acting locally, Gallagher brought his enthusiasm for reform to Alabama. The trustees of Talladega found a young idealist who reasoned that race relations could be transformed through education. They knew Gallagher believed that education could ameliorate the conditions of Black southerners without directly challenging Jim Crow.[15]

Gallagher's racial liberalism and socialist inclinations mirrored the trajectory of ecumenical Protestantism in the 1920s and 1930s. Organizations like the Federal Council of Churches established educational initiatives and promoted interracial contact in order to diminish prejudice without challenging Jim Crow. These meager initiatives were controversial enough in those decades that several denominations refused to take part. Similarly, during the Great Depression many ecumenical organizations revived their commitment to the Social Gospel and became important backers of the New Deal, a move that proved unpopular with many churchgoers.

Mirroring this national trend, Gallagher involved himself with respectable local organizations that agreed with his slow-paced, education-oriented program for fighting prejudice. Occasionally, these groups produced helpful results. After a 1939 study of conditions in the town of Talladega, faculty joined with local businessmen, labor leaders, and professionals to form the interracial Talladega Civic League. Thanks to the organization's lobbying, the African American neighborhood saw some improvements. A few streetlights were installed, several streets were paved, an extra teacher was hired, and a branch school was opened.[16]

Some ecumenical Protestants pushed their anti-racist agenda further in the 1940s by emphasizing access to jobs and eventually attacking the Jim Crow system. Gallagher joined them on the eve of World War II. The military buildup of the early 1940s moved the issue of the segregated workplace to the top of the civil rights agenda, as Black activists demanded that a fair share of defense jobs go to African Americans. When A. Philip Randolph threatened a march on Washington in 1940, Gallagher, who was a member of the board of directors of the NAACP, hesitated about the campaign because it might have incited racial violence.[17] But once the march was averted and Franklin Roosevelt responded to Randolph's demands by issuing an executive order that created the Fair Employment Practices Commission (FEPC), which monitored and publicized complaints about wartime employment discrimination, Gallagher wholeheartedly supported the endeavor. When several Black women from the town of Talladega told the Civic League they

Christian Globalism and the Ecumenical-Evangelical Rivalry

were denied jobs as sewing machine operators by a local company because the jobs were reserved for white women, the league appointed Gallagher to investigate the problem and to negotiate with local business leaders. The company agreed to hire Black women after Gallagher filed a complaint with the FEPC (and a second complaint at a later time, when the company tried to backslide on the original agreement). Thirty-nine Black women were hired as machine operators as a result of Gallagher's involvement.[18]

Like the views of his religious community, Gallagher's stance on segregation underwent a tectonic shift during World War II. Beginning in 1942, the Federal Council of Churches first took aim at segregation, a position that it would formally ratify when it called segregation a "sin" in 1946 and pledged to fight it both within and outside of Protestant churches. Prior to World War II, Protestant organizations had spoken out against the more violent manifestations of Jim Crow, especially lynching, but like southern liberals, they very rarely challenged segregation directly. Then, in 1946, the Federal Council of Churches, the YMCA and YWCA, and the Congregational denomination (to which Gallagher belonged) made a dramatic call for Jim Crow's end. The YMCA and YWCA desegregated their national organizations, and several denominations, including the Congregationalists, joined with the Federal Council of Churches in developing a concerted political program to combat racism. It was a transformation that was facilitated by the wartime enthusiasm for remaking the international order.[19]

Gallagher was among the architects of the wartime turn against segregation. He moved to California in 1944 to take a job as a social ethicist at the Pacific School of Religion in Berkeley. "It is my considered judgement that racial tensions are tighter in some spots on the West Coast than anywhere else in the nation," he observed, "and that at the same time, the situation is more fluid than in most other places. Strategically, the West Coast is an area calling for concentrated effort," Gallagher told NAACP executive secretary Walter White in 1944.[20]

In California he was in close contact with activists who were fighting to end Japanese internment, a priority for Congregationalists. He worked with Galen Weaver, who was a pastor at a multiracial church in Hawaii, in orchestrating a concerted effort by the denomination to combat racism from 1946 until 1948.[21] Among their more important contributions was the Congregationalists' amicus curiae briefs on behalf of pathbreaking civil rights cases, including *Takahashi v. Fish and Game Commission* and *Shelley v. Kramer*.[22]

The Alameda County NAACP, which included Berkeley and Oakland, elected Buell Gallagher vice president of the organization upon his arrival, and Gallagher worked closely with President C. L. Dellums, who also headed the regional branch of the Brotherhood of Sleeping Car Porters. Within his first year, Gallagher had placed himself at the center of several networks of local and national anti-racist activists, including developing ties to Black labor leaders.

Sensing the fluidity of racial politics in 1940s California, Gallagher helped broaden the institutional basis of the non-communist interracial left by helping create the South Berkeley Community Church.[23] It was one of several dozen experimental churches created in northern and western cities during World War II, a time when only 10 percent of the Congregational churches in the country had any Black members at all (and only a tiny fraction of this 10 percent had more than ten black members).[24] Gallagher regarded these churches as a "prophecy" of an unsegregated nation and hoped that integrated churches would be "the spiritual center of the integrated community."[25]

The Community Church began with about forty members but attracted outsized attention from the outset in 1943 as a center for interracial activism.[26] Sociologist Charles S. Johnson and activist Will W. Alexander gave speeches at the church's dedication, and W. E. B. Du Bois and Howard Thurman were among the many prominent activists who visited the church in later years.[27] Events at this small church, which grew to 300 members, were regularly covered by the Black press as far away as the *Chicago Defender*.[28] Gallagher would soon come to see his religiously inspired anti-racist activism as part of a global movement against white supremacy.

In the 1940s, Gallagher explicitly rooted his anti-racist work in an international context and became one of the leading spokespersons for Christian globalism. The links he drew between Protestant Christianity, the missionary movement, colonialism, and racism were most clearly expressed in his 1946 book, *Color and Conscience: The Irrepressible Conflict*. Written during wartime, it came out during a moment when ecumenical Protestants rallied for a new international order, one centered on a world government. Calling for a "true community of nations," the Federal Council of Churches announced in 1942 that "the interdependent life of nations must be ordered by agencies having the duty and the power to promote and safeguard the general welfare of all peoples." "A world of irresponsible, competing and unrestrained national sovereignties," it declared, "is a world of international anarchy."[29]

The drive for a world government was popular beyond the ecumenical Protestant community. Former Republican presidential candidate Wendell

Willkie endorsed the idea in his 1943 best-seller, *One World*, and hundreds of "world federalism" organizations formed in the 1940s. But ecumenical Protestants were among the idea's most enthusiastic backers. Under the leadership of future secretary of state John Foster Dulles, the Federal Council of Churches held rallies across the nation involving hundreds of thousands of churchgoers during the war years. Ecumenical Protestants called upon the Roosevelt administration and on Congress to forge a postwar peace along the lines of the "Six Pillars of Peace," which included a permanent international organization, a gradual end to colonialism, and disarmament. They played a leading role in creating the United Nations. But when the United Nations came into being in 1945, they were disappointed with the limits of the organization and advocated reforming it to give it greater power over the affairs of countries. Well into the 1950s and 1960s, American ecumenical Protestants, especially women's groups, continued to devote themselves to the institution through prayer, educational efforts, public ceremonies, and political advocacy.[30] Christian globalists often associated other progressive measures with their drive for world government, like diminishing poverty or demilitarization.

Gallagher's Christian globalism emphasized the need to combat racism and colonialism as part of the process of creating a community of nations. *Color and Conscience* marked his abandonment of the education-oriented racial liberalism and an embrace of politically active anti-racism. "Having been guilty, myself, of producing one book which conformed to these canons of the etiquette of caste," Gallagher lamented, referring to his earlier book, *American Caste and the Negro College*, "I am speaking somewhat more bluntly in these present pages."[31] *Color and Conscience* emerged at the same historical moment as Gunnar Myrdal's more famous *An American Dilemma*, and both books emphasized the chasm between American ideals and practices. As Gallagher put it, "Our difficulty is that, while we give theoretical assent to the idea [of racial equality], we postpone the day of ethical action until the irreversible course of history has carried us beyond the point where affirmative action is creative."[32] Gallagher's *Color and Conscience* was, in a way, an abridged Christian's guide to *An American Dilemma*.[33]

Unlike Myrdal, Gallagher emphasized the relationship between Jim Crow and colonialism. Centering the global dimensions of racism, Gallagher argued that Americans were witnessing "a march of world events which (particularly in the Near East and the Far East) have continued to expose the insistent pressures of color in the world scene."[34] Jim Crow, observed Gallagher, was part of a broader history of global white supremacy, which was coming to a quick end. "The Boxer Uprising was not an incident without an explanation," he wrote. "The Oriental Exclusion Act . . . did not endear America to Asiatics."[35] The long history of American colonialism in East Asia made the war in the Pacific much more difficult, he argued.

Gallagher was articulating an argument that would later be mobilized by Cold War liberals against Jim Crow: that racism at home undermined America's fight against totalitarianism abroad.[36] "The fanatical glee with which Radio Tokyo seized upon reports of racial difficulty in the United States and beamed them toward India and the Americans south of the Rio Grande is not accidental. [The race riots in] Los Angeles, Detroit, Houston, Beaumont, Sikeston, New York, Philadelphia, and other American cities have made headlines in the nonwhite world."[37] The history of American imperialism in East Asia and the news of white supremacy at home aided Japan, Gallagher told his readers. If the United States wanted to gain allies against fascism, it would have to jettison white supremacy more quickly than it was doing.

Gallagher remained optimistic about America's ability to renounce white supremacy, and he rooted that hope in the history of the Protestant missionary movement. He wrote, "After all allowance is made for the cultural imperialism and arrogant paternalism implicit (and often explicit) in much of the missionary effort of the nineteenth century, and after the connection of missions with the economic and political imperialism of Europe and North America has been fully acknowledged—to our shame—the story of missions remains one of the most heroic records of altruistic endeavor which history has yet unfolded."[38] As the missionaries went to China, Korea, and other nations, they were transformed by their experiences, forming friendships with locals and becoming increasingly embarrassed about white supremacy back home. Missionaries then set about to transform the United States, urging the country to disavow white supremacy.[39]

Gallagher's rosy depiction of missionaries was an elision of the long history of Christian imperialism. Yet his generous assessment was shared by many others in the 1940s, including the elder statesman of Pan-Africanism, W. E. B. Du Bois. In his slim 1945 book, *Color and Democracy: Colonies and Peace*, Du Bois began the chapter "Missions and Mandates" with a call for the creation of "a new mandates commission implemented by that unselfish devotion to the well-being of mankind which has often, if not always, inspired the missionary crusade."[40] Like Gallagher, Du Bois drew inspiration "especially in the Christian missions of the eighteenth and nineteenth centuries; in the suppression of slavery and the slave trade; and in the various attempts to alleviate, if not abolish, poverty and to do away with ignorance."[41]

Du Bois, a longtime acquaintance of Gallagher, also noted the long history of Christian imperialism and chauvinism but quickly moved past it. "It is all too clear today that if we are to have a sufficient motive for the uplift of backward peoples, for the redemption and progress of colonials, such a motive can be found only in the faith and ideals of organized religion; and the great task that is before us is to join this belief and the consequent action with the scientific knowledge and efficient techniques of economic reform."[42] Du Bois had publicly disavowed personal faith, but he believed in the potential of the Christian missionary project to undermine colonialism.

Du Bois evoked the missionary ethos in 1945 as he was contemplating the shape of international governance then coming to existence in the form of the United Nations. Gallagher, too, was thinking about the postwar international order. He was enthusiastic about the Atlantic Charter, which promised self-determination and human rights to "all the men in all the lands." But he echoed the *Christian Century*'s disappointment in 1944 that the document was an "idealistic hoax" as it became clear that the United States, Great Britain, and the USSR would dictate the postwar peace.[43] And, despite former presidential candidate Wendell Willkie's call for a Pacific Charter to bring self-determination to Asia, one never emerged.[44] The United Nations likewise was disappointing to Gallagher. And yet he was cautiously optimistic about the new organization's potential. It had not altered the prevalence of white supremacy across the world, but, unlike the earlier League of Nations, it did affirm the equality of all peoples. And he believed that the Commission on Human Rights would eventually be positioned to enforce this provision, even though it did not yet have that power.

The wartime debates over the United Nations also raised questions about the relationship between religion and government, both national and international. Should ecumenical Protestants really be giving enthusiastic support to an international organization that would take over some of the relief and reconstruction work that churches were doing? And should they participate in an organization that was attempting in its early days to be religiously neutral between Christians, Muslims, Buddhists, Hindus, and atheists by leaving out prayer and other religious ceremony from its proceedings? For Gallagher, the answer was a clear "yes." He urged his coreligionists to be more engaged in the world beyond the churches and, in particular, to help counteract injustices by taking on a public role that went beyond liturgy. The UN should be treated in the same way as the New Deal. Secular agencies, even radical ones, were best seen as "a challenge" to Protestants, pushing them to do more. "Critical comments and condemnation of the activities of the so-called 'secular' agencies which are 'invading the province of the Church' might legitimately be directed toward the institutions of religion," he wrote. Eschewing the boundary between the sacred and the secular, Gallagher urged his fellow Protestants to embrace all projects that were "of the essence of religious values." Even if these values were promoted by secular organizations, Gallagher wrote, "who shall say that the Spirit has not been at work?"[45]

Gallagher's Christian globalism had clear political implications, and his desire to move beyond the confines of the pulpit drove him to run for a congressional seat in 1948. He was recruited by labor groups in Oakland and Berkeley, California, who were on the defensive following the Oakland General Strike of 1946.[46] As the Cold War stigmatized labor organizations as insufficiently patriotic and potentially subversive, drafting a minister with a long track record of liberal political activism made sense for Berkeley and Oakland Democrats.

The congressional race began with a serious challenge, not from Gallagher's opponent but from the board of trustees and president of the Pacific School of Religion, where Gallagher continued to teach as a social ethicist. Gallagher requested a two-year leave of absence from the school to run for office and, if elected, to serve his term. Though other professors from the school had recently been given leaves of similar length, Gallagher's request was denied on grounds that his absence would be too detrimental to the students.[47] The Pacific School of Religion's president acknowledged that Gallagher was recognized as "the radical of the faculty," which likely affected the board's thinking.[48] Unhappy with the decision, Gallagher resigned his professorship and began his political campaign.

Gallagher belonged to the Democratic Party and referred to himself as a "liberal and responsible Democrat who has committed himself to carrying out the policies and principles of the late Franklin Delano Roosevelt."[49] Yet Gallagher cross-filed with the Republican Party and Henry A. Wallace's Independent Progressive Party.[50] He never made a serious attempt at the Republican nomination but did actively seek the endorsement of the Independent Progressive Party by appearing at its events and introducing Wallace at an Oakland rally.[51] Wallace was well known for opposing what was coming to be known as the "Cold War." Like Wallace, Gallagher called "for primary emphasis on strengthening the United Nations and correcting the immoralities of racism, narrow nationalism, and kindred evils which endanger permanent world peace."[52] Gallagher's platform was a testament to how much the New Deal, anti-racism, and opposition to the Cold War was intertwined for some ecumenical Protestants.

Gallagher's participation in the Wallace rally and his internationalist agenda set off accusations of communist sympathies. The *Oakland Tribune*, a staunchly Republican newspaper with connections to Gallagher's opponent, John Allen, repeatedly insinuated that Gallagher was a fellow traveler. The hectic campaign went on through the summer months of 1948 and into the fall. Gallagher's early momentum slowed as a result of his battle with the *Tribune*. The sympathetic coverage he received in the Berkeley press and union newspapers was not enough to overcome his opponent. The results of the November election were heartbreaking for Gallagher: he lost by two percentage points, 49 percent to 51 percent.

At the end of 1948, Gallagher reflected on the race he had so narrowly lost. The vote "was strictly along economic lines," Gallagher argued, torn between the "hill folk" who were "predominantly upper and middle class, and white," and "South and North and West Oakland, where 45,000 Negroes live and the homes of working class people boast no spacious lawns or imposing front porches."[53] Writing these words in the *Christian Century*, ecumenical Protestantism's flagship journal, the audience understood his message: the "hill folk" were mostly "mainline" Protestants who shared Gallagher's religion but not his politics.[54]

Gallagher was disappointed. "I had expected to win," he wrote; "I admit it."[55] But he was proud of his decision to run for office. For Gallagher, there was no looking back: "I have declined the protection of the pulpit . . . [and] stepped out from the cloistered halls of a theological seminary" in order to try to change, rather than merely condemn, government policy.[56] Others should do the same, he wrote.

By running for office, Gallagher took his political activism further than most ecumenical Protestant leaders. But in numerous other ways, ecumenical Protestants were involved politically in the 1940s on behalf of many of the same causes Gallagher supported. They organized letter-writing campaigns, held rallies, opened lobbying offices, testified before Congress, filed lawsuits, met regularly with elected officials, worked closely with the State Department, and used their international connections to press for reform at the United Nations.[57] Ecumenical Protestant activism was widespread in these years, and it was understood that leaders like Gallagher supported a reform movement centered on a new postwar international order. In the years before the Cold War became orthodoxy, Christian globalism was an outlook that was viable, politically potent, and popular.

Gallagher remained enthusiastic about his political career despite his election loss. "My present mind is not to go back into teaching, but to go forward in Government," he told Walter White.[58] And his commitment to Christian globalism made him covet a role at the United Nations. "If I had my choice of all the assignments in the world at this moment of history," Gallagher had written to White in 1946, "the one thing I would most like to do is to put my hand to the task before the Commission on Human Rights of the United Nations Organization. . . . Everything I have done in my preparation and experience up to this time points in a single straight line to this particular assignment."[59]

From 1946 onward, Gallagher mobilized every contact he had to place himself on the Human Rights Commission. He wrote repeatedly to White, collared Eleanor Roosevelt, and convinced Gordon Sproul, chancellor of the University of California, Berkeley, to lobby on his behalf.[60] It did not work. After losing the congressional race in 1948, Gallagher worked for a short time at the Pacific School of Religion, followed by an appointment in the education department in the Truman administration. As Truman left office in early 1953, Gallagher accepted a position as president of the City College of New York (today, the City University of New York) and then as chancellor of the California State College (later, University) system.[61] It would set him on a path toward a confrontation with Christian nationalism in Southern California.

As Gallagher and other ecumenical Protestants brought their Christian globalism into the political arena, evangelical Protestants mobilized increasingly on behalf of Christian nationalism. They viewed with great suspicion the coupling of liberal theology with desegregation and the New Deal, especially when it was tied together with calls for a world government. The National Association of Evangelicals (NAE) was created in 1942 to put forth an alternative religious voice in public and in politics to the ecumenical Protestant establishment. The upstart organization did just that, using its still-meager public platform to challenge Christian globalism. In 1949, the NAE was invited by the State Department to send a representative to discuss the Universal Declaration of Human Rights. At a meeting chaired by Eleanor Roosevelt, NAE representative Stephen W. Paine warned the State Department not to subscribe to an international covenant of human rights if it meant the inclusion of social and economic rights. Paine explained, "Knowing the constituency of the National Association of Evangelicals as I do, I feel confident in saying they would not at all concur in this feeling concerning the statement of social and economic rights." He decried the

Christian Globalism and the Ecumenical-Evangelical Rivalry

right to join a labor union as "forced unionization" and disparaged Article 25—the right to "food, clothing, housing, medical care, and necessary social services, and the right to security in the event of unemployment, sickness, disability, widowhood, old age, etc."—for being "socialistic."[62]

In the same way that Gallagher coupled together the UN with social and economic rights, so too did Paine—and he rejected all of it. The NAE objected to "the underlying assumption of the entire Declaration of Human Rights." Whereas the UN charter began with a personalist understanding of rights inhering in each individual person, "the founders of our nation started, not with certain rights *inherent in man*, but described man's rights as given by God." The UN's human rights, he charged, "simply go on and reinforce the picture of government as the big father upon whom the individual is dependent." And as scary as the U.S. government was becoming in the minds of many evangelicals, the UN had the potential to be yet more threatening to American liberty.[63]

The opposition to social and economic rights, the antipathy toward the UN due to its godlessness, and the identification of the founding of the United States as a Christian event marked evangelicals as Christian nationalists in the mid-twentieth century. It was an outlook that could be expressed in several registers. Evangelical intellectual Carl Henry could proclaim the UN to be "hostile to the historical Christian tradition" even if it may promote some goals evangelicals could support, like world peace.[64] In foreign policy, the NAE constantly warned government not to let American interests be beholden to UN approval. As late as 1962 it complained that "the growing influence of the United Nations in our national affairs, affecting our sovereign rights as a great nation, is a cause of mounting concern to many of our citizens and to many of our evangelical missionary agencies which are hampered by some of the programs and politics of this world organization."[65] Other evangelical leaders expressed the same sentiments in harsher tones. "From the very start we hail [the UN] as godless, as a child of illegitimate alliances, born lame and due to die in the further catastrophes that come upon the earth," wrote a columnist for the NAE's official journal in 1945.[66]

And it was widely understood that the UN's most forceful American backers were ecumenical Protestants and their powerful Federal Council of Churches. As Darren Dochuk explains, "Watching closely as liberal [Protestant] luminaries like G. Bromley Oxnam assumed a seat at the table at the UN's founding conference in San Francisco, evangelical pundits published reports exposing the UN as a godless society set on destroying America's Christian foundations."[67] Critics like Henry and Paine did not make distinctions between secular liberals and religious liberals, between humanism and Protestant personalism, or between the religious left and the communist left. Instead they dismissed ecumenical Protestants, in the language of the Cold War, as socialists, fellow travelers, or outright communists. Henry, for one, condemned the "trend toward Communism, as reflected in denominational committees on social action," on which Gallagher sat, "and especially in the Federal Council of Churches."[68]

Evangelicals who subscribed to premillennialism and were prone to prophesizing made the strongest links between opposition to Christian globalism and the United Nations. They accused ecumenical Protestants, who had created the World Council of Churches in 1948, of crafting a superchurch designed to abolish the autonomy of local churches in the same way the United Nations was seeking to abolish the autonomy of national governments. "Satan does not want any world-wide attack on his world-wide false church and beastly government," wrote Rev. Irwin W. Steele of the Bible Presbyterian Church. Those who refused to combat both the UN and ecumenical Protestantism in these "end-times" were "actually doing Satan's will."[69]

The coupling of conservative domestic politics, theological criticism of the UN, and fears that the genius of America's Christian founding was being undermined by sinister forces took root across the United States following World War II under the broad banner of anti-communism. Southern California was an especially important location of this phenomenon because it became a stronghold of conservative Republican politics. Los Angeles and the surrounding region had received an influx of migrants in the 1930s from the western edges of the American South—places like Oklahoma, western Texas, and Arkansas. These migrants brought with them a fundamentalist brand of Protestantism, which coalesced with Southern California's Pentecostalism and conservative politics among the region's business elite.[70]

In Los Angeles in 1952, a grassroots rebellion was underway against the use of United Nations Educational, Scientific, and Cultural Organization (UNESCO) pamphlets in the city's public schools. UNESCO had designed a curriculum that endorsed internationalism, criticized racism, and promoted peace. A series of pamphlets produced by the organization, titled *Toward World Understanding*, were critical of nationalism. "As long as the child breathes the poisoned air of nationalism, education in worldmindedness can produce only precarious results," UNESCO argued.[71] Verne Kaub, a longtime anti-ecumenical activist who had hounded Gallagher and other Congregationalists in the 1930s over their socialist politics, launched an attack against the international organization. In a book ostensibly about exposing

Christian Globalism and the Ecumenical-Evangelical Rivalry

the socialists and communists in the National Education Association, he focused intently on the sinister foreign forces the association was promoting. UNESCO was trying "to convince readers that world super-government is just around the corner and will make the earth a giant Utopia," Kaub stressed.[72] The collectivism of the UN stood in stark contrast to Christian nationalism. He wrote, "Christianity is the most individualistic of all religions, and as individuals were given more and more freedom to develop their possibilities, civilization advanced, reaching its highest plane in the United States, founded on the principles enunciated in the Preamble of the Declaration of Independence, but borrowed from the *New Testament*."[73] Instead of learning from the UN, Americans should be teaching the world "by sending Christian missionaries . . . to help people of other nations to seek and find the spiritual and material benefits to free government founded upon the principles of the Christian faith."[74]

Unsurprisingly, Kaub mixed antipathy toward world-mindedness with suspicion of the anti-racism Gallagher had promoted: "One of the 'touchy' points of the propaganda for world super-government is the One Worlders' contention that steps must be taken to put into practice the theories of race equality." The anti-racism that the UN was promoting was nothing short of "open advocacy for miscegenation and mongrelization." Along similar lines, Kaub lamented that public schools were "training the leadership for the planned economy which is to supplant our free competitive society."[75]

Kaub's book was one of many circulating among conservative grassroots activists in Southern California. His was just one articulation of Christian nationalism. As Michelle Nickerson shows, in greater Los Angeles housewives took the lead in attacking progressive educators, especially ones promoting the UN and UNESCO. Florence Fowler Lyons, a former journalist, led the Los Angeles campaign to keep UNESCO materials out of city schools. Speaking at the Southern California Republican Women's Club in 1951, she warned that "children are daily being fed doses of Communism, Socialism, New Dealism and other isms" by UNESCO. And the organization's views on race were especially abhorrent, according to Lyons. UNESCO "states there is but one race in the world—the human race—and implies the sooner it is bred and bended back to its original color the sooner the world will have peace."[76] Lyons summed up her Christian nationalism by claiming that UNESCO was an "alien enemy attacking innocent child minds . . . diabolically rooting up your children's faith in God, flag, country, and home."[77]

Women affiliated with ecumenical organizations fought back against the Christian nationalists. Bernice W. Harris, chairperson of the Los Angeles

YWCA's Public Affairs Committee, condemned the criticism of UNESCO as a deliberate attack on democracy and academic freedom. The nationalists' racial and religious intolerance, she wrote, "had done inestimable damage to American prestige abroad at a time when democracy was on trial in the world."[78] And other ecumenical organizations likewise defended the UNESCO curriculum and the UN more broadly. The Presbyterians of Los Angeles wrote to the school board expressing concern that right-wing activists like Lyons were "keeping our youngsters in ignorance of our government's activity in international cooperation for strengthening of the foundations of peace in our world."[79]

The Christian nationalist mobilization against the UN, desegregation, and the New Deal in the early 1950s had found champions among some members of the Republican Party in Southern California by the end of that decade. Increasingly, networks of activists began labeling themselves "conservatives" and seeing themselves as part of a singular movement. It was a transformation whose regional roots in Southern California soon had national consequences. The grassroots movements in Southern California found allies among the new respectable conservative organs, such as William F. Buckley's *National Review*, along with less reputable organizations like Billy James Hargis's Christian Crusade. And it was a transformation that was partly facilitated by the religious politics of Christian nationalists.

When Buell Gallagher returned to California in 1961, he became the perfect target for the Republican politics of Southern California. His progressive credentials, coupled with his support for the UN and his leading role in crafting policy of federal aid to education during the Truman administration, earned him the ire of Southern California politicians who had been whipped up into an anti-globalist frenzy in the years immediately preceding Gallagher's arrival.

Accusations of communist sympathies were not new for Gallagher. They had dogged him since at least the 1930s and worsened in the corrosive atmosphere of the early Cold War. Gallagher was on the House Un-American Activities Committee watchlist because of his 1948 run for office and the attacks by the *Oakland Tribune*, his defense of civil liberties, his continued opposition to laws that limited free speech, and his stance against legislation that created civil disabilities for communists. As a result, Gallagher was often banned from speaking in venues around the country in the 1950s even as he held the prestigious post of president of the City College of New York, one of the nation's leading universities at the time.[80]

Gallagher moved back to California at the age of fifty-seven to become the founding chancellor of the newly incorporated California State College system.[81] His stay in Inglewood, near Los Angeles, was short, lasting less than one year. As soon as he arrived, newspapers were flooded with accusations from conservative grassroots activists and Southern California politicians that he held communist sympathies.[82] Bruce Reagan, a Republican state assemblyman from nearby Pasadena, denounced Gallagher's "Fabian-Socialist philosophy" and asserted that his candidacy under the Democratic and Independent Progressive Parties made him the wrong person to head the colleges.[83] Virtually all of Gallagher's public acts during his brief return to California focused on defending himself from charges of communist sympathy.[84]

Gallagher "was pretty liberal," recalled a California State College trustee, "and I think that attracted most all of us, in a sense—new ideas and real regard for educational opportunities for the more deprived students."[85] But as Christian nationalists "jumped on him every chance they could," Gallagher "actually turned out to be too liberal in his political views and in his economic views for the board," another trustee suggested. Trustee Donald Hart observed, "The fact that he was carrying an NAACP card, and occasionally asked the color of God made some trustees wonder about him."[86]

By March 1962, Gallagher had resigned as chancellor of the California State College system. He was replaced by Glenn Dumke, a Republican from Orange County and a Nixon supporter. Gallagher soon returned to his old post at City College.[87] California's anti-communist politics was creating a yet more hostile atmosphere for ecumenical Protestants like him in the early 1960s.

As Gallagher headed back to the recently renamed City University of New York, he would encounter a different challenge that led to the end of his career. Student protesters on campus demanding greater enrollment of racial minorities occupied more and more of Gallagher's attention. Unlike many other university presidents, Gallagher welcomed some of the demands of the Black and Puerto Rican activists of the late 1960s. The *Chicago Defender* referred to one of his speeches in 1968 as "the first time a college president of the stature and academic prestige of Dr. Gallagher has come unequivocally to the defense of the Negro revolution."[88] When faced with budget cuts, Gallagher, along with twenty-three CUNY department heads, threatened to resign. "I am now asked by officers of government . . . to stand in the door and keep students out," he announced. "I shall not accede, I will not do it. I will not turn my back on the poor of all races. . . . I will be unfaithful to none of my brothers, black or white."[89]

Events continued to escalate at CUNY, as frustrated students occupied the buildings of the university in 1969. Hoping to avoid confrontation and to buy himself more time to negotiate, Gallagher closed the school. Almost as soon as he did, local politicians began protesting that students' education was being held hostage by demonstrators and demanded that the university reopen.[90] A court order forced Gallagher's hand, and, as he had predicted, violence ensued. Gallagher tendered his resignation after two campus buildings were burned, and this time the resignation was accepted. Years later, Albert H. Bowker, former president of the University of California, said Gallagher "was unable, in a way like [Berkeley chancellor] Clark Kerr was, to use violence, in his case particularly against black students. He simply was unable to discipline black students, and they had to be disciplined."[91]

The difficulties Gallagher experienced in his academic career mirrored in important ways the experience of his religious community. In the late 1960s, ecumenical institutions, like the National Council of Churches (formerly the Federal Council of Churches) and the World Council of Churches, were rocked by sit-ins by Protestant youth even as they continued to be attacked by religious conservatives.[92] Partly because of these political difficulties, church membership in ecumenical denominations began declining beginning in the late 1960s. Following a merger in 1957, Gallagher's Congregational Christian denomination had become the United Church of Christ, with more than 8,000 congregations and over 2 million members. By 2017, the number of churches shrank to less than 5,000 and membership to 853,778.[93] This demographic decline among ecumenical Protestant denominations worsened the financial hardship that was being imposed by religious conservatives who withheld donations from activist organizations. Broadly speaking, in the 1970s, ecumenical Protestant institutions began losing the resources they needed to maintain their public stature.

The very moment of crisis for ecumenical Protestant organizations saw the rise of evangelicals in American life and in international affairs. The ascendancy of the Christian right, in which evangelicals had a leading role, was punctuated by the election of Ronald Reagan to the presidency in 1980. Meanwhile, evangelical international engagement flowered with the 1974 First International Congress on World Evangelization, spearheaded by Billy Graham. Known popularly as the Lausanne Congress, after its meeting place in the Swiss town located just thirty-five miles away from the headquarters of the World Council of Churches, it marked a more cooperative and humanitarian-minded evangelicalism in the world.

With ecumenical Protestants a less-prominent presence by the 1970s, evangelical Protestants began dropping some of their oppositional posture toward their religious rivals and sometimes borrowed from them. While many evangelicals held on to segregationist views in that decade, others began adopting the racial liberalism that Gallagher had promoted in the 1930s—a view that stressed individualism and education. That Gallagher and other ecumenical Protestants moved on to a more structural criticism of racism opened up racial liberalism as a safe middle ground for evangelicals to occupy. In this way, Billy Graham could support some forms of racial liberalism while maintaining his opposition to the "radical" program of the National Council of Churches and the World Council of Churches.[94] In the international arena, evangelicals similarly took positions that were pioneered by ecumenical Protestants but had since been abandoned by them as insufficiently attuned to the needs of the Global South. World Vision, an organization dating back to 1950, reemerged in 1977 as World Vision International and as a close ally of the Lausanne Movement, which now dedicated itself to humanitarian and development work.[95] It was now safe to focus on the social dimensions of missionary work without drawing accusations, as ecumenical Protestants had earlier, of abandoning the essence of evangelism. By the 1980s evangelicals had largely dropped their opposition to human rights and worked closely with the Reagan administration to promote them— albeit without the emphasis on social and economic rights that ecumenical Protestants had promoted.[96] And a slew of evangelical groups today work closely with the United Nations. As ecumenical Protestants became a less prominent part of the U.S. political landscape in the late twentieth century, and as they slid further to the left politically, evangelicals took on many of the causes that ecumenical Protestants had once championed.

Beginning in the 1970s, American evangelicals were moving beyond the ecumenical-evangelical rivalry and were becoming shaped by other kinds of oppositional relationships, such as antipathy toward secular liberals and Islam. But their midcentury rivalry with ecumenical Protestants, like Buell Gallagher, and their opposition to Christian globalism had left a mark. The United Nations, to take one example, has remained less popular among white evangelicals than among any other religious group in the United States.[97] Christian nationalism has persisted among white evangelical Protestants and has found a range of political expressions, from the attacks on the UN and UNESCO during the Cold War to the election and presidency of Donald Trump.

Notes

1. His demise was not only dramatic and rapid but decisive and permanent. When he died nine years later, the *New York Times*, which had regularly reported his activities for many years, hardly took notice. He was given a three-paragraph obituary more than two months after his death. See "Obituaries," *New York Times*, November 6, 1978, 56.

2. George M. Marsden, *Reforming Fundamentalism: Fuller Seminary and the New Evangelicalism* (Grand Rapids, MI: Eerdmans, 1987), 3.

3. K. Healan Gaston, *Imagining Judeo-Christian America: Religion, Secularism, and the Redefinition of Democracy* (Chicago: University of Chicago Press, 2019); Lauren Frances Turek, *To Bring the Good News to All Nations: Evangelical Influence on Human Rights and U.S. Foreign Relations* (Ithaca, NY: Cornell University Press, 2020); Grant Wacker, *America's Pastor: Billy Graham and the Shaping of a Nation* (Cambridge, MA: Belknap Press of Harvard University Press, 2014), 120–36.

4. Gene Zubovich, *Before the Religious Right: Liberal Protestants, Human Rights, and the Polarization of the United States* (Philadelphia: University of Pennsylvania Press, 2022).

5. Michael G. Thompson, *For God and Globe: Christian Internationalism in the United States between the Great War and the Cold War* (Ithaca, NY: Cornell University Press, 2015); Or Rosenboim, *The Emergence of Globalism: Visions of World Order in Britain and the United States, 1939–1950* (Princeton, NJ: Princeton University Press, 2017); Susan Schulten, *The Geographical Imagination in America, 1880–1950* (Chicago: University of Chicago Press, 2002); Samuel Zipp, *The Idealist: Wendell Willkie's Wartime Quest to Build One World* (Cambridge, MA: Belknap Press of Harvard University Press, 2020).

6. Andrew L. Whitehead and Samuel L. Perry, *Taking America Back for God: Christian Nationalism in the United States* (New York: Oxford University Press, 2020), ix–x.

7. Daniel T. Rodgers, *As a City on a Hill: The Story of America's Most Famous Lay Sermon* (Princeton, NJ: Princeton University Press, 2018); Abram C. Van Engen, *City on a Hill: A History of American Exceptionalism* (New Haven, CT: Yale University Press, 2020).

8. Jonathan P. Herzog, *The Spiritual-Industrial Complex: America's Religious Battle against Communism in the Early Cold War* (New York: Oxford University Press, 2011); Kevin M. Kruse, *One Nation under God: How Corporate America Invented Christian America* (New York: Basic Books, 2015).

9. On the fundamentalist suspicion of international organizations, see Markku Ruotsila, *The Origins of Christian Anti-internationalism: Conservative Evangelicals and the League of Nations* (Washington, DC: Georgetown University Press, 2008).

10. Maxine Deloris Jones and Joe Martin Richardson, *Talladega College: The First Century* (Tuscaloosa: University of Alabama Press, 1990), 111–12.

11. Robert T. Handy, *A History of Union Theological Seminary in New York* (New York: Columbia University Press, 1987).

12. Buell Gordon Gallagher, "Religion and the Class Struggle in Ancient Greece" (B.D. thesis, Union Theological Seminary, 1929).

13. Brian Stanley, *The World Missionary Conference, Edinburgh, 1910* (Grand Rapids, MI: Eerdmans, 2009).

14. Melani McAlister, *The Kingdom of God Has No Borders: A Global History of American Evangelicals* (New York: Oxford University Press, 2018), 8.

15. On white attitudes in the South prior to World War II, see John Egerton, *Speak Now against the Day: The Generation Before the Civil Rights Movement in the South* (Chapel Hill: University of North Carolina Press, 1995); and Ira Katznelson, *Fear Itself: The New Deal and the Origins of Our Time* (New York: Liveright, 2014).

16. Jones and Richardson, *Talladega College*, 122–23.

17. Buell Gallagher to Eugene Link, undated [June 1942], Eugene P. Link Papers, 1907–1993 (APAP-025), M. E. Grenander Department of Special Collections and Archives, University at Albany, SUNY.

18. Jones and Richardson, *Talladega College*, 122–23.

19. Anne M. Blankenship, *Christianity, Social Justice, and the Japanese American Incarceration during World War II* (Chapel Hill: University of North Carolina Press, 2016); David A. Hollinger, *After Cloven Tongues of Fire: Protestant Liberalism in Modern American History* (Princeton, NJ: Princeton University Press, 2013); Zubovich, *Before the Religious Right.*

20. Buell G. Gallagher to Walter White, July 16, 1944, reel 7, frames 785–87, Papers of the NAACP, Supplement to Part 16, Board of Directors File, 1966–1970 [microform], eds. John H. Bracey Jr. and August Meier, University Publications of America, Bethesda, MD [hereafter, NAACP Papers].

21. Minutes, Intercultural Relations Committee Meeting of the Council for Social Action, November 1, 1945, RR-1, Council for Social Action Papers, Congregational Library, Boston, MA.

22. "Brief for Amici Curiae," "Writ of Certiorari," and "Brief of the Human Relations Commission," in folder 15, box 61, RG 18, Federal Council of Churches Papers, Presbyterian Historical Society, Philadelphia, PA.

23. Edward E. France, *A Long Stride Forward: A Brief History of South Berkeley Community Congregational Church in Commemoration of the Church's 20th Anniversary* (Berkeley: [publisher unknown], 1964).

24. Michael Emerson and Rodney Woo, *People of the Dream: Multiracial Congregations in the United States* (Princeton, NJ: Princeton University Press, 2006), 20. On interracial churches in the 1940s, see Homer A. Jack, "The Emergence of the Interracial Church," *Social Action* 13 (January 1947): 31–38.

25. Buell G. Gallagher, *Color and Conscience: The Irrepressible Conflict* (New York: Harper and Brothers, 1946), 230.

26. The church was founded in 1943 by Roy Nichols, an African America student at the Pacific School of Religion, and Robert Winters, a white student at a nearby Unitarian seminary.

27. France, *Long Stride Forward*, 1–2. Charles S. Johnson, like Gallagher, was a Congregationalist and had much of his work funded by a Congregationalist institution, the American Missionary Association. Will W. Alexander was then working for a commission sponsored by the Federal Council of Churches on race relations and had encouraged Gallagher to write his 1946 book, *Color and Conscience.*

28. For a sampling of coverage by the *Defender* and the many prominent speakers at the church, see the following in the *Chicago Defender:* [no title], November 27, 1943, 19A; [no title], January 22, 1944, 17; [no title], February 19, 1944, 17; [no title], March 4, 1944, 17A; Langston Hughes, "Here to Yonder," May 6, 1944, 12; "All Races Join in Interracial Church on Coast," November 25, 1944, 8; "Talks at Inter-Racial Church," April 27, 1946, 5.

29. "The Churches and a Just and Durable Peace," *Christian Century*, March 25, 1942, 391.

30. Gale L. Kenny, "The World Day of Prayer: Ecumenical Churchwomen and Christian Cosmopolitanism, 1920–1946," *Religion and American Culture* 27, no. 2 (2017): 129–58.

31. Gallagher, *Color and Conscience*, 144.

32. Gallagher, 13.

33. Myrdal cited Gallagher's 1938 book, *American Caste and the Negro College*, several times. "Many writers have employed the concept of caste as central to a study of some aspect of the Negro problem," Myrdal wrote. "Few have done this with such insight as Buell G. Gallagher." See Gunner Myrdal, *An American Dilemma: The Negro Problem and Modern Democracy* (New York: Harper and Brothers, 1944), 1377.

34. Gallagher, *Color and Conscience*, preface.

35. Gallagher, 98.

36. For a discussion of both the possibilities and the limits of Cold War discourses on race, see Mary Dudziak, *Cold War Civil Rights: Race and the Image of American Democracy* (Princeton, NJ: Princeton University Press, 2000). There has been a significant amount of writing on the close relationship between international affairs and the efforts of anti-racist activists in the Cold War era. See Azza Salama Layton, *International Politics and Civil Rights Policies in the United States* (New York: Cambridge University Press, 2000); and Penny M. Von Eschen, *Race against Empire: Black Americans and Anticolonialism, 1937–1957* (Ithaca, NY: Cornell University Press, 1997).

37. Gallagher, *Color and Conscience*, 98.

38. Gallagher, 56.

39. On Gallagher's missionary "boomerang," see David A. Hollinger, *Protestants Abroad: How Missionaries Tried to Change the World but Changed America* (Princeton, NJ: Princeton University Press, 2017).

40. Headnote in W. E. B. Du Bois, *Color and Democracy: Colonies and Peace* (New York: Harcourt, Brace, 1945), 123.

41. Du Bois, 123. See Thomas Borstelmann, *The Cold War and the Color Line: American Race Relations in the Global Arena* (Cambridge, MA: Harvard University Press, 2001), 41. Du Bois had been a sharp critic of American missionaries. In 1900, he railed against Christian missionaries at the first Pan-African Congress in London: "Let not the cloak of Christian missionary enterprise be allowed in the future as so often in the past, to hide the ruthless economic exploitation and political downfall of less developed nations, whose chief fault has been reliance on the plighted faith of the Christian church." Quoted in Edward J. Blum, *W. E. B. Du Bois: American Prophet* (Philadelphia: University of Pennsylvania Press, 2009), 122.

42. Du Bois, *Color and Democracy*, 136.

43. Editorial, *Christian Century*, January 26, 1944, 100.

44. Gallagher, *Color and Conscience*, 68.

45. Buell Gallagher, "Welfare Work: Ally or Alternative?," in *The Church and Organized Movements*, ed. Randolph Crump Miller (New York: Harper and Brothers, 1946), 125–28.

46. *Berkeley Daily Gazette*, May 28, 1948, 11; Robert O. Self, *American Babylon: Race and the Struggle for Postwar Oakland* (Princeton, NJ: Princeton University Press, 2003), 34–46.

Christian Globalism and the Ecumenical-Evangelical Rivalry

47. Harland E. Hogue, *Christian Seed in Western Soil: Pacific School of Religion through a Century* (Berkeley: Pacific School of Religion, 1965), 138 and 258n79.

48. Quoted in Hogue, 138.

49. *Berkeley Daily Gazette*, May 28, 1948, 11.

50. "Strictly Political," *Berkeley Daily Gazette*, May 20, 1948, 14.

51. "Strictly Political," *Berkeley Daily Gazette*, May 27, 1948, 17; Hogue, *Christian Seed in Western Soil*, 138–39.

52. *Berkeley Daily Gazette*, May 28, 1948, 11. For the ecumenical Protestant involvement in shaping the United Nations, see John Nurser, *For All Peoples and All Nations: The Ecumenical Church and Human Rights* (Washington, DC: Georgetown University Press, 2005). On the affinity of Protestant institutions with the United Nations, see Andrew Preston, *Sword of the Spirit, Shield of Faith: Religion in American War and Diplomacy* (New York: Knopf, 2012); William Inboden, *Religion and American Foreign Policy, 1945–1960: The Soul of Containment* (New York: Cambridge University Press, 2008); Jill K. Gill, *Embattled Ecumenism: The National Council of Churches, the Vietnam War and the Trial of the Protestant Left* (DeKalb: Northern Illinois University Press, 2011); T. Jeremy Gunn, *Spiritual Weapons: The Cold War and the Forging of an American National Religion* (Westport, CT: Praeger, 2009); and Heather A. Warren, *Theologians of a New World Order: Reinhold Niebuhr and the Christian Realists, 1920–1948* (New York: Oxford University Press, 1997).

53. Buell Gallagher, "The Honor of a Certain Aim," *Christian Century*, December 22, 1948, 1393.

54. On the gap between liberal Protestant leaders and the laity, see Elesha J. Coffman, *The Christian Century and the Rise of the Protestant Mainline* (New York: Oxford University Press, 2013).

55. Gallagher, "Honor of a Certain Aim," 1393.

56. Gallagher, 1396.

57. Preston, *Sword of the Spirit*; Gene Zubovich, "For Human Rights Abroad, against Jim Crow at Home: The Political Mobilization of American Ecumenical Protestants in the World War II Era," *Journal of American History* 105, no. 2 (September 2018): 267–90, https://doi.org/10.1093/jahist/jay144.

58. Buell Gallagher to Walter White, November 26 [?], 1948, reel 7, frame 808, NAACP Papers; Hogue, *Christian Seed in Western Soil*, 139.

59. Buell Gallagher to Walter White, March 11, 1946, reel 7, frame 796, NAACP Papers; "Charter of the United Nations and Statute of the International Court of Justice," online at https://treaties.un.org/doc/Publication/CTC/uncharter.pdf (accessed April 26, 2016). On the relationship between anti-racist activists and human rights, see Carol Anderson, *Eyes Off the Prize: The United Nations and the African American Struggle for Human Rights, 1944–1955* (New York: Cambridge University Press, 2003); Steven L. B. Jensen, *The Making of International Human Rights: The 1960s, Decolonization, and the Reconstruction of Global Values* (New York: Cambridge University Press, 2017).

60. Various, reel 7, frames 796–834, NAACP Papers.

61. "U.S. Education Aide Is Slated as President of City College," *New York Times*, June 14, 1952, 1; "U.S. Aide Elected City College Head," *New York Times*, June 17, 1952, 25.

62. James DeForest Murch, *Cooperation without Compromise: A History of the National Association of Evangelicals* (Grand Rapids, MI: Eerdmans, 1956), 142–43.

63. Murch, 143. On the Protestant personalist influence on the United Nations, see Gene Zubovich, "American Protestants and the Era of Anti-racist Human Rights," *Journal of the History of Ideas* 79, no. 3 (September 2018): 427–43.

64. Carl F. H. Henry, *The Uneasy Conscience of Modern Fundamentalism* (Grand Rapids, MI: Eerdmans, 1947), 14.

65. Stephen R. Rock, *Faith and Foreign Policy: The Views and Influence of U.S. Christians and Christian Organizations* (New York: Continuum International Pub. Group, 2011), 141.

66. "The San Francisco Charter," *United Evangelical Action*, August 1, 1945, 13.

67. Darren Dochuk, *From Bible Belt to Sunbelt: Plain-Folk Religion, Grassroots Politics, and the Rise of Evangelical Conservatism* (New York: W. W. Norton, 2011), 105.

68. Henry, *Uneasy Conscience of Modern Fundamentalism*, 21.

69. Quoted in Angela M. Lahr, *Millennial Dreams and Apocalyptic Nightmares: The Cold War Origins of Political Evangelicalism* (New York: Oxford University Press, 2007), 45.

70. Dochuk, *From Bible Belt to Sunbelt*; James N. Gregory, *American Exodus: The Dust Bowl Migration and Okie Culture in California* (New York: Oxford University Press, 1989).

71. Quoted in Michelle M. Nickerson, *Mothers of Conservatism: Women and the Postwar Right* (Princeton, NJ: Princeton University Press, 2012), 90.

72. Verne Paul Kaub, *Communist-Socialist Propaganda in American Schools* (Boston: Meador, 1953), 174.

73. Kaub, 174–75.

74. Kaub, 174–75.

75. Kaub, 8, 176–77.

76. Quoted in Nickerson, *Mothers of Conservatism*, 97.

77. Quoted in Carol Mason, *Reading Appalachia from Left to Right: Conservatives and the 1974 Kanawha County Textbook Controversy* (Ithaca, NY: Cornell University Press, 2009), 100.

78. Quoted in Glen Warren Adams, "The UNESCO Controversy in Los Angeles, 1951–1953: A Case Study of the Influence of Right-Wing Groups on Urban Affairs" (PhD diss., University of Southern California, 1970), 78–79.

79. Quoted in Adams, 80–81.

80. "Once-Barred Speaker Cites Student's 'Right to Learn,'" *Washington Post*, March 11, 1951, M10.

81. "N.Y. Educator to Head 15 California Colleges," *Los Angeles Times*, April 7, 1961, 7; "Gallagher to Head California Colleges," *New York Times*, April 7, 1961, 1.

82. On grassroots anti-communist activism in Southern California during this time, see Lisa McGirr, *Suburban Warriors: The Origins of the New American Right* (Princeton, NJ: Princeton University Press, 2001). On the affinities between religious and political conservatism in Southern California, see Dochuk, *From Bible Belt to Sunbelt*.

83. "Gallagher Opponent," *Los Angeles Times*, August 26, 1961, B4; "Educator Answers Charges of Red Softness," *Los Angeles Times*, October 1, 1961, B2; "Pro and Con," *Los Angeles Times*, October 7, 1961, B4; "Chancellor Flays Reds and Answers His Critics," *Los Angeles Times*, October 11, 1961, 14.

84. See Buell Gallagher, "Facts about the American Communist Party: Prepared for Delivery before the California Association of County Superintendents," October 10, 1961, California State Library, Documents Section, Sacramento, CA.

85. Quoted in John Benjamin Maschino, "'A Conservative Institution with Radical Functions': The Challenges to Liberal Higher Education on Three California Campuses, 1958–1969" (PhD diss., State University of New York, Stony Brook, 2002), 45–46.

86. Quoted in Maschino, 46.

87. "Resignation Surprises Gov. Brown, Trustees," *Los Angeles Times*, February 14, 1962, 30; "Gallagher to Return to City College Post," *New York Times*, February 14, 1962, 1.

88. "The Black Revolution," *Chicago Defender*, July 16, 1968, 13. See also "Backlash Forces Anger Gallagher," *New York Times*, June 11, 1968, 43.

89. Buell G. Gallagher, "Text of Gallagher's Letter to BHE," *The Campus*, April 2, 1969, 5, quoted in Christopher Gunderson, "The Struggle for CUNY: A History of the CUNY Student Movement, 1969–1999," 6–7, online at http://macaulay.cuny.edu/eportfolios/hainline2014/files/2014/02/Gunderson_The-Struggle-for-CUNY.pdf (accessed April 26, 2016).

90. "Court Test Due on City College," *New York Times*, May 2, 1969, 27.

91. Albert H. Bowker, "Sixth Chancellor, University of California, Berkeley, 1971–1980; Statistician, and National Leader in the Policies and Politics of Higher Education," p. 174, interviewed by Harriet Nathan, 1991, Regional Oral History Office, Bancroft Library, Berkeley, CA.

92. James F. Findlay Jr., *Church People in the Struggle: The National Council of Churches and the Black Freedom Movement, 1950–1970* (New York: Oxford University Press, 1993).

93. For further detail, see *United Church of Christ: A Statistical Profile*, Fall 2018, www.uccfiles.com/pdf/2018-UCC-Statistical-Profile.pdf.

94. Billy Graham, *World Aflame* (Tadworth, Surrey: World's Work, 1968).

95. David P. King, *God's Internationalists: World Vision and the Age of Evangelical Humanitarianism* (Philadelphia: University of Pennsylvania Press, 2019); David R. Swartz, *Facing West: American Evangelicals in an Age of World Christianity* (New York: Oxford University Press, 2020).

96. Turek, *To Bring the Good News to All Nations*.

97. Rock, *Faith and Foreign Policy*, 140–41.

CHAPTER SIX

The Greatest Opportunity since the Birth of Christ

American Evangelical Missionaries at the Dawn of Decolonization

Sarah Miller-Davenport

"There is a great undercurrent of feeling that we are on the verge of a new day," the Far Eastern Gospel Crusade's bulletin told its evangelical readers in the United States in 1948. Borneo would soon be "renouncing fetish worship of all kinds," Europeans were assuring American missionaries that God's word "will meet the need of the hour," and all over the Philippines "people are inquiring into the way of salvation." This "day of the open door" came at a moment of "crisis" as the world called out for Christ, but it also presented a "great opportunity" to witness to the world before God closed the door.[1] As such language suggests, the Far Eastern Gospel Crusade (FEGC), a pioneering American evangelical missionary organization, was founded in a moment of profound global upheaval. The FEGC was a product of World War II: established by American GIs stationed in the Philippines and Japan, it morphed into a permanent missionary organization after the war (eventually changing its name to SEND International in 1981). The end of the war brought about a dramatic transformation in international power relations, with the United States and the Soviet Union emerging as global superpowers and the worldwide movement for decolonization shifting into high gear and ultimately overturning generations of Western colonialism.

Among the first colonies to gain self-government after the war was the Philippines, which had been a U.S. possession since 1898. But to read FEGC literature from the immediate postwar years, one might never know about Philippine independence. While they railed against the obstacles posed by Catholicism and Protestant liberalism, the FEGC missionaries stationed in the former American colony were apparently untroubled by what the end of formal U.S. rule might mean for their work. How do we explain this absence of concern? Why wasn't Philippine independence—or global decolonization more broadly—a problem for the FEGC? As it turns out, the FEGC was right not to worry about what decolonization might mean for evangelical missions. The second half of the twentieth century would see "the greatest spurt of growth in the two-century career of modern missions," and this surge would be dominated by American evangelicals working in the Global South.[2] Decolonization, of course, coincided with the rise of the United States as the world's foremost military and economic power. Far from hampering American global expansion, decolonization helped to amplify it as the United States sought to shape the course of decolonization toward its own ends. FEGC and other American evangelical missionaries were on the front lines of this emerging phenomenon. To them, the shifting world order posed an opportunity, not a crisis—even as they often used the language of crisis to highlight the scale of opportunity.

This sense of opportunity was forged during a period of contingency and transition for American evangelicals, many of whom decided to reject separatism and champion American nationalism in a moment when Europe was ceding global authority to an ascendant United States. During the 1940s, many American evangelicals increasingly came to embrace U.S. global hegemony as a force for good. FEGC missionaries were vocal proponents of this view. With field offices in both the Philippines and Japan—key sites of American power projection in Asia in the postwar period—they witnessed the effects of American authority on the ground and saw that U.S. global expansion could help facilitate the opening of new mission fields. While they condemned the behavior of some U.S. servicemen abroad and railed against the sinfulness of secular U.S. society at home, they were generally supportive of the American military presence in the Pacific and around the world, as long as it could be channeled toward Christian ends.[3]

If decolonization was not a problem for the FEGC, neither was U.S. colonialism. While the organization barely mentioned Philippine decolonization, it also did not dwell on the nearly five decades of U.S. rule that preceded independence. American missionaries had benefited from colonial expansion and had occasionally worked directly with colonial authorities—whether U.S. or European—to varying levels of degree. Many liberal Protestant missionaries had begun to reckon with this legacy during the interwar period. By contrast, evangelical missionaries were much more resistant to turning a critical lens on their own historical role in abetting imperialism and racism in their work to convert the "heathen" peoples of Asia, Africa, and Latin America. This was due in large part to the fact that they did not see themselves as imperialists, even if their rhetoric and actions had often promoted empire. One of the reasons for this imperial myopia is that, compared to European missionaries, the links between American missionaries and U.S. colonial authorities during the pre–World War II era were relatively loose. In fact, the main mission fields for evangelicals and other American missionaries were not U.S. colonies.

With the end of colonialism around the world, however, American evangelical missionary work increased substantially. At the same time, evangelical missionaries forged tighter bonds with the U.S. state than they had during the height of U.S. colonialism.[4] These were related developments. The end of European colonialism in Africa and much of Asia—combined with the perceived need to battle the Soviet Union for the allegiance of the so-called Third World—led the United States to seek influence in new corners of the globe, whether through military or nonmilitary means. Evangelicals seized on the immense possibilities for missionary work created by this new set of global conditions. As the U.S. military extended its reach through warfare and base building, and as formerly colonized nations accepted American development aid and opened their markets to increased trade with the United States, evangelicals were often among the first Americans to establish a non-state presence in these newly accessible societies.

There is an emerging scholarship on American evangelical missionaries during the era of decolonization that analyzes their efforts to adapt to the changing environment for missions in the Global South.[5] And indeed, as American evangelicals were forced to confront the significance of global decolonization on the ground in the 1950s and 1960s, they acknowledged some of the challenges they faced in these new mission fields, one of which was their own association with the United States. In many parts of the world where U.S. evangelicals worked, local populations were suspicious of American intent, a problem that evangelicals increasingly reckoned with as they encouraged the indigenization of churches and worked to overcome their own racial and cultural biases. In response, they often talked about themselves as servants of God rather than as agents of the United States. As Melani McAlister reminds us, American evangelicals were not "puppets of the U.S. government," nor did they offer "unilateral endorsement for American military power or US policy" during the post–World War II period.[6] Nonetheless, evangelical missionaries were generally supportive of U.S. global expansion and were more willing to align themselves with U.S. power than they had been in previous decades. At the same time, their enthusiasm in taking advantage of U.S. expansion in the decolonizing world set them apart from other American missionaries, particularly mainline Protestants.

It was in the 1940s that evangelicals began actively preparing for what would become an explosion of evangelical missionary work in the latter half of the twentieth century, and the worldview they formed in this period would continue to shape evangelical practice over the next decades. The 1940s were formative for the American evangelical movement, both at home and abroad. The decade saw the establishment of Fuller Seminary; the Youth for Christ movement, which launched Billy Graham to global fame; the National Association of Evangelicals and its missionary arm, the Evangelical Fellowship of Mission Agencies; and numerous small missionary organizations like the FEGC. While mainline Protestants were dramatically rethinking what their global role should be and pulling back from traditional missionary work, American evangelicals were laying the institutional and ideological foundations for a renewed push to convert the world to conservative Christianity, which eventually propelled them to domination of the Protestant missionary scene. Central to this project was a resurgent nationalism, which took the form of increasing identification with the U.S. government and support for America's growing military power in the decolonizing world.

This was a notable change from evangelicals' pre–World War II stance toward the U.S. state, and especially the military, as many evangelical clergy had been pacifists before the United States entered World War II and often harbored a skeptical attitude toward the federal government.[7] But evangelicals carried into the postwar period some important ideological continuities from the preceding decades. Attention to Protestant missionaries' limited relationship to the U.S. government in the years before World War II can help to explain why evangelicals turned to collaboration with the American state so enthusiastically during the era of decolonization. While they relied on European empires to gain access to mission fields, American missionaries largely did not behave as if they themselves were part of a colonial empire. Their imperial denialism was reflective of broader American culture, and it provided an alibi for activities that reinforced global imperial structures. It allowed Americans, and American missionaries in particular, to see themselves as agents of morality and humanitarianism, which bolstered efforts to increase American global influence through "informal," non-state channels. This sense of righteousness was reinvigorated among evangelicals—and linked to state power—after World War II.

For British missionaries, decolonization posed a crisis as their role in colonization, however complicated, meant that they struggled to maintain their legitimacy among people working to overturn British rule.[8] Decolonization also forced a reckoning for French Christians, who split between defending colonialism and arguing that Christianity itself should be decolonized.[9] The situation was different for American missionaries in the era of decolonization because they were rarely formally linked to state power, in the form of either colonial authorities or established churches. While empire—and British empire in particular—had helped to expand their reach to some extent, it had usually done so in indirect fashion.

Decolonization was a problem for British and French missionaries because colonialism had been essential to furthering British and French missionary work in the period before World War II. The same cannot be said for American missionaries. While global imperialism enabled American missionary work, U.S. overseas colonialism was not central to the global expansion of U.S. Christianity. Indeed, in the nineteenth and early twentieth centuries, American Protestant missionaries did sometimes work directly with the U.S. state to promote mutual interests and often self-consciously aimed to spread Western culture abroad.[10] A notable example of this is the role of American missionaries in Hawai'i, who promoted a closer relationship between the United States and the Hawaiian Kingdom, which eventually led to Hawai'i's annexation to the United States.[11] However, unlike their European peers, American missionaries were never particularly dependent on U.S. colonial structures to establish and maintain most of their foreign posts—in Hawai'i, for instance, they created the conditions in the early nineteenth century that eventually led to American colonialism, not the other way around.

In 1898, when the United States acquired the Philippines, Puerto Rico, and Guam in the treaty that ended the Spanish-American War, evangelizing Americans did not exactly flock to the new colonies. Despite the fact that the Philippines was America's largest possession, with a population of some 10 million people, by 1925 fewer than 500 U.S. missionaries were stationed there—this at a time when American missionaries numbered well over 10,000 worldwide.[12] Part of the reason for this was the lukewarm support missionaries received from U.S. colonial officials. Missionaries in the colonial Philippines generally endorsed U.S. imperialism and in turn received some help from American authorities, with colonial governor William Howard Taft proving particularly adept at "cultivat[ing] their loyalty" by occasionally providing missionaries with funds, intervening in property disputes, and socializing with them.[13] But U.S. government assistance to missionaries in the Philippines was patchy and contingent, and many missionaries felt that American authorities in the predominantly Catholic colony were all too happy to accept "Romanism" as an unofficial state religion.[14] Meanwhile, in the Caribbean, in keeping with the relative lack of U.S. missionary engagement with the colonies, only a few hundred U.S. missionaries made their way to Puerto Rico in the first three decades of the twentieth century.[15] In short, American missionaries' engagement with U.S. formal empire was remarkably limited.

Compare this with European missionaries, where there was much greater geographical and ideological overlap between mission work and empire. For instance, unlike their American peers, British missionaries generally followed the flag: in 1916 there were nearly 4,200 British missionaries in India, out of around 7,700 British missionaries in total (with many of the rest located in other British colonies).[16] Although British missionaries did not begin the nineteenth century with a robust formal relationship to the British government—and in fact before 1813 they were not allowed to operate in areas controlled by the East India Company—by the end of the 1800s they were increasingly reliant on the Crown to help them gain access to new mission fields; by the same token, the British government looked to missionaries to promote the cause of empire.[17] British missionaries were not directly sponsored by the colonial state—and in some instances clashed with it, as when missionaries in South Africa complained to the colonial office about the poor quality of land accorded to indigenous Africans. Still, behind most of this kind of criticism was what one historian describes as a "burning commitment to the empire being based on higher standards."[18] French missionaries, meanwhile, enjoyed substantial direct support from the French colonial government, even if that relationship was often "both close and conflicted."[19] It was arguably closer than that between the British government and British missionaries since, until the separation of church and state in France in 1905, the French government had the authority to nominate colonial bishops and paid their salaries.[20]

In fact, American missionaries tended to shadow their British counterparts, often venturing to fields that were under British colonial control or after British missionaries had laid the initial groundwork. Beginning in the early and mid-nineteenth century, in the absence of a formal overseas U.S. empire, American missionaries had to rely on the British Empire for access to mission fields in Africa, Asia, and the Middle East. Inspired by British missionaries, their first overseas mission field was colonial India, where they joined their British peers in 1812 in what they viewed as a shared "single project" to "convert the whole world to an Anglo-American model of Protestant Christianity."[21] Two decades later they followed British missionaries to China, which would become one of the main sites for American missionary work in the decades before World War II.[22]

Although it might seem surprising that American missionaries would set their sights on British colonies rather than on those under U.S. dominion, their relative disinterest in converting American colonial subjects reflected broader sentiment at the time. Missionaries were steeped in a domestic culture of imperial denial. Colonialist fervor in the United States peaked with the Spanish-American War. But in the decades after 1898, metropolitan enthusiasm for U.S. formal empire gave way to ambivalence and a general inattention to the colonies. As Daniel Immerwahr argues, one of the distinguishing features of America's colonial empire was the fact that it was largely hidden from view for most Americans.[23] Newspaper coverage of the colonies was scant. Maps and textbooks listed the overseas territories as "foreign." Unlike in European metropoles, there was no dedicated colonial office in the United States or training program for American colonial administrators. While the British had an official Empire Day, which was celebrated throughout the United Kingdom, Americans had a day to honor the national flag, one that displayed "a star for each state but no symbol for territories."[24]

There was also a vocal anti-imperialist opposition within the United States that tempered public support for American colonialism and further discouraged any kind of strong association between missionaries and the U.S. state. While anti-imperialists in Europe at this time were largely confined to colonial expatriates in the metropole and the Far Left, the movement in the United States included high-ranking and influential adherents.[25] Among the

American Evangelical Missionaries

most prominent was William Jennings Bryan, a devout evangelical Christian, who was a fierce opponent of U.S. overseas colonialism and made anti-imperialism the central plank of his Democratic presidential campaign in 1900. Charles Sheldon, a popular preacher, a best-selling author, and an outspoken anti-imperialist, railed against U.S. counterinsurgency in the Philippines. More muted critiques of American colonialism were commonplace among evangelicals, including many missionaries—although they generally refused to condemn colonialism itself and argued instead that U.S. colonial practices were derailing missionary efforts.[26]

Anti-imperialism, however, ultimately helped Americans to hide their empire. While anti-imperialists brought attention to U.S. colonialism at certain moments, they also promoted the idea—contrary to the imperial reality—that America was essentially a republic, which ultimately nurtured continued imperial denial. Some anti-imperialists, fueled by racism and nativism, claimed that U.S. colonial subjects were incapable of shouldering the responsibilities of republicanism. They were among the core supporters of the Tydings-McDuffie Act of 1934, which mandated eventual independence for the Philippines while at the same time barring Filipinos from migrating to the United States.[27] This strain of anti-imperialism deliberately attempted to erase U.S. colonialism altogether by removing both the colonies and their inhabitants from the United States.

Imperial amnesia also allowed Americans to espouse a narrative of the United States as a force for democracy, humanitarianism, and morality in the world. This was a narrative that, paradoxically, served to promote America's informal empire and imperialist discourses. Missionaries were early proponents of imperial ways of thinking, even if they did not explicitly identify as imperialists and were generally uninterested in linking themselves to U.S. formal empire when the opportunity arose. As Emily Conroy-Krutz demonstrates, missionaries promoted a form of "Christian imperialism," and their approach to evangelism was, at base, "predicated on their position as Anglo-American Christians relative to foreign 'heathens' of supposedly inferior political, economic, cultural, and, of course, religious status."[28]

As the United States grew to be an increasingly important world power in the late nineteenth and early twentieth centuries through global trade, its growing military presence in the Western Hemisphere and the Pacific, and its cultural exports, many of these ventures were undergirded by a belief in the righteousness of the American cause and were bolstered by parallel, and sometimes entangled, efforts by U.S. missionaries and reformers to promote an American "moral empire." As Ian Tyrrell argues, American missionaries and reformers sought to center the United States and American nongovernmental organizations within a global reformist and humanitarian movement, in the process helping to produce "the broader sociopolitical context of American power abroad."[29] John Corrigan, in this volume, elaborates on how evangelical humanitarian discourse ultimately served empire by simultaneously distancing U.S. Protestants from "heathen" societies, which were supposedly more prone to humanitarian crisis, and envisioning their missionary targets as "just like us" and, therefore, capable of conversion and Americanization. And while U.S. Protestant missionaries did include the United States as an object of reform—particularly in the early twentieth century around the issues of alcohol and prostitution in the Philippines—U.S. global reformists increasingly focused their efforts on the colonies of Europe and, after World War I, on Europe itself.[30] In some cases, missionaries used reform and humanitarian work targeted at European colonies to deflect attention from the horrors of American colonial rule. For example, as Heather Curtis shows, reports of U.S. atrocities in the Philippines in 1900 helped fuel a massive fundraiser spearheaded by the *Christian Herald* to support U.S. missionaries working to address famine in India. In addition to offering humanitarian relief, Curtis writes, the campaign also sought to "reinforce evangelical solidarity and revitalize the United States' flagging reputation as the Almoner of the World."[31]

However much U.S. missionaries had wanted to avoid confronting their role in U.S. empire in the early twentieth century, they found themselves in an increasingly tricky position as anti-colonial movements gained momentum after World War I.[32] Global anti-colonialism also forced a confrontation within American Protestantism at home, as the interwar period coincided with the intensification of the modernist-fundamentalist split. Conservative evangelicals adopted a separatist stance and rejected their liberal counterparts' emphasis on ecumenism, Darwinism, biblical criticism, and the Social Gospel.[33] The two factions also were also divided over the future of missions. For liberal Protestants, the worldwide struggle against colonialism posed a challenge to their missionary endeavors, and during the interwar period many began to question whether they could promote Christianity in the non-European world in an anti-colonial way. Conservatives, by contrast, did not see why anti-colonialism should change their approach to missionary work.

Missionaries, as we have seen, witnessed the effects of colonialism firsthand, and they often faced pushback from indigenous populations, who were becoming increasingly radicalized and vocal in their resistance to all forms of Western domination. Meanwhile, the horrors of World War I chastened many liberal Protestants, who were now reassessing the idea of Western supremacism. Over the course of the 1920s, a number of mainline Protestant missionaries published searching treatises on the central dilemma of missionary work: the mandate to convert people to Christ, which assumed the superiority of Christianity, without casting non-Christians as inferior. This "paradox of power relations" had already led some missionaries to alter their approach by conceding more authority to indigenous Christian leaders.[34]

Then, in 1932, a multivolume report titled *Re-thinking Missions* shook the American missionary world. The report—the result of a study directed by Harvard philosopher William Hocking and commissioned by John Rockefeller and seven major denominations—condemned missionaries' Western cultural biases, calling on them to cooperate with other world religions and focus on the "secular needs of men" rather than on direct evangelism.[35] It suggested that non-Christian religions should be respected, even actively encouraged. Writer and missionary Pearl Buck—author of the Pulitzer Prize–winning *The Good Earth*, a sympathetic portrait of Chinese peasants—wholeheartedly endorsed this stance in a review in the *Christian Century* and would later go on to describe most missionaries as "narrow, uncharitable, unappreciative, ignorant."[36]

The Hocking Report, David Hollinger argues, transformed mainline thinking on missionary work. It was formally supported by the leadership of six major mainline Protestant denominations and went through ten printings in six months.[37] But while many liberal Christians in the United States were attempting to reconcile their proselytizing with a burgeoning cultural pluralism, most fundamentalist and conservative Protestants did not recognize this as a problem during the interwar period. In contrast to mainline Protestant missionaries, evangelical missionaries did not go through a process of rigorous self-evaluation over the relationship between imperialism and Christian evangelism. As Hollinger writes, "Fundamentalists had no doubt that the gospel had to be preached unapologetically to the multitudes all over the world, no matter what their inherited faith."[38] Instead, when the Hocking Report came out, a number of prominent evangelicals called on the Board of Foreign Missions to denounce it and also to remove Buck as a missionary of the Presbyterian Church.[39] The board refused to do either, further angering fundamentalists and deepening the rift between liberal and conservative Protestants. For conservatives, the Board of Foreign Missions' tepid response to the Hocking Report—along with the national humiliation of the 1925 Scopes trial, the repeal of Prohibition in 1933, and the Democratic

Party's embrace of urban Catholics— reaffirmed the sense that they were "ideological strangers in their own land."[40]

And so evangelical missionaries entered the post–World War II period mostly unburdened by new structural limitations on evangelizing foreign populations, or by ideological concerns over doing so. Meanwhile, the war itself both aided and inspired American evangelical missionaries. It also facilitated a much closer relationship with the U.S. state. Using the language of military conquest, evangelicals talked about "invading" other nations with the word of God and establishing "beachheads" from which to spread the gospel.[41] The FEGC exemplified the links between U.S. military activity and renewed evangelical purpose, as military service itself created the conditions for its formation. Several other evangelical missionary organizations—including the New Tribes Mission and the Missionary Aviation Fellowship—were also founded during the war by members of the armed forces. Many of these new groups benefited materially from America's military victory by purchasing surplus stockpiles of war materials "at bargain basement prices" for use in setting up their new missions.[42]

It was the war, rather than U.S. colonialism, that brought huge numbers of Americans—among them the founders of the FEGC—into contact with the Philippines. At the height of America's postwar military occupation of the Philippines in 1946, over 800,000 U.S. troops were stationed there.[43] By contrast, before the war, when the Philippines was a U.S. colony, only around 4,000 U.S. military personnel and another 8,700 American civilians were based in the colony.[44] A strong American presence would remain in the Philippines after its independence from the United States in the form of dozens of military bases, which would play a significant part in the wars in Korea and Vietnam and in the "exertion of U.S. military power in Asia and the Pacific" more broadly.[45] Philippine independence, in short, did not lead to the expulsion of the U.S. government or of American residents. Quite the opposite: the number of Americans in the Philippines *increased* after independence. Among the American civilians who moved to the Philippines after 1946 were Protestant missionaries, who numbered nearly 1,200 strong by 1972, with the Philippines ranking among U.S. missionaries' top five recipient countries.[46]

For FEGC missionaries, the highly visible U.S. military in both the Philippines and Japan reinforced American supremacy—as well as their belief in America's providential role in the world. Allied success was directly linked to the fact that the United States was a Christian nation singled out by God. While all the Allied countries had been the recipients of divine help, in the end it took the United States, "a nation with a living God," to secure victory and "thwart the evil purposes of those who denied the Deity and power of our Lord."[47] The FEGC frequently criticized the military over troops' behavior—for their drinking, dancing, and introducing local women to lipstick and other immoral consumer goods from America. Yet the FEGC's qualms about certain elements of the U.S. military were outweighed by its positive assessment of American military power, which was embodied by the "Christian GI," the organization's revered founding hero. In their correspondence, and in the evangelical press's coverage of FEGC activities, Christian GIs were portrayed as agents of divine benevolence—ministering to the material needs of local communities, distributing candy to orphans, and, of course, spreading the Word.

FEGC missionaries also appreciated that they were in Japan and the Philippines only because American troops had opened the way, and they were well aware of the connection between American military power and what they called "the greatest opportunity since the birth of Christ for reaching the peoples of the Pacific with the story of God's transforming love." While suggesting that years of war had left people in Japan and the Philippines "eager, curious, receptive" to evangelical proselytizing, the FEGC also emphasized the importance of the American postwar presence in Asia as a catalyst to revival. "International conditions allow unhindered missionary effort," the FEGC proclaimed. "Military leaders, government authorities encourage missionary occupation of the islands."[48]

The statement about encouraging military leaders was an obvious reference to General Douglas MacArthur, who, according to Lawrence Wittner, used his position as Supreme Commander of the Allied Powers in occupied Japan to aggressively promote Christianity without formal government sanction. Believing that "the Occupation has every right to propagate Christianity," MacArthur abolished Shintoism as Japan's state religion, and he gave preferential treatment to American missionaries, granting them entry to Japan before other civilians unconnected with the occupation and even allowing them to use military transportation.[49] To the FEGC, MacArthur represented American military power combined with Christian evangelistic purpose, and the organization frequently celebrated the fact that "General MacArthur is carrying forward the Occupation on Christian principles" in its correspondence.[50]

While the FEGC was spreading the gospel in Asia, other American evangelicals were turning to a new mission field, one far removed from the "heathen" societies usually associated with missionary work. Europe—the traditional source of Christian missionaries—now appeared desperate to be saved itself. The war in Europe, many believed, was part of a larger civilizational crisis in which Christianity was being eroded by secularism, communism, Catholicism, and other religions, with Nazism a prime example of what happened when people turned away from Christ.[51] Europe's established churches, meanwhile, were staid and ineffective. By 1952, missionary literature sent to evangelicals back home had begun to identify Europe as a separate mission field.[52]

As in the Philippines, the U.S. military presence in Europe after the war gave evangelicals a new level of access to the unsaved. During the U.S. occupation of Germany, it was estimated that at one point some 100 Youth for Christ rallies—to which English-speaking Germans were invited—were held every weekend at bases throughout the American zone, coordinated with the active support of military chaplains. The immense opportunity for evangelization provided by U.S. military power in Germany was celebrated by Youth for Christ founder Torrey Johnson, who spoke of "an army of occupation for the purposes of establishing YOUTH FOR CHRIST" and offered an implicit reference to America's defeat of Germany when he characterized Youth for Christ's German mission as "'blood and guts' spiritual warfare."[53]

The European mission field, in comparison to other regions, was not a major object of focus for American evangelicals in the postwar period. But it is significant that it became a missionary field at all, and evangelical revival efforts in Europe were an important part of the story of U.S. evangelicals' global ascent. It was in postwar Europe where Billy Graham conducted his first major tour (a few months before his first official crusade in Michigan), which served as the model for the hundreds of global crusades he would do over the next decades. During the course of half a year in 1946–47, Graham, along with other members of Youth for Christ, spoke at hundreds of meetings throughout England, Scotland, Ireland, Norway, and Sweden—"almost every one packed to capacity"—in an effort to convert audiences to Graham's brand of neo-evangelicalism.[54]

Youth for Christ activity in these years was emblematic of the broader shift in the balance of power between the United States and Europe and between American and European global religious leadership. Americans had surpassed the British among Protestant missionaries by 1910 (and by then represented around one-third of all Protestant missionaries).[55] But their postwar growth was exponential, with North Americans constituting 70 percent of the worldwide missionary force by 1969. The majority of Protestant missionaries, meanwhile, belonged to evangelical parachurch groups or conservative denominations.[56]

Billy Graham's early postwar tour and the missionary work of Youth for Christ in occupied Germany and elsewhere in Europe came at a time when the United States was engaged in a larger campaign to reconstruct Europe by exporting American consumer culture and its particular brand of modernity.[57] Graham himself linked salvation to modernity and presented evangelism as another form of consumerism in his many revival meetings in Europe in the 1950s.[58] Although the war had ended the Great Depression in the United States and reinvigorated its manufacturing sector, European recovery was a much longer process—the rebuilding of industry and physical infrastructure took the better part of a decade, with food rationing ending in Britain only in 1954.[59] Evangelicals in the United States personally assisted in European recovery by funding the reconstruction of churches and other aid efforts.[60] The steady stream of images and stories of a war-ravaged and starving Europe would have reinforced for them the Old World's descent, with once-great powers now struggling to hold onto their empires and in dire need of the gospel.

The FEGC, meanwhile, was determined to root out one of the most enduring European influences on the newly independent Philippines: Catholicism—or as evangelicals often called it, "Romanism." Catholics had long served as the ultimate foil for evangelicals, who believed that veneration of the saints and prayers for the dead were vestiges of paganism. Bias against Catholics historically had been linked to the growth of evangelicalism in America—revivalist movements flourished in the nineteenth century by promoting an antiestablishmentarian brand of popular religion that disdained traditional church hierarchies, which were associated with feudal Europe. Drawing on this anti-Catholic tradition, the FEGC portrayed Filipino Catholics as led astray by a corrupt church. Unfortunately, the FEGC told its followers back home, Catholic missionaries in the Philippines had been highly successful. "Catholics use education to the advantage of their cause," wrote Betty Honeywell, the wife of the FEGC's Philippines field chairman, Russell Honeywell. "It makes my heart sick to see the lovely institutions they have all repaired and operating while the fundamental Protestants are so slow!"[61]

Spain might have been successful in converting Filipinos to the wrong brand of Christianity, according to the FEGC, but many other American evangelicals during the era of decolonization tended to view European colonialism as largely ineffective when it came to evangelizing indigenous populations. European missions in the Belgian Congo—mostly Catholic—"went in for quantity at the expense of quality," as one Presbyterian missionary wrote in *Christianity Today*. Although they managed to convert some 30 percent of the population, their "eagerness to break the crust of pagan life inclined missionaries to impose the minimum of conditions on those brave enough to break away from stark heathenism."[62] Colonists' willingness to compromise was even more egregious in Malaysia, the influential evangelical leader Carl F. H. Henry explained to readers in another *Christianity Today* article, which asserted that "Christian penetration [was] ruled out" in the former colony when "the British empire, as a price for its colonial foothold, promised protection of Malay religion and custom, intrinsically Moslem."[63]

European failures in Asia and Africa were something of a running theme in the evangelical magazine, conveying the challenges posed by the scale of work to be done in the decolonizing world but also the opportunity for American Protestants to repair Europe's mistakes. In cases where the former colonizers had attempted to inculcate Christianity, their style of imperial rule undermined the missionary cause by linking Christianity with Western domination. India was a notable example, as *Christianity Today* informed readers in 1958. Although Christianity had reached South Asia in the fourth century, "once Christianity was identified with the West, its progress was severely hindered." Now, however, "different circumstances" meant that "all Christian nations have renewed opportunity to manifest His name to those who know not Christ as Saviour nor worship him as King."[64]

U.S. evangelicals during the 1940s and 1950s framed themselves as representatives of a new Christian front poised to take the reins from the old guard—embodied by Europe, Catholicism, and mainline Protestantism. And indeed, during this period, evangelicals could legitimately espouse a kind of outsider status. Compared with Catholics and mainline Protestants, evangelicals were relatively small in number outside the United States and did not have the same kind of well-established international religious networks.[65] This posed obvious disadvantages. But it also provided evangelicals with important rhetorical tools. More so than their liberal and Catholic counterparts, evangelicals saw (and had) tremendous room for missionary growth, and they frequently emphasized both the opportunity and the challenge of the postwar moment as a way to galvanize domestic support. According to the FEGC, for instance, evangelicals in the late 1940s had been blessed with an "unparalleled opportunity for the cause of Christ," yet it was one that "seems largely to remain unmet." Meanwhile, "the mere trickle of evangelical missionaries is far overbalanced by the activity of our spiritual enemies" (that is, liberalism, communism, and "Romanism").[66] This emphasis on opportunity—a word evangelicals used a lot in this period—followed by raising the alarm over "unmet" demands and formidable opponents was typical of the language in evangelical mobilization efforts in the decolonizing world.

Despite their professed conservatism, many postwar evangelicals thought of themselves as young and innovative. They might have been "overbalanced" by their enemies, but this gave them an edge, allowing them to take the stance of "pugnacious underdogs" in opposition to the international ecumenical status quo.[67] This was an identity already well-honed during the modernist-fundamentalist debate of the interwar years. But it took on new valence among "neo-evangelicals" like Billy Graham and FEGC missionaries who were determined to go beyond lamenting the sorry state of secular society and instead convert through persuasion rather than condemnation those who seemed lost to Christ. Youth for Christ was particularly adept at projecting an image of itself as a friendly and modern challenger to a moribund establishment. One Youth for Christ missionary claimed in 1955 that "more people have been converted to Christianity [in India] in the past eight years than in the hundred years prior to 1947."[68]

It was in the decolonizing world that U.S. evangelical missionaries set out to prove the novelty of their approach—and to do what European colonizers could not by winning the Global South for Christ. By 1972, over half of all North American Protestant missionaries were serving in Africa, Asia, and the Middle East.[69] Their spending in these regions was likewise substantial, with $35 million per year going to Africa alone in the mid-1960s.[70] These were parts of the globe that the U.S. government was also seeking to win over by proclaiming itself to be a new kind of world power for the postwar world—one in which European empire would give way to a global system of nation-states loosely overseen (and sometimes not so loosely) by the United States. As American evangelicals were forging a similar identity in the context of the global missionary movement, both parties were eager to exploit each other's resources. The FEGC, Youth for Christ, and other groups formed in the crucible of World War II had established a model for how missionaries could take advantage of U.S. expansion to advance the evangelical cause. As other evangelical missionaries continued to extend their reach in the decolonizing world, they likewise often did so with the help of the U.S. military. For instance, at the height of the Korean War, U.S. Army chaplains invited Billy Graham and Bob Pierce, founder of the evangelical aid organization World Vision, to South Korea, where they traveled the country under military protection and held a series of revival meetings and hospital visits.[71] Evangelicals, meanwhile, identified the military as a prime vehicle for increasing their influence both at home and abroad and worked to enlarge the number of evangelical chaplains in the armed forces.[72] The number of evangelical chaplains had been negligible during World War II; by 1955 there were over 150.[73] This development corresponded with an unprecedented buildup of the U.S. military, kicked off by the Korean War. Evangelicals were becoming more influential within the armed forces just as the military itself was increasing its own global footprint.

Evangelical missionaries also formed mutualistic relationships with other branches of the American foreign policy apparatus. From the fledgling years of postwar U.S. foreign assistance programs, religious groups were identified by Congress as "an essential counterpart" to administering aid, and in the early 1950s religious aid agencies relied more heavily on government support than did secular organizations (both received significant federal funding and would continue to do so).[74] Evangelicals, meanwhile, came to play a progressively significant role in foreign assistance, with nearly half of all religious aid groups identified as evangelical by the beginning of the twenty-first century and some 75 percent of them receiving federal funding (compared to only 50 percent of mainline Protestant aid organizations).[75] Unlike many other religiously affiliated aid organizations, which increasingly eschewed missionary work, evangelical groups tended to engage in evangelism in addition to providing material aid—and the self-proclaimed goal of their federally subsidized humanitarian activities was to bring people to Christ. These foreign assistance efforts, in turn, served American Cold War policy, as the United States hoped that development aid would help "modernize" newly independent nations along capitalist lines and secure their allegiance in the ideological battle against the Soviet Union.[76] Evangelical aid workers and missionaries also more directly promoted U.S. interests in the regions where they served, for instance by functioning as mediators between U.S. diplomats and local leaders.[77]

As decolonization progressed, American evangelicals working in the Global South became more nuanced in their understandings of global power relations and their own racial and cultural biases.[78] Unfortunately, according to missionary Ross Coggins in *Christianity Today* in 1964, colonialism meant that Christianity "came to be identified with a system under which the control of 'natives' was deemed 'the white man's burden.'" Missionaries must avoid any hint of the "'Great White Father' image of the missionary," which was now "dangerously anachronistic," Coggins argued. To counteract that stereotype, missionaries in Asia and Africa needed to confront their own prejudice, and "any effective ministry must be deferred" until they solved their own "race problem." Moreover, the missionary must ensure "a careful distinction between his timeless Gospel and his Western cultural trappings" and not confuse "Christianizing with Americanizing."[79] Coggins adopted the language of racial liberalism when he admonished U.S. evangelical missionaries who "resisted any adaptation of the presentation of the Gospel to indigenous cultural patterns" and who believed "in world missions abroad and racial discrimination at home"—thereby reinforcing the image of missionaries as colonialists. But while Coggins suggested that colonialism and missionary worked had been historically linked, he failed to acknowledge the ways in which evangelical missionaries continued to promote U.S. empire.

While American evangelical missionaries may have relinquished some of their racism and cultural chauvinism as part of their effort to globalize Christianity and appease indigenous Christians and would-be converts, they were willing to go only so far. If they engaged in too much accommodation to local conditions, they risked falling into the trap of many former colonizers who had sold out Christianity for reasons of political expediency. And although decolonization offered tremendous opportunity to correct European failures, it also posed significant threats to the missionary project. As decolonization unfolded in Asia and Africa in the 1950s and 1960s, American evangelicals grew increasingly rattled by Third World critiques of neocolonialism and nationalist calls for cultural autonomy. In Asia, *Christianity Today* warned in 1959, the scourge of communist encroachment was matched by "antipathy for Christianity on the professed ground that 'the Asian religions are best for the Orient.'"[80] A *Christianity Today* article published in 1960 on decolonization in Africa struck an even more alarmist tone. It forecast great "shocks and disappointments" if too many Africans were "thrown off center by the tides of nationalism sweeping their countries." Readers were told to look no further than "Germany during the heyday of national socialism" if they needed a reminder of nationalism's dire consequences.[81] Yet even accounts full of warnings and alarms about the problems posed by decolonization still tended to emphasize the potential for missionary intervention to steer the decolonizing world toward Christ. In Asia, many people were beginning to seek out "a spiritual answer to communism," so that, "in mysterious ways, the Christian witness faces new openings through the Communist challenge."[82] In Africa, Black nationalism was a response to white "color bias"; evangelical churches could counter both through the promise of "racial peace" by way of Christian universalism.[83]

American evangelicals approached decolonization as an opportunity for worldwide evangelism—an opportunity made all the more realizable because of how the U.S. government worked to influence decolonization's trajectory to align with U.S. foreign policy. Along the way, they were forced to grapple with the legacies of European colonialism and the ongoing challenge of how to decouple Christianity and imperialism. But although American evangelicals may have themselves been serving the interests of a new global empire, their own sense of righteousness was rooted in an imperial denial that washed away any doubts. Like the United States itself, U.S. evangelicals tended to behave on the world stage as if they were representatives of a benevolent power: unwilling to confront the sins of American empire and innocent of any complicity.

Notes

Thanks to John Corrigan, Melani McAlister, Axel Schäfer; the anonymous readers of this chapter; and all the participants who provided feedback at the Global Faith conference that inspired this volume.

1. "The Open Door," *Crusade Bulletin*, 1948, Billy Graham Center (BGC) Archives, Wheaton, IL, collection 406, box 1.

2. Joel A. Carpenter, *Revive Us Again: The Reawakening of American Fundamentalism* (New York: Oxford University Press, 1997), 177.

3. I explore the role of evangelical missionaries in promoting U.S. nationalism in the 1940s in more depth in "'Their Blood Shall Not Be Shed in Vain': American Evangelical Missionaries and the Search for God and Country in Post–World War II Asia," *Journal of American History* 99, no. 4 (March 2013): 1109–32.

4. It is important to note that U.S. colonialism did not end during the broader global movement for decolonization. After World War II, the U.S. maintained a formal colonial relationship with Puerto Rico, the Virgin Islands, Guam, Samoa, the Marshall Islands, and Micronesia, most of which are still U.S. colonies to this day.

5. The major works on this are Melani McAlister, *The Kingdom of God Has No Borders: A Global History of American Evangelicals* (New York: Oxford University Press, 2018); and David P. King, *God's Internationalists: World Vision and the Age of Evangelical Humanitarianism* (Philadelphia: University of Pennsylvania Press, 2019). See also Heather J. Sharkey, *American Evangelicals in Egypt: Missionary Encounters in an Age of Empire* (Princeton, NJ: Princeton University Press, 2008), 179–214.

6. McAlister, *Kingdom of God Has No Borders*, 3.

7. T. Jeremy Gunn, *Spiritual Weapons: The Cold War and the Forging of an American National Religion* (Westport, CT: Praeger, 2009), 91.

8. John Stuart, *British Missionaries and the End of Empire: East, Central, and Southern Africa, 1939–64* (Grand Rapids, MI: Eerdmans, 2011).

9. Darcie Fontaine, *Decolonizing Christianity: Religion and the End of Empire in France and Algeria* (New York: Cambridge University Press, 2016); Elizabeth A. Foster, *African Catholic: Decolonization and the Transformation of the Church* (Cambridge, MA: Harvard University Press, 2019).

10. Emily S. Rosenberg, *Spreading the American Dream: American Economic and Cultural Expansion, 1890–1945* (New York: Hill and Wang, 1982).

11. Patricia Grimshaw, *Paths of Duty: American Missionary Wives in Nineteenth-Century Hawaii* (Honolulu: University of Hawai'i Press, 1989); Sally Engle Merry, *Colonizing Hawai'i: The Cultural Power of Law* (Princeton, NJ: Princeton University Press, 2000); Jennifer Thigpen, *Island Queens and Mission Wives: How Gender and Empire Remade Hawai'i's Pacific World* (Chapel Hill: University of North Carolina Press, 2014).

12. U.S. Bureau of the Census, *Fourteenth Census of the United States Taken in the Year 1920* (Washington, DC: Government Printing Office, 1923). Missionary statistics taken from Frank Charles Laubach, *The People of the Philippines: Their Religious Progress and Preparation for Spiritual Leadership in the Far East* (New York: George H. Doran, 1925), 481–82. I could not track down an exact worldwide figure for 1925, but the number for 1935 is nearly 12,000. See Mark Noll, *The New Shape of World Christianity: How American Experience Reflects Global Faith* (Downers Grove, IL: InterVarsity Press, 2009), 80. Evidence suggests that the 1935 figure was in fact a decrease from 1925, due to the effects of the Great Depression and a general decline in interest in missionary work during this period. See Robert T. Handy, "The American Religious Depression, 1925–1935," *Church History* 29, no. 1 (March 1960): 4.

13. Kenton J. Clymer, "Religion and American Imperialism: Methodist Missionaries in the Philippine Islands, 1899–1913," *Pacific Historical Review* 49, no. 1 (February 1980): 39.

14. Clymer, 41–44.

15. Ellen Walsh, "Advancing the Kingdom: Missionaries and Americanization in Puerto Rico, 1898–1930s" (PhD diss., University of Pittsburgh, 2008), 2.

16. The 4,200 figure comes from Rosemary Seton, who writes that there were 2,500 British female missionaries in India in 1916, and from Jeffrey Cox, who asserts that around 60 percent of British missionaries in India were women (2,500 is 60 percent of 4,166). See Seton, *Western Daughters in Eastern Lands: British Missionary Women in Asia* (Santa Barbara, CA: Praeger), 33; and Cox, *The British Missionary Enterprise since 1700* (New York: Routledge, 2008), 269. See Cox, 267, for 7,700 figure.

17. John Gascoigne, "Religion and Empire, an Historiographical Perspective," *Journal of Religious History* 32, no. 2 (June 2008): 167–8.

18. Gascoigne, 169.

19. Jennifer Dueck, "Flourishing in Exile: French Missionaries in Syria and Lebanon under Mandate Rule," in *In God's Empire: French Missionaries in the Modern World*, ed. Owen White and J. P. Daughton (New York: Oxford University Press, 2012), 152.

20. Fontaine, *Decolonizing Christianity*, 29.

21. Emily Conroy-Krutz, *Christian Imperialism: Converting the World in the Early American Republic* (Ithaca, NY: Cornell University Press, 2015), 22.

22. Jane Hunter, *The Gospel of Gentility: American Women Missionaries in Turn-of-the-Century China* (New Haven, CT: Yale University Press, 1984).

23. Daniel Immerwahr, *How to Hide an Empire: A History of the Greater United States* (New York: Farrar, Straus and Giroux, 2019).

24. Immerwahr, 112.

25. On anti-imperialism in Britain, see Priyamvada Gopal, *Insurgent Empire: Anticolonial Resistance and British Dissent* (New York: Verso, 2019); and Stephen Howe,

Anticolonialism in British Politics: The Left and the End of Empire (New York: Oxford University Press, 1993). For France, see Michael Goebel, *Anti-imperial Metropolis: Interwar Paris and the Seeds of Third World Nationalism* (New York: Cambridge University Press, 2015). On anti-imperialism in the United States, see Michael Patrick Cullinane, *Liberty and American Anti-imperialism* (New York: Palgrave Macmillan, 2012); and Ian Tyrrell and Jay Sexton, eds., *Empire's Twin: U.S. Anti-imperialism from the Founding Era to the Age of Terrorism* (Ithaca, NY: Cornell University Press, 2015).

26. For evangelical critics of colonialism, see Heather D. Curtis, *Holy Humanitarians: American Evangelicals and Global Aid* (Cambridge, MA: Harvard University Press, 2018), 129–31.

27. Paul A. Kramer, *The Blood of Government: Race, Empire, the United States, and the Philippines* (Chapel Hill: University of North Carolina Press, 2006), 347–432.

28. Conroy-Krutz, *Christian Imperialism*, 10.

29. Ian Tyrrell, *Reforming the World: The Creation of America's Moral Empire* (Princeton, NJ: Princeton University Press, 2010), 9.

30. Tyrrell analyzes the temperance and anti-prostitution campaigns in the Philippines in depth in *Reforming the World*. For more on humanitarianism's imperial roots, see Michael Barnett, *Empire of Humanity: A History of Humanitarianism* (Ithaca, NY: Cornell University Press, 2011). On reform and humanitarian efforts directed at Europe, see Julia Irwin, *Making the World Safe: The American Red Cross and a Nation's Humanitarian Awakening* (New York: Oxford University Press, 2013).

31. Curtis, *Holy Humanitarians*, 126.

32. For World War I as a galvanizing moment for anti-colonialism, see Erez Manela, *The Wilsonian Moment: Self-Determination and the International Origins of Anticolonial Nationalism* (New York: Oxford University Press, 2007).

33. George Marsden, *Fundamentalism and American Culture* (New York: Oxford University Press, 1980).

34. Jay Riley Case, *An Unpredictable Gospel: American Evangelicals and World Christianity, 1812–1920* (New York: Oxford University Press, 2012), 7–8.

35. Milton Coalter et al., *The Re-forming Tradition: Presbyterians and Mainstream Protestantism* (Louisville, KY: Westminster/John Knox Press, 1992), 169. For more on the Hocking report and liberal missionary reassessments in the interwar period, see David A. Hollinger, *Protestants Abroad: How Missionaries Tried to Change the World but Changed America* (Princeton, NJ: Princeton University Press, 2017), 59–93.

36. Hilary Spurling, *Pearl Buck in China: Journey to "The Good Earth"* (New York: Simon and Schuster, 2019), 206.

37. Hollinger, *Protestants Abroad*, 71.

38. Hollinger, 72.

39. James A. Patterson, "Robert E. Speer, J. Gresham Machen and the Presbyterian Board of Foreign Missions," *American Presbyterians* 64, no. 1 (Spring 1986): 58–68.

40. Marsden, *Fundamentalism and American Culture*, x.

41. Carpenter, *Revive Us Again*, 178.

42. Carpenter, 180–81.

43. Hal Friedman, *Creating an American Lake: United States Imperialism and Strategic Security in the Pacific Basin, 1945–1947* (Westport, CT: Greenwood, 2001), 129.

44. Catherine Porter, "Preparedness in the Philippines," *Far Eastern Survey* 10, no. 6 (April 7, 1941): 67; Gerald Wheeler, "The American Minority in the Philippines: Prewar Commonwealth Period," *Asian Studies* 4, no. 2 (1966): 363.

45. Colleen Woods, *Freedom Incorporated: American Imperialism and Philippine Independence in the Age of Decolonization* (Ithaca, NY: Cornell University Press, 2020), 5.

46. Edward R. Dayton and Samuel Wilson, *Mission Handbook: North American Protestant Ministries Overseas* (Monrovia, CA: Missions Advanced Research and Communication Center, 1977), 37.

47. *The GI Gospel Hour Monthly Bulletin*, no. 5, September 1945, BGC Archives, collection 406, box 3.

48. FEGC pamphlet on its second annual convention, 1948, BGC Archives, collection 406, box 2.

49. Lawrence S. Wittner, "MacArthur and the Missionaries: God and Man in Occupied Japan," *Pacific Historical Review* 40, no. 1 (February 1971): 78.

50. *The Far Eastern Gospel Crusader*, May 1947, BGC Archives, collection 406, box 1. Emphasis in original.

51. Thomas E. Bergler, "Youth, Christianity, and the Crisis of Civilization, 1930–1945," *Religion and American Culture* 24, no. 2 (2014): 259–96.

52. Hans Krabbendam, "The Lost Continent? The Discovery of Europe by American Evangelicals, 1940–1980," transcript of the Billy Graham Center Annual Lecture given on September 27, 2012, www.wheaton.edu/media/billy-graham-center-archives/2012-Annual-Lecture-Transcript.pdf (accessed July 7, 2020). See also Krabbendam, *Saving the Overlooked Continent: American Protestant Missions in Western Europe, 1940–1975* (Leuven, Belg.: Leuven University Press, 2020).

53. James Enns, *Saving Germany: North American Protestants and Christian Mission to West Germany, 1945–1974* (Montreal: McGill-Queen's University Press, 2017), 114–15.

54. Billy Graham, *Just As I Am* (New York: HarperCollins, 1997), 100.

55. Wilbert R. Shenk, *Changing Frontiers in Mission* (Maryknoll, NY: Orbis Books, 1999), 142; Richard Pierard, "Pax Americana and the American Evangelical Advance," in *Earthen Vessels: American Evangelicals and Foreign Missions, 1880–1980*, ed. Joel A. Carpenter and Wilbert R. Shenk (Grand Rapids, MI: Eerdmans, 1990), 158.

56. Pierard, "Pax Americana and the American Evangelical Advance," 158.

57. Victoria de Grazia, *Irresistible Empire: America's Advance through Twentieth-Century Europe* (Cambridge, MA: Belknap Press of Harvard University Press, 2005); Reinhold Wagnleitner, *Coca-Colonization and the Cold War: The Cultural Mission of the United States in Austria after the Second World War*, trans. Diana M. Wolf (Chapel Hill: University of North Carolina Press, 1994); Kristin Ross, *Fast Cars, Clean Bodies: Decolonization and the Reordering of French Culture* (Cambridge, MA: MIT Press, 1995).

58. Uta Balbier, "'Selling Soap and Salvation': Billy Graham's Consumer Rhetoric in Germany and the United States in the 1950s," *Amerikastudien* 59, no. 2 (2014): 137–52.

59. For more on U.S. reconstruction of Europe, see Michael J. Hogan, *The Marshall Plan: America, Britain, and the Reconstruction of Western Europe, 1947–1952* (New York: Cambridge University Press, 1987).

60. Hans Krabbendam, "Opening a Market for Missions: American Evangelicals and the Re-Christianization of Europe, 1945–1985," *Amerikastudien* 59, no. 2 (2014): 154.

61. "News Flashes for Deputational Workers," letter from Mrs. Russell Honeywell, February 26, 1948, BGC Archives, collection 406, box 2.

62. John Morrison, "Too Little and Too Late," *Christianity Today*, February 4, 1957.

63. Carl F. H. Henry, "Malayan Workers Set Task in New Focus," *Christianity Today*, August 3, 1959.

64. J. C. Pollock, "Christian Imperialism," *Christianity Today*, June 23, 1958.

65. Krabbendam, "Opening a Market for Missions," 153–75.

66. "FEGC News Release," December 29, 1948, and *Pacific News Letter*, [1948?], BGC Archives, collection 406, box 2.

67. McAlister, *Kingdom of God Has No Borders*, 8.

68. Eileen Luhr, "Cold War Teenitiative: American Evangelical Youth and the Developing World in the Early Cold War," *Journal of the History of Childhood and Youth* 8, no. 2 (Spring 2015): 306.

69. Edward R. Dayton, *Mission Handbook: North American Protestant Ministries Overseas* (Monrovia, CA: Missions Advanced Research and Communication Center, 1976), 36.

70. Peter Duignan and L. H. Gann, *The United States and Africa: A History* (New York: Cambridge University Press, 1987), 359.

71. Robert Bruns, *Billy Graham: A Biography* (Westport, CT: Greenwood Press, 2004), 50–51.

72. Anne C. Loveland, *American Evangelicals and the U.S. Military, 1942–1993* (Baton Rouge: Louisiana State University Press, 1996).

73. Gunn, *Spiritual Weapons*, 91.

74. Axel R. Schäfer, "Evangelical Global Engagement and the American State after World War II," *Journal of American Studies* 51, no. 4 (2017): 1074.

75. Schäfer, 1078, 1079.

76. Odd Arne Westad, *The Global Cold War: Third World Interventions and the Making of Our Times* (Cambridge: Cambridge University Press, 2005).

77. Schäfer, "Evangelical Global Engagement," 1081.

78. On evangelical missionaries and race, see McAlister, *Kingdom of God Has No Borders*, 17–29.

79. Ross Coggins, "Missions and Prejudice," *Christianity Today*, January 17, 1964.

80. "The Gospel in Modern Asia," editorial in *Christianity Today*, September 28, 1959.

81. Ben J. Marais, "The Church's Role in Africa (Part I)," *Christianity Today*, May 23, 1960.

82. "Gospel in Modern Asia."

83. Marais, "Church's Role in Africa."

CHAPTER SEVEN

Race and the Korean War Origins of World Vision Inc.

Helen Jin Kim

Korea was indispensable for the revival of modern evangelical America, as exemplified by the Korean War origins of World Vision Inc., the largest evangelical humanitarian nonprofit in the world.[1] Yet World Vision's founding is usually solely attributed to Bob Pierce. World Vision's origins in Korean creativity and suffering is largely forgotten.[2] Along with that memory loss, the history of war and its racialized dimensions have been under-analyzed in the organization's founding narrative in the context of the Korean War.[3] This chapter corrects that oversight, narrating the rise of World Vision through the inconvenient history of Cold War America's entanglements with Korean Christianity and Korean people in a war turned "hot." It showcases a transpacific lens through which to study global Christianity and the Cold War.[4]

World Vision Inc. is an organization that began with the idea of Kyung Chik Han (1902–2000), which Bob Pierce (1914–78) then incorporated into a 501c3. Two months before the outbreak of the Korean War—traditionally recorded as June 25, 1950—Han, a northern Korean Presbyterian minister, met Pierce, a white evangelist from the fundamentalist Sunbelt, in the southern region of Korea. Pierce had formative transpacific encounters as a missionary in China, but his alliance forged with Han, annealed in the fire of war, was arguably the most impactful in his career, as Han gave him the idea to create the largest evangelical humanitarian organization. Though Pierce carried greater national status as a representative from the "big brother" nation of the United States, Han tutored Pierce in the business of evangelical humanitarian care.[5]

In Seoul, Han and Pierce preached revivals and engaged in humanitarian work that drew thousands of Koreans. Han and Pierce sought to care for Korean Protestant martyrs' families, especially that of Kim Ch'anghwa and Paek Okhyŏn's, the inaugural family that World Vision financially sponsored. The blood shed by Kim Ch'anghwa—his martyrdom—sowed the seeds for the creation of World Vision. Thus, World Vision's origins were connected to the rise of global Christianity in the non-Western world, especially in Korea. Pierce leaned on Han's ideas and Kim's sacrifice to make his Christian humanitarian vision a reality. Thus, highlighting the story of Korean Protestants like Kyung Chik Han, Paek Okhyŏn, and Kim Ch'anghwa modifies the myth that World Vision was created by one white man and reveals how much Pierce also needed them. So indebted was Pierce to Korea that, even at the end of his life, when he had contracted leukemia, he painfully longed to be buried in South Korea, with Han at the helm of his funeral. Han instead persuaded him to be buried in California and spoke at his service there.[6]

However, World Vision was built upon a troubling paradox. The U.S. militarization of Korea in the aftermath of World War II, and the onset of the "religious Cold War" thereafter, connected a new generation of white fundamentalists to the peninsula, which not only remade institutions that would exemplify modern evangelical America but also renewed the racial politics that accompanied its rise as a religious phenomenon.[7] Indeed, Cold War South Korea and the United States had been intertwined in a "religious Cold War" against global communism—matters of faith permeated the war as a political struggle for legitimacy and a global rivalry between divergent ideas of governance in Cold War America's battle against the Soviet Union. In spite of Harry Truman and Dwight D. Eisenhower's differences, Eisenhower expanded Truman's belief that Cold War America had a divine mandate to save the world from "the spiritual evil of atheistic communism."[8] That religious Cold War extended into Asia.[9] The U.S. paved a militarized highway into Korea through its Cold War in Asia, laying the groundwork for the business of evangelical humanitarianism at mid-twentieth century.

Race and the Korean War Origins of World Vision Inc.

In this context, while Korean Protestants founded and built World Vision, and were glorified for doing so, they were simultaneously erased, their narratives and faces nowhere to be found in the organization's origins. Pierce and Han's reliance on the superiority of the salvific power of the American Cold War state short-circuited the full effect of the transnational, intimate, and existential exchanges between two men from vastly different worlds. When Pierce rendered what he saw in Korea to a white audience in the United States, as in his film *Dead Men on Furlough*, he regrettably mistranslated the story of Kim Ch'anghwa and his wife Paek Okhyŏn, representing them as flat characters that perpetuated racial stereotypes about Asians. Kim Ch'anghwa's death was rendered Christian martyrdom with little acknowledgment of the tragedy of war. Han was also made a martyr as he was erased from this film, nowhere to be seen in the image of the "new" evangelicalism he helped to build. A new generation of white fundamentalists and Korean Protestants transnationally remade evangelical America but conserved ideas of race and anti-communist politics through the glorification and martyrdom of Korean Protestants.

World Vision's Korean Founder: Kyung Chik Han

Pierce is widely known as the founder of World Vision Inc. However, his daughter Marilee Pierce Dunker named Kyung Chik Han as its progenitor. She recalls, "Pastor Han was already doing the work of World Vision when my dad met him, and Pastor Han was someone who showed my father how to meet the practical needs of the hungry and homeless and the widows and the orphans." Having had a near-death experience while living abroad in the United States, Han had used this experience to serve the disadvantaged in northern Korea. When Han was a pastor at Second Sinuiju Presbyterian Church, he met Bok Soon, an orphaned child who had lost one of her legs. Inspired by her story, he created Borinwon, a home for orphans, which launched his lifelong social welfare ministry.[10] He also created a *kyungnowon*, a home for the elderly.[11]

Amid the war, and in the southern region of Korea, Han continued to translate these social welfare ministries into Tabitha Mojawon or Tabitha Widows Home, established for families whose male heads of household were martyred during the war.[12] Han recalled, "During the Korean War . . . so-called fatherless families came into being more in the church. As they lost their husbands, the church had to take care of them, that is, widows."[13] Marilee Pierce Dunker remarked that when her father arrived during the war, "Pastor Han had already begun the arduous task of organizing the church to feed, clothe and care for the homeless and the widows and the orphans."[14] Han showed Pierce how to connect U.S. resources to war-torn Korea. Pierce Dunker concluded, "So, you see, my father's vision to engage the world, to provide for the needs of those who have not—my father received his education about how to do that from Pastor Han."[15]

Pierce came to Korea with Christian American ideas of heroism and rescue. But he also encountered seasoned Korean Protestants like Han, whom he described as a "Korean saint," a spiritual role model whose "depth of patience" he marveled at, and whom he observed "hour upon hour." He studied Han "tirelessly" evangelizing, ministering "to the multitudes," caring for "men's souls irregardless of their station in life," and showing "mercy to refugees."[16] Han tutored Pierce in evangelical humanitarianism, laying the groundwork for World Vision.

Yet Pierce also described Han as a man of "slight stature." As he juxtaposed Han's grand faith, which would "stagger any clergyman I know in America," with his smaller physical build, Pierce painted Han in extremes, romanticizing his faith as exceptional, placing him on a pious pedestal, in stark contrast with his diminutive body. Indeed, U.S. Protestants like Pierce looked to Han with admiration as he was "an early sign of the evolving relationships between the two groups," in which Americans "increasingly looked to Korean Christianity as a source to revitalize their own institutions and congregations at home."[17] But that desire to emulate also entangled him in a paradoxical process of Korean glorification and erasure that would haunt Han and Pierce's alliance and, therefore, the founding of World Vision.

For further background, Kyung Chik Han emerged out of the lineage of Protestantism in northern Korea. Born and raised on a farm near Pyongyang, he attended a church founded in 1907 by Samuel Moffett (Mapo Samyul), an early American Presbyterian missionary to Korea. As Han grew up under Japanese colonialism (1910–45), he learned to use Protestantism for Korean nation building. Han attended Osan High School, which was known for its nationalist leaders, including Cho Mansik, the school's principal. Yi Sŭng-hun, another Korean Independence leader, was a key teacher and role model for Han. Han vividly remembered how Yi Sŭnghun showed students his wounds from the 105 Persons Incident in December 1911, when he was tortured by the Japanese. When Yi Sŭnghun helped lead the March First Movement for Independence in 1919, the Japanese government burned down Osan High School.

Han went on to Soongshil College in Pyongyang, where Moffett was president. While Han initially studied science, he had a transformative spiritual experience that shifted his interest to theology. Contemplating his future near the ocean at Hwang Hae Do, he pondered what he could do for his nation, at which point he stopped to pray. He reported hearing a divine voice urging him to shift his educational focus: "If I want to serve my country's people, rather than science, I need to, more fundamentally, devote my life to help revive their mind and spirit."[18] He decided to study theology, in part as a tool for national uplift. Yun Chi'ho helped Han with the fees to travel across the Pacific, and he studied education and religion at the College of Emporia in Kansas. After receiving his master of divinity degree at Princeton Theological Seminary, he had hoped to attend Yale for his doctoral studies, but he shed those dreams when he caught tuberculosis and spent two years in a Presbyterian sanatorium in New Mexico.

Upon returning to northern Korea, which was still occupied by the Japanese, he became a pastor at the Second Presbyterian Church of Sinuiju.[19] Eventually, with the outbreak of the Korean War, Han would meet Pierce, who traveled to South Korea in the spring of 1950. They preached in the cities of Pusan, Taegu, and Seoul, and Han helped translate his sermons and Bible studies from English into Korean. They reportedly attracted hundreds of people, often preaching open-air revivals, including at Namdaemun Park in Seoul.[20] To further understand the historical forces that led to the meeting of two men from unlikely places, which would transform modern evangelical America, one must understand the larger backdrop of war.

The Historical Backdrop of Korean Nationalism, Division, and War

In 1945, the Japanese Empire surrendered. As Koreans shed the shackles of colonialism, they rid the nation of Shintoism such that "nothing remain[ed] of Shinto" in Japan's former colonies.[21] Though the 1919 March First Movement for Korean Independence had begun to lay a foundation for a movement for Korean sovereignty, most Koreans could only imagine their liberation. So few had expected to actually see their liberation that some Koreans actively collaborated with the Japanese, finding favor in their eyes, and with it elevated status, even as their fellow Koreans suffered the empire's brutality. With the end of the empire, those Korean collaborators experienced a reversal of fortune, now being deemed traitors. Those who had protested the lure of empire and its privileges, even engaging in the most public forms of protest, were rewarded respect as nationalists and rose to the ranks of leadership in postcolonial Cold War Korea as they jockeyed for national power. These leaders included Kim Il Sung and Syngman Rhee, both part of the Korean Provisional Government during the imperial period.

Kim Il Sung and Syngman Rhee had divergent ideas about national leadership for postcolonial Cold War Korea. Whereas Kim Il Sung pursued a vision aligned with international socialism, Syngman Rhee pursued one aligned with international democratic capitalism. Some scholars have seen Syngman Rhee's and Kim Il Sung's adoption of these divergent worldviews as evidence that they were puppet leaders, manipulated by the United States and the Soviet Union. Though this point has been extended to scholarship that rendered the Korean War as nothing more than a proxy war for the United States and the Soviet Union, Bruce Cumings has strongly critiqued this position, viewing the war as rooted in a civil war between forces of revolution and anti-revolution, national liberation and reactionary forces represented respectively by North and South Korea.[22]

Syngman Rhee and Kim Il Sung were influenced by the United States and the Soviet Union respectively, but as others have shown, their drive for a unitary nation-state, or ethnic unity, previously thwarted by the 1945 division of the nation, was a key factor in the outbreak of war. The North's and South's respective desire to liberate the other from foreign powers, whether U.S. or Soviet, toward national unity, and therefore ousting those "black sheep" deemed national traitors, was a core impetus for war within a relatively ethnically homogeneous nation.[23] As Gi-Wook Shin writes, "Seen in this way, the Korean War was a war of national liberation of fellow nationals from foreign powers and their collaborators for *both* Kim and Rhee."[24]

But, of course, the two superpowers cannot be ignored in considering the onset of the Korean War. As Korean leaders debated the direction of the nation, with large differences surrounding Kim Il Sung and Syngman Rhee, the United States and the Soviet Union also intervened in 1945. As a result of the 1945 Potsdam Conference, Korea was divided at the 38th parallel, with the Soviet Union taking control of the northern region and the United States taking control of the southern region. By 1948, two separate nations were created: Democratic People's Republic of Korea (DPRK) to the north and the Republic of Korea (ROK) in the south. The polarizing beliefs among Korean nationalists, with some espousing international socialism and others capitalist democracy, were exacerbated by the intervention and military presence of the two rival superpowers that represented those worldviews.

When North Korean leader Kim Il Sung, with the support of Joseph Stalin, attempted on June 25, 1950, to force North and South Korean reunification,

Race and the Korean War Origins of World Vision Inc.

he believed the skirmish would likely last three days, not result in a three-year war. Kim and Stalin had not anticipated that the United States, under the auspices of UN troops, would defend its interests in the Korean civil conflict as one of its first efforts to contain communism in the region. Historically, the U.S. state had few political interests in Korea, the nation sandwiched between China and Japan. In fact, through the Taft-Katsura Agreement (1905), the United States permitted Japan's annexation of Korea in exchange for colonial rule over the Philippines.[25] In the aftermath of World War II, however, the geopolitical landscape of Asia shifted. Thirty-five years of Japanese imperialism in Korea ended, and the United States relinquished colonial rule in the Philippines. The U.S. military then occupied Korea in 1945.

With Mao Tse-Tung's 1949 communist triumph in the People's Republic of China, the United States eagerly sought to contain communism through its new military position in South Korea, which escalated the Korean civil conflict onto the global stage of the Cold War.[26] On April 7, 1950, the U.S. Department of State's Policy Planning Staff issued National Security Council Paper NSC-68, "United States Objectives and Programs for National Security," a top-secret fifty-eight-page report, which was declassified in 1975 and is among the most influential documents drafted by the United States during the Cold War period. Its authors argued that one of the most pressing threats confronting the United States was the "hostile design" of the Soviet Union. They concluded that the Soviet threat would soon be augmented by the addition of more weapons, including nuclear weapons. To respond to this threat, NSC-68 argued that the optimal course of action for Truman was a massive buildup of the U.S. military and its weaponry.

Syngman Rhee and Kim Il Sung espoused divergent philosophical and religious commitments. Both grew up Christian, though Rhee remained a Methodist and the latter developed *juche* ideology as his core political and philosophical frame.[27] Han sided with the model of Western capitalist democracy as a path toward Korean liberation, not only because of his education in the United States but also because of his particular religious position. He had established the Christian Democratic Social Party to defend Christianity and democracy against communist ideals in northern Korea.[28] "Considering our ideology had nothing in common with theirs and none of our members agreed with their socialist ideals," Han recalled, "there was no way for us to not fight them at every step."[29] Han's party, however, was unsuccessful.[30] In November 1945, Korean Protestants clashed violently with the Korean communist army in the north, rendering many a martyr on both sides of the conflict.

Han and his family fled from the northern city of Sinuiju to Seoul. Other northern Korean Protestants followed suit. Amid the waves of southern migration, Korean Christianity's center shifted from the north to the south.[31] Protestantism became ever more concentrated in South Korea as the nation came under U.S. influence. Han translated his vision against communism into politics, revivalism, and humanitarianism, activities through which he met Pierce.

New Transpacific Networks: From Bible Belt to Sunbelt and across the Pacific to Asia

The war forged a militarized transpacific highway between the United States and Asia-Pacific, built not only upon a militaristic foundation but also upon that of anti-communist faith. Via this highway, anti-communist Protestants in South Korea and white fundamentalists from the U.S. Sunbelt and Bible Belt fused their ideas and practices, with Han and Pierce serving as a prime example.[32] Orientalist fascination, humanitarian interest, and fear marked the U.S. gaze toward Asia-Pacific at mid-twentieth century. Sunbelt evangelicals, located in California, the "gateway to Asia," were eager to spread the gospel to mitigate the communist threat into their sunny, free world.[33] California's proximity to Asia fueled anti-communist political fervor and religious anxiety, solidifying a desire to preserve their ideas about religion, race, and free-market capitalism.

At this time, anti-communist sentiment was commonplace among Americans, religious Americans in particular. U.S. Catholics, under the leadership of the pope, were among some of the most fervent anti-communists.[34] The meaning of communism and the degree to which it was feared, however, differed among U.S. religious traditions. Liberal Protestant leaders such as Reinhold Niebuhr held communism at arm's length for unjustly manipulating the poor and for failing to "understand the ambiguity of all human virtue and the foolishness of all human wisdom."[35] He critiqued those Christians who professed faith "but claim[ed] [God] too simply as an ally of their purposes." He had the moralism of U.S. secretary of state John Foster Dulles in mind and suggested that such Christians, too, were people "who bring evil into the world."[36]

Americans associated with fundamentalism, and the emerging neo-evangelicalism, believed anti-communism was inextricably linked with soul saving.[37] They differentiated themselves from the Social Gospel orientation of their liberal counterparts and framed soul saving as an alternative to communist (and secular) identity.[38] Moreover, the psychological menace of "Red China" and California's proximity to Asia fueled not only anxiety but also action on the part of white fundamentalists. For instance, while preaching at Church of the Open Door in Pasadena, Pierce first heard about the outbreak of the Korean War, and he rushed preparations to return to Korea.[39] Sunbelt fundamentalists like Pierce traveled to South Korea for evangelism, humanitarianism, and alliance building. They met with American missionaries and soldiers, Korean Protestants and soldiers, and U.S. and Korean government officials to combat communism through Christian conversion.

Unlike modern Judaism or Hinduism, evangelicalism was, since its eighteenth-century origins, a missionary religion seeking global converts; for twentieth-century fundamentalists like Pierce, ideally the whole world would heed his understanding of faith—that Jesus Christ is the only means to humanity's salvation and freedom from the damnation of sin. When white fundamentalists had seemingly lost in the fundamentalist-modernist controversy, they sought revival not only through domestic allies but also through global allies beyond the U.S. nation-state. As such, movements like Youth for Christ (YFC), a missionary organization with roots in the fundamentalist strand of the fundamentalist-modernist controversy, remained core for young fundamentalists. In spite of the post–World War II concerns that the evangelical thrust of Western Christianity was, in part, responsible for propagating imperialism, leaders of YFC continued to send out missionaries due to their stalwart faith in biblical literalism and, therefore, the literal command to follow the Great Commission to make disciples of all nations.[40]

While from two different nations, with vast power differentials between them, Han and Pierce shared the belief that the Korean War was a religious war between good and evil. Though relatively unknown pastors, from Seoul and the Sunbelt, Han and Pierce's vision aligned with Cold War America's faith-based argument against communism, amplifying their power as non-state actors. Once in Seoul, Han, together with twenty-seven other northern Protestant refugees, founded a new church called Young Nak Presbyterian Church.[41] "Young Nak" meant "everlasting joy" and signified their belief that, though they had "lost everything," they still possessed "everlasting joy in Jesus Christ."[42] If the war was a religious war, Han believed that with each new church, the south also grew stronger as a nation, and so did Pierce.

With the emerging global Cold War, the geopolitical landscape of East Asia shifted and with it the U.S. missionary presence in the region. In light of the communist triumph in China in 1949, the "communists were kicking everyone out," including Pierce, who was working in China as a YFC missionary.[43] For Pierce, the geopolitics of the emerging Cold War in Asia restricted access to China but also paved new routes into South Korea. Pierce first traveled to Korea when, in the summer of 1949, Oriental Mission Society missionaries invited him to join them—they believed he knew "how to reach across the pulpit to touch the people."[44]

U.S. dominance was never more powerful in Korea than in the midst of the Korean War. Yet, at mid-twentieth century, Koreans were not merely potential converts for white fundamentalists. Korean Protestants had for decades indigenized their tradition, making it their own through revival, ritual, and anti-imperial protest. Pierce basked in the experience of learning indigenous practices such as *t'ongsŏng kido* (audible prayer in unison) and *saebyŏk kido* (dawn prayer).[45] He recalled, "Attending those prayer meetings was an indelible experience. These people pray with fervency, with a faith that reaches out and believes God from the moment of a prayer's utterance."[46]

Pierce's vision for revival intensified because of his encounter with Korean Protestants' spirituality. Pierce reflected, "Do you wonder why I have such an overpowering love for these dear people? They are my seniors in the Gospel! They walk with God in a fellowship which I yet long for! To think that they yet cry out so hungrily for more of His power! After I had witnessed some of these things, it was not difficult to believe that there is not a more vigorous church on the face of the earth." In casting Korean Protestant spirituality as more mature and earnest than his, he gained greater hope for a revived church. But his admiration also cast Koreans as exceptional: "No wonder the Koreans, differing from all the Orient, sent missionaries to fellow lands like China. No wonder the Korean church is so staunchly indigenous."[47] Pierce was especially impressed with how Korean Protestants' faith had been proven through "great testing," especially under Japanese imperialism and North Korean communism. He reflected, "No wonder I so constantly found myself feeling embarrassment, as I realized what they had done for the Lord in comparison to the scant service I, and so many of my fellow Christians back in America, have offered in appreciation of Calvary." From the perspective of the work "for the Lord," Pierce believed Korean spirituality to be exemplary for Americans. But it was that exceptionalism that also served as a means of rendering them invisible and martyrs in the eyes of white fundamentalists. At the same time that Pierce genuinely learned from Korean Protestant fervor, the exceptionalist lens through which he viewed them also romanticized their spirituality. But that very dance, between Korean Protestant exceptionalism and white fundamentalists' romanticization of them, sustained the embrace between the two nations.

In the spring of 1950, Han introduced Pierce to Kim Ch'anghwa, a northern Protestant refugee and elder at his Young Nak church, who helped Pierce lead Bible studies.[48] On June 25, 1950, one month after the outbreak of the Korean War, North Korean communist officials arrested Kim Ch'anghwa. Pierce declared in pamphlets that because Kim Ch'anghwa had established a Bible study with him, he was accused of collaborating with "American imperialists," replacing "ancient oriental culture" with the "new Western superstition of Christianity." On August 4, 1950, Kim Ch'anghwa was executed.[49] When pressured to recant his faith publicly, he resisted, with Pierce later recounting that Kim declared, "I do believe that Christ himself and his truth are the hope of the world, and I believe in everything that I taught these young people and I'm willing to die for the hope I have in Christ."[50] Pierce hailed Ch'anghwa's death a "tragic—yet heroic—death," a martyr's death. Kim Ch'anghwa's martyrdom connected closely with the U.S. fundamentalist vision of Protestantism in terms of the belief that faith could, indeed, call for the sacrifice of one's whole life. Korean martyrdom also served as a first line of Christian defense for Americans who feared the international threat of communism. Shortly thereafter, in September 1950, Kim Ch'anghwa's death compelled Pierce to incorporate World Vision into a 501(c)3, described as "an evangelical inter-denominational missionary service organization meeting emergency world needs through established evangelical missions." He opened a small office in Portland, Oregon, and the work of World Vision Inc. had begun.

Kim Ch'anghwa's death was glorified as martyrdom, but it was undoubtedly also a tragedy. He left behind his wife, Paek Okhyŏn, and their four young daughters. In January 1951, when North Korean troops pressed harder into the south, Paek Okhyŏn and their daughters fled the advances of the North Korean Communist Party for Pusan, the southernmost city of South Korea. She carried the youngest on her back and held hands with the two middle girls, while the eldest carried a bundle of coverlets on her back.[51] With their home now twice demolished because of national division and

Paek Okhyŏn and her four daughters. Paek's husband,
Kim Ch'anghwa, was martyred during the war.
Courtesy of World Vision Korea, Seoul, Korea.

then war—from Sinuiju to Seoul, and now Pusan—Paek Okhyŏn placed her daughters in an orphanage called Home of Birds while she sold rice cakes on the streets of Pusan.[52] She found an alternative means of financial survival when she discovered that Kyung Chik Han, whose church she had attended in Seoul, had established Tabitha Widows Home for war widows. At Tabitha, Paek Okhyŏn relied on the paternal comfort of her heavenly "Father's house."[53] The war rendered her dependent on Han's patriarchal hearth.

In June 1951, Pierce visited Tabitha Widow's Home in Pusan with Han, where he met Paek Okhyŏn and her four daughters. Upon learning of her husband Kim Ch'anghwa's death, Pierce immediately sponsored Paek Okhyŏn and her daughters for fifteen dollars and then twenty-five dollars per month.[54] It is unclear whether Pierce had felt especially eager to commit to them because his association with Kim Ch'anghwa had led to his death. What is clear is that he did so in part as a result of Han's request. As Pierce recalls, Han, the pastor of "the largest Presbyterian Church in Korea, was the first to ask me, 'Can you find someone in America to sponsor some of the widows and orphans that my church is trying to help?'"[55] Paek Okhyŏn used this money to purchase burlap bags and army uniforms, which she unraveled to sell as thread at marketplaces and war-torn streets in Pusan.[56] The money Paek Okhyŏn received was insufficient to challenge the U.S. interests in

Race and the Korean War Origins of World Vision Inc.

Korea that fueled the war or the polarizing vilification of communists and Christians. It did, however, provide a temporary means of financial survival.

Korean Erasure and *Dead Men on Furlough*, 1954

Yet Pierce mistranslated Koreans in his cultural productions, erasing their narratives and names. South Korean Protestants were not just martyrs to religious sacrifice or the tragedies of war but also ultimately martyrs to the racialized dimensions of a religious Cold War. If a transatlantic network of communication was crucial for the eighteenth-century growth of evangelicalism in the Anglo-American world, then the transpacific network forged between the United States and Korea depended on skillfully leveraging visually based media.[57] Pierce relentlessly gazed upon and involved himself in ameliorating suffering, especially that of children, and it led to a collection of tracts, films, and photos. In the midst of the war, one could often see him connecting with an orphaned or bedridden child, or kneeling down to sympathize with malnourished babies sleeping on the floor. He used technology to see more closely: dark-rimmed spectacles, a camera, and a Pathe brand three-lens video camera, which he carried around with his bare hands even in the dead of winter.[58] The projects Pierce produced to portray the people of Korea, however, reflected his theological imagination and entrepreneurial impulse more than it did the empirical stories and ideas of Koreans themselves—though much of his American audience embraced the veracity of his work. His very best effort to see clearly ironically resulted in a blurry image of reality. A prime example is his translation of the story of Kim Ch'anghwa and Paek Okhyŏn in the 1954 black and white film *Dead Men on Furlough*. In spite of his attempts to "see," Pierce was often blind to the geopolitical nightmare of the Korean War.

When Pierce returned to the United States, he publicized Kim Ch'anghwa's martyrdom to elicit action, especially from fundamentalist Christians. He created *Dead Men on Furlough*, a forty-minute film, based on the symbolism of Kim Ch'anghwa's Cold War martyrdom; it was directed by Dick Ross of Great Commission Films.[59] Ross noted that the figure of Pastor Chai is "really Mr. Chang Hwa Kim, but 'names and places have been changed to protect the innocent from Communist retaliation.'"[60] As a work of creative nonfiction, the film is a "factual dramatic story," as the media reported, or an early version of the "docudrama."[61] It was also the only World Vision movie shot in black and white, which World Vision thought was "better suited psychologically to some story lines," which had "a lot of Cold War era rhetoric." A poster for the film declared, "See the growing struggle between godless Communism and Christianity!"[62] Publicity excitedly suggested that Pastor Chai's "confession . . . will thrill the hearts of the audience in the stand against Communism."[63] *Dead Men on Furlough* is a window into Pierce's understanding of the war. He used it to motivate fundamentalist Americans into action.[64] The film imagines a polarized debate that conflated a binary fundamentalist theology of good versus evil with the Cold War politics of democratic capitalism versus communism.[65]

The anonymity of Kim Ch'anghwa's story provided considerable creative license. Thus, loosely based on Kim Ch'anghwa's story, the plot centers on the North Korean military's infiltration of South Korea during the Korean War when Pastor Chai, Mrs. Chai, their newborn, and the rest of the villagers in their town are captured by North Korean officials. Pastor Chai encounters the North Korean official Major Koh, who demands he recant his faith to save his wife and child; when Pastor Chai refuses to recant, he is killed by North Korean communists, leaving behind his family and the villagers who, nevertheless, are proud of him for defending his faith. The polarized debate between Pastor Chai and Major Koh exemplified the theological battle that Pierce imagined between the Cold War enemy and ally.

Because Pastor Chai and his community refuse to follow Major Koh's directions, they engage in a tense theological and political argument that pits communism against Christianity and socialism against capitalism. Major Koh attempts to persuade Pastor Chai to give up his faith, since Koh sees communism as liberation from the "yoke of capitalism" and "bourgeois tyranny." Chai's Christian worldview is an opiate of the masses, he says. In spite of Koh's challenge, Chai believes that preaching and stalwart belief in "God's word," which "never changes," is the most powerful antidote to Koh's atheistic belief system. As they continue to debate, Chai argues that Koh's communist worldview is a form of enslavement, a denial of the "spirit" and "soul" of man who was "made in the image of God." Koh, however, articulates that the re-education system in "labor camps," as Chai calls them, or "hospitals," as Koh calls them, is the best means to "heal" the "sick" from "capitalistic disease." Both believe they have an antidote for the other's sickness, a means of salvation for the other's sin.

The climax arrives when Pastor Chai stands at the podium to declare the central motivating message of the film: he will not renounce his faith for godless communism. Pastor Chai's defense against the communists is a declaration of faith, but more specifically a theological declaration in the

Race and the Korean War Origins of World Vision Inc.

belief that the "Bible is God's word" and that Jesus Christ is "the way, the truth, and the life." Pierce then looks into the camera: "I cannot deny Christ and his truth. He is the way, the truth, and the life." He defends the Bible: "The Bible is God's word and his promises are true. And I am willing to die . . . for righteousness . . . for the Savior . . . the one true hope of the world. God's day of judgment will come. But all of us must make some kind of decision now. Jesus said, 'He that is not with me is against me.'" He links theology with anti-communism, revealing his belief that faith, in the tradition of fundamentalism, was a core strategy for the United States to win the Cold War: "There are times when no man can be neutral when the choice is between democracy and communism, God and devil. On these issues no man can just decide not to decide. The faith of the communist must be surpassed by our deeper faith, their labor by our harder and better labor, their consecration by our greater consecration."

Pastor Chai became a symbol of the Christian triumph over communism and, relatedly, the global triumph of democratic capitalism over Sino-Soviet communism. Pierce's theological paradigm that divided God and the devil, democracy and communism, capitalism and socialism, made a clear, binary challenge to other fundamentalists who desired to be on the side of God. Moreover, in an era when the inerrancy of the Bible and Christianity as the sole path to salvation were debated in liberal and conservative theological communities in the United States, Pastor Chai represented a defense of a conservative interpretation of Christian scripture. When Pastor Chai is killed, he dies not only for defending the Christian God against godless communism but also for being a transpacific spokesperson for fundamentalist Christianity in the United States.

But note that the sacralization of a Korean martyr depends on multiple racial elisions and erasures. Though the film is set in war-torn Korea, it uses the English language from beginning to end. Neither the Korean language nor Korean actors and actresses are central. In an article titled "Communism in Korea Portrayed by Film," Torrance Press reported that *Dead Men on Furlough* would feature "a number of Hollywood's most competent actors and actresses, including Keye Luke, Richard Loo, Jean Wong, Don Harvey, Victor Sen Yung, and scores of all ages from a Korean colony in Los Angeles."[66] While the article notes the names of the prominent actors, it does not mention that they are all Chinese American. Dick Ross recalled that these actors "were hard to direct and 'unresponsive'" and found "their delivery of lines somewhat stilted."[67] Their "stilted"—unnatural or wooden—lines were as stilted as the racial imagination in the film that suggested that English-speaking Chinese Americans could stand in for Kim Ch'anghwa and Paek Okhyŏn, the foreign "others." The film associated Chinese American actors with war-torn Korea, a nation with which they had no roots, relying on the extant racial imagination of Asians in the United States as "perpetual foreigners," unassimilable and ineligible for American citizenship.

Kyung Chik Han is also nowhere to be seen in the film. Instead, Pierce plays the role of narrator and actor. Pierce shifts between these roles in a scene in the Korean village of Inkok, encouraging villagers to "live for godliness as the communist lives for godlessness" and to follow and rely on their leader, Pastor Chai, a "man of godliness." "Follow him as he follows Christ," Pierce declares. The Korean flag in the background and the Koreans wearing traditional clothing indicate that the scene is set in Korea; however, the Western straw cowboy hats that the villagers wear betray that *Dead Men on Furlough* was filmed in a U.S. studio, most likely in Southern California. Pastor Chai's first words are a hymn sung in English, titled "I Must Tell Jesus All of My Trials":

> I must tell Jesus all of my trials;
> I cannot bear these burdens alone;
> In my distress He kindly will help me;
> He ever loves and cares for His own.

The film makes the normative assessment that, like Pastor Chai, "good" Koreans are those who rely on Jesus in the midst of the trials of war, who sing hymns that reflect this belief, and who combat godless communism with Christian faith. Pastor Chai seems to be a stand-in figure for Kim Ch'anghwa and Kyung Chik Han, but neither are actually acknowledged as individual historical figures, rendering both martyrs for the transnational Christian cause against communism.

Han and Pierce's alliance had a seesaw effect. At its highest point, Korean Protestants like Kyung Chik Han and Kim Ch'anghwa served as an example to Americans; at its lowest point, Korean Protestants like Kim Ch'anghwa and Paek Okhyŏn were not only reduced to caricatures but also hidden from the American gaze. As much as Pierce and Han's partnership complicated the white-over-Korean hierarchy, they could not escape the Orientalist trappings of the Cold War era. When Pierce communicated his message to other white fundamentalists, he did so, in part, through stilted and inaccurate renderings of Kim and Paek's lives. As historian William Yoo has noted, Han possessed a "rising stature" that directed American attention to the proliferation of Christians in the Global South; yet he was also the "object of American affection" because Americans could "project their values" onto him and "advance their agendas at home."[68]

Indeed, World Vision's "founding myth" does not usually begin with Koreans or the Korean War. But Han and Pierce disputed the origins of World Vision. When Han recounted World Vision's beginnings, he related its indelible transpacific origins, pointing to the location of the organization's founding in Seoul during "the spring of 1950 when the Korean War broke out." And he named the "young Pastor Pierce" as the founder. Han told Pierce, "Even though I told you that World Vision was needed and I told you that we should do World Vision in your name, you are the one who founded World Vision." Pierce replied, "No, you, *hyungnim* [older brother], are the founder of World Vision." Kwang Soon Lee recalls that they "went back and forth like this" and "at the end, Pierce said, 'You were the one that came up with all of these ideas' . . . that this world needs World Vision . . . and that World Vision is a name that Rev. Han created. But [Han said that] since Han is a Korean person . . . 'I cannot do this work.' He told Pierce to do it in his name. . . . That's how today's World Vision was created."[69] Han saw that Pierce's national status as an American could make his vision a reality. Han and Pierce both influenced each other, however unevenly.

Yet to forget Korean names such as Kyung Chik Han, Paek Okhyŏn, or Kim Ch'anghwa in the historical origins of World Vision is to forget the Pacific-facing career of U.S. Cold War empire in Korea. The trope of martyrdom both glorified and erased South Korean Protestants from the narrative of the emerging American evangelical empire, as sacrificing one's self—via invisibility—was hailed pious amid a holy war. As South Korean Protestants were both glorified and forgotten in the eyes of Americans, World Vision grew as a global organization.

Notes

1. See David P. King's comprehensive study on the origins and historical development of World Vision, *God's Internationalists: World Vision and the Age of Evangelical Humanitarianism* (Philadelphia: University of Pennsylvania Press, 2019).

2. Please see David R. Swartz's helpful reconstruction of World Vision's Korean origins, *Facing West: American Evangelicals in an Age of World Christianity* (New York: Oxford University Press, 2020), 35–65. See also my reconstruction of the Korean and Korean War origins of World Vision, Helen Jin Kim, "Gospel of the 'Orient': Koreans,

Race and the Rise of American Evangelicalism in the Cold War Era, 1950–1980" (PhD diss., Harvard University, 2017).

3. Though intersecting with King's and Swartz's histories of World Vision, this chapter also emphasizes the transpacific racialized dimensions of the Korean War origins of the organization and employs Korean language sources to analyze this forgotten past. Moreover, it highlights the non-elite figures, such as Paek Okhyŏn and Kim Ch'anghwa, who were crucial to World Vision's origins.

4. For a helpful study of World Vision's global context as connected to other regions of the world, see Melani McAlister, *The Kingdom of God Has No Borders: A Global History of American Evangelicals* (New York: Oxford University Press, 2018).

5. William Yoo, *American Missionaries, Korean Protestants, and the Changing Shape of World Christianity, 1884–1965* (New York: Routledge, 2017), 182. Yoo notes especially Pierce's admiration for Han as an example of someone who confirmed his own orientation toward faith. Note that Han was twelve years older than Pierce, a significant marker of rank in Confucian societies.

6. "12. Docu Movie—Kyung Chik Han," in *The Complete Collection of Rev. Kyungchik Han: Visual Materials No. 5 Docu 2* (DVD collection in Korean), The Kyungchik Han Foundation, Seoul, Korea.

7. On the "religious Cold War," please see the following: Andrew Preston, "Introduction: The Religious Cold War," in *Religion and the Cold War: A Global Perspective,* ed. Philip E. Muehlenbeck (Nashville, TN: Vanderbilt University Press, 2012), xi–xxii; Dianne Kirby, ed., *Religion and the Cold War* (New York: Palgrave Macmillan, 2003); and Angela M. Lahr, *Millennial Dreams and Apocalyptic Nightmares: The Cold War Origins of Political Evangelicalism* (New York: Oxford University Press, 2007).

8. William Inboden, *Religion and American Foreign Policy, 1945–1960: The Soul of Containment* (New York: Cambridge University Press, 2008), 261–62. For Inboden's discussion of the Cold War as a religious Cold War, see 1–25; for a specific attention to Truman and Eisenhower's religious vision of the Cold War, see 105–57, 257–311.

9. For religion, as it pertains to the Cold War in Asia, see Seth Jacobs, *America's Miracle Man in Vietnam: Ngo Dinh Diem, Religion, Race, and U.S. Intervention in Southeast Asia* (Durham, NC: Duke University Press, 2005). For discussion on Korea in particular, see Kai Yin Allison Haga, "An Overlooked Dimension of the Korean War: The Role of Christianity and American Missionaries in the Rise of Korean Nationalism, Anti-colonialism, and Eventual Civil War, 1884–1953" (PhD diss., College of William and Mary, 2007).

10. "3. Kyung Chik Han, the Volunteer," in *The Complete Collection of Rev. Kyungchik Han: Visual Materials No. 5 Docu 2* (DVD collection in Korean), The Kyungchik Han Foundation, Seoul, Korea.

11. "12. Docu Movie—Kyung Chik Han."

12. "Case History of Lee-Kim Duck Hei (widow in Tabitha Home). H#6 A#411," Korea Projects 1956–1978, World Vision Inc., Central Records, Monrovia, CA.

13. *Kyung Chik Han Collection: Volume 1* (Seoul: Kyung-Chik Han Foundation, 2010), 455–56.

14. "12. Docu Movie—Kyung Chik Han."

15. "12. Docu Movie—Kyung Chik Han."

Race and the Korean War Origins of World Vision Inc.

16. Bob Pierce, *The Untold Korea Story* (Grand Rapids: Zondervan Publishing House, 1951), 45–46.

17. Yoo, *American Missionaries*, 182.

18. "12. Docu Movie—Kyung Chik Han."

19. "12. Docu Movie—Kyung Chik Han."

20. "8. World Vision and Pastor Kyung Chik Han," *The Complete Collection of Rev. Kyungchik Han: No. 4 Docu 1 Visual Materials* (DVD collection in Korean), The Kyungchik Han Foundation. Seoul, Korea.

21. Helen Hardacre, *Shinto: A History* (New York: Oxford University Press, 2016), 434. Note also Jolyon Thomas's caution against stereotyping Japan as a Shinto state, reinforcing incorrect perceptions of modern Japan as religiously intolerant. Jolyon Baraka Thomas, *Faking Liberties: Religious Freedom in American-Occupied Japan* (Chicago: University of Chicago Press, 2019).

22. Bruce Cumings, *The Origins of the Korean War*, vols. 1 and 2 (Princeton, NJ: Princeton University Press, 1981, 1991).

23. Gi-Wook Shin, *Ethnic Nationalism in Korea: Genealogy, Politics, and Legacy* (Stanford: Stanford University Press, 2007), 161–65.

24. Shin, 162.

25. The Taft-Katsura Agreement was established in the aftermath of Japan's victory in the Russo-Japanese War (1904–5).

26. Sheila Miyoshi Jager, *Brothers at War: The Unending Conflict in Korea* (New York: W. W. Norton, 2013). See also Bruce Cumings, *The Origins of the Korean War, Volume 1: Liberation and the Emergence of Separate Regimes, 1945–1947* (Princeton, NJ: Princeton University Press, 1981); and Bruce Cumings, *The Korean War: A History* (New York: Modern Library, 2010).

27. *Juche*, literally "self-reliance," is a combination of Marxist and neo-Confucian thought, which has over time become a national North Korean religion.

28. Established in September 1945, it was the first political party in the country since liberation, established to promote democracy and reform the nation according to Christian ideals. Haga, "Overlooked Dimension of the Korean War." See also Kai Yin Allison Haga, "Rising to the Occasion: The Role of American Missionaries and Korean Pastors in Resisting Communism throughout the Korean War," in Muehlenbeck, *Religion and the Cold War*, 88–113.

29. *Kyung Chik Han Collection: Volume 1*, 285.

30. Haga, "Overlooked Dimension of the Korean War," 148–51.

31. Pyongyang was historically the center of Korean Christianity.

32. This is a reference to Darren Dochuk's book *From Bible Belt to Sunbelt: Plan-Folk Religion, Grassroots Politics, and the Rise of Evangelical Conservativism* (New York: W. W. Norton, 2011).

33. Dochuk, 188–89.

34. Patrick Allitt, *Religion in America since 1945: A History* (New York: Columbia University Press, 2003), 22.

35. Inboden, *Religion and American Foreign Policy*, 64. He warned other American intellectuals for allowing communism to infiltrate their minds at the cost of rejecting the American values of democracy. See also Jonathan P. Herzog, *The Spiritual-Industrial*

Complex: America's Religious Battle against Communism in the Early Cold War (New York: Oxford University Press, 2011).

36. Inboden, *Religion and American Foreign Policy*, 69. Dulles served as U.S. secretary of state under President Dwight D. Eisenhower from 1953 to 1959 and was an aggressive anti-communist whose religious discourse, Inboden argues, strongly shaped the course of the Cold War between the Christian United States and the atheistic Soviet Union; Dulles, he provides, was not a fundamentalist, but his religiopolitical worldview created a moralistic discourse of good and evil between the United States and the Soviet Union.

37. For further discussion on neo-evangelicals and anti-communist rhetoric during the Cold War, see Elizabeth Barstow, "'These Teen-agers Are Not Delinquent': The Rhetoric of Maturity for Evangelical Young Adults, 1945–1965" (PhD diss., Harvard University, 2010).

38. William R. Hutchison, *Errand to the World: American Protestant Thought and Foreign Missions* (Chicago: University of Chicago Press, 1987).

39. Marilee Pierce-Dunker, *Man of Vision: The Candid and Compelling Story of Bob and Lorraine Pierce, Founders of World Vision and Samaritan's Purse* (Waynesboro, GA: Authentic Media, 2005). See also Marilee Pierce-Dunker, "Korea Is Transformed into a Nation That Blesses Others," World Vision Online, April 21, 2015 (updated), www .worldvision.org/christian-faith-news-stories/korea-transformed-nation-blesses-others.

40. By comparison, the liberal Protestant corollary to YFC, the Student Christian Movement, tended to place missionaries in university or health care settings with a focus on socially engaged ministries.

41. It was first called Bethany Church when they started it in December 1945.

42. *Kyung Chik Han Collection: Volume 1*, 414.

43. Gwen Wong, Inter-Varsity Christian Fellowship Archives, Oral History, provided courtesy of InterVarsity USA archivist Ned Hale. InterVarsity began as a British movement among evangelical students in Cambridge and London in the late nineteenth century; it was a conservative evangelical alternative to the Student Christian Movement. The U.S. branch of InterVarsity, however, did not begin until 1939. Keith Hunt, *For Christ and the University: The Story of InterVarsity Christian Fellowship, 1940–1990* (Downers Grove: Intervarsity Press, 1991).

44. Phone conversation with Bob Pierce's daughter Marilee Pierce-Dunker, August 2015.

45. See Sung Deuk Oak's discussion of how these became indigenous Korean Christian practices. Sung-Deuk Oak, *The Making of Korean Christianity: Protestant Encounters with Korean Religions, 1876–1915* (Waco, TX: Baylor University Press, 2013), 271–305.

46. Pierce, *Untold Korea Story*, 10–11.

47. Pierce, 66–67.

48. Kyung Bae Min, *World Vision 50 Year History, 1950–2000* (Seoul: World Vision Korea, Hong Ik Jae Publishers, 2001), 178–79.

49. For an overview of Kim Ch'anghwa and Paek Okhyŏn's story, see "Our Daddy Died for Truth: A Radio Show by Bob Pierce," World Vision Inc., Central Records, Monrovia, CA; Min, *World Vision 50 Year History*, 178–81; "Christmas in Korea," in *World Vision Pictorial*, 68 (the publication year of the *World Vision Pictorial* is not recorded on the publication, but it was most likely 1953); and "My Daddy Died for Truth," *World Vision Magazine*, June 1959, 12.

50. "Our Daddy Died for Truth." Kim Ch'anghwa was a high school math teacher, a father of four, and a North Korean refugee. He taught at Seoul National University Attached Middle School.

51. Kim Ok Hyun, "God Leads Me," 2, Testimony of the First Sponsorship: Widow Ok Hyun Kim and Her Four Daughters Were the First to Be Sponsored by World Vision, 1951, World Vision Inc., Central Records, Monrovia, CA. (Note that this source incorrectly gives Paek Okhyŏn her husband's last name—Kim Ok Hyun.)

52. War widows often had to abandon their children at orphanages and could not afford to return for their children once they left them. As historian Arissa Oh reports, war widows were especially vulnerable, sometimes by coercion, to recruitment into sex work: "In 1952, the U.S. State Department reported that 2,658 'UN Aunties'—one of the many terms used to describe prostitutes who served foreigners—had been arrested in a five-month period in Seoul alone; of this number, half were widows." Arissa Oh, *To Save the Children of Korea: The Cold War Origins of International Adoption* (Stanford, CA: Stanford University Press, 2015), 49. Since the U.S. military first entered the southern region of Korea in 1945, camp towns or *kijich'on* providing sexual services for troops emerged nearly simultaneously. The number of Korean women working at camp towns increased to about 2,000 during the war. Ji-Yeon Yuh, *Beyond the Shadow of Camptown: Korean Military Brides in America* (New York: New York University Press, 2002),19–23.

53. Her favorite verses were from John 14:1–4. Kim Ok Hyun, "God Leads Me." This source cites the King James Version: "Let not your heart be troubled: ye believe in God, believe also in me. In my Father's house are many mansions: if it were not so, I would have told you. I go to prepare a place for you. And if I go and prepare a place for you, I will come again, and receive you unto myself; that where I am, there ye may be also. And whither I go ye know, and the way ye know."

54. There is some discrepancy in the amounts Bob Pierce gave to Paek Okhyŏn. In the following source, it says that after Paek met Pierce with Han in 1951 at the Tabitha Widows Home in Pusan, she and her four daughters received twenty-five dollars per month and then fifty dollars every other month from World Vision. Kim Ok Hyun, "God Leads Me." Also note that World Vision began its official child sponsorship program in 1953, historically the organization's main program, but before that they sponsored a war widow—Paek Okhyŏn—whose husband died because of his collaboration with Pierce.

55. Bob Pierce and Dorothy Clark Haskin, *Orphans of the Orient: Stories That Will Touch Your Heart* (Grand Rapids: Zondervan Publishing House, 1964), 86.

56. Kim Ok Hyun, "God Leads Me."

57. Susan O'Brien, "A Transatlantic Community of Saints: The Great Awakening and the First Evangelical Network, 1735–1755," *American Historical Review* 91, no. 4 (1986): 811–32.

58. See images of Bob Pierce in "BGEA Korea 1952 Visit Photo File": Images 52, 68, 182, 179, 328, 202, and 179, 319, 457, Billy Graham Center Archives, Wheaton, IL. Pierce's video camera had at least three lenses—for short, medium, and long shots—through which to record footage. See also John Hamilton, "An Historical Study of Bob Pierce and World Vision's Development of the Evangelical Social Action Film" (PhD diss., University of Southern California, 1980), 19–22. Hamilton notes that Pierce's first camera, a 16mm, was purchased in 1941. On it, he filmed home videos of his daughters. He filmed two movies before he went to China for China Challenge. *38th Parallel* was

his first film of Korea. Dick Ross produced or directed the first nine of the Bob Pierce films for World Vision from 1948 to 1956, under the name Great Commission Films, which eventually became World Wide Pictures under the BGEA in 1956.

59. Hamilton, "Historical Study of Bob Pierce," 71–73. Great Commission Films spent nearly $200,000 to film *Dead Men on Furlough,* significantly more than on later films in the $30,000–40,000 range. Great Commission Films' first film, *The Flame,* was also about Korea, which cost about $200,000. *Of Such Is the Kingdom,* Great Commission's last film with Pierce, was also about Korea.

60. Quoted in Hamilton, "Historical Study of Bob Pierce," 83.

61. Historian Catherine Ceniza Choy might categorize such a 1950s film as such. See Catherine Ceniza Choy, *Global American Families: A History of Asian International Adoption in America* (New York: New York University Press, 2013).

62. Hamilton, "Historical Study of Bob Pierce," 81.

63. "Communism in Korea Portrayed by Film," November 22, 1954, Torrance Press, 11.

64. Choy, *Global American Families,* 31.

65. "Our Daddy Died for Truth."

66. Loo, Keye, and Wong are Chinese American actors who played relatively prominent roles in films throughout their careers. See the following IMDB profiles to follow their careers: Richard Loo, www.imdb.com/name/nm0519618/?ref_=nm_mv_close; Keye Luke, www.imdb.com/name/nm0525601/bio?ref_=nm_ov_bio_sm; and Jean Wong, www.imdb.com/name/nm0939134/bio?ref_=nm_ov_bio_sm.

67. Hamilton, "Historical Study of Bob Pierce," 83.

68. Yoo, *American Missionaries,* 196, 199.

69. "12. Docu Movie—Kyung Chik Han."

CHAPTER EIGHT

Moral Minorities

Decolonization and the
Global Evangelical Left

David C. Kirkpatrick

"Choose life!" The words trumpeted across the chapel and lingered in the rafters at Andover Newton Theological School in 1987.[1] This pro-life slogan, commonly found on billboards, bumper stickers, and license plates, reflects the lockstep loyalty between many white American evangelicals and the Republican Party. Yet, in his annual dean's address, the Puerto Rican progressive evangelical Orlando Costas wielded the phrase not as an anti-abortion cudgel but with an edge that was sharpened on both sides of the Rio Grande: Costas called evangelicals to *choose life* in the face of perceived American global imperialism.[2] "The Pro-Life Movement constitutes a crusade for the defense of life before birth. But have you noticed how little emphasis is put on life before death?" Costas asked. For him, the violence of the global status quo was the *real* pro-life crisis: "The poor struggle for justice in order to survive an economic, social and political holocaust. For them life without justice means death," Costas billowed.[3] He also refused to leave white evangelicals within a comfortable and familiar narrative, indicting them for supporting Cold War state crimes. The Reagan Doctrine was deeply implicated as the archetype of American intervention in Latin America and the centerpiece of American foreign policy. In striking language, Costas called for "pro-life" Christians to be truly "converted from the path of injustice" with its "idol of military power" and "god of war." The call was clear: "There is still time for us and our children to choose life—to obey God and become peacemakers by struggling for justice."[4]

In the 1970s, American evangelicals often heard stories of unjust governments, endemic poverty, and communist violence from missionary prayer letters and popular print media. Yet, these descriptions often arrived with a prescription: that American evangelicals should intervene or share material resources to save souls abroad. In the film *Tortured for Christ* (1967), for example, Richard Wurmbrand, the founder of the Voice of the Martyrs and leading figure in the "global war on Christians," famously stripped his clothes and revealed scars from torture under the communist regime in Romania. "Communists torture those who believe in Christ. . . . Christians are happy to suffer like this," he testified. Wurmbrand then turned to his evangelical audience: "But it is your duty to fight to stop these sufferings."[5] Today, the Voice of the Martyrs flashes a similar phrase on its online donation page: "Many Christians are forced to flee persecution. *You* can help them" (italics mine).[6] In another prominent example, Bob Pierce, the U.S. founder of World Vision, presented images of global poverty with a probing question: "What are you going to do about it?"[7] Pierce's solution was "sponsored children," their photos stuck on refrigerators in millions of American homes and supported financially for "just a few dollars a day." The world was suffering and Americans had a unique responsibility to intervene.

In a sharp reversal, the emerging evangelical *left* told stories of global violence not to arouse an American public to intervention but to rebuke it. In a sense, these evangelicals showed images of violence with a probing question of their own: "*You* did this—now what are you going to do about *yourself?*" This was a "global war on Christians" of a significantly different kind. Members of a global evangelical left named and shamed the United States abroad, providing a dissenting voice to the support of many American evangelicals for the Republican Party. These perspectives contrasted heavily with widespread white evangelical belief in the God-given role of the United States to shape the world in its image. In this way, stories of global violence in the Cold War reversed trajectory from fundamentalism at the turn of the twentieth century and dampened nationalism rising in the evangelical ranks.

During the Cold War, fractures and fissures erupted not only at the margins of evangelicalism but at its very core. White power brokers including Billy Graham, Harold Lindsell, and Carl F. H. Henry clashed with an emerging Latin American evangelical left over the issue of violence and the role of the United States in perpetuating it. A fresh, clear, and complex picture of American religion and politics arises with a view of the evangelical left on both sides of the Rio Grande.

The Cold War made strange bedfellows. Progressive Latin American evangelicals negotiated intimate proximity to American missionaries, Catholic and mainline Protestant liberation theologians, and a violent social context. The tumult and instability of the Cold War provided shared raw materials with Catholic liberation theology and an entire generation of Latin American theologians. In the case of the Latin American evangelical left, the Cuban Revolution (1959) called into question long-standing assumptions about evangelical politics, mission, identity, and theology. In particular, the triumph of Fidel Castro's forces inspired a restless generation with a luminous example: the cancer of American imperialism could be thoroughly excised. This political victory also magnified ideologies that supported decolonization and nationalization. As a result, religious thinkers across many denominations and traditions rejected paternalistic structures and foreign control of institutions. Rather than responding to the emergence of Catholic theologies of liberation, progressive Latin American Protestant evangelicals appear to have been primarily reacting to a cluster of social and political forces that were reshaping postwar Latin America.[8] Religion intersected economic, educational, and political theories that called for liberation from an unjust status quo; it was not exempt from waves of change lapping onto the shores of Latin American life.

Latin American intellectual and religious elites also wielded "theories of dependency" that rejected the global economic status quo. For religious leaders, these theories applied equally to an unjust *religious* structure and the persistent foreign influence smuggled across Latin American borders.[9] South of the Rio Grande, then, the Latin American evangelical left emerged from the same social and political context as Argentine pope Francis and Peruvian Dominican priest Gustavo Gutiérrez, author of the monumental *Teología de la liberación* (1971). What global evangelicals needed, then, was not *development* within the worldwide religious system but *liberation* from a violent context and a Christian mission that saved disembodied souls still hungering for justice. In fierce debates with their American coreligionists, the language of decolonization and violence became the dividing line. Could righteous ends justify violent means? Were American evangelicals implicated in their government's role in assassinations and regime change? Was alleviating the violence of poverty a central mission of the church?

This global voice joined a growing chorus from the American evangelical left in the 1970s.Flagship publications such as *Sojourners* and the *Other Side* covered a panoply of cross-border topics from the Cuban Revolution, the Salvadoran civil war, Brazilian military prisons, Uruguayan government torture, and the crimes of the U.S.-backed Argentine military junta, alongside American Latinx features and figures such as the United Farm Workers and Cesar Chavez.[10] The American evangelical left, by adopting a fierce critique of U.S. foreign relations, listened intently to the voices and experiences of evangelicals of color and those living in current and former colonial contexts. As a result, they were well positioned to hear, be shaped by, and respond to ideologies emanating from the Global South and an increasingly diverse United States. A significant marker of the evangelical left in the postwar period was either proximity to global violence or their attention to voices emanating from decolonizing contexts.

Evangelicals of color present a subaltern and alternative history of American evangelicalism and its diverse political and theological convictions. Their "testimonies" cut against the grain of a "global war on Christians," painting a contrasting picture of America in the world. For them, American global hegemony was deeply implicated in the sufferings of Christians in the Global South—a marked contrast to pleas for "sponsored children" and evangelical internationalism. Evangelicalism faced a new reality as it grew and diversified in the Global South. As the movement shifted southward, the agency of global violence shifted alongside it. It moved multidirectionally, shaping biographies and carving coalitions. Yet, shifts in immigration patterns, accelerated by the 1965 Hart-Celler Immigration Act, meant Africa, Asia, and Latin America were no longer simply "over there" but represented an increasing diversity at home. Bilingual actors became bridges, ushering religious materials across borders. By examining hybridized biographies *and* battles, we can account for the agency of global violence in an increasingly diverse movement. For many white American evangelical power brokers, the "testimonies" of their global coreligionists presented a frustrating contradiction for their audience, challenging binaries and boundaries that many American evangelicals took for granted in both religion and politics.

The evangelical left burst onto the global stage in the early 1970s. In the United States, however, inconspicuous origins belied a later meteoric rise. On Thanksgiving weekend in 1973, an emerging coalition of progressive evangelicals gathered in the basement of the YMCA in downtown Chicago. The delegates of the "Thanksgiving Workshop of Evangelical Social Concern" included Anabaptist Ron Sider (who took a leading and organizing role), theologian Carl F. H. Henry, Sojourners president Jim Wallis, Fuller Theological Seminary professor Richard Mouw, and Peruvian evangelical Samuel Escobar, who was then general secretary of the InterVarsity Christian Fellowship in Canada. Together, they produced the influential 1973 Chicago Declaration, which called for a resurgence of social justice among evangelicals. They also caught the eye of the *Washington Post*, which highlighted their primary goal: to "launch a religious movement that could shake the political and religious life in America."[11] Much of the narrative surrounding this emerging evangelical left has focused on political defeat at the hands of the Moral Majority and religious right. But a global lens refocuses this story, uncovering victories and defeat, negotiation and resistance. The gathering deepened channels for the flow of social Christian ideas and dissenting politics through members' global friendships and networks. This emerging coalition also pressed American evangelical power brokers to reject a global status quo of U.S. hegemony, soul-saving myopathy, and affinity for conservative politics. On global stages and in American publications, evangelicals of color drew from Cold War sources to negotiate for change.

On July 26, 1974, Ecuadorian evangelical René Padilla implicated the U.S. State Department in the Chilean coup d'état, where General Augusto Pinochet had deposed Marxist, democratically elected president Salvador Allende the year before.[12] The provocative article appeared in *Christianity Today*, the flagship American evangelical magazine known for its conservative bent. Padilla also rebuked evangelical leadership—in both Latin America and the United States—for baptizing the coup d'état in anti-communist waters: "As soon as the military had taken over, several evangelical leaders expressed . . . that God had directly intervened to deliver the country from Communism . . . a widespread view among evangelical Christians."[13] Padilla was not confused by anti-communism or corresponding conservative political loyalties; he grew up alongside missionaries in Ecuador, graduated from the conservative evangelical Wheaton College in Illinois, and married an American evangelical missionary, Catharine Feser. Padilla wondered, however, why American evangelicals preferred law and order at *home* but violence *abroad*. As a result, he rebuked their conservative "political views [that led] them to overlook crimes that they would not have overlooked under the Marxist government." He exclaimed, "One need not be a leftist to see that the cruelty of an anti-Communist government is *also* an abomination before God!"[14] In these waning days of the Nixon presidency, Padilla and many young evangelicals of color called into question long-standing political and theological loyalties.

The timing of Padilla's article was significant; this fierce critique of Americans abroad followed his plenary speech at the epochal Lausanne Congress of 1974 that had adjourned the day prior. *Time* magazine called Lausanne "a formidable forum, possibly the widest-ranging meeting of Christians ever held," with nearly 2,500 Protestant evangelical leaders from over 150 countries and 135 denominations.[15] *Time* also singled out Padilla among noteworthy "Third World Evangelicals" as having "one of the meeting's most provocative speeches."[16] His visibility, influence, and notoriety were cresting as waves of change swept over global evangelicalism. While Billy Graham summoned leaders to evangelize of the world, Padilla nearly ushered in an evangelical civil war. Padilla rebuked Americans for exporting a deadly cocktail of capitalist rhetoric and evangelical salvation. Once again, Padilla blamed the political loyalties of American evangelicals for their complicity: evangelical loyalty to the Republican Party was a deal with the devil himself.[17]

For Padilla, colonialism had not disappeared; it had simply rebranded under the banner of "the American Way of Life." As a result, "American culture Christianity integrate[s] racial and class segregation into its strategy for world evangelization."[18] Padilla's nascent brand of social Christianity and harsh rebuke of American evangelical politics drew vocal support from members of an emerging American evangelical left, exposing fault lines and growing pains of this eclectic religious coalition. The tapestry of global evangelicalism was beginning to fray.

The loudest and most influential voices at Lausanne came from Latin American and Latinx evangelicals, whose proximity to U.S. missionaries and Cold War interventionism provided tools for a sharp critique. In his plenary speech, Peruvian Samuel Escobar implicated missionary-exported Christianity in siding with the ruling class and called out missionaries for "explain[ing], justify[ing], and back[ing] whatever the Western nations do."[19] Echoing Padilla, Escobar also challenged allegiance to law-and-order policies with a bit of sarcasm: "Are there groups with strong racist tendencies? Well, we should not bother their prejudice with teaching about equality before

God. Any reference in the Bible to race can be interpreted in a way that does not disturb the established law and order."[20] Orlando Costas, at the time a missionary with Latin America Mission, led a breakout session and called for a rejection of a soul-saving mission so that it will "no longer be a superficial, commercial, manipulative whitewash."[21] The Latin American evangelical left broke a common mold of reporting from so-called mission fields. In John Stott's words, they had "put the cat among the pigeons."[22]

While it may be tempting to view these challenges exclusively through bordered or directional perspectives (Global South to Global North, for example), challenges to American managerial control arose not only from the Global South but also from the unique Latinx evangelical experience in the United States and its territories. Hybridized biographies and bilingual actors played an integral role in selling Cold War materials in a postwar American religious marketplace. While many are familiar with American evangelicals exporting their religious and political goods around the world, fewer acknowledge the reverse—Christians in the Global South sending resources northward. In a way, the "global war on Christians" marketed violence for mass consumption. The evangelical left competed for market share, attempting to reshape the habits of the American evangelical consumer.

Bridging Worlds

Orlando Costas waged war against the white evangelical establishment. His life and work represented, perhaps more than anyone else's, an emerging global evangelical left and fraught negotiation with white evangelical power brokers. In his chapel speech above, Costas did not throw stones from afar; he was thoroughly evangelical in education and orientation, navigating intimate relationships with such conservatives as Bob Jones, Billy Graham, and Carl F. H. Henry and with key members of the evangelical left such as Ron Sider and Tony Campolo, who later became Costas's colleagues at Eastern University and Eastern Baptist Theological Seminary in Pennsylvania. Costas became a leading voice in the American evangelical left as the first Hispanic evangelical endowed chair in the United States, cutting his teeth as an activist during the civil rights movement in Milwaukee in the 1960s.[23] Prior to his untimely death in 1987, Costas was in the vanguard of evangelicals of color and their efforts to sound alarms about American evangelical political loyalties.

Costas's life is a story of whiplash and surprise: forced migration, shifting religious identity, and unlikely encounters with evangelical power brokers.

He found his voice in the heart of the Cold War and in his identity as a Puerto Rican—particularly with the island's fraught history with American colonization. While his closest colleagues also were shaped by the Cold War, Costas's intimacy with American imperialist ambitions contributed a sharper edge and sensitivity to foreign incursion. In this way, the Puerto Rican experience is an untold story and an interpretive bridge between Latin American evangelicalism and the mainland United States.

Puerto Ricans have long occupied a tenuous existence between their Latinx identity and American citizenship. Some Latin Americans have perceived Puerto Ricans—U.S. citizens—as "Yankees" or less than Latin American. Yet, within racialized U.S. borders, their Latinx identity can mark them as "other" and less than American, as well. They often walk a path as a minority *within* a minority. By wielding his own personal biography, Costas targeted American influence—political and religious—that labeled him as dangerous in the evangelical imagination and blunted his influence in the broader community. Yet prior to his political awakening, Costas had embraced an opposing message: the gospel of "law and order," shaping his life around its contours.

As a child, Costas was part of a wave of Puerto Rican migration to the mainland (by 1970, more Puerto Ricans lived in New York City than in the capital city of San Juan). Costas was born in 1942 in Ponce, Puerto Rico, but his journey would quickly be defined by his relationship to perceived U.S. imperialism and the violence of forced migration. When he was twelve years old, his father's grocery business failed in mainland Puerto Rico, and the family immigrated to Bridgeport, Connecticut. Costas recalled his childhood in stark racialized language: "As a member of a forgotten minority, I experienced the awfulness of ethnic prejudice, the harshness of poverty (in a country where the great majority have over and beyond their needs), and the oppression of an impersonal, culturally alienating educational system."[24] In Costas's memory, this led him to embrace a life of crime at a young age. As a fourteen-year-old self-described "juvenile delinquent," Costas was invited to the now-famous Billy Graham crusades at Madison Square Garden in 1957.[25] These New York crusades represented the peak of Graham's influence in the United States—a media spectacle that propelled his political and religious celebrity.

During these years, Costas shaped his "testimony" in evangelical language with a racialized edge. In a biographical piece titled "Teólogo en la encrujijada" (Theologian at the crossroads), Costas described himself as a "juvenile delinquen[t]" in need of personal salvation but also the victim of racial discrimination: "For three years I suffered the impact of a foreign cultural environment, full of hostility and prejudice. I developed strong feelings of shame, scorn and hatred for myself and for all that we Hispanics represented. I tried to overcome the stigma of being Puerto Rican through aggressive social behavior bordering on what some American sociologists call 'juvenile delinquency.'"[26] In Costas's recollection, he turned self-hatred into antisocial behavior within a racist American society. In his colleague Samuel Escobar's words, this was Costas's "restless and turbulent youth."[27] Perhaps more importantly for this story, his own dabbling in youthful crime led him to this "strange and marvelous" encounter with Billy Graham on the floor of the iconic New York stadium.[28]

Prior to a wider embrace of "law and order" policies under Richard Nixon, Billy Graham pounded the drum of crime, violence, and rebellion, as well as the solution of personal salvation.[29] Graham laid out his argument in a *Washington Post* feature promoting the 1957 Madison Square Garden crusades, declaring that "lawlessness has become the spirit of our age."[30] In the year leading up to the crusades, Graham raised the alarm on his radio program *Hour of Decision*: juvenile crime was a nationwide epidemic. Graham argued that "a veritable avalanche of crime, drunkenness, and immorality is sweeping the length and breadth of America." As a result, God was suspending his hand over a lawless nation, threatening to wipe it off the map. Graham later shared a grim diagnosis with a potentially macabre solution: "Sex, sadism, and violence continue to dominate the screens of both theaters and television. . . . 'It may take an atomic bomb to wake us up to reality.'"[31] These themes—crime and violence—resonated with an uneasy American public, selling out Madison Square Garden for over two months—the longest consecutive sellout in its history to that point.

On the floor of Madison Square Garden, Graham's focus on crime and violence captured the young Costas's attention and helped usher him into the evangelical fold. In 1957, Costas responded passionately to Graham's appeal, reflecting that the "encounter marked a new beginning in my life."[32] Perhaps ironically, Graham would play a prominent role in this evangelical "conversion" and Costas's leftist politicization. Costas found an uneasy home in American evangelicalism, situating himself and his story within established religious language and structures. The following year, Costas enrolled at the fundamentalist Bob Jones Academy in Greenville, South Carolina. Unbeknownst to the young Latino, he had stepped onto the battlefield of the raging civil war between Billy Graham and Bob Jones that had erupted that year. Jones was particularly offended by Graham's practice at Madison

Square Garden of "cooperative evangelism," in which decision cards of those who "accepted Christ" were shared with mainline Protestant pastors and denominations—those Jones considered "theologically liberal." Thus, Jones made Graham the dividing line: cooperating with Graham was dabbling in watered-down, compromised Christian belief. On the campus of Bob Jones, Costas knew he had to choose a side: "Like many of my friends, I started to take a fundamentalist posture. . . . Without understanding everything that was involved in the controversy, I became an enemy of both the liberals and the neo-evangelicals."[33]

Costas soon became uneasy with his identity as an evangelical of color in what he called "the Deep South." He would later diagnose Bob Jones Academy with a "racist and triumphalistic Anglosaxon subculture."[34] Conversations with other Latino students confirmed his unease, accelerated his search for Latinx identity, and widened his distance from a white evangelical subculture. After brief studies at Nyack College in Nyack, New York, Costas transferred to the Inter-American University of Puerto Rico in 1966.[35] In Puerto Rico, Costas rediscovered his heritage and a sharper critique of U.S. foreign policy in Latin America—its state crimes and global hegemony. During his return to Latin America, American political *and* religious interventionism appalled him. This crucial intersection of perceived political and religious imperialism paved the way for his contribution to global evangelicalism.

In the late 1960s, Costas was shocked to find a dual American intervention at play in the Caribbean: the U.S. military and the Billy Graham Evangelistic Association. Costas's discovery set him on a crash course with those who had shaped him—Bob Jones, Billy Graham, Carl Henry, and the white evangelical establishment.[36] As a college student in Puerto Rico, he traveled to the Dominican Republic during Operation Power Pack, the U.S. military occupation from 1965 to 1966: "I had a chance to see for myself how a powerful nation quenched the hopes and aspirations of a people who had been dominated . . . by oligarchies and foreign powers."[37] This encounter with U.S. foreign relations pushed Costas leftward as he uncovered evidence of American violence: "The story repeats itself over and over," he recalled. Yet, more than a reflection on U.S. foreign policy, Costas wondered aloud about the implications for *Christianity*: "The sad thing is that these countries have been largely responsible for the expansion of Christianity in the Third World. . . . It ought not surprise us to see coming out of the same land a movement of domination and exploitation together with the message of freedom imbedded in the gospel."[38] For Costas, Christianity itself was deeply implicated in an unjust global status quo. A political and religious awakening, then, required a new mission: decolonizing Christianity. It was here that violence would take on new life. Costas rebuked the American role in global violence but defended colleagues who endorsed the possibility of violence for social change. Violence became a departure point for Costas from colleagues on both sides of the border—American conservatives and progressive Latin Americans.

Orlando Costas represents the complex and hybridized biographies of many progressive Latin American and Latinx evangelicals. But his story also diverges in significant ways from those of key members of the Latin American evangelical left, especially René Padilla and Samuel Escobar. South of the Rio Grande, Latin American Protestant evangelicals often negotiated their identities between personal relationships with American missionaries and growing anti-American attitudes around them. Indeed, anti-American sentiment was thick on Latin American university campuses in the 1950s and 1960s where Padilla and Escobar worked as staff members with the International Fellowship of Evangelical Students (the global representative body that included InterVarsity Christian Fellowship). While many of their friends, pastors, teachers, and financial backers were Americans, broad antipathy toward the interventionist foreign policy and paternalistic role of the United States was endemic to the region.

René Padilla's encounter with decolonization and American evangelical-ism, while radically different in terms of geography, held striking similarities to Costas's. Both revolved around minority status—Costas as a racial minori-ty in the United States and Padilla a religious minority in Latin America. Both were also economic migrants at an early age: Padilla's family moved to Colombia in 1934, when he was two and a half years old, where his father sought a better market for their tailoring business.[39] Proximity to the Cold War, however, would produce strikingly divergent experiences and religious products. Padilla was the recipient of anti-Protestant violence as a child, his home firebombed, his back stoned as he attempted to enroll in a local school, and his life nearly taken by an assassination attempt while open-air preaching. Escobar shared the religious minority path as a Protestant in Peru, and his home was searched by a hostile right-wing military regime in Argentina years later, as well.

For Padilla and Escobar, this was an entrance card that Costas lacked—intimate proximity to Cold War sociopolitical tumult and global violence. Escobar identified Costas's affinity for Marxist class analysis, for example, in his distance from its rebellious political offspring in Latin America.[40] Even within this emerging coalition, issues of citizenship, country of origin, and even race flavored their contributions and perceptions of each other. Monolithic renderings of a Latin American evangelical left, then, do not paint an accurate picture of its internal diversity. While they lacked a shared social and political context, they shared a growing restlessness with the state of global evangelicalism and American managerial control.

The frustration of an emerging progressive coalition was undoubtedly aided by Catholic intellectual developments emanating from the Second Vatican Council (Vatican II, 1962–65). The awakening of Latin American Catholic Christianities from dependence on Western methods and themes can be identified quite precisely in the career of Gustavo Gutiérrez and his *Teología de la liberacíon* mentioned above. The documents of Vatican II itself, such as *Gaudium et spes*, and Pope Paul VI's encyclical *Populorum progressio* of 1967 had begun to accelerate a wider shift toward the poor, alongside a call for liberation from oppression and dependency. In Latin America, many Catholic theologians viewed these developments as license and endorsement of their construction project of truly local and contextual Christianity rather than foreign importation. For example, on August 26, 1968, the Latin American Episcopal Conference met in Medellín, Colombia, to develop and apply Vatican II to the Latin American sociopolitical context. In this prominent case, Catholics and Protestants overlapped in a shared intellectual space. When the conference took place in Medellín, American evangelicals were planning their own intervention into the same sociopolitical context. These stories and biographies intersected at the invitation of the Billy Graham Evangelistic Association, provoked by violence, tumult, and anti-communist sentiment. The surprising result was an emerging *progressive* coalition and an intellectual framework for a global evangelical left. Once again, American intervention provoked unintended consequences, dissenting voices, and generative religious production.

War with the White Establishment

The structures of global evangelicalism buckled under the weight of the global Cold War. For the evangelical left, this project of decolonization aimed at religious ideas and influence that had been imported from the United States. But these ideas were also embedded in institutions that carried tremendous cultural power—institutions often operated by Americans in the region or by proxy across the border. Given the change sweeping across Latin America, the status quo of American managerial control was stamped with an expiration date. Key American evangelicals were caught in the crossfire,

as local battles foreshadowed a global war. Could the use of violence be justified in fomenting social change? Disagreement over this question became a
catchall conflict for broader struggles and frustrations between Latin America
and the United States, and left versus right. The most influential evangelical
seminary in Latin America became the proxy battlefield and symbol of a
global religious struggle.

From its founding in 1924, an unbroken line of American missionaries
had led the flagship institution Seminario Bíblico Latinoamericano (SBL)
in San José, Costa Rica.[41] This took place both in person through American
faculty in Costa Rica and via the Miami-based board of the organization
Latin America Mission. While conversations regarding nationalizing the
institution percolated for decades, they reached full boil in the late 1960s.
Shortly after, in the early 1970s, Costas arrived from Milwaukee, alongside
two Latin American rectors, the Argentine Plutarco Bonilla and the Cuban
Rubén Lores. Costas's arrival placed him within accelerating conversations
regarding missionary leadership, perceived paternalism, and local control
in Latin America.

At the SBL, Costas was known for a consistently fierce protest of missionary oversight and a take-no-hostages approach to American influence in
the region. In a recent interview, Mike Berg, former president of the Latin
America Mission board, recalled long diatribes from Costas's "soap box." Even
when the American board was taking steps toward nationalization, Costas
issued strong warnings: "Orlando was always banging down hard on, we
have to be careful of imperialism, organizational imperialism, we have to be
careful of paternalism, and he mentioned even in the process . . . we have
to be sure, absolutely sure, there are no paternalistic overtones."[42] Costas
took a leading role as these conversations quickened. He presented a paper,
"On the Path toward an Autochthonous Seminary," to the annual assembly
of the board and gave the board two choices, both potentially unpalatable:
either nationalize the seminary and release it into Latin American hands, or
be hopeless paternalists unwilling to reject an unjust status quo. In sharp
language, Costas wrote, "Someone, certainly a missionary . . . has said that
the [SBL] is a child that has grown and now doesn't want to recognize her
mommy. I would say [that we are] like a 48-year-old man whose mother,
for reasons of cultural conditioning, has not been prepared to recognize
her son's maturity with the promptness that it should, but that is gradually
becoming conscious of his duties and possibilities."[43] Costas was eventually
successful; the seminary won its independence, and leaders spoke publicly
of a dawning era of Latin American national leadership. Yet, when the SBL

could least afford it, its funding took a direct hit from the white evangelical establishment in the United States. To gain intellectual and institutional independence, the SBL first had to emerge from the white evangelical gaze across the border. Once again, violence and crime arose as a dividing line in these religious and institutional battles.

In July 1973, Harold Lindsell wrote to Rubén Lores, the Cuban rector of the newly nationalized seminary. Lindsell expressed concern about the leftist politics emerging from the influential institution, saying, "MY IMMEDIATE CONCERNS have to do with the question of revolution and socialism. . . . It is not only unacceptable, it is also unbiblical. I am fully aware of the effort on the part of some Roman Catholics to synthesize Christianity and Marxism. . . . I have reason to believe that your Seminary is involved in this movement and that at least some members of your faculty have been or are involved."[44] At the time, Lindsell was editor of *Christianity Today*, the flagship evangelical magazine in the United States founded by Billy Graham. (Lindsell, a self-identified fundamentalist, was certainly not a newcomer to U.S.–Latin American relations; he held a PhD in the subject from New York University.) While the SBL had recently wrested institutional control from American missionary hands, it continued to operate with two competing paradigms: a rejection of American evangelical oversight *and* financial dependency on American evangelicals' donations.[45] Seen in a different light, the school required approval from conservative American evangelical households while fiercely guarding its institutional and theological turf.

Lindsell tapped his former colleague Carl F. H. Henry to investigate the SBL's perceived leftward shift. Henry, one of the chief architects behind fundamentalism's renovation as "neo-evangelicalism," was already planning a forty-day trip to eight Latin American countries that year. Thus, Henry agreed but privately would regret being brought into the mess. Costas arranged to host Henry during his SBL visit but was also unaware of Henry's covert, fact-finding mission from Lindsell. After Henry left, Costas wrote that Henry seemed pleased and approving. Yet, Henry's friendly demeanor masked private reservations. When Henry returned to the United States, he wrote a critical public report confirming Lindsell's fears, identifying Latin American faculty's affinity for socialism, theologies of liberation, rejection of missionary influence, and ambivalence toward the use of violence.[46] Henry also published his findings in the *Evangelical News Service*, assuring the news would reach the American evangelical faithful. Henry's phrase "violence as a Christian possibility for social change" was particularly damaging, shaking the foundation and fragile fundraising structure of the SBL.

Decolonization and the Global Evangelical Left

In the Cold War era, evangelical leaders from the United States sought to police the borders of global evangelicalism while suspending their hand over a considerable financial spigot. Latin American faculty thus responded swiftly. On September 26, 1973, Escobar already doubted that any intervention would help: "Unfortunately, clarifications in the press have a very limited effect and I am really concerned about the reactions that Henry's report might produce."[47] Despite his concern of effectiveness, Escobar responded firmly in a published letter to the editor of *Evangelical News Service*. In particular, he focused on clarifying violence for North American readers: "Words like 'violence' have to also be understood in the context of very unstable institutional life," Escobar argued. "There are countries in Latin America that have had had more coup d-etats [*sic*] than years of independent life. Probably many conservative Protestants who reject violence will applaud the violent overthrow of a democratically elected government in Chile," he wrote, echoing Padilla's *Christianity Today* article mentioned above. As for "affinity for socialism," Escobar equivocated. Rather than addressing it directly, he called for American evangelicals "to not impose on them, or any brother in Christ, a determined political viewpoint." Overall, a broader point needed to be made: "There is a growing weariness of police attitudes from persons and institutions in North America who have made themselves the watchdogs of orthodoxy around the world."[48] White evangelicals were blinded by conservative political loyalties and distance from a context of violence, he argued. Together, those on the evangelical left curated their own images of violence and formed their own narrative of acceptable responses—including violence as a possibility for social change. Decolonization hung in the air, an unmistakable odor for progressive Latin Americans.

The SBL faculty also responded to Henry's report defensively and directly in an open letter. Like Escobar, they spent considerable time challenging and clarifying any endorsement of violence: "The [Henry] report states, again without definition or interpretation, that some professors support 'violence as a Christian possibility for social change' without indicating whether it refers to approval of the American revolution, the assassination attempt on Adolph Hitler, American participation in World War II, the Viet Nam War, Castro-inspired guerrilla warfare, the torture of political prisoners in Brazil, the forceful overthrow of the Allende Government in Chile, law enforcement, or what have you." In other words, SBL faculty argued that American evangelicals *also* support the possibility of violence for social change; this was the core of white evangelical hypocrisy, they contended—the affinity for violence abroad but stability at home. Ultimately, this duplicity was driven by a contrasting context for political and social life: "We recognize that it is difficult for some of our white North American evangelical brethren who live in a relatively free, democratic, and wealthy society to understand how Christians living in Latin America might prefer one of the socialist parties here to the military dictatorships or feudal oligarchies of the political right." Proximity to unrest, or violence, was *generative*, and distance-blurring.[49]

In concluding, SBL faculty members turned up the temperature and made their argument personal for evangelicals like Billy Graham: "Many Latin American evangelicals have at least as much difficulty understanding how so many North American brethren can continue to support Nixon and believe in capitalism after the Watergate debacle." Once again, American evangelical loyalties to the Republican Party were on trial, and Latin Americans found them guilty of hypocrisy. The Latin American faculty put a final and unmistakably political stake in the ground: "We affirm the right of certain brethren to support socialist parties, just as we affirm the right of other professors to vote Republican." The evangelical status quo was shifting, and Americans had lost control of the narrative.[50]

Carl Henry, for his part, followed the protesting letters and articles closely but remained unmoved. He wrote to Escobar on October 15, 1973, arguing that Latin Americans had produced more heat than light: "The comments I made were not rebutted, but . . . an emotional public relations job was ventured."[51] Henry clashed with the Latin American evangelical left on both sides of the border in these crucial years. This hidden and overlooked controversy in the Global South signaled fractures and fissures under the surface of American evangelicalism.

Costas diagnosed Henry's critique as a festering colonial wound.[52] Costas was also deeply offended that Henry questioned Costas's ability to speak for Latin America because he was a Puerto Rican.[53] On the broader controversy, Costas wrote, "No sooner had we begun to take a few steps toward the development of a Latin American theology and a contextual missiological reflection than we began to feel the heat from North America, particularly the United States. Since I was one of the most vocal of the San José LAM [Latin America Mission]–related theologians, I began to be quoted—and misquoted." Costas blamed the language barrier and intentional mistranslation for some of the controversy: "The fact that our writings were mainly in Spanish complicated the matter further. Our so-called constituency was getting questionable reports from some missionary circles, often quoting us out of context. I decided to take the bull by the horns."[54] For Costas, taking the "bull by the horns" meant turning northward to an emerging and eclectic coalition of the evangelical left. In 1980, he left Latin America to join perhaps the most prominent and productive institution of the American evangelical left—Eastern University and its Eastern Baptist Theological Seminary in Philadelphia, where Ron Sider and Tony Campolo had taken leading roles. Sider had just released his best-selling *Rich Christians in an Age of Hunger* (1978), while Campolo had run for the U.S. House of Representatives as a Democrat two years earlier. Campolo later spearheaded the "Red Letter Christians" coalition with best-selling author and New Monastic activist Shane Claiborne. Costas joined these conversations, raising Latin American issues with the most influential leaders of the American evangelical left.

Diversifying Movement

The emerging American evangelical left watched these developments with marked anticipation. Some even participated south of the border. The American ethicist John Howard Yoder was living in Buenos Aires in the early 1970s, collaborating with the leading minds of the emerging Latin American evangelical left. In Buenos Aires, Yoder taught at the ecumenical seminary ISEDET (Instituto Superior Evangélico de Estudios Teológicos) while workshopping ideas in Spanish journals and local think tanks. British professor Andrew Kirk, who was Yoder's colleague at ISEDET in 1971, recalled controversy and protest surrounding Yoder's work. Kirk remembered that year as "the height of student radicalization." Denoting the importance of the issue, Kirk, Yoder, and José Míguez Bonino, the Argentine Methodist and leading liberation theologian, co-taught a seminar on the issue of violence. According to Kirk, Yoder "endured a huge amount of opposition because of his non-violent leanings," as "students at the time didn't see any problem with violence as long as it was righteous violence, the violence of the oppressed."[55] Yoder, at the time, was also writing *The Politics of Jesus*, a book that would solidify his place in evangelical intellectual life and the leadership of the American evangelical left. *Christianity Today* later named it the fifth most important Christian book of the twentieth century.[56] These conversations south of the border undoubtedly shaped the American Anabaptist, as well as leading minds in the Latin American evangelical left. Kirk reflected on Yoder's time in Latin America: "His Spanish was good, he was fairly fluent in Spanish, and you know his influence was quite long lasting. . . . He certainly influenced René [Padilla]."[57]

More recently, emerging church movement leader Brian McLaren, whom *Time* magazine called one of the "25 Most Influential Evangelicals in America," completed his groundbreaking book *Everything Must Change* while living with Padilla in Buenos Aires.[58] McLaren later credited Latin American evangelical ideas with providing an intellectual framework for the movement. In a 2013 interview, McLaren called Padilla's social Christianity "a new theological ecosystem" and the means through which McLaren rejected white evangelical theology.[59]

While key Americans traveled southward, influential Latin Americans migrated northward. Many global evangelicals from these conflict zones moved to the United States, as in the case of Costas and Escobar, participating in strategic collaboration with their U.S. mainland counterparts. Jim Wallis, perhaps the most prominent American progressive evangelical political activist, later credited migration and proximity to Latin American ideas with providing an intellectual framework for the movement. These ideas, in turn, shaped his own thinking: "René [Padilla] and Samuel [Escobar] talked for a long time [about social Christianity] and now it's coming to the Western world. I didn't have the words for it then, but I do now." He also spoke to the future of American churches and the continuing role of a diversifying evangelicalism: "Traditional liberalism is dying, mainline churches in the USA are dying, many won't be here in 25 years. I'm seeing among a new generation, an integral Gospel growing up all over the country—particularly among people of color."[60] These dissenting voices from Latin America gained a crucial hearing among progressive evangelicals in the United States. In doing so, they shared intellectual sources for constructive ends. The differences between thinkers and locations were immense. Yet, the theme of violence was magnetizing. In particular, they shared a stinging rebuke of American foreign policy from the Cold War to the present.

A shared critique of American foreign relations bridged cultural and theological differences. Wallis, for his part, used *Sojourners* magazine to highlight synergies across borders. In a clear example, he interviewed Samuel Escobar for its pages in 1976, focusing on the rise of theologies of liberation.[61] Together, they critiqued American evangelicalism for missing a prophetic voice from Latin America and honed in on the issue of hypocrisy over violence. Wallis wrote, "Obviously one of the reasons that North Americans don't understand liberation theology is that they have no conception of the reality of poverty and violence in Latin America."[62] He later expanded on what he saw as hypocrisy in white evangelicalism over the issue of violence: "Much evangelical theology is at one with liberation theology over questions of power and violence. Established evangelical theology points to the stand against violence by Latin American evangelicals and will play that off against the violence of liberation movements in Latin America while they themselves are clearly comfortable with the violence and the power of this society and in their own theology. That is a real contradiction, a real use of a position that they themselves don't want to be criticized by."[63] While Escobar initially hesitated, he later agreed: "Evangelicals often claim to have no ideology. But that's not true. Recent events are showing that. I think we are seeing it operative in such literature as Hal Lindsay's and Harold Lindsell's [apocalyptic literature]. They seem to be saying, 'We are for power and for the right of the powerful to exist and impose their rules.' This is a kind of theology of domination."[64] In the aftermath of the SBL controversy and Lausanne, Escobar certainly had in mind earlier clashes with white evangelical power brokers. Channeling this controversy, he argued that the issue was not *actually* violence but rather whether violence produced desired ends. This was the heart of American evangelical hypocrisy, and the patience of the Latin American evangelical left had grown thin.

As noted above, this impatient, global voice joined a growing chorus from the American evangelical left; publications such as *Sojourners* and the *Other Side* covered a plethora of Latin American topics, from the Cuban Revolution to the Salvadoran civil war and U.S.-backed military regimes in Brazil and Argentina.[65] Members of the American evangelical left, by adopting a fierce critique of American foreign policy, were often more sensitive to the voices and experiences of evangelicals of color and those living in former colonial contexts. As a result, they were more likely to hear and be shaped by these religious ideas emanating from the Global South. A significant marker of the evangelical left, then, has arisen as clear and complex: proximity to global violence or empathizing with a violent foreign context. In a broader sense, the Latinx and Latin American evangelical story of battling for inclusion—for themselves and their ideas—has been challenged, obscured, and even whitewashed. When seen through the lens of transnational intellectual history, the story of the evangelical left arises as one of global diffusion rather than local American decline.

Conclusion

After the Second World War, key architects of American evangelicalism clashed with an emerging evangelical left in the Global South. Violence and decolonization arose as a dividing line, carving coalitions and separating thinkers. For many evangelicals of color, violence—perhaps more than any other theme—exposed political hypocrisy in white American evangelicalism.

During the Cold War, white evangelicals preferred law and order at home but accepted, or even endorsed, violence abroad if it produced desired outcomes. For many, their endorsement of conservative U.S. foreign policy *hardened* even as their anti-communism *softened*. In the wake of anti-Protestant violence and Marxist revolutions, then, American evangelicals intervened—baptizing their work in a nascent "global war on Christians." A fresh perspective on U.S. culture wars emerges through a sustained lens of violence on both sides of the Rio Grande. Monolithic renderings and white monologues arise insufficient and incomplete alongside. The contemporary picture of American evangelicalism, then, comes into fuller view from a recast foundation and refocused development.

The legacy of evangelicals in the world is not primarily one of child sponsorship programs but rather one of global evangelicals producing their own answers and solutions—often with conflicting political loyalties. Evangelicals of color, in particular those with hybridized biographies, reversed a trajectory set by their forebears at the turn of the twentieth century. During this period, American evangelicals were accustomed to hearing stories of unjust governments, endemic poverty, and communist violence from missionary prayer letters or evangelical print media. Through these stories, they often longed for the faith of impoverished Africans, Asians, and Latin Americans who appeared undisturbed by the temptations of modernity. As Third World evangelicals shared their "testimonies," American evangelicals sought to "enchant" their own faith, to use the language of Melani McAlister, and to revive their own spirituality perceived to be tainted by a secularizing North.[66] Hearing these stories of injustice and persecution also allowed American evangelicals to identity with victims and embody their suffering. This complex contortion allowed white American evangelicals to wield enormous power in the public square while simultaneously decrying persecution by the broader American culture.[67] Perhaps more importantly, these global descriptions often arrived with a prescription: that American evangelicals should intervene or share material resources to save souls abroad.

Though widely overlooked, key members of the American evangelical left drew inspiration from the testimonies of their coreligionists and strategic gatherings in Latin America. Cutting across the grain of wider scholarship on American religion, these stories short-circuited victim identification as they linked their testimonies with a fierce rebuke; the "testimonies" of Latin American progressive evangelicals, then, presented a frustrating contradiction for conservatives and inspiration for progressives. Stories of persecution and violence, far from an invitation for intervention or rescue, arrived with a warning. In particular, descriptions of global violence often came prepackaged with a rebuke and a call for repentance from blind loyalty to conservative politics. Any discussion of the influence of the evangelical left in the Cold War era, then, requires grappling with the diversity of the coalition and raw ingredients exported from the Global South. As Latin American and Latinx theologians awoke to dependency on the North, they turned inward to their social context—one marked by endemic violence and unrest. On this construction site, they built the scaffolding of their political dissent, throwing into question long-standing evangelical loyalties. The interconnectedness of global evangelicalism, however, also blunted the influence of the evangelical left, as most forms of evangelical Christianity landed right of the political spectrum. This contributed to a sense among many that evangelical left ideas were either foreign to evangelicalism or a threat to Christian orthodoxy. The story, then, is not one of either victory or defeat but rather one of a complex diffusion of hybridized ideas.

Evangelicals of color cut across U.S. political divides that calcified during the Reagan years. In doing so, they challenged binaries and boundaries that many white American evangelicals took for granted. Within the "global war on Christians," then, white American evangelicals often preferred an imagined global community to a real, but dissenting, one. This represents a culmination of white Christian nativism, rather than a departure from our story, and an interpretive crux for many evangelicals of color regarding their identity and belonging within American evangelicalism.

Notes

1. Orlando Costas was appointed the dean and the Adoniram Judson Professor of Missiology at Andover Newton Theological School in Newton Centre, Massachusetts, in 1984. Andover Theological Seminary was founded in 1807 and merged with Newton Theological Institution in 1931. Andover Newton, which calls itself "the oldest graduate school in the country," closed it's historic campus in 2017 and is now based at Yale Divinity School in New Haven, Massachusetts.

2. Orlando Costas, "Choosing Life," *Judson Bulletin* 6, no. 2 (1987): 40–46. *Judson Bulletin* is a journal of the American Baptist Churches USA.

3. Costas, 40.

4. Costas, 42.

5. For more, see Melani McAlister, *The Kingdom of God Has No Borders: A Global History of American Evangelicals* (New York: Oxford University Press, 2018).

6. See the Voice of the Martyrs website, www.persecution.com.

7. In 2015, World Vision was the eleventh largest charity in the United States, with revenue of over $1 billion that year alone. David P. King, *God's Internationalists: World*

Vision and the Age of Evangelical Humanitarianism (Philadelphia: University of Pennsylvania Press, 2019), 32.

8. David C. Kirkpatrick, "C. René Padilla and the Origins of Integral Mission in Post-War Latin America," *Journal of Ecclesiastical History* 67, no. 1 (January 2016): 351–71.

9. Brian Stanley, *The Bible and the Flag: Protestant Missions and British Imperialism in the Nineteenth and Twentieth Centuries* (Leicester, Eng.: Apollos, 1990), 21–26.

10. See, for example, *Sojourners* 6, no. 8 (June 1977); and *Sojourners* 5, no. 6 (July/August 1976).

11. Marjorie Hyer, "Social and Political Activism Is Aim of Evangelical Group," *Washington Post*, November 30, 1973, D17, cited in David R. Swartz, *Moral Minority: The Evangelical Left in an Age of Conservatism* (Philadelphia: University of Pennsylvania Press, 2012), 1.

12. C. René Padilla, "The Church and Political Ambiguity," *Christianity Today*, July 26, 1974), 41–42. For more on this history, see Tanya Harmer, *Allende's Chile and the Inter-American Cold War* (Chapel Hill: University of North Carolina Press, 2011). Padilla noted in a 2013 interview that classified documents released decades later revealed this was true. René Padilla, interview and translation by author, Buenos Aires, September 10, 2013; Samuel Escobar, interview and translation by author, Valencia, October 22, 2013.

13. Padilla, "Church and Political Ambiguity," 41.

14. Padilla, 41.

15. "A Challenge from Evangelicals," *Time*, August 5, 1974.

16. "Challenge from Evangelicals."

17. C. René Padilla, "Evangelism and the World," in *Let the Earth Hear His Voice: International Congress on World Evangelization, Lausanne, Switzerland*, ed. J. D. Douglas (Minneapolis: World Wide Publications, 1975), 137.

18. Padilla, 137.

19. Samuel Escobar, "Evangelism and Man's Search for Freedom, Justice, and Fulfillment," in Douglas, *Let the Earth Hear His Voice*, 311, 305.

20. Escobar, 305.

21. Orlando Costas, "Depth in Evangelism—an Interpretation of 'In-Depth Evangelism' around the World," in Douglas, *Let the Earth Hear His Voice*, 675–97.

22. John Stott, "The Significance of Lausanne," *International Review of Mission* 64, no. 255 (July 1975): 289.

23. In 1980, Costas became the first Hispanic endowed chair at an evangelical institution in the United States as Thornley B. Wood Professor of Missiology at Eastern Baptist Theological Seminary in Pennsylvania (later renamed Palmer Theological Seminary).

24. Orlando Costas, *The Church and Its Mission: A Shattering Critique from the Third World* (Wheaton, IL: Tyndale House, 1974), 12.

25. See Costas, chap. 3.

26. Orlando Costas, "Teólogo en la encrucijada," in *Hacia una teología evangélica Latino-americana*, ed. C. René Padilla (San José: Editorial Caribe, 1984), 15.

27. Samuel Escobar, "Orlando Costas: In Memoriam," *Transformation* 5, no. 3 (1988): 1.

28. Costas, "Teólogo en la encrucijada," 15.

29. Aaron Griffith, "Jesus Christ Is the Only Control: Crime, Delinquency, and Evangelical Conversion in the Early Postwar Era," *Fides et Historia* 50, no. 1 (Winter/Spring 2018): 53.

30. Historian Aaron Griffith's analysis of Graham's sermons at crusades reveals that Graham focused on crime and juvenile delinquency with marked emphasis. Griffith, "Jesus Christ Is the Only Control," 42; Billy Graham, "What's Wrong with American Morals," *Washington Post*, May 12, 1957, cited in Griffith, 42. Griffith estimated that in his ninety sermons at Madison Square Garden, Graham brought up crime in over thirty of them.

31. Billy Graham, "Christian Attitude toward World Crisis," *Hour of Decision* radio program, February 4, 1968.

32. Costas, "Teólogo en la encrucijada," 15.

33. Costas, 17.

34. Costas, 17.

35. Nyack College is the flagship institution of the Christian and Missionary Alliance denomination.

36. Bob Jones embraced the fundamentalist moniker and would not have associated himself with Graham and Henry's neo-evangelical nomenclature.

37. Costas, *Church and Its Mission*, 12–13.

38. Costas, 12–13.

39. C. René Padilla, "My Theological Pilgrimage," *Journal of Latin American Theology* 4, no. 2 (2009): 127. See also René Padilla, interview by Paul Ericksen, March 12, 1987, Billy Graham Center Archives, collection 361, T1.

40. See Costas, *Church and Its Mission*, chap. 4.

41. This section expands on David C. Kirkpatrick, "Reforming Fundamentalism in Latin America: The Evangelical Left and Universidad Bíblica Latinoamericana," *Journal of the American Academy of Religion* 87, no. 1 (March 2019): 122–55.

42. Mike Berg, interview by Paul Ericksen, July 23, 2001, Billy Graham Center Archives, collection 473, T1-T8.

43. Orlando Costas, "En el camino hacia un seminario autóctono notas de viaje: 1970," 15, Seminario Bíblico Latinoamericano (SBL) Archives, San José, Costa Rica.

44. Harold Lindsell to Ruben Lores, 1972, recorded in H. L. Fenton to SBL Board of Trustees, October 10, 1973, SBL Archives.

45. See Allen Duble to Ruben Lores, July 29, 1972, letter in author's possession.

46. Carl F. H. Henry, "Evangelical Leader Reports on Religion in Latin America," August 21, 1973, René Padilla Papers, Buenos Aires, Argentina.

47. Escobar to Wagner, September 26, 1973, Samuel Escobar Papers, Valencia, Spain.

48. Samuel Escobar, "Evangelical Theology in Latin America," letter to the editor, October 6, 1973, Padilla Papers.

49. Escobar.

50. Escobar.

51. Henry to Escobar, October 15, 1973, Padilla Papers.

52. Costas saved much of his public comment on the SBL controversy for a 1982 book, *Christ outside the Gate*.

53. Carl F. H. Henry, *Confessions of a Theologian: An Autobiography* (Waco, TX: Word Books, 1986), 346.

54. Orlando Costas, *Christ outside the Gate*, xiii, cited in Samuel Escobar, "The Legacy of Orlando Costas." *International Bulletin of Mission Research* 25, no. 2 (2001): 52.

55. Andrew Kirk, Skype interview by author, December 1, 2014.

56. John Howard Yoder, *The Politics of Jesus* (Grand Rapids, MI: Eerdmans, 1972); "Books of the Century," *Christianity Today*, April 24, 2000.

57. Andrew Kirk, Skype interview by author, December 1, 2014.

58. "The 25 Most Influential Evangelicals in America," *Time*, January 20, 2005.

59. Brian McLaren, Skype interview by author, November 20, 2014.

60. McLaren, Skype interview; Jim Wallis, public lecture and question and answer session at St. John's Episcopal Church, Edinburgh, Scotland, August 29, 2013.

61. Jim Wallis, "Interview with Samuel Escobar," *Sojourners* 5, no. 7 (September 1976): 16.

62. Wallis, 16.

63. Wallis, 18.

64. Wallis, 18.

65. For El Salvador and jails, see *Sojourners* 6, no. 8 (1977); for torture, see *Sojourners* 5, no. 6. (July/August 1976); for Argentina, see *Sojourners* 7, no. 9 (September 1978).

66. McAlister, *Kingdom of God Has No Borders*, 290.

67. This is the wider argument of new works such as John Corrigan, *Religious Intolerance, America, and the World: A History of Forgetting and Remembering* (Chicago: University of Chicago Press, 2020); and McAlister, *Kingdom of God Has No Borders*.

CHAPTER NINE

Evangelical Empire

Christian Nationalism and U.S. Foreign Policy in a Postcolonial World

Lauren F. Turek

In 1983, in the midst of the Contra war in Nicaragua and an unfolding geno-cide in Guatemala, the evangelical magazine *Christianity Today* published an editorial titled "The Central American Powder Keg: How Can Christians Keep It from Exploding?" In the piece, *Christianity Today* editor and theologian Kenneth Kantzer urged readers to understand the root causes of unrest in the region, including poverty, rampant human rights abuses, and economic injustice, while also cautioning against "Marxist" solutions to those prob-lems.[1] Although he noted that "we must not seek to treat the problem of Central America as merely a sinister communist plot" and even applauded leftist governments for bringing land reform and some measure of justice to their people, he nonetheless raised the alarm about revolutionary move-ments in the region, which he viewed as inherently duplicitous, oppressive, and undemocratic.[2] In laying out his argument for evangelical attention to these issues, Kantzer depicted the conflicts in Central America as pitched battles for freedom against the forces of communist tyranny and oppression. Yet Kantzer did not just address political freedom in Central America. He also paid particular attention to advancing the cause of *spiritual* freedom.

Indeed, Kantzer made the case that evangelicals should concern themselves with social and political unrest in Central America both because of the growth of the evangelical population in Guatemala, Nicaragua, El Salvador, Honduras, and Costa Rica and because of the suffering there. He called on evangelicals in the United States to "covenant to pray" for the people and pastors of Central America who "witness faithfully to the gospel" despite the risk they faced from "guerilla insurgents" as well as government agents.[3] In his opening salvo to his readers, he stressed that "Christians see, too, that their own freedom to bring the gospel to people in need cannot be taken for granted. They must battle for freedom for all if they wish to preserve freedom to witness to the redemption Christ alone can give."[4] Through such assertions, he connected the "right" to evangelize with broader concepts of freedom and U.S. foreign policy objectives, including the Cold War aims of promoting democratic capitalism and battling the spread of communism abroad. Drawing attention to issues related to Christian witness and injustice in other countries also underscored ongoing tensions within evangelical circles about the proper balance between evangelism and social action. In addition to informing his readers about strife, affliction, and threats to Christian life in other countries, Kantzer also sought to mobilize them to take political action. As such, he implored evangelicals to support the Reagan administration and what he described as its stated policy of seeking "peace with justice" in Central America.

Kantzer's piece, written for a U.S. audience about suffering and injustice occurring abroad—suffering and injustice that, as he well noted, the United States had abetted through its foreign policy priorities—reveals the power and underlying motivations of U.S. evangelical foreign policy engagement during the Reagan era. In the late 1970s and early 1980s, politically conservative evangelicals became an increasingly powerful foreign policy constituency, one that helped to shape the role of the United States in the world as it negotiated the vicissitudes of the late Cold War and an era of rising globalization and decolonization.[5] Evangelicals involved in missionary and humanitarian activity abroad, particularly those working in regions that the White House deemed strategically important, provided information to policy makers as well as to their fellow believers in the United States about the situation on the ground. This information, coupled with core Christian beliefs, including the biblical mandate for global evangelism, shaped the policy perspectives and lobbying agenda of evangelicals in the United States. The concerns that this group articulated in Christian media, fundraising and advocacy letters, and congressional testimony often (though not always) overlapped with and complemented those of the Reagan administration. As such, evangelical leaders formed a base of grassroots conservative advocacy on a range of policy issues, including trade, foreign aid, and military interventions in Central America, during the 1980s.

A sense of urgency surrounding the missionary imperative informed evangelical foreign policy objectives and compelled evangelicals to seek greater influence in foreign affairs in this era. This is not to say that they were not involved in or concerned with foreign relations issues earlier. Evangelicals and other politically conservative Christians had long evinced concern about the threat that communism and the expansion of the "godless" Soviet Union posed to the Christian faith.[6] Furthermore, even in the nineteenth century, earlier generations of Protestants had pushed the U.S. government to ensure religious freedom for missionaries in South and Central America.[7] Yet, as evangelical engagement in policy advocacy matured and grew more effective during the 1970s and 1980s, evangelicals became increasingly helpful to the Reagan administration as it worked to implement its vision for exporting U.S. influence and ideology abroad. Although evangelical political pressure was never the sole causal factor in foreign policy making, conservative Christian lobbying and notions of Christian nationalism and internationalism played into congressional debates, public opinion, and presidential strategy regarding U.S. foreign relations and national security. The political and cultural power that the religious right had amassed by the early 1980s ensured that even when policy makers did not share specific evangelical beliefs, they recognized the opportunity to make common cause with evangelical leaders to achieve their desired policy ends.[8] In this way, evangelicals integrated themselves into the foreign policy–making process and contributed to decisions of great consequence in international relations.

This chapter will explore these dynamics through a case study of U.S. evangelical involvement in building congressional and public support for the Reagan administration's policies toward Nicaragua during the Contra war. After discussing the religious beliefs that shaped how evangelicals understood their Christian responsibility to engage with the world, it will explain how that viewpoint translated into an evangelical vision for U.S. foreign relations and human rights. A chief part of that vision involved the promotion of religious liberty and evangelism abroad. During the Contra war, evangelicals collaborated with White House officials to frame U.S. support for repressive and counterrevolutionary forces using the language of human rights and religious liberty. Reagan faced tremendous (and deserved) push-back for his record on human rights from liberal members of Congress. Congressional resistance hindered the administration's ability to pursue its desired policy aims—in this case shoring up security in the Western Hemisphere by removing the perceived threat that leftist governments posed to U.S. interests and predominance in Latin America and the Caribbean. Adopting the limited human rights ethos that evangelicals articulated—a human rights perspective that privileged religious liberty as the foundational human right and condemned regimes that persecuted Christians—gave the Reagan administration a useful moral rhetoric to use to counter congressional activism against the administration's support for brutal military dictatorships. Examining evangelical political activism in a global context helps us to better understand the power of religious belief to shape foreign policy opinion as well as the role that motivated grassroots non-state actors have played in influencing policy at the state and international level.

For evangelicals in the 1970s and 1980s, as in decades (indeed centuries) past, the Great Commission—the scriptural mandate to "go into all the world and proclaim the good news to the whole creation" in order to "make disciples of all nations"—was a core tenet of faith as well as the basis for their internationalism.[9] Evangelical Christians believed earnestly that by following this biblical command to share the gospel throughout the world, they offered all of mankind the opportunity to receive eternal salvation through faith in Jesus Christ. Since billions of people had not heard the "good news" though, either because they lived in remote parts of the world or under the thrall of governments perceived as hostile to Christianity, evangelicals felt great pressure to increase their missionary work and make it more effective.[10] Yet the contours of national and international politics, economics, and social relations delimited the means by which evangelicals carried out these efforts to fulfill the Great Commission.

By the 1970s, the post–World War II movements for self-determination and decolonization in the Global South, with their attendant critiques of colonialism and imperialism, had led both nationalist and indigenous Christian leaders to inveigh against Western missionary work. This meant that U.S. evangelicals seeking to spread the gospel in Latin America, Africa, Asia, and the Middle East faced significant resistance, particularly from indigenous Christians in these regions, and had to adapt their missionary strategies accordingly.[11] Decolonization had also quite literally redrawn the geopolitical map. Political leaders in the United States and the Soviet Union viewed the decolonized world through the prism of their superpower rivalry. The advent of strategic parity had ushered in a period of détente and Cold War stalemate yet had not dampened the fierce competition to win allies and ideological influence throughout the Global South.[12] Furthermore, the reemergence of an international human rights movement had opened up new avenues for fighting the Cold War, as it inspired grassroots activism and dissidence movements as well as novel legal and rhetorical means for the superpowers to use against each other.[13] Evangelicals, eager to spread the gospel abroad, used human rights language to condemn regimes that persecuted Christians and limited evangelism.[14] This approach proved effective in shaping public opinion about the issue of international religious liberty as well as in encouraging Congress to restrict trade and foreign aid to regimes deemed guilty of religious persecution, especially communist governments. It also opened space to defend missionary work (Western as well as indigenous) as contributing to the spread of human rights more broadly.

Evangelical foreign policy activists developed this rhetorical strategy through their campaigns on behalf of persecuted Christians in the Soviet bloc during the 1970s. By the 1980s, they had established a cogent conservative human rights perspective, which they could apply to a number of foreign policy issues beyond fighting communism.[15] Evangelical opinion leaders, such as Robert P. Dugan Jr. of the National Association of Evangelicals, made clear in editorials as well as in congressional testimony that they believed that freedom of conscience was the primary human right. Further, in conceptualizing the freedom of conscience, they characterized their ability to practice their faith by evangelizing the unreached and also the freedom of people abroad to hear evangelicals share the Christian gospel as core components of that fundamental human right.[16] This conceptualization proved quite powerful. During the Reagan era, this merger of human rights language with core American values such as religious freedom, individual civil liberties, and democratic governance helped conservative policy makers overcome challenges to their foreign policy agenda from liberal opponents in Congress.

In his campaign for the presidency as well as during his time in office, Reagan adopted this religious rhetoric when discussing his foreign policy agenda. He infused his calls to abandon détente and pursue a more forceful approach to dealing with the Soviet Union with religiously inflected human rights language. During the 1980 presidential campaign, Reagan attacked incumbent Jimmy Carter's human rights policies for targeting violations in friendly authoritarian regimes while ignoring religious persecution and other abuses in totalitarian states.[17] Reagan pledged to upend this approach, highlighting religious liberty in the communist world as a matter of paramount concern.[18] Part of his plan for combating global totalitarianism involved shoring up security in the Western Hemisphere by removing the perceived threat that leftist governments posed to U.S. interests and predominance in Latin America and the Caribbean.[19] These aims aligned neatly with evangelical policy goals; greater religious liberty abroad would presumably ease hostility toward and restrictions on evangelistic activities. As noted earlier, the Contra war in Nicaragua provides an example of how the strands of evangelical foreign policy lobbying, missionary objectives, and human rights language wove together with Reagan's strategic vision to shape U.S. extraterritorial interventions during his time in office.[20]

When the Frente Sandinista de Liberación Nacional (FSLN) overthrew the reviled dictator Anastasio Somoza DeBayle in July 1979 and established a revolutionary government, Nicaragua became a major flashpoint in the Cold War between the United States and the Soviet Union. U.S. leaders perceived the Nicaraguan revolution as evidence of Soviet and Cuban interference in Central America. Eager to counter communist incursions in the region, Ronald Reagan committed his administration to providing military aid to the nascent anti-Sandinista counterrevolutionary movement, known as the Contras, when he took office in 1981.[21] The ensuing war between the U.S.-backed Contras and the Sandinistas lasted until 1988. Tens of thousands of Nicaraguans died in the fighting, and many more suffered atrocities ranging from torture, maiming, and rape to forcible relocation and the loss of their property. Christian groups within Nicaragua and the United States involved themselves in the conflict; Catholics and evangelicals in both countries found themselves divided over which side to support, and regardless of denomination or nationality, supporters of both the Contras and the Sandinistas claimed the mantle of Christianity and country.[22] For this reason, Christian nationalist rhetoric infused the debate in the United States and in Nicaragua over the war and proved particularly resonant with the public and with legislators in discussions about religious persecution and U.S. military aid for the Contra forces.

At the outset of Reagan's first term in office, though, members of the State Department and Reagan's national security advisors were divided over how to best respond to the Nicaraguan revolution.[23] During a meeting of the National Security Council on November 16, 1981, the Reagan administration

Christian Nationalism and U.S. Foreign Policy

worked to come to an agreement on an appropriate policy response. Through these discussions, the president and the National Security Council developed National Security Decision Directive 17 (NSDD 17), which Reagan signed on January 4, 1982. NSDD 17 affirmed U.S. "support for those nations which embrace the principles of democracy and freedom for their people" and as such declared that the Reagan administration would "support democratic forces in Nicaragua" as well as lend assistance to anti-insurgency groups throughout Central America.[24] In April 1981, the Reagan administration had suspended U.S. economic assistance to Nicaragua and, later that year, authorized the CIA to train and arm the Contras, a group of counterrevolutionaries that included former members of Somoza's National Guard. As historian David Painter notes, although Reagan claimed that the goal of these polices was to halt Sandinista aid to a growing leftist insurgency in El Salvador, "[their] main objective quickly became the overthrow of the Nicaraguan government."[25] By the time that Reagan signed NSDD 17 in 1982, Contra forces had begun to launch attacks in Nicaragua, leading the Sandinistas to seek support from the Soviet Union and Cuba to shore up their defenses and to declare an official state of emergency.

In addition to laying the groundwork for the covert counterinsurgency war against the Sandinistas, NSDD 17 also set the stage for a pro-Contra public relations campaign in the United States, a campaign that would ultimately draw heavily on evangelical activism and human rights rhetoric. Reflecting Reagan administration concern about congressional and public opinion against lending support to counterrevolutionary groups, NSDD 17 placed the National Security Council's plan to "create a public information task force to inform the public and Congress of the critical situation in the area" first in its enumerated list of decisions.[26] The passage of the first Boland Amendment in December 1982, which prohibited the use of congressionally appropriated funds to "furnish military equipment, military training or advice, or other support for military activities . . . for the purpose of overthrowing the government of Nicaragua," bore out the Reagan administration's concerns about congressional resistance to its policy agenda.[27] When Congress passed a second Boland Amendment in late 1983 prohibiting "covert assistance for military operations in Nicaragua" and then banned aid for military and paramilitary operations in Nicaragua entirely in 1984, the administration launched a concerted effort to bring congressional and public opinion around to supporting the Contras.[28]

Allegations that the Sandinistas violated the human rights of their political opponents and persecuted nonrevolutionary Christians formed the centerpiece of White House outreach on behalf of the Contras. Faith Ryan Whittlesey, the director of the Office of Public Liaison, explicitly discussed this strategy to mobilize public opinion as she and her staff considered how to best communicate the president's aims in Central America. Department memoranda called for a strategy that would "trigger humanitarian emotions" by sharing the details of "the utter inhumanity and unspeakable cruelties of Marxist guerillas in Central America."[29] They also incorporated religious themes, such as emphasizing the incompatibility of revolutionary activities and Christianity.[30] The Office of Public Liaison noted that "nongovernment support must be recruited and prepositioned for activation" by inviting key groups to the White House for foreign policy seminars and following up with regular policy updates, which would provide them with information to incorporate into letter-writing and lobbying campaigns.[31]

In May 1983, the Office of Public Liaison began holding weekly briefings on U.S.–Central American relations for religious leaders.[32] For a seminar on religious persecution in Nicaragua, Whittlesey invited a number of "eye-witnesses," including a self-described Pentecostal preacher and Sandinista torture victim named Prudencio de Jesus Baltodano, to share their experiences. In this way, the department hoped to elicit the desired "humanitarian emotions" from the religious leaders in attendance; in line with the argument that John Corrigan advanced in his chapter in this volume, this affective response helped to stir empathy for persecuted Christians abroad, which in turn created support for the Reagan administration's policy aims.[33] When introducing the speakers, Whittlesey argued that "the Sandinista leadership is following a two-track policy of persecution and subversion" designed to weaken conservative Christian churches, especially Protestant denominations, while cultivating ties with more sympathetic churches.[34] Such messaging struck at the heart of the missionary agenda, as it suggested the introduction of barriers to spreading the evangelical gospel in Central America. She also stated that "believers have been harassed, arrested, and even tortured" by the Sandinistas, allegations that her guest speakers elaborated on in detail.[35] Baltodano, for example, described Sandinistas tying him to a tree, torturing him, cutting his ears off, and leaving him for dead because they suspected him of supporting the Contras.[36] Whittlesey noted that his testimony "unfailingly effect[ed] a dramatic change in the attitude in the audience."[37] For evangelical audience members, it made manifest the peril that indigenous evangelists faced in their efforts to share the "good news" with their compatriots and thus the broader threat the Sandinistas posed to the achievement of the Great Commission.

Christian Nationalism and U.S. Foreign Policy

Evangelical organizations in the United States, already publishing actively about religious persecution throughout the world and in Central America, amplified these messages from the Reagan White House. Christian publications and news services that focused on religious freedom, such as *Jesus to the Communist World* and the Open Doors News Service, shared regular updates with their readers about evangelicals who faced arrest and torture at the hands of the Sandinistas.[38] *Christianity Today* treated the Sandinistas' early promises of religious freedom skeptically and began reporting more regularly about persecution against evangelicals as the situation in Nicaragua deteriorated, particularly after the government there declared a state of emergency in 1982.[39] The Institute on Religion and Democracy and other Christian organizations incorporated reports about Sandinista attacks on religious liberty into their fundraising campaigns.[40] In all cases, these groups conveyed the impression that the Sandinistas engaged in widespread yet selective religious repression, targeting only those "true" Christians who rejected Marxism and the FSLN. In this way, they attacked the many Nicaraguan Protestants and Catholics who sought revolutionary change and supported the Sandinista government while promoting an American Christian nationalist ideology rooted in democratic and liberal capitalist principles. Furthermore, by casting the Sandinistas as the sole perpetrators of religious persecution, they framed the conflict in Nicaragua as a battle to defend global religious freedom, with the Contras and their U.S. supporters acting as champions of human rights.

Yet despite the allegations that the Reagan administration and its religious surrogates made about Sandinista religious persecution, U.S.-backed Contra forces committed extensive and appalling human rights abuses, which opponents of Reagan's policies publicized extensively.[41] Politically progressive and moderate Catholics, mainline Protestants, and numbers of evangelicals spoke out against the war in Nicaragua through pamphlets, newspaper editorials, letter-writing campaigns to their representatives, and testimony before Congress. These religious leaders focused on the Contras' poor human rights record and questioned the Reagan administration's foreign policy objectives in Central America. One brochure from the Inter-Religious Task Force, an interdenominational activist organization, compiled statements from a wide range of religious leaders who argued that the firsthand experiences of their missionaries and affiliated churches in Nicaragua made clear "that poverty, oppression and injustice are the primary causes of unrest in the region," not "Soviet and Cuban-directed agitation and aggression," as the Reagan administration claimed.[42] The prominent evangelical social justice activist Jim Wallis also drew on firsthand experience in a searing piece in *Sojourners* about his trip to Nicaragua with the anti-Contra organization Witness for Peace, in which he recounted, "I will not easily forget another mother who tearfully told us how her 13-year-old daughter was decapitated by a *contra* mortar, or the Baptist pastor who could not understand the brutality of the *contras* who hacked to death with machetes a whole group of evangelical teenagers who were simply teaching campesinos how to read. . . . Every Witness for Peace volunteer can tell stories of terror, torture, rape, pillage, and murder carried out by the *contras*."[43] Such essays aimed to counter the narratives of Sandinista brutality against Christians that conservative organizations shared, seeking to undermine their portrayal of the Contras as defenders of religious liberty and American political values.

The fierce disagreements among and within Christian denominations over U.S. policy in Nicaragua greatly intensified the debates in Congress over Reagan administration requests for Contra funding in 1985 and 1986. As historian Theresa Keeley has shown, the testimony of Catholic anti-Contra activists, including Maryknoll Sisters and Jesuit priests, played a significant role in shaping congressional attitudes against Contra funding, yet also pushed the Reagan administration to recruit conservative Catholic allies to lend moral support to his cause.[44] These allies, along with conservative Protestant and evangelical activists, proved effective at softening congressional resistance, particularly after FSLN leader Daniel Ortega sought direct aid from the Soviet Union and extended the state of emergency, further restricting civil liberties, which bolstered Contra supporters' negative claims about the Sandinistas.[45] Evangelical and Christian fundamentalist media personalities such as Jerry Falwell and Pat Robertson, whom the White House invited to receive special briefings from Oliver North on U.S.-Nicaraguan relations, urged their followers to contact Congress in advance of pending votes on Contra funding.[46] The Reagan administration's public relations efforts to undermine its liberal adversaries bore fruit in June 1985, when Congress passed a measure to extend humanitarian aid to the Contras. This aid did not include any funds for military purposes, however, so the White House shifted its religious outreach and lobbying efforts into high gear in advance of a March 1986 congressional vote over military funding.

Christian nationalist and evangelical human rights rhetoric took center stage in this campaign as Reagan pressured Congress to extend an additional $100 million in aid to Contra forces, most of it expressly intended for military purposes. On March 5, 1986, President Reagan sat down in the White House library to film a five-minute video message about the Contra war in Nicaragua. The message, recorded specifically for broadcast on Christian television and radio programs, was part of a larger Reagan administration effort to wrangle military funding from Congress to support the Contras, the U.S.-backed counterrevolutionary forces fighting to oust the FSLN from power. Reagan used explicitly Christian language to condemn the Sandinistas, accusing them of infringing on religious liberty in Nicaragua and suggesting that their social reforms threatened liberal democratic capitalism in the Western Hemisphere. He argued that, in a time when freedom and democracy had "flashed out like a great astonishing light" elsewhere in the world, it was "nothing less than a sin to see Central America fall to darkness." In addition to using the language of sin to describe the threat of communism, the speech referenced Matthew 4:16 ("The people which sat in darkness saw great light") to identify democracy as the force of national salvation. Reiterating this theme, Reagan told his Christian audience that "if we work together . . . we can save Central America."[47] He ended the video by asking viewers to contact their representatives and urge them to provide military funding for the Contras. The core message was clear: politically conservative Christians—especially evangelicals—had a key role to play in advancing U.S. national security objectives and extending the reach of American power.[48]

This video message blended national and religious ideals as Reagan castigated Sandinista restrictions on civil liberties, particularly religious freedom, and connected the Christian faith with American democracy and anti-communism explicitly. These media pieces mobilized evangelical Christians, many of whom had already donated money directly to the Contras through the fundraising campaigns that Pat Robertson coordinated through his aid organization Operation Blessing and advertised on his television show, *The 700 Club*.[49] In addition to the aforementioned video, Reagan also recorded a sixty-second audio message that went out to over 1,500 Christian radio stations across the country.[50] These messages included instructions for listeners to call a 1-800 number, which would connect them with the contact information for their congressional representatives so that viewers and listeners could call or write letters urging them to support the president's policies.[51] These constituent letters and phone calls poured in to Congress, providing additional moral backing to legislators who supported White House policy on Central America.

Reagan's approach of conflating Sandinista victory with "sin" and "darkness" in contrast to American democracy and freedom also proved effective in the congressional debate that followed. Senators and representatives who supported the president's foreign policy agenda in Nicaragua reiterated these points, sharing details on Sandinista persecution of Christians; some even participated in hearings on the threats that communism and liberation theology posed to the survival of the church in Central America.[52] Opponents of the military aid measure also appealed to religious themes, marshaling evidence of Contra human rights violations and religious persecution and incorporating statements and testimony from anti-Contra Catholic and Protestant leaders into the proceedings.[53] In the end though, the Contra supporters edged out their opponents. Congress approved the $100 million spending measure.

This military support for the Contras did not end the religious controversy over the conflict in Nicaragua, of course, which continued throughout the rest of the Contra war and only intensified as the details of the Iran-Contra scandal emerged. Still, in 1987, evangelical news sources reported that "the Sandinista government has recently adopted a more relaxed approach toward the Church and that evangelistic activities within the country are at an all-time high."[54] Yet they also noted that the National Association of Evangelicals had announced its intention to participate in a worldwide prayer campaign to protest Sandinista religious repression, including the closure of religious radio stations and limitations on church publications, which it argued made evangelism "extremely difficult."[55] Conflicting reports about the extent of ongoing Sandinista persecution abounded.

The Contra war led to widespread economic and social dislocation in Nicaragua, not to mention the deaths of tens of thousands of people. In 1987, the Sandinistas signed the Esquipulas Peace Agreement, in which they and the other Central American leaders committed to pursue economic cooperation, democratic reforms, and conflict resolution. By January 1988, the Sandinistas had ended the six-year-long state of emergency, a move that conservative Christians in the United States and Nicaragua welcomed, though with some skepticism.[56] The democratic elections that followed in 1990 ousted the Sandinistas from power, but the damage from the war was extensive.[57] U.S. efforts to bring about the overthrow of the Nicaraguan government through its support for the Contras was both destabilizing and deadly. Despite the rhetoric of democracy and freedom that evangelical activism helped propagate, the intervention revealed the imperial character of U.S. national security and power projection in the hemisphere.

Yet evangelicals still celebrated the spread of Christianity in post-conflict Nicaragua. *Christianity Today* reported on Christian life in Nicaragua in the early 1990s, noting that Violeta Chamorro—leader of the National Opposition Union (the UNO or Unión Nacional Opositora) who defeated Daniel

Ortega in the 1990 election—had promised Nicaraguan evangelical pastors that she would protect their religious liberty and right to worship.[58] The proportion of evangelicals in Nicaragua had grown from less than 8 percent in 1978 to over 20 percent by 1991, making them an increasingly "strong political electoral group" in the country.[59] Evangelistic outreach seemed to be paying escalating dividends. A 1990 *Christianity Today* article shared statistics about what it described as "border[ing] on the spectacular" church growth in the war-torn country, noting that "more than 20,000 people made first-time professions of faith in Christ [in 1989] during a nationwide outreach coordinated by the Nicaraguan Institute of Evangelism-in-Depth."[60] Evangelical organizations such as the National Council of Evangelical Pastors of Nicaragua claimed that this remarkable church growth, spurred on by evangelism, along with the concomitant rise in evangelical influence in Nicaragua would hold the Roman Catholic Chamorro to her pledge to support religious freedom.[61] The linkages between human rights, religious freedom, democratic capitalism, and the evangelical missionary imperative seemed clear to U.S. evangelicals.

Nor was the Contra war the only U.S. intervention into another sovereign state that involved this merger of evangelical aims, human rights language, and notions of democracy promotion. During the Reagan administration, many of the same evangelical leaders who contributed to the crusade to fund the Contras also lent support to U.S.-backed regimes in Guatemala, El Salvador, Honduras, South Africa, Angola, and Lebanon.[62] They used similar language and public advocacy strategies (though different foreign policy instruments) to encourage dissident and anti-communist movements in the Soviet bloc during this time as well. Evangelical foreign policy activism, rooted in a commitment to creating a world that would be open to evangelism, had tangible, significant effects on international relations during the Reagan era. Although evangelical lobbying was just one of many factors that shaped U.S. policy, it nonetheless contributed to the Reagan administration's ability to implement its agenda—including its capacity to gain congressional approval for military spending for violent counterrevolutionary groups operating in other countries.[63]

Even though Reagan was not actively seeking to foster the Great Commission through his foreign policy, conservative evangelical activists saw an opportunity to work toward their biblical mandate for global evangelism through his stated objectives for international relations. They provided the rhetorical tools and the active constituency necessary for the Reagan administration to achieve its ends. In so doing, evangelicals, with their commitment to global evangelism and anti-communism, along with their conservative and limited human rights vision, played a small yet still consequential role in the monumental geopolitical changes that unfolded in the last decade of the Cold War.

Notes

1. Kenneth S. Kantzer, "The Central American Powder Keg: How Can Christians Keep It from Exploding?," *Christianity Today*, July 15, 1983, 12–13.

2. Kantzer, 13.

3. Kantzer, 13.

4. Kantzer, 12.

5. This is the history that I trace in my book. See Lauren Frances Turek, *To Bring the Good News to All Nations: Evangelical Influence on Human Rights and U.S. Foreign Relations* (Ithaca, NY: Cornell University Press, 2020).

6. Turek, 73–75.

7. John Corrigan, *Religious Intolerance, America, and the World: A History of Forgetting and Remembering* (Chicago: University of Chicago Press, 2020), 125–38.

8. The religious right played an important role in electing Reagan to the presidency and served as a crucial constituency during his time in office (though his policy decisions did not always align with conservative Christians' political aims). Evangelicals constituted an important population within the religious right, which also included fundamentalist Christians as well as conservative Catholics and Protestants of other denominations. Politically conservative evangelicals exerted an influence on U.S. foreign policy, particularly during the late 1970s and 1980s, and are thus the focus of this chapter and my other work on this topic. That said, evangelicals in the United States are not and were never monolithic in their political views. Over the course of the 1970s, white evangelicals began to coalesce into a reliably Republican voting bloc, but there remained a small yet important evangelical left that, along with many African American and Latinx evangelicals, tended to vote for Democratic candidates. For some of the many excellent works on the rise of the religious right and the role of evangelicals within it in American politics and foreign policy, see William C. Martin, *With God on Our Side: The Rise of the Religious Right in America* (New York: Broadway Books, 1996); Lisa McGirr, *Suburban Warriors: The Origins of the New American Right* (Princeton, NJ: Princeton University Press, 2001); Daniel K. Williams, *God's Own Party: The Making of the Christian Right* (New York: Oxford University Press, 2010); Darren Dochuk, *From Bible Belt to Sunbelt: Plain-Folk Religion, Grassroots Politics, and the Rise of Evangelical Conservatism* (New York: W. W. Norton, 2011); Axel R. Schäfer, *Countercultural Conservatives: American Evangelism from the Postwar Revival to the New Christian Right* (Madison: University of Wisconsin Press, 2011); and Angela M. Lahr, *Millennial Dreams and Apocalyptic Nightmares: The Cold War Origins of Political Evangelicalism* (New York: Oxford University Press, 2007).

9. Mark 16:15 (New Revised Standard Version) and Matthew 28:19 (NRSV), the "Great Commission."

10. One of the ways this manifested was through the proliferation of global conferences on evangelism in the late 1960s and early 1970s, including the World Congress

on Evangelism in 1966, Key '73, and the International Congress on World Evangelism in 1974, as well as through the myriad publications on the "crisis in missions." For some examples of the debates over this perceived crisis, see Günter Linnenbrink, "Witness and Service in the Mission of the Church," *International Review of Mission* 54, no. 216 (October 1965): 428–36; Harold Lindsell, "A Rejoinder," *International Review of Mission* 54, no. 216 (October 1965): 437–40; and Donald McGavran, "Wrong Strategy: The Real Crisis in Missions," *International Review of Mission* 54, no. 216 (October 1965): 451–61. See also Kaj Baago, "The Post-colonial Crisis of Missions," *International Review of Mission* 55, no. 219 (July 1966): 322–32. See also the published proceedings of the International Congress on World Evangelism, J. D. Douglas, ed., *Let the Earth Hear His Voice: International Congress on World Evangelization, Lausanne, Switzerland* Official Reference Volume (Minneapolis: World Wide Publications, 1975).

11. An issue that exploded in global evangelical discourse in the 1970s and especially at the International Congress on World Evangelism. See Melani McAlister, *The Kingdom of God Has No Borders: A Global History of American Evangelicals* (Oxford: Oxford University Press, 2018); Al Tizon, *Transformation after Lausanne: Radical Evangelical Mission in Global-Local Perspective* (Eugene, OR: Wipf and Stock, 2008), 54–58; and Dana Robert, "The Great Commission in an Age of Globalization," in *The Antioch Agenda: The Restorative Church at the Margins; Celebrating the Life and Work of Orlando Costas*, ed. D. Jeyaraj, R. Pazmino, and R. Petersen (New Delhi: Indian Society for the Promotion of Christian Knowledge, 2007).

12. As evidenced by the many Soviet and American interventions during this era in Southeast Asia, the Middle East, Africa, and Latin America. For background on détente, strategic parity, and the Cold War competition in the Global South, see Odd Arne Westad, *The Global Cold War: Third World Interventions and the Making of Our Times* (Cambridge: Cambridge University Press, 2005); Raymond L. Garthoff, *Détente and Confrontation: American-Soviet Relations from Nixon to Reagan* (Washington, DC: Brookings Institute, 1985), 25–36; Robert S. Litwak, *Détente and the Nixon Doctrine: American Foreign Policy and the Pursuit of Stability, 1969–1976* (Cambridge: Cambridge University Press, 1984), 82; and Keith L. Nelson, *The Making of Détente: Soviet-American Relations in the Shadow of Vietnam* (Baltimore, MD: Johns Hopkins University Press, 1995), 71, 54–55.

13. On the rise of the international human rights movement and how it shaped the late Cold War, see Sarah Snyder, *Human Rights Activism and the End of the Cold War: A Transnational History of the Helsinki Network* (Cambridge: Cambridge University Press, 2011); and Sarah Snyder, "The Rise of the Helsinki Network: 'A Sort of Lifeline' for Eastern Europe," in *Perforating the Iron Curtain: European Détente, Transatlantic Relations, and the Cold War, 1965–1985*, ed. Poul Villaume and Odd Arne Westad (Copenhagen: Museum Tusculanum Press, University of Copenhagen, 2010), 179–80.

14. Carl F. H. Henry, "The Fragility of Freedom in the West," *Christianity Today*, October 15, 1956, 8–10; Robert P. Dugan Jr., "Prepared Statement of Robert P. Dugan, Jr.," Senate Committee on Foreign Relations, *Nomination of Ernest W. Lefever: Hearings before the Committee on Foreign Relations, United States Senate, Ninety-Seventh Congress, First Session, on Nomination of Ernest W. Lefever, to be Assistant Secretary of State for Human Rights and Humanitarian Affairs, May 18, 19, June 4, and 5, 1981*, 97th Cong., 1st sess. (Washington, DC: Government Printing Office, 1981), 307.

15. I develop this argument in detail in my book. See Turek, *To Bring the Good News to All Nations*, chaps. 3 and 4.

16. Henry, "Fragility of Freedom," 8–10; Dugan, "Prepared Statement," 307.

17. Ronald Reagan, "1980 Ronald Reagan/Jimmy Carter Presidential Debate," October 28, 1980, Ronald Reagan Presidential Library, www.reaganlibrary.gov/archives /speech/1980-ronald-reagan-and-jimmy-carter-presidential-debate. I address this aspect of his campaign in more detail in chapter 4 of my book. Turek, *To Bring the Good News to All Nations*, 99.

18. Ronald Reagan, "Republican National Convention Acceptance Speech," July 17, 1980, Ronald Reagan Presidential Library, www.reaganlibrary.gov/archives/speech /republican-national-convention-acceptance-speech-1980; H. W. Brands, *Reagan: The Life* (New York: Doubleday, 2015), chap. 31, Kindle.

19. Ronald Reagan, "Televised Address by Governor Ronald Reagan: A Strategy for Peace in the 80s," October 19, 1980, Ronald Reagan Library, www.reaganlibrary.gov /archives/speech/televised-address-governor-ronald-reagan-strategy-peace-80s; Ronald Reagan, "Election Eve Address—A Vision for America," November 3, 1980, Ronald Reagan Presidential Library, www.reaganlibrary.gov/archives/speech/election-eve -address-vision-america.

20. The following case study on Nicaragua comes from previously published work. I have condensed and edited it somewhat for the purposes of this chapter, but much of it is verbatim from the original. For the full version, see Lauren Frances Turek, "Ambassadors for the Kingdom of God or for America? Christian Nationalism, the Christian Right, and the Contra War," *Religions* 7, no. 12 (December 2016): 151 (6–11). *Religions* is an open access journal and provides authors with full copyright to work and with permission to reuse the published material with proper accreditation under the Creative Commons Attribution License. For more information, see MDPI Open Access Information and Policy, www.mdpi.com/about/openaccess (accessed February 16, 2022).

21. There is a wealth of scholarship on the Contra war and U.S.–Central American (and U.S.-Nicaraguan) relations during the Reagan administration. For background, see William M. LeoGrande, *Our Own Backyard: The United States in Central America, 1977–1992* (Chapel Hill: University of North Carolina Press, 1998); Walter LaFeber, *Inevitable Revolutions: The United States in Central America* (New York: W. W. Norton, 1993); Greg Grandin, *Empire's Workshop: Latin America, the United States, and the Rise of the New Imperialism* (New York: Metropolitan Books, 2006); and Evan McCormick, "Freedom Tide? Ideology, Politics, and the Origins of Democracy Promotion in U.S. Central American Policy, 1980–1984," *Journal of Cold War Studies* 16, no. 4 (Fall 2014): 60–109.

22. Much of the existing literature on religion and the Contra war focuses either on denominational change and political involvement in Nicaragua itself or on the Catholic and Protestant left's activism against Reagan's foreign policy. For the former, see Henri Gooren, "The Religious Market in Nicaragua: The Paradoxes of Catholicism and Protestantism," *Exchange* 32, no. 4 (October 2003): 340–60; and Christian Smith and Liesl Ann Haas, "Revolutionary Evangelicals in Nicaragua: Political Opportunity, Class Interests, and Religious Identity," *Journal for the Scientific Study of Religion* 36, no. 3 (1997): 440–54. For the latter, see Charles T. Strauss, "Quest for the Holy Grail: Central American War, Catholic Internationalism, and United States Public Diplomacy in Reagan's America," *U.S. Catholic Historian* 33, no. 1 (Winter 2015): 163–97; Christian Smith,

Resisting Reagan: The U.S. Central America Peace Movement (Chicago: University of Chicago, 1996); Sharon Erickson Nepstad, *Convictions of the Soul: Religion, Culture, and Agency in the Central America Solidarity Movement* (New York: Oxford University Press, 2004); Roger Peace, *A Call to Conscience: The Anti-Contra War Campaign* (Amherst: University of Massachusetts Press, 2012); and Theresa Keeley, "Reagan's Real Catholics vs. Tip O'Neill's Maryknoll Nuns: Gender, Intra-Catholic Conflict, and the Contras," *Diplomatic History* 40, no. 2 (June 2016): 530–58. Unlike these works, this chapter takes a different tack by examining how U.S. evangelicals used Christian nationalist rhetoric and the language of religious freedom in their public diplomacy and policy advocacy, with the aim of shoring up support for the Reagan administration's goals in Central America. Sara Diamond's work on the Christian right reflects some of these themes, and though she completed and published her research before the Contra war ended and devotes only part of a chapter to the conflict, her book remains a very useful primer. See Sara Diamond, *Spiritual Warfare: The Politics of the Christian Right* (London: Pluto, 1989).

23. McCormick, "Freedom Tide?," 75, 77.

24. National Security Decision Directive 17, "National Security Decision Directive on Cuba and Central America," January 4, 1982, 1–2, www.reaganlibrary.gov/public /archives/reference/scanned-nsdds/nsdd17.pdf.

25. David S. Painter, *The Cold War: An International History* (New York: Routledge, 1999), 99.

26. National Security Decision Directive 17, 1.

27. "Amendment Offered by Mr. Boland," *Congressional Record*, 97th Cong., 2nd sess., December 8, 1982, vol. 12, pt. 21: H 29468–69.

28. "Amendment Offered by Mr. Boland," *Congressional Record*, 98th Cong., 1st sess., October 20, 1983, vol. 129, pt. 20: H 28560, H 28572; Continuing Appropriations for the Fiscal Year 1985, P.L. 98-473, Stat. 1935–1937, sec. 8066 (October 12, 1984).

29. "Mobilizing Public Opinion," ca. 1983, 4, folder "Central America: Responses from Ambassadors," Whittlesey, Faith Ryan: Records, 1983–1985 Series III: Subject File, box 36, Ronald Reagan Library, Simi Valley, CA. Underlining in original.

30. "Mobilizing Public Opinion," 5.

31. "Mobilizing Public Opinion," 12, 15, 18. Underlining in original.

32. "The Central American Outreach Effort," ca. 1984, 1, folder "Central America: Materials (1 of 7)," Whittlesey, Faith Ryan: Records, 1983–1985 Series III: Subject File, box 34, Ronald Reagan Library.

33. For more on the role of affect in shaping U.S. evangelicals' identification with persecuted evangelicals abroad, see McAlister, *Kingdom of God Has No Borders*. On the links between victim testimonials, empathy, and the broader international human rights movement, see Mark Philip Bradley, *The World Reimagined: Americans and Human Rights in the Twentieth Century* (NY: Cambridge University Press, 2016), 137–48.

34. Outreach Working Group on Central America, "Religious Persecution in Nicaragua," transcript (May 4, 1984), 2, folder "Central America: Materials (3 of 7)," Whittlesey, Faith Ryan: Records, 1983–1985 Series III: Subject File, box 34, Ronald Reagan Library.

35. Outreach Working Group on Central America, 2.

36. Outreach Working Group on Central America, 7. Some critics questioned whether Baltodano was actually a minister or even a lay preacher; John Stam reported

that when he confronted Baltodano, the man confessed that at the time the Sandinistas tortured him, he had only just converted to Pentecostalism. See Barbara Thompson to Doug Coe and interview with John Stam, January 7, 1987, BGC [Billy Graham Center] Collection 459—Fellowship Foundation, box 245, folder 61: Nicaragua 1984, BGC Archives, Wheaton, IL.

37. Faith Ryan Whittlesey to Terence A. Todman, August 7, 1984, folder "Central America: Responses from Ambassadors," Whittlesey, Faith Ryan: Records, 1983–1985 Series III: Subject File, box 36, Ronald Reagan Library.

38. "Entire Churches Jailed in Nicaragua," *Jesus to the Communist World, Inc.* newsletter, December 1984, 1, Intercessors for the Suffering Church Collection, 1971–1997, SC #79, box 4, folder 12: Jesus to the Communist World—"The Voice of the Martyrs" 6/82–10/93, Wheaton College Buswell Library Special Collections, Wheaton, IL; Dan Wooding and Kate Rafferty, "'Only Contras Are Preventing Shut-Down of Nicaraguan Church,' Claim Fleeing Refugees Now in Guatemala," *Open Doors News Service*, June 28, 1985, and Dan Wooding, "Nicaraguan Evangelical Leaders Arrested in Sandinista Crackdown," *Open Doors News Service*, December 24, 1985, Intercessors for the Suffering Church Collection, 1971–1997, SC #79, box 6, folder 7: Open Doors News Service 9/84–8/86, Wheaton College Buswell Library Special Collections.

39. For an example of the progression of reporting in *Christianity Today*, see Stephen R. Sywulka, "Aftermath of Nicaragua's Civil War: Church and State Regroup," *Christianity Today*, September 21, 1979, www.christianitytoday.com/ct/1979/september -21/aftermath-of-nicaraguas-civil-war-church-and-state-regroup.html; Tom Minnery, "Why the Gospel Grows in Socialist Nicaragua," *Christianity Today*, April 8, 1983, www .christianitytoday.com/ct/1983/april-8/why-gospel-grows-in-socialist-nicaragua.html; Beth Spring, "Does the Sandinista Regime Promote Religious Freedom?," *Christianity Today*, November 23, 1984, www.christianitytoday.com/ct/1984/november-23/does -sandinista-regime-promote-religious-freedom.html; and Beth Spring, "Nicaragua: The Government's Heavy Hand Falls on Believers," *Christianity Today*, December 13, 1985, www.christianitytoday.com/ct/1985/december-13/nicarauga-governments-heavy-hand -falls-on-believers.html.

40. Institute on Religion and Democracy to Doug Coe, fundraising letter, July 1984, BGC Collection 459—Fellowship Foundation, box 245, folder 61: Nicaragua 1984, BGC Archives.

41. As Greg Grandin recounts, the Contras killed, kidnapped, and tortured thousands of civilians. He quotes one advisor to the Joint Chiefs of Staff describing them as "'just a bunch of killers'" and notes the Contras themselves admitted to vast atrocities. See Grandin, *Empire's Workshop*, 115. The Sandinistas also committed atrocities.

42. Inter-Religious Task Force, "Different Convictions: What the Religious Community Is Saying about Central America" (Chicago: Inter-Religious Task Force, ca. 1984–85), Chicago Religious Task Force on Central America Records, 1982–1992, M93-153, M2004-170, box 2, folder: "Interreligious Task Force," Wisconsin Historical Society, Madison.

43. Jim Wallis, "Christians and Contras," *Sojourners* 14, no. 9 (October 1985): 4.

44. Keeley, "Reagan's Real Catholics," 548, 554; Theresa Keeley, *Reagan's Gun-Toting Nuns: The Catholic Conflict over Cold War Human Rights Policy in Central America* (Ithaca, NY: Cornell University Press, 2020).

Christian Nationalism and U.S. Foreign Policy

45. Keeley, "Reagan's Real Catholics," 548; Joe Renouard, *Human Rights in American Foreign Policy: From the 1960s to the Soviet Collapse* (Philadelphia: University of Pennsylvania Press, 2016), 226; Margaret Hornblower, "Ortega, in N.Y., Defends State of Emergency," *New York Times*, October 21, 1985.

46. J. Douglas Holladay to Oliver North, May 3, 1985, memorandum, folder: Evangelical Press on Freedom Fighters and Budget, 04/19/1985, Holladay, J. Douglas: Files, Series V: Events OA 12267, box 13, Ronald Reagan Library.

47. Ronald Reagan, "Taping: Message on Contra Aid for Religious Programs," transcript, March 5, 1986, folder "OA 17967: RR/Nicaragua Videotape for Christian Media 03/05/1986," Anderson, Carl: Files, Series III: Events, box 10, Ronald Reagan Library. The Bible verse is from the King James Version.

48. Evangelicals made up a significant subset of that larger body of politically conservative Christians that Reagan targeted in his message. Many of the media stations that the White House sent tapes of the recording to, including the Christian Broadcasting Network, Trinity Broadcasting Network, and Word of Faith World Outreach, attracted large evangelical audiences. See Pat Youstra to Linas Kojelis, "Central America Support Checkup," memorandum, March 12, 1986, 1–2, folder "OA 17967: RR/Nicaragua Videotape for Christian Media 03/05/1986," Anderson, Carl: Files, Series III: Events, box 10, Ronald Reagan Library.

49. Much to the great dismay of liberal, anti-contra evangelicals. See "Christians Oppose TV Evangelist's Aid to Right-Wing Groups in Central America," *Synapses* press release, April 13, 1985; "The Christian Broadcasting Network: Unholy Alliances," memorandum (ca. 1985); and "Pat Robertson Publicly Questioned on Operation Blessing Aid to Contras," *Synapses* press release, June 27, 1985, all from Chicago Religious Task Force on Central America Records, 1982–1992, M93-153, M2004-170, box 1, folder: Christian Broadcasting Network (1/7), Wisconsin Historical Society.

50. Youstra to Kojelis, "Central America Support Checkup"; Carl Anderson to William B. Lacy, "Christian Media Coverage for Central America," memorandum, March 5, 1986, folder "OA 17967: RR/Nicaragua Videotape for Christian Media 03/05/1986," Anderson, Carl: Files, Series III: Events, box 10, Ronald Reagan Library.

51. Youstra to Kojelis, "Central America Support Checkup"; Anderson to Lacy. "Christian Media Coverage for Central America."

52. Senator Jeremiah Andrew Denton Jr., "Sandinista Religious Oppression," *Congressional Record*, 99th Cong., 2nd sess., March 18, 1986, vol. 132, pt. 33: S 2970.

53. Representative Barbara Mikulski, "Opposing Aid to the Contras," Extension of Remarks, *Congressional Record*, 99th Cong., 2nd sess., March 18, 1986, vol. 132, pt. 35: E 919; Representative Barney Frank, "Nicaragua," *Congressional Record*, 99th Cong., 2nd sess., April 10, 1986, vol. 132, pt. 43: H 1765.

54. Chris Woerh, "NAE Rallies behind Nicaragua's Evangelicals," *Open Doors News Service*, April 1, 1987, 9, Intercessors for the Suffering Church Collection, 1971–1997, SC #79, box 6, folder 8: Open Door News Service 7/86–7/87, WCSC.

55. Woerh, 10.

56. Representative Jim Lightfoot to Mary Ann Gilbert, April 15, 1988, Intercessors for the Suffering Church Collection, 1971–1997, SC #79, box 5: Serials Correspondence Liv-Ni, folder 16: Nicaraguan Refugees, WCSC.

57. Ortega returned to power in Nicaragua in 2007 and remains at odds with the United States; it is an understatement to say that the effects of U.S. efforts to bring regime change have been long-lasting.

58. John Maust, "Nicaragua: The Honeymoon Begins," *Christianity Today*, April 9, 1990, www.christianitytoday.com/ct/1990/april-9/nicaragua-honeymoon-begins.html.

59. Gustavo Sevilla, "Interview: Winds of Change Warm Churches in Nicaragua," *Christianity Today*, January 14, 1991, www.christianitytoday.com/ct/1991/january-14/interview-winds-of-change-warm-churches-in-nicaragua.html.

60. Maust, "Nicaragua."

61. Sevilla, "Interview."

62. I discuss these cases (in varying levels of detail) in my book.

63. Though, as the Iran-Contra scandal revealed, even when congressional funding was not forthcoming, the Reagan administration found other means to finance its adventurism.

PART THREE

Evangelicals in the Neoliberal Order

CHAPTER TEN

Global Evangelicalism and U.S. Foreign Policy, 1940s–1970s

A Review of Recent Transnational Research

Axel R. Schäfer

In recent decades the growing scholarly interest in the relationship between religion and U.S. foreign policy has generated a plethora of new publications that analyze the role evangelicalism has played in constituting U.S. empire and, conversely, the salience of U.S. global power in cementing the influence of the Christian right at home. A number of authors in this volume contribute to these conversations through case studies of previously unexamined events, actors, and entanglements in the history of the relationship between evangelicals and foreign policy. This chapter adopts a somewhat different approach: it takes stock and critically reviews the existing historiography on the connections between U.S. empire and (primarily white) evangelicalism.

In particular, it finds that much of the newer research has retained standard nation-centric perspectives on U.S. foreign policy, as well as interpretations of conservative Protestantism as exclusively right-wing. In contrast, transnational perspectives on evangelical investments in the imperial project situate U.S. evangelicalism in a global frame in ways that challenge these established narratives in diplomatic and religious history. Transnational scholarship highlights the contestation of U.S. foreign policy as well as the contingency of evangelicalism, opening up new perspectives on the interpretation of their relationship. It also sheds new light on the mutual construction of U.S. empire and the conservative Protestant resurgence.

The chapter first reviews recent religious and foreign policy research on the connections between U.S. empire and evangelicalism, focusing on the period from World War II to the 1970s. The second section reviews relevant transnational approaches, investigates evangelicals' interactions with the non-Western world in the twentieth century, and discusses their significance for both the politics of modern evangelicalism and U.S. foreign policy. In the third section, the chapter picks up the central themes of contingency and contestation. It argues that they provide a frame through which scholars can integrate the exercise of U.S. power with instances of indigenization, resistance, transactional relations, and feedback effects within the United States. At the same time, it suggests that the ambivalence of religion is structurally relevant for consolidating empire, while the instabilities of foreign policy are crucial for shoring up conservative Protestantism at home. In the end, transnational perspectives thus frequently end up affirming what they had set out to challenge.

New Perspectives on Evangelicalism and Foreign Policy

Filled with ambitions to return to the global arena and viewing the United States' rise to global power as providential, many white evangelicals after World War II eagerly took advantage of the opportunities of the "American century" to pursue vigorously overseas religious revivalism, missions, and institution building. While the desire to convert the world has always been at the heart of the evangelical project, the war and the postwar years proved a particular boon for the expansion of foreign missions, humanitarian aid, global crusades, and Bible tourism, particularly in Asia and Africa. In turn, the massive growth of evangelical missionary activism meant that in the decades after 1945, conservative Protestants became the dominant mission group. By the 1980s, 90 percent of U.S. Protestant missionaries were evangelicals.[1] Whereas in 1940 evangelical foreign aid agencies had made up 10 percent of religious organizations in the field, by 2004 they constituted close to half.[2] And by 2010, close to 70 percent of evangelicals lived outside of the United States.[3]

This "international turn" of American evangelicalism is a crucial part of the domestic resurgence of white conservative Protestantism in the United States in the second half of the twentieth century. Considering the close connection between U.S. evangelicals' interactions with the non-Western world and the movement's engagement with foreign policy, it is also a significant aspect of U.S. international relations and diplomatic history since 1945. For a long time, however, religion in general and evangelicalism in particular have received little serious attention among diplomatic historians. The dominant "realist" school put the focus on state-to-state relations, national interest, and diplomatic elites; the secular bias of academics dismissed religion as a formative element in international affairs; and historians frequently lacked the conceptual tools for dealing with religion as an analytical category.[4] Indeed, as historian Jon Butler has argued, scholars treated religion as a historical "jack-in-the-box" that, popping up intermittently, provided the occasional unsettling spiritual scare in otherwise resolutely secular accounts of the American century.[5] "However devout presidents and secretaries of state may be," historian Leo Ribuffo cautioned in 2014, "they discuss tariffs at meetings of the Organization of Economic Cooperation and Development . . . not biblical inerrancy at conferences of the World Council of Churches."[6]

Similarly, among many scholars of religion the question of how the new global evangelical consciousness and activism have shaped the domestic revival since World War II has in the past generated a collective shrug. Instead, the majority of studies of the rise of the New Christian Right in the United States have located the political resurgence of evangelicalism in the domestic "backlash" against the civil rights and anti-Vietnam movements, Lyndon Johnson's Great Society, growing secularism, and the counterculture. Since foreign policy has traditionally been underrepresented within the field of religious studies, this body of research also often missed how Cold War politics and culture in the 1940s and 1950s brought conservative Protestant groups back into the political arena and contributed to their partisan mobilization.[7] Indeed, as late as 2013, religious scholar Sylvester Johnson noted that understandings of both evangelicalism and U.S. foreign policy have largely been isolated on separate tracks: "Of the hundreds of studies of US empire that have emerged over the past decade, only a mere handful examine the intersection with religion." Likewise, "for the vast majority of scholars of US religion, it seems to matter little if at all that the US is an empire."[8]

Much has changed in recent years, however, as a range of new studies have placed resurgent evangelicalism and its "international turn" in the context of America's rise to global power. Foreign policy scholarship, in part inspired by the "new diplomatic history," has explored how religious convictions and institutions shaped U.S. international relations during and after World War II—to the extent that religion has been declared the "missing piece" in understanding the Cold War.[9] Andrew Preston, for example, shows that most U.S. presidents have "framed and justified their foreign policies in religious terms."[10] David Ziemtsma maintains that a "Christian realist" narrative that imagined the United States as a righteous nation opposing evil in the world was the key to establishing the legitimacy of intervention in World War II.[11] Jonathan Herzog argues that efforts to mobilize the resources of religion for the exercise of America's global power were very much at the heart of the "spiritual-industrial complex" of the Cold War.[12] And William Inboden, a former White House staffer, regards religion itself as a key causal factor for the Cold War.[13] Further research has explored how religious interpretations and imagery permeated U.S. foreign policy, traced the development of new partnerships between religious organizations and the federal government, examined the connection between religion and the military-industrial complex, and looked at religion in relation to the sociocultural dynamics that challenged established racial hierarchies, gender roles, and sexual norms in postwar America.[14]

Similarly, the revival of religious history has generated a range of studies that reveal the close connection between the evangelical resurgence at home and the movement's engagement with foreign policy and international relations. Darren Dochuk, Angela Lahr, Kevin Kruse, Matthew Sutton, and others explore how Cold War ideology, political economy, and foreign policy were key factors in re-politicizing conservative Protestantism, shoring up its institutions, and providing access to government. They largely view the Christian right as a product of World War II and the Cold War rather than as a result of the post-sixties backlash. They delineate how evangelicals understood, accommodated, embraced, or resisted global U.S. power; how they participated in divisive debates about the nation's role in the world; and how their international experiences reverberated in the organizational dynamics of the domestic revival.[15] Lauren Turek, for example, illuminates the extent to which evangelical policy advocacy helped the Reagan administration implement its vision for exporting U.S. influence and ideology.[16]

Global Evangelicalism and U.S. Foreign Policy

David King shows that evangelical foreign aid organizations, who, with the help of the American government, found themselves on the front line of Cold War expansionism, shaped both U.S. policies and the domestic evangelical movement through their encounter with peoples abroad.[17] And John Corrigan examines how evangelicals connected their domestic intolerance of other religious groups with the denunciation of infringements on religious freedom and human rights abroad.[18]

In mapping the dynamics of global evangelical engagement onto the terrain of U.S. international power, this body of recent research has thus introduced new ways of understanding both the domestic resurgence of evangelicalism and the role of religion in foreign policy. On the one hand, it has helped to bring evangelicalism back into foreign policy, challenging the tendency to relegate religion to the sidelines. On this basis it has established the significance of religious ideologies, practices, and institutions in the development of an internationalist mindset, an organizational infrastructure to deliver foreign policy goals, and a knowledge base for foreign policy decisions—all key to ensuring the effective exercise of U.S. global power. On the other hand, it has put international relations back into religion, placing overseas activities squarely at the center of research on U.S. evangelicalism. On this basis researchers have shown that the domestic evangelical mobilization cannot be understood in isolation from the movement's efforts to return to the global arena and its engagement with foreign policy.

In short, while the Cold War state and foreign policy governance became evermore reliant on evangelical resources, the political formation of postwar evangelicalism likewise became increasingly connected to religious foreign policy engagement. These findings also provide the historical context for the *post*–Cold War rise of a "religious foreign policy regime" and the emergence of a "postsecular consciousness" in U.S. foreign policy that Gregorio Bettiza diagnoses. While policy makers sought to harness the power of faith in support of U.S. interests and values abroad, religious players, particularly evangelicals, used the new access to government to spread the faith. The ever closer ties between religion and politics that have emerged since the end of the Cold War are characterized by institutional continuity across presidential administrations; a shared effort to "elevate" religion as an interpretive filter to "categorize" international conflicts; an ideological notion of religion as a positive good that offers unique humanitarian resources; and mutual efforts to relax rules mandating the separation of church and state.[19]

This body of research has clearly enriched our understanding of the evangelical movement as it unfolds in the context of the rise of U.S. global power. At times, however, it has been marred by conceptual myopia. Foreign policy scholars tend to reduce the issue to the question of how important religion in general, and evangelicalism in particular, was in shoring up the national foundations of U.S. foreign policy. Likewise, scholars of religion have in the main explored evangelical foreign policy engagements in terms of their significance for the rise of the New Christian Right at home. At the same time, other researchers have questioned these understandings of both evangelicalism and U.S. foreign policy. In regard to conservative Protestantism, they have highlighted that the period from the early 1940s to the mid-1970s was not simply a prelude to the New Christian Right but a time when opportunities for rather different political alignments offered themselves. Indeed, the large-scale expansion of evangelical foreign engagement happened at a time when diverse voices within the movement vied with conservatives for political influence.[20] Particularly the 1960s and 1970s were the heyday of left-wing evangelicalism, which formed a small but outspoken minority within resurgent conservative Protestantism. Many left evangelicals had organized in groups such as Evangelicals for McGovern, Evangelicals for Social Action, Sojourners, the People's Christian Coalition, and the Christian World Liberation Front. They championed women's rights, pacifism, social justice, and civil rights.[21]

Indeed, observers in the mid-1970s could hardly be faulted for thinking that a type of liberal evangelicalism, rather than the militant Christian right, had emerged triumphant. In 1976, Jimmy Carter, a liberal born-again Southern Baptist, was elected to the U.S. presidency. Meanwhile, a sequence of colorful conversions, ranging from Black Panther Eldridge Cleaver and *Hustler* magazine's Larry Flynt to Watergate villain Charles Colson and musician Eric Clapton, made front-page news and established what pundit George Wills called "evangelical chic."[22] As evangelical theologian Carl Henry noted, conservative Protestantism had a "new aura of acceptability among parents who prefer that their teen-agers take up with the Jesus movement or with the charismatics rather than join the Moonies."[23]

Likewise, in terms of U.S. foreign policy, recent scholarship reveals a much more conflicted setting than is commonly recognized in the literature. Looking beyond political elites and official foreign policy ideas, it exposes a more incoherent process made up of diverse and conflicted reactions to U.S. empire-building and a rich legacy of alternative ideas about the country's global engagement, interests, and obligations. The 1940s to the 1970s were crucial decades when the rise to global power awakened tensions present in U.S. political culture at home and Western hegemony was challenged by anti-colonial movements abroad. Empires require ideologies of cultural superiority, effective bureaucracies, technological supremacy, and a commitment to military capacities in order to ensure access to resources, suppress subaltern insurgencies, compete with other imperial aspirants, and assert domestic social control. Yet in the United States, establishing the ideological, institutional, and economic prerequisites of empire clashed with deeply embedded traditions of anti-colonialism, anti-statism, anti-monopolism, anti-militarism, exceptionalism, and distrust of centralized control. While the United States traced its origins back to a struggle against British colonial rule, it had by the end of World War II become a hegemon itself. Whereas the United States had had one of the smallest armies at the beginning of the war, by 1945 it had become the only country that owned—and had used—the most powerful weapon in the world. Having in the past prided itself on avoiding "entangling alliances," the nation was now in charge of constructing an international collective security system. And a country that had a long tradition of limited government and strict civilian control of the military found that its economic fortunes were ever more tied to vast defense expenditures. In short, domestically the country's postwar role was not yet ideologically and culturally established, and the transition from "isolationism" to "internationalism" was politically contested and culturally fought over.[24]

What is more, in the international arena the United States had to take cognizance of postwar global challenges to imperialism and capitalism. After all, America's rise to global power happened at a time when the German invasion of France and the Japanese conquest of British Singapore, the Dutch East Indies, French Indochina, and the American Philippines had severely weakened the old centers of imperialism. The postwar collapse of the old imperialist system opened up opportunities to anti-colonial activists, including Mahatma Gandhi in India, Kwame Nkrumah in Ghana, Sékou Touré in Guinea, and the Mau Mau fighters in Kenya. Meanwhile, postwar efforts by Britain and France to restore their global influence remained mostly haphazard, ill-conceived, and largely unsuccessful.[25]

In summation, this second body of scholarship has challenged the reified conceptions of both religion and foreign policy that tended to dominate among the first group of authors. Instead, it depicts both religion and foreign policy as highly unstable forms characterized by built-in fragilities, tensions, and contradictions. At the same time, it outlines pathways for the transnational "de-centering" of evangelicalism and foreign policy, opening up new perspectives on the contingency of religion as well as the contestation of U.S. foreign policy. This was picked up by a third group of scholars who have employed transnational approaches and perspectives in their analyses. Foreign policy looks different when seen through the angle of transnationalism. It turns our attention toward, for example, processes of decolonization, experiences from the "Global South," and grassroots counter-narratives. It thus recovers alternative visions of foreign relations and shifts the focus from the consolidation to the challenges of empire building. In an era shaped by anti-colonial movements, many U.S. Protestant missionaries returned to the homeland as advocates of foreign peoples and as agents of anti-racist and anti-imperialist causes. In turn, the interactions of everyday U.S. missionaries, ecumenists, relief workers, and lay Protestants with the non-Western world became part and parcel of bringing the "Global South" to North American shores.[26]

By the same token, evangelicalism looks different when placed in a transnational context. Transnational perspectives shed new light on the significance of global transfers, connections, networks, agencies, activism, and ideologies in redefining the content and boundaries of the faith. As evangelical voices from Africa, Asia, and Latin America have become more vocal and assertive within the movement, conservative Protestantism emerged as a more pluralistic, multidirectional enterprise characterized by instances of indigenization, anti-colonial resistance, and "reverse missions."[27] Transnational research thus reveals a movement whose center is increasingly located abroad and transports non-Western and subaltern perspectives. It shows how evangelicals of all ethnic and racial backgrounds—including white, Black, Hispanic, African, and Asian believers—influenced domestic theological and political debates and transformed the global movement. As David Swartz put it, "In the 1950s and 1960s Christians from India and many African nations condemned racial segregation in the United States. In the early 1970s Latin Americans criticized American imperialism at a global gathering on evangelism led by Billy Graham. In the late 1970s Majority World Christians encouraged World Vision to internationalize its organizational structure, an act that radically transformed its methods of poverty relief. These intense challenges reshaped sectors of American evangelicalism in the twilight of the twentieth century."[28]

Transnationalism and the Study of Global Evangelicalism

In the course of its short history, the term "transnationalism" has acquired a plethora of meanings and has become fuzzy and overused. Nonetheless, I would argue that the term does have a conceptual core that offers crucial impulses for the study of global religious movements and their relationship with politics. Broadly speaking, the transnational project can be defined as an effort to critique and transcend the nation-centric focus in historical writing, which has dominated the nineteenth and twentieth centuries. It speaks out against the tyranny of the national and the fiction of isolation and exceptionalism in U.S. historiography. In contrast, it constitutes a way of "seeing" history from its borders, confluences, entanglements, exchanges, and cross-fertilizations. It assumes that the nation is a highly unstable political form that is ever in flux and forged in the very process of transnational encounters. On this basis, transnationalism pursues a dual agenda: it moves away from nation-centric narratives and toward a concern with the international and the global. At the same time, the term implies that deconstructing the national also involves finding out how international experiences fed back into constructing the nation-state.[29]

For our purposes we can distinguish between four interconnected dimensions of the transnational project. I want to use the terms "networks," "ecologies," "diasporas," and "subalternities" to describe them. The focus on *networks* in transnational research offers a historiographical perspective that considers circulations, interactions, connections, and transfers beyond the nation state. This involves, for example, the study of nongovernmental organizations and multinational linkages. The emphasis of network analysis is often on the material and institutional means of transoceanic connectivity. It examines such topics as the material and physical realities of nineteenth-century transportation (railways, shipping routes, ports), means of communication (such as national postal services), and communicative forms (editorial practices, subscriptions, venues, and audiences). While the network perspective engages closely with processes of both state and nation building, it looks at the intercultural transfer of ideas across oceans, regions, and continents through personal friendships, webs of exchanges, organizational ties, and the like.[30]

The term *ecology* describes the epistemological implications of network analysis, namely, a shift toward the notion of interconnectedness, relationality, and co-constitution. From this perspective, nothing exists as an isolated "object" independent of its context. Ecological approaches conceive of knowledge in terms of connectivity and mutual construction (for example, hydroscapes, landscapes). Indeed, some of the best transnational history is written by environmental historians, ranging from Albert Crosby's *Ecological Imperialism* to Ian Tyrrell's *True Gardens of the Gods*.[31] Seen from this perspective, not only do we need to understand evangelicalism on the basis of its transportation and communication networks that connect communities of believers across oceans, nations, or regions. We also need to recognize that the decentralized and pluralist evangelical network culture, including media ministries, periodicals, colleges, coffee shops, and family ties, defines and constructs religious content. In other words, the "connective tissue," rather than set doctrines and fixed ethno-national identities, constitutes the emotional, social, political, and cultural worlds of evangelicalism.

Closely connected to this is the *diasporic* perspective of transnationalism. It shifts the gaze from relationships and connectivity to in-between spaces and interstices as the true locus of our being—the "no-places" Randolph Bourne described in his July 1916 essay in *Atlantic Monthly* that first introduced the concept of a "trans-national America."[32] Diasporic consciousness means that we recognize ourselves as inter-beings and affirm syncretic, hybrid, mixed identities against the myths of ethno-racial purity and homogeneity. In turning our attention from "place" to "movement" and in asserting that the experience of mobility is more fundamental to identity formation than "roots," the diasporic gaze combines two dimensions. On the one hand, it describes a sense of displacement, homelessness, alienation, and liminality.[33] On the other hand, however, it is linked to the religious concept of diaspora, which regards the longing for a lost homeland and the experience of uprootedness as the necessary prerequisites for redemption. W. E. B. Du Bois's famous concept of "double consciousness," for example, combines these two dimensions in a secular imaginary. The "twoness," "second sight," and "seeing oneself through the other world" he speaks of are not simply analytical categories for understanding the African American experience. Following Hegelian reasoning, he also regards them as facilitating a deeper understanding of liberty required for substantive social transformation.[34]

Finally, building upon a diasporic perspective, *subalternity* seeks to give voice to those not represented or made invisible by nation-states, particularly colonized people and noncitizens. It emphasizes subaltern self-assertion within a social and political order that alternately employs strategies of inclusion and exclusion. Anchored in a postmodern and postcolonial outlook, this dimension of transnationalism on the one hand exposes the extent to which coercion, racism, and exploitation are built into the very foundations of liberal capitalism, the democratic order, and U.S. nation-state formation. On the other hand, it recovers fundamental counternarratives of marginalized people seeking their own language, cultural expressions, rituals, and ways of seeing beyond established forms of cognition, rationality, and literacy embedded in the Western canon.[35]

Applied to the study of evangelicalism, transnational research and its emphasis on networks, ecologies, diasporas, and subaltern groups highlight how global perspectives have entered U.S. religious lives. They have done so via many avenues, including missionary and professional assignments, military deployment, marriage, immigration, educational sojourns, travel, and media. Two regions in particular—Africa and the Middle East—increasingly came into focus during and after World War II. On the one hand, Africa became the center of the postwar evangelical missionary reengagement with "unreached peoples," social justice–oriented "kingdom work," and human rights campaigns focused on protecting Christians. In turn, it also became the site of the most explosive growth of world Christianity. Likewise, the continent's devastating humanitarian crises—including epidemics, famines, civil wars, and military coups—mobilized many evangelicals. Africa also emerged as a key battleground in the fight against secular communism and later against Islam. On the other hand, politics in the Middle East drew evangelicals into that region's orbit because many invested the creation of the state of Israel with prophetic meaning as part of the end-times scenario.[36] Below, I'll take a closer look at examples of how transnational research, in highlighting evangelicalism's international experiences, recognizes the diversity of the movement and the struggles for authority within the global evangelical church. It reveals how evangelical interaction with U.S. foreign policies challenges established racial and ethnic divisions, organizational structures, and theological contents of evangelicalism.

The first dimension of the transnational project provides new insights into the significance of global *networks and transfers* for both the evangelical movement and U.S. foreign policy. In the post–World War II period, policy planners and politicians faced the problem of the systematic underfunding of the foreign policy infrastructure during a time of expanding U.S. international involvement. In addressing this need for administrative capacities for the exercise of global might, they fell back upon what Emily Rosenberg argues has historically been part of the political economy of expansion, namely, the experiences and resources of nongovernmental organizations.[37] In particular, planners designed policies that made federal funds available to private businesses and nonprofit organizations via subsidies, tax exemptions, loans, vouchers, grants-in-aid, and purchase-of-service agreements. Recent research has shown that the expanding networks between the state and nongovernmental agencies helped forge the ideological and institutional infrastructure for America's pursuit of international relief, commercial access, military penetration, and containment.[38]

Religious organizations were at the very heart of these new "hybrid ventures." Faith organizations brought a number of important resources to the table. Globally, their missionary knowledge base, institutional presence, and role as transcultural mediators facilitated U.S. entries into the Third World, which many policy makers considered the key to winning the Cold War. In contrast to diplomatic and military personnel, missionaries engaged in long-term and intimate ties with foreign cultures and interacted closely with native populations. They were fluent in their languages and present in areas that were initially peripheral to U.S. interests. Regarded locally with less suspicion than government agencies while largely subscribing to the same faith in the universality of Western values and institutions, they frequently prepared the ground for pro-American sympathies at the grassroots and elite levels and gained political access where the U.S. government failed to do so.[39]

Keen to tap into both the institutional and ideological resources of religion, policy makers in the late 1940s and 1950s leveraged the trending ecumenicalism of the times in engineering new ties between faith groups, bureaucrats, and political elites—in ways that increasingly benefited evangelicals. Africa in particular was a key continent where an established evangelical missionary presence coalesced with Cold War government interests, and evangelical missionaries became a nexus between religious and diplomatic circles, as Philip E. Dow has shown. A wide range of informal exchanges, including picnics, holiday celebrations, sports events, and hunting trips, linked missionaries and primary government agents, who often lacked other viable intelligence sources. Close contacts between missionaries and U.S. diplomatic staff remained the norm throughout the postwar period. Indeed, in the superheated ideological atmosphere of the Cold War, missionaries often saw a relationship with government as part of their calling. Among the most active organizations with evangelical leanings in Africa were the Billy Graham Evangelistic Association, Moral Re-Armament, and International Christian Leadership. The latter, led by Abraham Vereide, had long cultivated ties between politicians and religious leaders through breakfast prayers, conferences, and informal meetings. It had also set up an effective political network of evangelical Christians in the military. In particular, Dwight Eisenhower's right-hand man, Kansas senator Frank Carlson, a prominent figure in the domestic religiopolitical scene, encouraged close ties between the Ethiopian branch of International Christian Leadership and Washington congressional chapters. Likewise, the influence of Moral Re-armament missionaries, such as William Close (father of actress Glenn Close), combined "evangelical missionary ethos, zealous anti-communism, and connections to

Global Evangelicalism and U.S. Foreign Policy

the international diplomatic elite."⁴⁰ Or, as Eisenhower put it, "What is our battle against communism if it is not a fight against anti-God and a belief in the Almighty. When God comes in, communism has to go."⁴¹

Similarly, public funding for religious humanitarian aid transformed traditional evangelical church-state separationism into a new engagement with governance, international politics, and empire building. In particular, the decision to distribute U.S. surplus food abroad and President Truman's Point Four Program led to increasing cooperation between the state and religious agencies. In turn, by the early 1950s, the share of revenue from federal sources was greater for religious aid agencies than for secular ones. Despite a tradition of evangelical aversion to the close intertwining of church and state, conservative Protestant aid agencies became increasingly willing to participate in these church-state networks. By the 1960s, Seventh-Day Adventists, the Salvation Army, World Vision, and the National Association of Evangelicals' World Relief Corporation had become major players in the government-funded distribution of surplus foods, hospital building, and land reclamation programs. In addition, many other evangelical NGOs, including Compassion International, Cru, and Samaritan's Purse, became ever more reliant upon public funds. By the 1990s, only a quarter of evangelical international aid organizations received no government funds, as opposed to half of mainline Protestant agencies. Although evangelical loyalty to that project has not been immutable and unconflicted, the voluntarist enterprise of global American evangelicalism was constitutive of U.S. influence in the world in ways that, left to its own devices, the U.S. government could not have achieved.⁴²

As mentioned above, these networks between grassroots activists, experts, and policy makers ultimately laid the foundation for ever-closer cooperation between religious agencies and foreign policy after the end of the Cold War that transferred significant public resources to religious leaders, institutions, and communities around the world. For example, the 1998 International Religious Freedom Act, which mandated that U.S. foreign policy had to monitor religious persecution and promote religious liberty throughout the world, resulted in growing administrative and financial support for religious programs, especially during George W. Bush's administration. The act also framed religious intolerance primarily in terms of the persecution of Christians. Similarly, the administration's overseas HIV/AIDS program involved religious providers in abstinence and faithfulness policies at the expense of condom distribution and work with high-risk groups. Likewise, the Bush administration's faith-based initiative, passed in 2001, removed restrictions on public funds flowing to religious organizations. It tilted the playing field further in favor of religious organizations, particularly in the humanitarian aid arena. The Obama administration deepened and broadened this relationship, and the U.S. Agency for International Development's partnerships with religious groups, including African American church-based aid organizations, increased by more than 50 percent.[43]

The second dimension of the transnational project utilizes an *ecological perspective* that shows how foreign engagement redefined who is an evangelical. In particular it focuses on how global media, outreach, and communication technology constitute or disrupt the beliefs, practices, and institutions of American evangelicalism. In a faith tradition that is organizationally pluralist but theologically centralizing, the labor of representation via the nodes and modes of communication and exchange is crucial in creating that which evangelicals speak of. Evangelicalism is thus not just a belief system but a way of operating in the world. The rich and complex evangelical network culture, ranging from conferences, TV ministries, magazines, radio programs, and Christian music to Bible colleges, prayer groups, and study tours, in many ways constructs knowledge that defines who could be regarded as belonging or admissible to the evangelical fellowship.[44] This includes conscious attempts to generate and choreograph enthusiasm, emotion, and empathy; to shrink the distance between home and abroad; and to shape and sustain patterns of engagement, association, and authority across the global evangelical movement.

Exploring mission manuals, statements, letters, magazine articles, and a range of other sources, Melani McAlister, for example, shows how evangelicals "construct an image of themselves through a particular image of others." On this basis she identifies two different but interconnected postures toward the rest of the world. "Enchanted internationalism" describes the evangelical longing for emotionally powerful forms of religious experience associated with the Global South. It also indicates a significant change in missionary perceptions and representations, as Christians in Africa, Latin America, and Asia are no longer presented as heathens to be saved and "modernized" but as embodiments of authentic, passionate, "vibrant, healing worship" meant to invigorate stale and shallow Western practices. "Victim identification," meanwhile, galvanizes believers in the defense of the faith with persecution narratives and images of tortured bodies. It taps into the rich emotional resonance of Christian stories of martyrdom and Jesus's sanctified suffering on the cross.[45] In turn, McAlister shows how the evangelical politics of affection and the "circulation of feeling" provide the emotional frames and aesthetic structures that determine the way of relating to the world. Evangelical "rituals of intensification" that seek to awaken the heart out of the slumber of "desultory faith," for example, locate authority and legitimacy in fervent preaching, emotional expressiveness, ecstatic forms of worship, heart-wrenching conversion, and displays of suffering. These forms of public discourse run counter to the premises of rational actor theory that continue to dominate the study of international relations.[46]

Third, viewing evangelicalism through the lens of *diaspora* studies shifts the focus from the domestic to the foreign arena, from the center to the margin, from the hegemon to the colonized. It uncovers how the deep engagement with religious thought, rituals, institutions, cultures, and places abroad has furthered the emergence of perspectives markedly different from the strident nationalism of the Christian right in the United States. In an era of decolonization, many Protestant missionaries, having engaged with indigenous movements and ecumenical thought, returned to the United States as critics of global poverty, economic injustice, imperialism, and discriminatory race and gender politics. Ian Tyrrell traces how the colonial experiences of missionaries infused anti-racist and anti-imperial activism in the United States. David Swartz shows how leading evangelicals in the 1950s and 1960s, such as E. Stanley Jones, in part through his friendship with Mahatma Gandhi, took evangelicals to task over issues of domestic racism and international colonialism. Intermittent voices denouncing evangelical complicity in racial oppression and discrimination in the 1960s were followed in the 1970s by more insistent demands from the Global South that evangelicals should commit themselves to "social concern" and focus more fully on the poverty and injustices faced by vast numbers of people in the world. Other studies reveal that the growing reliance on an indigenous workforce in international aid challenged American evangelicals' neglect of issues of racial discrimination and social exclusion.[47]

These so-called feedback effects of reverse missions were more frequent than is often recognized. They informed an insurgent evangelical agenda that powerfully challenged the Christian right's avowedly pro-Israel stance, embrace of anti-communist foreign dictators, and defense of military intervention in Southeast Asia. Many Black, Latino, and white liberal evangelicals supported anti-apartheid campaigns, the Palestinian right to statehood, and the anti–Vietnam War movement. A broad range of activists, including Samuel Escobar, Michael Cassidy, Clarence Hilliard, Tom Skinner, Ron Sider, Jim Wallis, Caesar Molebatsi, and Steven Biko, demanded that evangelicals realize their own complicity in a global capitalist system of racial oppression, colonialism, and war. Organizations such as the Women's Missionary Union in the Southern Baptist Convention and periodicals such as InterVarsity Christian Fellowship's *His* magazine emerged as leading voices for social justice and racial liberalism. Similarly, venues such as the 1966 World Congress on Evangelism and the 1974 Lausanne Congress offered forums for attacking "plantation politics," materialism, white racial power, and the sins of "middle-class captivity." Evangelical mission work, especially in Latin America, helped create what Nancy Wadsworth has called "epiphanal spaces" that enabled evangelicals to develop the social reflexivity and cultural empathy required for dismantling racist attitudes and structures at home and abroad. In her view, this represents "gradual challenges to social hierarchies" in a faith where rituals of admitting and forgiveness have "continually repressed cognitive reflection, inquiry, and open conversation about power and politics"—or, as one white pastor who features in her study notes, "You talk to black Christians, they want to talk about justice; you talk to white evangelicals, they want to talk about reconciliation."[48]

By the 1970s, many of the hopes of the "American century" had been shattered as authoritarian governments, poverty, and economic dependency showed that foreign assistance was often used as an instrument of capitalist expansion and naked national self-interest. Growing fears about compromising the religious mission led to efforts to prohibit cooperation with U.S. intelligence agencies abroad. Oregon senator and evangelical Mark Hatfield, in particular, supported congressional legislation aimed at making such contacts illegal.[49] Likewise, the issue of immigration began to challenge conservative Protestantism's alignment with the right when religiously based relationships with ("illegal") immigrants (often evangelicals themselves) changed many evangelicals' view on punitive policies. As one evangelical pastor noted, "Watching a third grader cry because her dad is deported" opened his eyes to the injustices of the exiting policy regime: "And I talk about 'family values.'"[50]

The diasporic dimension of global evangelicalism, however, largely confines the discussion to the repercussions in the United States. In contrast, in employing a *subaltern perspective* scholars have explored how global evangelicalism makes visible the voices that have been marginalized in the context of the nation-centric focus of much scholarship on religion and politics. In particular, they show that the political visions and actions of Asian, African, and Latin American evangelicals were not simply pale reflections of Western religion. Instead, they grew out of combinations of indigenous and imported concepts. In the case of World Vision, for example, as David Swartz has shown, Korean pastor Kyung Chik Han should really be recognized as its cofounder (with American Bob Pierce), as he provided much of the inspiration and logistic prowess for the organization.[51] (See also Helen Jin Kim's chapter in this volume.) Likewise, the key to understanding the power of Pentecostalism in the Global South is that it both validates and transcends indigenous spiritual practices (including witchcraft, sorcery, evil spirits, reincarnation, and ancestor worship).

This opens up horizons for a different understanding of global evangelicalism that ties it to the growing transnational literature on subaltern self-assertion emanating from colonized spaces. The radical egalitarian logic of Protestant conversionism and nonhierarchical church governance frequently fed into movements asserting indigenous pride and challenging the established order. As Philip Dow maintains, the expansion of evangelical influence in Africa, as well as the rise of indigenous elites educated at mission schools, helped establish democratic structures. In pre-independence Congo, for example, where the symbiosis of Christian and African practices was a core ingredient in the anti-colonial struggle, the experience with church governance was "virtually the only training in Western-style democratic institutions available." Likewise, in Ethiopia evangelical education nurtured independence among evangelicals and promoted "democratically-friendly values of individualism and egalitarianism." Particularly during the Ethiopian revolution of 1974, this meant that radicalized Christian converts from marginal areas (who had been taught at mission schools and had been discriminated against by the Haile Selassie regime) formed the leading cadres of the insurgency.[52] Similarly, Heather Sharkey delineates how evangelical missionary activity in Egypt in the twentieth century inadvertently helped foster the rise of anti-imperialist sentiments and organizations. And David Kirkpatrick reveals how in Latin America, missionary paternalism, repressive U.S.-backed military regimes, and a growing restlessness over foreign incursion mobilized a generation of progressive evangelicals.[53]

In summation, the transnational historiography on evangelicalism, by shifting the focus toward global networks, ecologies of identities, diasporic gazes, and subaltern assertions, has deepened (and complicated) our understanding of the movement as it unfolds in the context of the rise of U.S. global power. By showing that U.S. evangelicalism cannot be fully understood through the domestic lens, transnational religious history (1) challenges the standard narrative of a consolidated Christian right, (2) recovers the diversity of evangelical voices, and (3) sheds new light on the global interchanges that construct evangelical theologies and beliefs. First, viewing evangelicalism from the vantage point of its global engagement questions the notion of evangelicalism as exclusively white and right-wing and shifts the focus from telling the story of conservative Protestantism primarily through the perspective of the "backlash." As U.S. evangelicals expanded rapidly across the globe via missions, crusades, humanitarian aid organizations, and overseas institution building, they interacted with, shaped, and were influenced by both "empire building" and processes of decolonization, particularly those set in motion by both world wars. Global engagement generated a measure of political diversity, cultural complexities, and sociocultural contestations within the movement that is often overlooked by traditional interpretations. Second, the newer research into evangelicalism facilitates a broader global reimagining of conservative Protestantism as a polycentric and multilayered enterprise. The movement is less rooted in U.S. ethno-nationalism than in the religious, political, and emotional orientations that emanate from global exchanges and interactions. It not only encompasses evangelical tenets and practices that grew in American soil but also includes foreign voices critical of America's corruptibility and worldliness. In turn, white, Black, Hispanic, African, and Asian believers were entangled with asserting or questioning American power abroad, became voices of indigenous protest, and shaped the way the United States related to the rest of the world. Third, transnational scholarship shows how U.S. evangelicalism has itself been reformed by its encounters with the world. As international missions and humanitarian organizations became fertile sites of spiritual and cultural exchange, they opened up opportunities for global battles over the meaning and content of the faith in which diasporic and subaltern voices within the movement redefined who is an evangelical.

When we place these transnational perspectives alongside established research on evangelicalism and its relationship with foreign policy, what emerges is the image of a deeply divided movement. On the one hand, many of its followers displayed a deep attachment to the righteousness of the American nation and to the militarized globalism of the Cold War. Evangelical NGOs often saw their work as part of a Cold War project of simultaneously winning souls and spreading the American way of life. They frequently embraced the growing reach of American power as a protector of Christians abroad. As Robert Wuthnow has observed, "It becomes hard to disentangle the Christian message from images of U.S. wealth and power."[54] And as "God's machine gun," Billy Graham, exclaimed, "If you would be a true patriot, then become a Christian. If you would be a loyal American, then become a loyal Christian."[55]

On the other hand, many conservative Protestants involved in mission and foreign aid work regarded themselves not as citizens of a particular country but as members of the kingdom of God. They were less interested in instilling democratic or capitalist values than in converting souls and frequently expressed discomfort with exporting American secular culture.[56] Transnational approaches show how global evangelicals constituted a counternarrative to a state-centric, technocratic, national-interest-led politics that permeated the United States' pursuit of humanitarian aid, international relations, and commercial access. The movement's orientation toward evangelizing, proselytizing "unreached peoples," and conveying the "good news" to all according to the Great Commission emphasizes concepts of relationality and connectivity, locating authority and legitimacy in, for example, the "circulation of feeling" and "emotional healing." Rooted in the religious, political, and emotional orientations that emanate from global exchanges and interactions, this "politics of affect" constitutes an alternative vision of foreign relations.

The key contribution of the transnational perspective, however, is not simply to tell the other side of the story and to recuperate a dimension missed by the focus on national diplomacy and the New Christian Right. It also does more than simply depict religion and foreign policy as more diverse, conflicted, and ambivalent than is commonly recognized. In emphasizing contingency and contestation, transnationalism actually dissolves notions of foreign policy and religion as distinct and clearly defined entities. It sees them as interdependent and mutually constructed. Evangelicalism, including the instabilities and tensions within the faith tradition, is thus deeply intertwined with the fabric of U.S. globalism in the fluid process of "doing empire." Conversely, U.S. foreign policy, with all its paradoxes and incoherences, is intimately connected to the fluid process of "doing religion." This is the focus of the next section.

"Doing Empire" and "Doing Evangelicalism"

Transnational research conceptualizes both the nation-state and evangelicalism as sets of relationships constituted via complex processes of negotiating between conflicts, rather than as fixed doctrines or ideologies. In these entangled webs and gyrations, elements of co-optation, absorption, and mutual instrumentalizing are intertwined with oppositional voices and counternarratives. In emphasizing "relations" rather than "fixity," transnationalism thus opens up new perspectives on how engagement with global

U.S. power was constitutive of the beliefs, practices, and institutions of American evangelicalism—and vice versa. It suggests that the story of the resurgence of evangelicalism since World War II cannot be separated from the formation of the ideologies, institutions, and political economy of American global power during and after the war. Conversely, the story of U.S. global hegemony cannot be disentangled from the structures and dynamics of the postwar religious awakening.

These concepts of co-constitution, in turn, raise the question of whether the contingencies and contestations that transnational research uncovers actually need to be understood as stabilizing factors, rather than as disruptions, of both evangelicalism and foreign policy. Seen from this dialectical perspective, global evangelicalism channels and defangs adversarial positions within a U.S. public that often remained skeptical of U.S. hegemony. It helped adjust Americans to their nation's new global role in ways that reinforced boundaries of race, religion, and nation. The ideologies, practices, and institutions of global evangelicalism thus continued to help ensure the effective exercise of U.S. power in the world. By the same token, this perspective suggests that U.S. international engagement was key to consolidating the Christian right and helped cement its dominance within a diverse American evangelical setting. Evangelical global engagement and foreign policy involvement thus ultimately marginalized or co-opted insurgent voices that continued to crop up within the missionary discourses and fieldwork of an increasingly internationalized movement.

Newer research on mission history in particular illustrates this process. It shows that missionary dialogues with indigenous history, traditions, and experiences forged (often contradictory) justifications for empire and imperial power. The faith tradition thus simultaneously acted as a conduit for transporting and preserving insurgent perspectives and as key agent of negotiating contradictions and tensions within U.S. imperialist thought and practice. As Tom Smith concludes in his study of missionaries in the Philippines and in Hawai'i, missionary historiography simultaneously offered a platform for the indigenous voice and nullified it, alternately using suppression and appropriation in efforts at erasure and censorship.[57]

This pattern also prevailed in the period after the Second World War. Clearly the revival of global evangelical missionary and humanitarian engagement since the war changed in fundamental ways the relationship of evangelicals with human rights issues and economic justice crusades. Nonetheless, post–World War II evangelical missionaries often channeled their newfound affective attachments to colonized and oppressed peoples

Global Evangelicalism and U.S. Foreign Policy

back into conservative norms and values at home. As Hannah Waits argues, they constructed racial discrimination as a problem of personal feelings in ways that gave U.S. evangelicals the spiritual blueprint for color-blind racism. They taught their fellow believers to view foreign people as the raw material for white Americans' spiritual self-actualization. And they used humanitarian and AIDS campaigns to moralize the health discourse and to export U.S. culture warring.[58]

What is more, evangelical global engagement in the second half of the twentieth century went hand in hand with a distinct "business turn" of the movement. This included the cultivation of corporate ties, the rise of Christian corporations, the notion of religious marketplaces, an ethic of economic individualism, and the embrace of a global free-trade agenda. Many evangelical NGOs abroad promoted individualistic notions of personhood centered on the promise that entrepreneurship, microloans, and hard work would forge routes out of deepening poverty. In their encounter with foreign people, they frequently linked the gospel of Christianity to the gospel of capitalism. As much as religious narratives emphasized kinship with "unreached peoples," they were ultimately infused with affective concepts that centered on heteronormative marriage, acquisitive individualism, and Christian views of proper sexuality that abetted the construction of U.S.-style neoliberal subjects abroad, as John Corrigan argues in this volume. Similarly, evangelical efforts to choreograph global empathy at times ended up replicating market-driven consumerist models. Church Growth ideologies and the prosperity gospel, for example, combined a commitment to spirituality with a firm belief in the entrepreneurial self. The "invasion teams" of the short-term mission movement sold a commodified spiritual adventure designed to make Western religious customers feel good about themselves. Requiring neither cultural immersion nor language skills, short-term missions "petted the poor," reduced mission work to a self-help trip, and failed to generate insights into the structural causes of poverty. As Melani McAlister writes, "There was a kind of willful determination to be enchanted rather than disturbed by the poverty of the people they met."[59]

In the same vein, diasporic consciousness can open people's hearts and minds to the suffering of others, but it can also be cruelly dichotomous and rigidly self-righteous when it comes to those outside of the "body of Christ." Its emphasis on conversion, new beginnings, uprootedness, and liminality— indeed, on "emptiness"—transports a narrative of erasure. In merging with the emotional and spiritual resonance of nationalist imagery of "virgin land," the "geography of hope," or the "New American Adam," it has reinforced colonialist imaginaries that eclipse, silence, or erase indigenous people and their history, traditions, and cultures.[60] Missionary texts thus viewed native peoples either as part of a dying, degraded race or as healthy, vigorous "noble savages." Whichever image they used, however, they constructed and aestheticized Natives within a landscape simultaneously exotic and American.

Diasporic self-conceptions can also contribute to an imperialist gaze. The biblical call to "go and make disciples of all nations" is an admonition that joins religious impulses with the agenda of empire. Hence, the very mechanisms that generate global evangelical engagement with the world, including persecution imagery, "enchanted internationalism," and human rights campaigns, cannot be disaggregated from growing Islamophobia and "clash of civilization" thinking. Evangelical silence on the atrocities at Abu Ghraib and Guantanamo Bay, as well as support for the Iraq War and "extraordinary rendition," attests to this. Indeed, this raises the question of whether evangelicalism, despite (or because of) its global mission and commission, remains at its core a highly nationalistic endeavor of white evangelicals in America who single-mindedly pursue domestic power and are not much shaped by the transnational.[61]

Likewise, the "politics of affect" can mask, and even perpetuate, inequalities between donors and recipients. Recent scholarship on the significance of affective sentiment to the economic relationships that underlie humanitarian aid shows how evangelical religious practices give shape to the inequalities inherent in dominant forms of global humanitarian "care." The "compassion economy," in imbuing images of pain and suffering with productive value, replicates the ways government aid was conceived of, that is as a means of ensuring greater accountability and responsibility on the part of poor recipients. Similarly, the confluence of mysticism and metrics, of evangelizing and church growth ideologies, suggests that the politics of affection can be understood as furthering neocolonial dependency, rather than as a cultural enabler that empowers recipient populations.[62] "Most liberal injunctions for greater affective knowledge," Carolyn Pedwell notes, "avoid confronting how a positivist rhetoric linking empathy, accuracy, and prediction can become fully complicit with the interconnected logics of Western imperialism, capitalist accumulation and war."[63]

Subaltern assertion along evangelical lines can equally result in the affirmation of racial hierarchies, religious divides, and oppressive practices. In the case of Uganda, for example, anti-gay campaigns, which included threats to LGBT+ rights, "corrective rape," and even murder, should not be understood as simply the result of an American right-wing import. Instead, they grew out of Ugandan anti-colonialism rooted in the abstinence orientation of East African revivalism, campaigns against sexual enslavement, suspicions about Western liberalism, and resentment toward paternalist NGOs. And in their struggle against Islam, many southern Sudanese regarded themselves as Black and Christian and constructed their northern Sudanese enemies as Arab, Muslim—and white.[64] Likewise, the evangelical "theology of submission" frequently reinforced traditional deferential attitudes to the governing authority and reasserted authoritarian structures. The prime example of this is Kenya, where President Daniel arap Moi, mission-educated and zealously committed to missionary-inspired anti-communism, effectively used Christian images to defend his increasingly conservative philosophy and authoritarian style.[65]

In summation, even in light of new evidence on global evangelicalism, the jury is out on whether a faith tradition that is so intimately connected to U.S. power truly has the internal capacity to challenge fundamentally global hierarchies and power relations. Evangelicals from the Global South might ask uncomfortable questions about the extent to which racism, exploitation, exclusion, and resource depletion are built into the very foundations of the American liberal order. Indeed, throughout the postwar decades, significant groups within the evangelical movement voiced pacifist sentiments, retained a strong aversion to civil religion, rejected the spiritual sanctification of U.S. foreign policy, denounced the arms race, and demanded nuclear disarmament. The jeremiad tradition clearly continued to put a damper on the bombastic confidence of imperialist cant: a 1956 *Christianity Today* poll of evangelical clergy, for example, showed significant support for "world security built on a trusting spiritual level, and less on military spending."[66] Even conservatives, such as Fuller Theological Seminar's Harold Lindsell, insisted in 1967 that the church should avoid becoming "the voice of those who have managed to seize control of the power structures."[67] As George Marsden notes, "The vision more critical of nation and self-interest is an equally venerable part of a heritage that goes back at least to Roger Williams."[68] Despite these valiant efforts, however, disentangling the Christian message from U.S. wealth and power remains a challenging project. In the end, global evangelicalism owes a debt "to the stimulus of American investment capital or the servicing of American markets, to the allure of an Americanized modernity, or to the apparatus of 'hard power,' with its occupying forces and military installations." In such overseas contexts, evangelicals have all too frequently "enlisted as auxiliaries in the expansion and consolidation of the *Pax Americana*."[69]

In essence, transnational research thus rescues missionaries from being stereotyped as cultural imperialists—but simultaneously shows that they were key to making empires "legible" at home. It suggests that the contingencies and contestations that characterize the religious resurgence can be understood as stagings and performances that spiritualized politics for evangelicals on the one hand, and brought people into relationship with the Cold War order via religious beliefs, institutions, and norms and practices on the other.[70] In the end this feeds into a reading of evangelicalism that scholars of the domestic movement have advanced all along. As many of them contend, evangelical religion serves as a conceptual vocabulary for mediating between the inherent contradictions in the U.S. civic, cultural, and economic order, and has had centuries of experience in doing so.[71] In the specific context of the postwar period, evangelicalism helped negotiate the conflicts between popular isolationist sentiments and the exigencies of postwar global power; anti-statist sentiments and the growth of the national security state; anti-monopolist impulses and the rise of the corporate-controlled military industrial complex; and established race and gender hierarchies and unhinged consumer capitalism. Ideologically, postwar neo-evangelicalism's combination of a universalistic message with a profoundly nationalistic faith was crucial in mobilizing a largely skeptical public for the new global struggle. This has been central to the endeavor of sustaining an American "anti-colonialist" empire and has helped to narrate the Cold War in an anti-imperialist vein. Institutionally, the involvement of evangelical voluntary organizations in federal funding arrangements paved the way for the "anti-statist statism" that helped make the expansion of the state palatable to a public committed to limited government. Socioeconomically, evangelicals simultaneously supported the military-industrial complex and upheld an insurgent message of free enterprise in a kind of "libertarian corporatism." This appealed to an electorate particularly in the south and the west of the country that had benefited from federal defense spending and the social service expansions but clung to the vision of self-made entrepreneurs and frontier individualism. And socioculturally, evangelicals combined morality politics and freewheeling capitalism into a form of "reactionary modernism." This spoke to people who were comfortable with the new technological and consumerist society but felt besieged by the race and gender challenges it had generated. In other words, only in the context of the neo-evangelical revival did a conception of American empire come into its own in the postwar period.[72]

Conversely, the ideological fragilities and institutional openness of U.S. empire building helped consolidate evangelicalism. World War II and the

Cold War period witnessed extensive efforts by policy makers to mobilize evangelicalism's ideological and institutional resources for the domestic legitimation and global assertion of empire. Eager to launch spiritual weapons against America's foes, they encouraged a commitment to the "redeemer nation" and the religious sanctification of liberal capitalism and American-style democracy. This not only provided conservative Protestants with access to political power brokers and decision-making processes in Washington but also meant that the very elements that had previously pushed conservative Protestantism to the margins of U.S. politics—obscure prophetic pietism, church-state separationism, and old-fashioned moral revivalism—ironically ended up enabling evangelicals to thrive under the conditions of the postwar period. World War II and the Cold War helped make arcane biblical concepts meaningful for the unconverted, bestowed national political importance on the experience of conversion, and established evangelical themes and sentiments as valid and coherent interpretive concepts for understanding the new world order. They strengthened evangelical institutions, shored up the material basis for revivalism, enabled conservative Protestants to invest heavily in overseas proselytizing, and affirmed the moral codes of the old-time religion as part of the civic foundations of American society.

This new closeness to worldly power benefited the conservative wing within the movement more than the left-leaning evangelicals. After all, the statist merger of "throne and altar" had historically been more characteristic of the Protestant right, whereas pietism, church-state separatism, and revivalism were more characteristic of the left. In the same vein, the resurgent right within the U.S. movement used the new ideological, institutional, and socioeconomic linkages to the wartime and Cold War state to develop a coherent political ideology, foster ties to secular conservatism, and sideline or co-opt evangelical liberals and the left. They did this, however, not solely by sacralizing America's new global power, military-industrial complex, free enterprise ideology, Cold War nationalism, and liberal capitalism. Instead, they formulated an ideology that addressed the contradictions within a movement whose adherents simultaneously were at home in the "American century" and historically expressed sentiments deeply critical of worldly culture, society, and power. Conservative Protestants combined an "outsider" message of righteousness, anti-elitism, and morality politics with the sanctification of the both the Cold War order and global U.S. power. In this theo-ideology, religious pietism became associated with militant anti-communism and Cold War nationalism; church-state separation meant rejecting intrusive state control while embracing government funding of faith-based aid agencies;

and spiritual revivalism associated moral awakenings with the embrace of entrepreneurial selves and liberal capitalism.[73]

Conclusion

The post–World War II revival of international evangelical missionary and humanitarian engagement increasingly brought conservative Protestants into global politics. By the same token, U.S. foreign policy elites, engaged in constructing the foundations of American empire, progressively involved evangelicals in cementing the ideological, institutional, cultural, and socio-economic foundation of global power. Researching this interrelationship on the basis of transnational perspectives opens up a range of new vistas on both the evangelical resurgence and U.S. foreign policy history.

Transnationalism challenges established narratives in the history of both religion and foreign policy between the 1940s and the 1970s on two levels. First, it reveals the emergence of visions markedly different from the strident nationalism of the Christian right in the United States and an evangelical reservoir of alternative concepts for U.S. international engagement. After all, these were decades when postwar evangelicalism was coming into its own but had not yet coalesced into the New Christian Right. Becoming more embroiled with the world outside of the United States redefined the content and boundaries of evangelicalism. Decolonization, mission work, and humanitarian aid confronted many missionaries with their complicity in racism, capitalist exploitation, and global hierarchies.

Second, in contrast to the standard trope of the postwar consolidation of the ideologies and institutions of U.S. foreign policy, transnational approaches highlight the instabilities and contestations of empire building. They open up new vistas on the anti-imperial threads woven into domestic U.S. political culture and the country's emergence as a "reluctant hegemon." Similarly, they remind us that the ascent of the United States as a global power went hand in hand with the postwar weakening of the old imperialist rulers Britain and France. This provided opportunities for anti-colonial movements for self-determination, especially in Asia and Africa, and for the questioning of the social, cultural, and political foundations of nineteenth-century imperialism.

Crucially, the "transnational turn" not only takes cognizance of the diversity of evangelicalism and the contested terrain of foreign policy, but also opens up new ways of understanding the relationship between religion and foreign policy in general, and between evangelicals and empire in particular. Concepts of co-constitution provide new insights into the significance of religious ideologies, practices, and institutions in constructing U.S. international power. Likewise, they reveal the role of U.S. global engagement and foreign policy in constituting conservative Protestantism.

In exploring this mutual construction, however, transnational research—ironically — tends to folds concepts of diversity and contestation back into an established story of the rise of the New Christian Right and the consolidation of U.S. global power. It suggests that the very instabilities and contradictions that transnationalism uncovers end up being constitutive of empire and of conservative evangelicalism. In regard to global evangelicalism, scholars show that it played a conflicted role: it acted simultaneously as a conduit for transporting and preserving insurgent perspectives and as a key agent of negotiating contradictions and tensions within U.S. imperialist thought and practice in ways that stabilized the emerging American world order. Though frequently challenging racism and colonialist exploitation, evangelical global activism tended to further social inequality and neocolonial dependency rooted in capitalism, particularly as the U.S. movement continued to cultivate corporate ties, replicate market-driven consumerist models, and sacralize capitalist agendas friendly to broader U.S. economic interests.

In regard to foreign policy, transnational perspectives show that the lack of fully operational ideologies and institutions for the exercise of political, economic, and cultural power abroad offered manifold opportunities to evangelical groups for linkages with the state—in ways that primarily benefited the conservative wing within the movement. Indeed, only in the context of World War II and the Cold War did the New Christian Right come into its own. U.S. foreign policy making, including its contestations, ultimately enabled the New Christian Right to assert its dominance at home during a time of a diversifying and fragmenting evangelical movement.

Transnational perspectives thus open up new perspectives on both evangelicalism's challenges to global U.S. power and the movement's political and cultural diversity beyond the embrace of right-wing politics. Yet they also reveal how evangelical tenets and practices that grew in American soil impose limitations and blind spots on the global movement, how evangelical relations with the outside world largely remained a facet of U.S. empire building, and how deeply reliant U.S. empire is on evangelical religion. In particular, transnational research exposes how ideologies of empire were legitimized in domestic U.S. society and politics via the religious engagement with subaltern peoples, traditions, and histories.

Sustaining truly alternative visions, however, requires an imaginative space that transcends nations, capitalism, individualism, and liberalism as the dominant territorial form, socioeconomic mode, cultural trope, and political ideology. Or, to quote James Baldwin, "The oppressor and the oppressed are bound together within the same society; they accept the same criteria; they share the same beliefs; they both alike depend on the same reality. Within this cage it is . . . meaningless to speak of a 'new' society as the desire of the oppressed, for that shivering dependence on the props of reality which he shares with the *Herrenvolk* makes a truly 'new' society impossible to conceive."[74]

Notes

1. Philip E. Dow, "The Influence of American Evangelicalism on US Relations with East and Central Africa during the Cold War" (PhD diss., University of Cambridge, 2012); Robert Coote, "The Uneven Growth of Conservative Evangelical Missions," *International Bulletin of Missionary Research* 6, no. 3 (July 1982): 119.

2. Rachel M. McCleary and Robert J. Barro, "U.S.-Based Private Voluntary Organizations: Religious and Secular PVOs Engaged in International Relief and Development, 1939–2004," NBER Working Paper No. 12238, May 2006, www.nber.org/papers /w12238.pdf, 3. For example, in 2005, the International Mission Board of the Southern Baptist Convention sponsored more than 5,000 full-time foreign missionaries, a five-fold increase from 1955. See Robert Wuthnow and Stephen Offutt, "Transnational Religious Connections," in *Sociology of Religion: A Reader*, ed. William A. Mirola, Michael O. Emerson, and Susanne C. Monahan (New York: Routledge, 2016), 434–36.

3. "Christian Movements and Denominations," in *Global Christianity—A Report on the Size and Distribution of the World's Christian Population*, Pew Research Center, December 19, 2011, www.pewforum.org/2011/12/19/global-christianity-movements-and -denominations/.

4. See, for example, Frank Ninkovitch, "Interests and Discourse in Diplomatic History," *Diplomatic History* 13, no. 2 (April 1989): 135–61; Andrew Preston, "Bridging the Gap between the Sacred and the Secular in the History of American Foreign Relations," *Diplomatic History* 30, no. 5 (November 2006): 783–812; Walter A. McDougall, "Religion in Diplomatic History," Foreign Policy Research Institute, March 2, 1998, www.fpri.org /article/1998/03/religion-in-diplomatic-history/; and Walter A. McDougall, "The Myth of the Secular: Religion, War, and Politics in the Twentieth Century," Templeton Lecture on Religion and World Affairs, Foreign Policy Research Institute, October 17, 2019, www.fpri.org/article/2019/10/the-myth-of-the-secular-religion-war-and-politics-in-the -twentieth-century/.

5. Jon Butler, "Jack-in-the-Box Faith: The Religion Problem in Modern American History," *Journal of American History* 90, no. 4 (March 2004): 1357–78.

6. Leo Ribuffo, "Why You Can't Ignore Religion If You Want to Understand Foreign Policy," History News Network, July 14, 2014, http://historynewsnetwork.org /article/156246.

7. Among some of the exceptions are Michael Cromartie, ed., *Evangelicals and Foreign Policy: Four Perspectives* (Lanham, MD: University Press of America, 1989); and

Angela M. Lahr, *Millennial Dreams and Apocalyptic Nightmares: The Cold War Origins of Political Evangelicalism* (New York: Oxford University Press, 2007). See also Bruce Ellis Benson and Peter Goodwin Heltzel, eds., *Evangelicals and Empire: Christian Alternatives to the Political Status Quo* (Grand Rapids, MI: Brazos Press, 2008); and Dean C. Curry, "Where Have All the Niebuhrs Gone? Evangelicals and the Marginalization of Religious Influence," *Journal of Church and State* 36, no. 1 (Winter 1994): 97–114.

8. Sylvester A. Johnson, "Religion and US Empire," *Religion in American History: A Group Blog on Religion in American Culture and History*, October 17, 2013, http://usreligion.blogspot.com/2013/10/religion-and-us-empire.html.

9. See Paul Mojzes et al., eds., *North American Churches and the Cold War* (Grand Rapids, MI: Eerdmans, 2018); Patricia R. Hill, "Commentary: Religion as a Category of Diplomatic Analysis," *Diplomatic History* 24, no. 4 (October 2000): 633–40; Philip E. Muehlenbeck, ed., *Religion and the Cold War: A Global Perspective* (Nashville, TN: Vanderbilt University Press, 2012); Dianne Kirby, ed., *Religion and the Cold War* (New York: Palgrave Macmillan, 2003); Walter McDougall, *Promised Land, Crusader State: The American Encounter with the World since 1776* (New York: Houghton Mifflin, 1997); Mark Edwards, *Faith and Foreign Affairs in the American Century* (Lanham, MD: Lexington Books, 2019); and Elliot Abrams, ed., *The Influence of Faith: Religious Groups and U.S. Foreign Policy* (Lanham, MD: Rowman and Littlefield, 2001). Insightful articles on this issue include Andrew J. Rotter, "Christians, Muslims and Hindus: Religion and U.S.–South Asian Relations, 1947–1954," *Diplomatic History* 24, no. 4 (October 2000): 593–613; Seth Jacobs, "'Our System Demands the Supreme Being: America's Religious Revival and the Diem Experiment, 1954–1955," *Diplomatic History* 25, no. 4 (October 2001): 589–624; Leilah Danielson, "Christianity, Dissent, and the Cold War: A. J. Muste's Challenge to Realism and U.S. Empire," *Diplomatic History* 30, no. 4 (September 2006): 645–69; George J. Hill, "Intimate Relationships: Secret Affairs of Church and State in the United States and Liberia, 1925–1947," *Diplomatic History* 31, no. 3 (June 2007): 465–503; and Mark Edwards, "'God Has Chosen Us': Re-membering Christian Realism, Rescuing Christendom, and the Contest of Responsibilities during the Cold War," *Diplomatic History* 33, no. 1 (January 2009): 67–94.

10. Andrew Preston, *Sword of the Spirit, Shield of Faith: Religion in American War and Diplomacy* (New York: Knopf, 2012), 610. See also Walter Russell Mead, "God's Country?," *Foreign Affairs* 85, no. 5 (September/October 2006): 24–43.

11. David Ziemtsma, "'Sin Has No History': Religion, National Identity, and U.S. Intervention, 1937–1941," *Diplomatic History* 31, no. 3 (June 2007): 531–65.

12. Jonathan P. Herzog, *The Spiritual-Industrial Complex: America's Religious Battle against Communism in the Early Cold War* (New York: Oxford University Press, 2011).

13. William Inboden, *Religion and American Foreign Policy, 1945–1960: The Soul of Containment* (New York: Cambridge University Press, 2008).

14. See, for example, T. Jeremy Gunn, *Spiritual Weapons: The Cold War and the Forging of an American National Religion* (Westport, CT: Praeger, 2009); Anna Su, *Exporting Freedom: Religious Liberty and American Power* (Cambridge, MA: Harvard University Press, 2016); Gary Scott Smith, *Faith and the Presidency* (Oxford: Oxford University Press, 2007); Raymond Haberski, *God and War: American Civil Religion since 1945* (New Brunswick, NJ: Rutgers University Press, 2012); and Bethany Moreton, *To Serve God and Wal-Mart: The Making of Christian Free Enterprise* (Cambridge, MA: Harvard University Press, 2010).

15. On the role of the Cold War in the religious resurgence, see Matthew Avery Sutton, *American Apocalypse: A History of Modern Evangelicalism* (Cambridge, MA: Belknap Press of Harvard University Press, 2014); Kevin M. Kruse, *One Nation under God: How Corporate America Invented Christian America* (New York: Basic Books, 2015); Darren Dochuk, *From Bible Belt to Sunbelt: Plain-Folk Religion, Grassroots Politics, and the Rise of Evangelical Conservatism* (New York: W. W. Norton, 2011); Daniel K. Williams, *God's Own Party: The Making of the Christian Right* (New York: Oxford University Press, 2010); Steven P. Miller, *Billy Graham and the Rise of the Republican South* (Philadelphia: University of Pennsylvania Press, 2009); and John G. Turner, *Bill Bright and Campus Crusade for Christ: The Renewal of Evangelicalism in Postwar America* (Chapel Hill: University of North Carolina Press, 2008). See also Sarah Miller-Davenport, "'Their Blood Shall Not Be Shed in Vain': American Evangelical Missionaries and the Search for God and Country in Post–World War II Asia," *Journal of American History* 99, no. 4 (March 2013): 1109–32; Uta A. Balbier, "Transnationalizing US Religious History and Revisiting the European Case," *Journal of American Studies* 51, no. 1 (2017): 249–54; and Mark R. Amstutz, *Evangelicals and American Foreign Policy* (New York: Oxford University Press, 2013). Useful recent dissertations that explore the role of foreign policy in the political mobilization of evangelicals include Jeremy R. Hatfield, "For God and Country: The Religious Right, the Reagan Administration, and the Cold War" (PhD diss., Ohio University, 2013); and Chan Woong Shin, "America's New Internationalists? Evangelical Transnational Activism and U.S. Foreign Policy" (PhD diss., Syracuse University, 2014).

16. Lauren Frances Turek, *To Bring the Good News to All Nations: Evangelical Influence on Human Rights and U.S. Foreign Relations* (Ithaca, NY: Cornell University Press, 2020). See also her chapter in this volume.

17. David P. King, *God's Internationalists: World Vision and the Age of Evangelical Humanitarianism* (Philadelphia: University of Pennsylvania Press, 2019).

18. John Corrigan, *Religious Intolerance, America, and the World: A History of Forgetting and Remembering* (Chicago: University of Chicago Press, 2020).

19. Gregorio Bettiza, *Finding Faith in Foreign Policy: Religion and American Diplomacy in a Postsecular World* (New York: Oxford University Press, 2020).

20. On postwar neo-evangelicalism, see, for example, George Marsden, *Understanding Fundamentalism and Evangelicalism* (Grand Rapids, MI: Eerdmans, 1991); Joel A. Carpenter, *Revive Us Again: The Reawakening of American Fundamentalism* (New York: Oxford University Press, 1997); James Davison Hunter, *American Evangelicalism: Conservative Religion and the Quandary of Modernity* (New Brunswick, NJ: Rutgers University Press, 1983), 41–45; Nathan O. Hatch and Michael S. Hamilton, "Taking the Measure of the Evangelical Resurgence, 1942–1992," in *Reckoning with the Past: Historical Essays on American Evangelicalism from the Institute for the Study of American Evangelicals*, ed. D. G. Hart (Grand Rapids, MI: Baker Books, 1995), 395–412; and Axel R. Schäfer, *Countercultural Conservatives: American Evangelicalism from the Postwar Revival to the New Christian Right* (Madison: University of Wisconsin Press, 2011).

21. On left evangelicalism, see David R. Swartz, *Moral Minority: The Evangelical Left in an Age of Conservatism* (Philadelphia: University of Pennsylvania Press, 2012); Craig Gay, *With Liberty and Justice for Whom? The Recent Evangelical Debate over Capitalism* (Grand Rapids, MI: Eerdmans, 1991); and Robert Booth Fowler, *A New Engagement: Evangelical Political Thought, 1966–1976* (Grand Rapids, MI: Eerdmans, 1987). On the

range of evangelical debates about foreign policy, see also Timothy Padgett, "Warmongers? Continuity and Complexity in Evangelical Discourse on United States Foreign Policy, 1937–1973" (PhD diss., Trinity International University, 2016).

22. Quoted in Hunter, *American Evangelicalism*, 46. See also Leonard I. Sweet, "The 1960s: The Crisis of Liberal Christianity and the Public Emergence of Evangelicalism," in *Evangelicalism and Modern America*, ed. George Marsden (Grand Rapids, MI: Eerdmans, 1984), 29–45.

23. Carl F. H. Henry, "Evangelicals: Out of the Closet but Going Nowhere?," *Christianity Today*, January 4, 1980, 17.

24. On these issues, see Christopher McKnight Nichols, "The Enduring Power of Isolationism: An Historical Perspective," *Orbis* 57, no. 3 (Summer 2013): 390–407; James Sparrow, *Warfare State: World War II Americans and the Age of Big Government* (New York: Oxford University Press, 2011); Nancy Beck Young, *Why We Fight: Congress and the Politics of World War II* (Lawrence: University Press of Kansas, 2013); Michael Hunt, *Ideology and U.S. Foreign Policy* (New Haven, CT: Yale University Press, 2009); and Walter Hixson, *The Myth of American Diplomacy: National Identity and U.S. Foreign Policy* (New Haven, CT: Yale University Press, 2008). See also Michaela Hoenicke Moore, *The Varieties of American Patriotism* (forthcoming).

25. For recent books on this subject, see, for example, Odd Arne Westad, *The Cold War: A World History* (London: Allen Lane, 2017); Leslie James and Elisabeth Leake, eds., *Decolonization and the Cold War: Negotiating Independence* (London: Bloomsbury, 2015); David Ryan and Michael Patrick Cullinane, eds., *U.S. Foreign Policy and the Other: Transatlantic Perspectives* (New York: Berghahn Books, 2014); and Petra Goedde, *The Politics of Peace: A Global Cold War History* (Oxford: Oxford University Press, 2019).

26. On the feedback effects of foreign missions (though in this case in regard to mainline Protestants), see also David A. Hollinger, *Protestants Abroad: How Missionaries Tried to Change the World but Changed America* (Princeton, NJ: Princeton University Press, 2017).

27. Among recent books on the international activism of U.S. religious groups and the global history of American evangelicalism are Robert Wuthnow, *Boundless Faith: The Global Outreach of American Churches* (Berkeley: University of California Press, 2009); Ian Tyrrell, *Reforming the World: The Creation of America's Moral Empire* (Princeton, NJ: Princeton University Press, 2010); Emily Conroy-Krutz, *Christian Imperialism: Converting the World in the Early American Republic* (Ithaca, NY: Cornell University Press, 2015); Heather D. Curtis, *Holy Humanitarians: American Evangelicals and Global Aid* (Cambridge, MA: Harvard University Press, 2018); Melani McAlister, *The Kingdom of God Has No Borders: A Global History of American Evangelicals* (New York: Oxford University Press, 2018); David R. Swartz, *Facing West: American Evangelicals in an Age of World Christianity* (New York: Oxford University Press, 2020); and Mark Hutchinson and John Wolffe, *A Short History of Global Evangelicalism* (Cambridge: Cambridge University Press, 2012). See also Kendrick Oliver, Uta A. Balbier, Hans Krabbendam, and Axel R. Schäfer, "Special Issue: Exploring the Global History of American Evangelicalism— Introduction," *Journal of American Studies* 51, no. 4 (2017): 1019–42.

28. Swartz, *Facing West*, 55.

29. The literature on transnationalism is voluminous. For good introductions covering the breadth of the field, see, for example, Ian Tyrrell, *Transnational Nation:*

United States History in Global Perspective since 1789 (Basingstoke: Palgrave Macmillan, 2007, 2015); Akira Iriye, *Global and Transnational History: The Past, Present, and Future* (Basingstoke: Palgrave Macmillan, 2012); Emily Rosenberg, ed., *A World Connecting, 1870–1945* (Cambridge, MA: Harvard University Press, 2012); Thomas Bender, *A Nation among Nations: America's Place in World History* (New York: Hill and Wang, 2006); Eric Rauchway, *Blessed among Nations: How the World Made America* (New York: Hill and Wang, 2006); Matthew Frye Jacobson, *Barbarian Virtues: The United States Encounters Foreign Peoples at Home and Abroad* (New York: Hill and Wang, 2001); and David Thelen, "The Nation and Beyond: Transnational Perspectives on United States History," *Journal of American History* 86, no. 3 (1999): 965–75. See also Akira Iriye and Pierre-Yves Saunier, eds., *The Palgrave Dictionary of Transnational History* (Basingstoke: Palgrave Macmillan, 2009). On defining transnationalism, see Ian Tyrrell, "Reflections on the Transnational Turn in United States History: Theory and Practice," *Journal of Global History* 4, no. 3 (November 2009): 453–74; "Interchange: Globalization and Its Limits between the American Revolution and the Civil War," *Journal of American History* 103, no. 2 (September 2016): 400–433; and Patricia Clavin, "Defining Transnationalism," *Contemporary European History* 14, no. 4 (November 2005): 421–39.

30. On transnational networks, see, for example, Daniel T. Rodgers, "An Age of Social Politics," in *Rethinking American History in the Global Age*, ed. Thomas Bender (Berkeley: University of California Press, 2002), 250–73; Kiran Klaus Patel, *The New Deal: A Global History* (Princeton, NJ: Princeton University Press, 2016); and Carola Hein, "Crossing Boundaries: The Global Exchange of Planning Ideas," in *Making Cities Global: The Transnational Turn in Urban History*, ed. A. K. Sandoval-Strausz and Nancy H. Kwak (Philadelphia: University of Pennsylvania Press, 2018), 114–29.

31. Alfred W. Crosby, *Ecological Imperialism: The Biological Expansion of Europe, 900–1900* (New York: Cambridge University Press, 1986); Ian R. Tyrrell, *True Gardens of the Gods: Californian-Australian Environmental Reform, 1860–1930* (Berkeley: University of California Press, 1999). On the ecological perspective in transnationalism, see also Paul Sutter, "Seeing beyond Our Borders: US and Non-US Historiographies," in *A Companion to American Environmental History*, ed. Douglas Cazaux Sackman (Chichester: Wiley-Blackwell, 2010), 635–52; Ian Tyrrell, "Beyond the View from Euro-America: Environment, Settler Societies, and the Internationalization of American History," in Bender, *Rethinking American History in the Global Age*, 168–91; David Igler, *The Great Ocean: Pacific Worlds from Captain Cook to the Gold Rush* (Oxford: Oxford University Press, 2013); and Regina Schober, "America as Network: Notions of Interconnectedness in American Transcendentalism and Pragmatism," *Amerikastudien* 60, no. 1 (2015): 97–119. See also Jared Diamond, *Guns, Germs, and Steel: The Fates of Human Societies* (New York: W. W. Norton, 1997).

32. Randolph Bourne, "Trans-National America," *Atlantic Monthly* 118 (July 1916): 86–97. On the diasporic dimension, see, for example, Matthew Fry Jacobson, "More 'Trans-,' Less 'National,'" *Journal of American Ethnic History* 25, no. 4 (Summer 2006): 74–84; Donna R. Gabaccia, "'Is Everywhere No Where?' Nomads, Nations, and the Immigrant Paradigm of American History," *Journal of American History* 86, no. 3 (December 1999): 1115–34; Donna R. Gabaccia, *Foreign Relations: American Immigration in Global Perspective* (Princeton, NJ: Princeton University Press, 2012); Dirk Hoerder, "From Euro- and Afro-Atlantic to Pacific Migration System: A Comparative Migration

Approach to North American History," in Bender, *Rethinking American History in the Global Age*, 195–235; A. K. Sandoval-Strausz, "Latino Landscapes: Postwar Cities and the Transnational Origins of a New Urban America," *Journal of American History* 101, no. 3 (December 2014): 804–31.

33. An early example of the way diasporic consciousness shaped the writing of U.S. history is Oscar Handlin, *The Uprooted: The Epic Story of the Great Migrations That Made the American People* (Philadelphia: University of Pennsylvania Press, 1952).

34. W. E. B. Du Bois, "Of Our Spiritual Strivings," in *The Souls of Black Folk: Essays and Sketches* (Chicago: A. C. McClurg, 1903), 3.

35. Examples of the subaltern focus include Saskia Sassen, "The Global City: Strategic Site/New Frontier," *American Studies* 41, no. 2/3 (Summer/Fall 2000): 79–95; Celeste-Marie Bernier, "'The Slave Ship Imprint': Representing the Body, Memory, and History in Contemporary African American and Black British Painting, Photography, and Installation Art," *Callaloo* 37, no. 4 (2014): 990–1022; Robin D. G. Kelley, "How the West Was One: The African Diaspora and the Re-mapping of U.S. History," in Bender, *Rethinking American History in the Global Age*, 123–47; and Andrew Zimmerman, "Africa in Imperial and Transnational History: Multi-sited Historiography and the Necessity of Theory," *Journal of African History* 54, no. 3 (November 2013): 331–40.

36. McAlister, *Kingdom of God Has No Borders*. See also Daniel G. Hummel, "Religious Pluralism, Domestic Politics, and the Emerging Jewish-Evangelical Coalition on Israel, 1960–1980," in *The Cold War at Home and Abroad: Domestic Politics and US Foreign Policy since 1945*, ed. Andrew L. Johns et al. (Lexington: University Press of Kentucky, 2018), 100–122.

37. Emily S. Rosenberg, *Spreading the American Dream: American Economic and Cultural Expansion, 1890–1945* (New York: Hill and Wang, 1982).

38. See, for example, Michael S. Sherry, *In the Shadow of War: The United States since the 1930s* (New Haven, CT: Yale University Press, 1995); Peter Dobkin Hall, "The Welfare State and the Careers of Public and Private Institutions since 1945," in *Charity, Philanthropy, and Civility in American History*, ed. Lawrence J. Friedman and Mark D. McGarvie (New York: Cambridge University Press, 2003), 363–83; Gary R. Hess, "Waging the Cold War in the Third World: The Foundations and the Challenges of Development," in Friedman and McGarvie, *Charity, Philanthropy, and Civility in American History*, 319–39; and Helen Laville and Hugh Wilford, eds., *The US Government, Citizen Groups and the Cold War: The State-Private Network* (New York: Routledge, 2006).

39. Philip E. Dow, "Romance in a Marriage of Convenience: The Missionary Factor in Early Cold War U.S.-Ethiopian Relations, 1941–1960," *Diplomatic History* 35, no. 5 (November 2011): 859–95; Bruce Nichols, *The Uneasy Alliance: Religion, Refugee Work, and U.S. Foreign Policy* (New York: Oxford University Press, 1988).

40. Dow, "Influence of American Evangelicalism," 148–50. Despite this focus, however, U.S. evangelicalism in Africa remains an under-researched aspect of transnational religion, reflecting the political power imbalance between the United States and Africa.

41. Eisenhower quoted in Richard V. Pierard and Robert D. Lindner, *Civil Religion and the Presidency* (Grand Rapids, MI: Academic Books, 1988), 189, 197–98.

42. Stephen V. Monsma, *When Sacred and Secular Mix: Religious Nonprofit Organizations and Public Money* (Lanham, MD: Rowman and Littlefield, 1996), 10, 72–73; McCleary and Barro, "Religious and Secular PVOs," 14–15. See also David P. King, "The

New Internationalists: World Vision and the Revival of American Evangelical Human-itarianism," *Religions* 3, no. 4 (October 2012): 922–49. I have explored this further in Axel R. Schäfer, "Evangelical Global Engagement and the American State after World War II," *Journal of American Studies* 51, no. 4 (November 2017): 1069–94.

43. Bettiza, *Finding Faith in Foreign Policy*, 119.

44. See, for example, Oliver Scheiding and Anja-Maria Bassimir, eds., *Religious Periodicals and Publishing in Transnational Contexts: The Press and the Pulpit* (Newcastle upon Tyne: Cambridge Scholars Publishing, 2017); and Anja-Maria Bassimir, *Evangelical News: Politics, Gender, and Bioethics in Conservative Christian Magazines of the 1970s and 1980s* (Tuscaloosa: Alabama University Press, 2022).

45. McAlister, *Kingdom of God Has No Borders*, chaps. 8, 9, 11.

46. McAlister, chaps. 12–15. See also Mark Philip Bradley, *The World Reimagined: Americans and Human Rights in the Twentieth Century* (New York: Cambridge University Press, 2016).

47. Tyrrell, *Reforming the World*, esp. chap. 8; David Swartz, "Christ of the American Road: E. Stanley Jones, India, and Civil Rights," *Journal of American Studies* 51, no. 4 (2017): 1117–38; Melani McAlister, "The Global Conscience of American Evangelicalism: Internationalism and Social Concern in the 1970s and Beyond," *Journal of American Studies* 51, no. 4 (November 2017): 1197–220. On "reverse missions," see also Patrick Harries and David Maxwell, eds., *The Spiritual in the Secular: Missionaries and Knowledge about Africa* (Grand Rapids, MI: Eerdmans, 2012); and David Hollinger, "The Protestant Boomerang: American Missionaries and the United States," November 15, 2010, Washington History Seminar, Wilson Center, Washington, DC, www.wilsoncenter.org/event /the-protestant-boomerang-american-missionaries-and-the-united-states.

48. Nancy D. Wadsworth, *Ambivalent Miracles: Evangelicals and the Politics of Racial Healing* (Charlottesville: University of Virginia Press, 2014), 147, 219.

49. "Minutes-Business Meeting of ESAC [Evangelical Social Action Commission] at NAE Convention," February 23, 1976, National Association of Evangelicals [NAE] Records (SC-113), Buswell Library Special Collections, Wheaton College, IL.; H. Wilbert Norton to Martin H. Schrag, June 11, 1976, NAE Records.

50. Quoted in Wadsworth, *Ambivalent Miracles*, 253. On this issues, see also Ulrike Elisabeth Stockhausen, *The Strangers in Our Midst: American Evangelicals and Immigration from the Cold War to the Twenty-First Century* (New York: Oxford University Press, 2021).

51. Swartz, *Facing West*, chap. 2.

52. Dow, "Influence of American Evangelicalism," 97, 76, 65.

53. Heather J. Sharkey, *American Evangelicals in Egypt: Missionary Encounters in an Age of Empire* (Princeton, NJ: Princeton University Press, 2008); David C. Kirkpatrick, *A Gospel for the Poor: Global Social Christianity and the Latin American Evangelical Left* (Philadelphia: University of Pennsylvania Press, 2019). For the nineteenth century, see, for example, Stephen Warren, "Rethinking Assimilation: American Indians and the Practice of Christianity, 1800–1861," in Friedman and McGarvie, *Charity, Philanthropy, and Civility in American History*, 107–27.

54. Wuthnow, *Boundless Faith*, 94.

55. Graham quoted in Anne C. Loveland, *American Evangelicals and the U.S. Military, 1942–1993* (Baton Rouge: Louisiana State University Press, 1996), 37.

56. Miller-Davenport, "American Evangelical Missionaries," 1117, 1127.

57. On this theme see, for example, Tom Smith, "'History,' 'Unwritten Literature,' and U.S. Colonialism in Hawai'i, 1898–1915," *Diplomatic History* 43, no. 5 (November 2019): 813–39; Tom Smith, *Across God's Vast Lake: American Missionaries, Pacific Worlds, and the Making of Imperial Histories* (forthcoming); and Lanny Thompson, *Imperial Archipelago: Representation and Rule in the Insular Territories under U. S. Dominion after 1898* (Honolulu: University of Hawai'i Press, 2010). See also Tom Smith's chapter in this volume.

58. Hannah Waits, "Missionary-Minded: American Evangelicals and Power in a Postcolonial World, 1945–2000" (PhD diss., University of California Berkeley, 2019). See also Melissa Borja and Jacob Gibson, "Internationalism with Evangelical Characteristics: The Case of Evangelical Responses to Southeast Asian Refugees," *Review of Faith and International Affairs* 17, no. 3 (September 2019): 80–93; Sarah E. Ruble, *The Gospel of Freedom and Power: Protestant Missionaries in American Culture after World War II* (Chapel Hill: University of North Carolina Press, 2012); and Rodney A. Coeller, "Beyond the Borders: Radicalized Evangelical Missionaries in Central America from the 1950s through the 1980s" (PhD diss., American University, 2012).

59. McAlister, *Kingdom of God Has No Borders*, 208. On the intersection of faith, market ideology, and social conservatism, see also Linda Kintz, *Between Jesus and the Market: The Emotions That Matter in Right-Wing America* (Durham, NC: Duke University Press, 1997); and Moreton, *To Serve God and Wal-Mart*.

60. John Corrigan, *Emptiness: Feeling Christian in America* (Chicago: University of Chicago Press, 2015).

61. On this issue, see also Andrew Preston, "Evangelical Internationalism: A Conservative Worldview for the Age of Globalization," in *The Right Side of the Sixties: Reexamining Conservatism's Decade of Transformation*, ed. Laura Jane Gifford and Daniel K. Williams (New York: Palgrave Macmillan, 2012), 221–40.

62. Oliver et al., "Special Issue," 1019–42. On the link between church growth and capitalism, see also Jesse Curtis, "White Evangelicals as a 'People': The Church Growth Movement from India to the United States," *Religion and American Culture* 30, no. 1 (Winter 2020): 108–46.

63. Quoted in Carolyn Pedwell, "Carolyn Pedwell on Empathy, Accuracy, and Transnational Politics," *Theory, Culture, and Society*, December 22, 2014, www .theoryculturesociety.org/carolyn-pedwell-on-empathy-accuracy-and-transnational -politics/. See also Caroline Pedwell, *Affective Relations: The Transnational Politics of Empathy* (Basingstoke: Palgrave Macmillan, 2014); Amalia Ribi Forclaz, *Humanitarian Imperialism: The Politics of Anti-slavery Activism, 1880–1940* (Oxford: Oxford University Press, 2015); and Johannes Paulmann, ed., *Dilemmas of Humanitarian Aid in the Twentieth Century* (Oxford: Oxford University Press, 2016).

64. McAlister, *Kingdom of God Has No Borders*; Lydia Boyd, *Preaching Prevention: Born-Again Christianity and the Moral Politics of AIDS in Uganda* (Athens: Ohio University Press, 2015). See also her chapter in this volume.

65. Dow, "Romance in a Marriage of Convenience," 859–95; Dow, "Influence of American Evangelicalism," 97, 76, 65, 166–67.

66. "Where Do We Go From Here?," *Christianity Today*, November 12, 1956, 17.

67. Harold Lindsell, "An Evangelical Evaluation of the Relationship between Churches and the State in the United States," Consultation on the Church in a Secular World, October 11–13, 1967, NAE Records, 14–15.

68. Marsden, *Understanding Fundamentalism and Evangelicalism*, 97.

69. Oliver et al., "Special Issue," 1037, 1025.

70. Uta A. Balbier, "The World Congress on Evangelism 1966 in Berlin: US Evangelicalism, Cultural Dominance, and Global Challenges," *Journal of American Studies* 51, no. 4 (2017): 1171–96; Ruble, *Gospel of Freedom and Power*.

71. On this issue see, for example, Molly Worthen, *Apostles of Reason: The Crisis of Authority in American Evangelicalism* (New York: Oxford University Press, 2013); Mark A. Noll, *The Old Religion in a New World: The History of North American Christianity* (Grand Rapids, MI: Eerdmans, 2002); Christian Smith, *American Evangelicalism: Embattled and Thriving* (Chicago: Chicago University Press, 1998); and Jerome L. Himmelstein, *To the Right: The Transformation of American Conservatism* (Berkeley: University of California Press, 1990). See also Shin, "America's New Internationalists?"

72. I have explored this in more detail in Axel R. Schäfer, "Evangelicals and Empire: White Conservative Protestants in U.S. Cold War Politics and Society," in Mojzes et al., *North American Churches and the Cold War*, 375–403.

73. Axel R. Schäfer, *Piety and Public Funding: Evangelicals and the State in Modern America* (Philadelphia: University of Pennsylvania Press, 2012), chap. 5.

74. James Baldwin, "Everybody's Protest Novel," in *James Baldwin: Collected Essays*, ed. Toni Morrison (New York: Library of America, 1998), 17.

CHAPTER ELEVEN

PEPFAR, AIDS Prevention, and the Politics of American Compassion in Uganda

Lydia Boyd

At the 2004 International AIDS Conference in Bangkok, Thailand, President George W. Bush's new global AIDS policy was a focal point of debate and discussion. Introduced during Bush's 2003 State of the Union address, PEPFAR—the President's Emergency Plan for AIDS Relief—was a $15 billion global health program that sought to provide care and treatment to people living with AIDS in resource-poor countries, especially in Africa. It had the potential to radically expand access to effective antiretroviral therapy, which had until then been severely limited in Africa, the continent hardest hit by the epidemic. While a celebrated investment in global health, the policy was also deeply controversial because of the Bush administration's decision to earmark spending on prevention programs, directing $1 billion, a third of the monies pledged for prevention, to abstinence-and-faithfulness-only projects.

In Bangkok, the efficacy of abstinence programs was widely debated, and PEPFAR's prevention guidelines drew ridicule from many researchers and activists. President Bush's Global AIDS Coordinator, Randall Tobias, faced so much criticism during one public appearance that reporters speculated that he had considered abandoning his participation in the conference entirely.[1] But there was also vocal support for the policy, and especially of abstinence as a prevention strategy. American evangelical Christians, who had until then largely stayed on the sidelines of AIDS advocacy, were key political supporters of Bush's decision to promote abstinence as AIDS prevention. In Bangkok a new brand of AIDS activists joined panels, shared experiences, and touted the effectiveness of the United States' new approach. Pastor Rick Warren, the American evangelical author of the wildly successful best-seller *The Purpose Driven Life*, sent his son to the Bangkok conference. And one panel featured a young Ugandan Christian activist who defended abstinence against criticisms raised by other more prominent panelists, including Steven Sinding, the director general of the Planned Parenthood Federation.[2]

The participation of Warren and the Ugandan activist was the result of a new awareness among evangelical Christians that the global HIV/AIDS epidemic should be a humanitarian problem of significance to their communities. As recently as 2000, a survey conducted by the international Christian aid group World Vision revealed widespread resistance among American Christians to the idea of serving HIV-positive individuals.[3] One Christian missionary I interviewed in Uganda in 2004 explained that the U.S. community funding his work considered AIDS the result of "immoral behavior" and an inappropriate cause for a Christian mission to take up. Yet these attitudes were changing quickly in the mid-'00s. Bush had repositioned the issue of AIDS in many believers' minds, describing PEPFAR as a "work of mercy"[4] that not only could address suffering among the most vulnerable (especially poor African women and children) but also could become a vehicle for social programs long considered important to Christians, including abstinence-only education and policies emphasizing family values, like the support of heterosexual marriage.

This repositioning of AIDS provoked religious organizations, like the one headed by the missionary whom I interviewed in 2004, to grapple with questions of whether to apply for U.S. grants to provide AIDS prevention services in foreign communities. Should AIDS be a problem addressed—at least in part—by American Christians, working with and funded by the U.S.

government? The answer to this question was often yes, as both global Christian aid organizations, like Franklin Graham's Samaritan's Purse, and small local Christian organizations in both the United States and donor-recipient countries like Uganda, quickly mobilized in response to PEPFAR and applied for funds that helped them to deploy a U.S. AIDS prevention policy focused on abstinence and faithfulness. This shift—from viewing AIDS as a problem outside the scope of Christian concern to an issue of importance that became a key mode of American Christian global engagement—was dramatic in both its scope and speed.

Evangelical American support for PEPFAR in the opening years of the twenty-first century can be read as a barometer not only of shifting Christian interest in the AIDS epidemic but also of changing attitudes about the scope and reach of American humanitarian work and the church's role in such projects. While American Christians have taken part in actions that have helped shape American engagement with a global sphere since at least the nineteenth century,[5] in recent decades the desire of American evangelicals to play a larger role outside U.S. borders, and in U.S. international policy and humanitarian endeavors, has only intensified.[6] Neoliberal economic policies seemed to accelerate this shift, as government social programs in the 1980s and 1990s were defunded, and a private sector powered by the charitable impulses of volunteers—many of them Christian—were called upon to shore up communities in need.

President Bush in many ways exemplified this shift. Having been elected in 2000 with the strong backing of evangelical Christians, his initial policy efforts outlined a view of government working together with faith organizations in ways that many considered pushed the boundaries between church and state, forging new ground for the role of religious organizations in public life. Early in his administration he had created the White House Office of Faith-Based and Community Initiatives, a program that sought to shift more federal funding for social services to religious organizations. This domestic program aimed to increase the participation of faith-based service providers in federally funded projects, such as foster care and housing programs.

The administration of PEPFAR represented an extension of this effort to engage the religious sector in government work. Not only were policy decisions that were considered friendly to Bush's evangelical base written into PEPFAR—such as the emphasis on sexual abstinence—but faith-based organizations were involved in and targeted for inclusion in the policy's initial implementation. Samaritan's Purse reviewed grant applications for PEPFAR, and smaller Christian organizations were motivated to apply for, and received, such funding. In the early years of my research in Uganda, where I conducted fieldwork on AIDS prevention programs from 2004 to 2010, representatives of small Christian aid groups regularly spoke with me about their realization that the U.S. government was suddenly interested in funding Christian groups to provide AIDS services, and a number of churches took up the issue of AIDS prevention with new intensity, many for the first time.

The involvement of religious groups in both domestic and international programs funded by the U.S. government was characterized in Bush's speeches as the natural result of the sentimental bonds forged between people through religious belief. For Bush, religion famously brought "compassion" to the conservative policies of the Republican Party. In a speech accepting an award for his humanitarian work from Rick Warren, Bush emphasized the important contribution of faith in the work of government: "'Government is justice, and love comes from a higher government, higher calling—from God. . . . People from across America, motivated by faith . . . are already involved in the process' of bringing faith and government together."[7] Anthony Petro, in his study of American Christian HIV/AIDS activism, notes that "Bush elevated to a new level faith-based approaches to humanitarian concerns."[8]

Bush was particularly adept at deploying language familiar to evangelical Christians to argue for the integration of faith into government. "Compassionate conservativism," the label he is perhaps best associated with, was not simply about bringing a redeeming dose of care to the work of a government that by the beginning of the twenty-first century was associated with neoliberal austerity and a resulting decline in social services. Compassion signaled the role that faith could play in transforming governance and, in turn, society. As Rebecca Sager argues in her study of the role of Christianity in Bush's domestic policies, programs like the White House Office of Faith-Based and Community Initiatives "were more about changing culture and politics by altering the relationship between religion and government" than they were ever about simply channeling more money to religious organizations.[9]

Evangelical engagement in humanitarian projects like PEPFAR reveals how such work was about more than just the changing status of evangelicals in political and social projects in the last decades of the twentieth century. The empathy of American evangelicals that gave shape to humanitarian projects like PEPFAR was also instrumental to the cultivation of a broader neoliberal economic ethos that shaped public responses to social problems at home and abroad during these decades (see also John Corrigan in this volume).

This chapter considers the ways that American evangelical compassion was deployed in one of the countries that was the target of the PEPFAR program, Uganda, and the ways Ugandan Christians engaged with and understood the material and spiritual intentions of the program. An emphasis on "compassion" was not incidental to a program like PEPFAR; it helped to structure what kinds of care and what approaches to AIDS prevention the U.S. government favored. Compassion, as I discuss more fully below, signaled not just "mercy" for others but an expectation about what Christian mercy might achieve and the transformation it was believed to elicit in communities and individuals subjected to Christian care. Compassion was often paired in Bush's rhetoric with an emphasis on the *accountability* of recipients of aid. The use of empathy to shape expectations of responsibility, self-sufficiency, and autonomy in turn helped to emphasize a broader ethos of economic and moral behavior that undergirded American neoliberal policies of this period.

Drawing on multiyear fieldwork within a Christian community of AIDS activists in Uganda who received PEPFAR grants, this chapter also examines the impact of this humanitarian approach on an African community. While Ugandans were supportive of abstinence as AIDS prevention, the American Christian emphasis on accountability and personal autonomy that was part of the PEPFAR program was more controversial, mainly for the conflicts it produced involving locally meaningful ideas about the moral obligations and expectations of reciprocity that many Ugandans believe to be inherent in charitable relationships. This conflict is revealing not only of the limits of PEPFAR's success but also of the broader implications of American evangelical aspirations for global influence and connectivity.

PEPFAR and the Political Mobilization of American (and Ugandan) Evangelicals

As with all government policies, PEPFAR was shaped by various interest groups and lobbying constituencies that sought to imprint their agenda onto one of the largest peacetime humanitarian projects deployed by the United States since World War II. In its initial iteration, PEPFAR was a pledge of $15 billion over five years, directed toward fourteen countries, all but two of them in Africa. It was a policy that took up an issue of pressing human importance—in 2003 there were more than 26 million people living with HIV in Africa, only a small percentage of whom had access to any effective treatment—that had long been politically volatile in the United States. President Reagan, in office in the first frantic years of the epidemic, was ridiculed for all but ignoring the virus's existence, failing to say the word "AIDS" in public until 1986, five years into the crisis.[10] But it was also Reagan's administration that recognized the political power of AIDS. As Jennifer Brier has written in her history of the U.S. federal response to AIDS, Reagan's administration was more than just silent on the issue. It was a topic heavily debated within his administration, viewed as an opportunity both for those on the religious right to corral public discussion of AIDS toward a reassertion of a shared "family"-based morality that emphasized heterosexual unions and abstinence and for another constituency that warned of the danger of the public health crisis and advocated for access to politics-free health education.[11]

A similar tension was revealed during the congressional debates that authorized the funding for PEPFAR. Several Christian advocates who supported abstinence as a key funding initiative, many with ties to the Bush administration, spoke alongside others who argued for the funding of more diverse strategies. During the 2003 congressional hearings on PEPFAR, Shepherd Smith, a missionary with ties to the Bush administration, and Anne Patterson, a "former missionary doctor" and then current U.S. Agency for International Development employee, both spoke of the essential importance of funding abstinence-only approaches to AIDS prevention, especially in Africa. Their testimony was refuted by many others, most testifying on behalf of the Democrats, who argued that abstinence-only programs were linked to stagnant or increased HIV-prevalence rates.[12]

Unlike the behind-the-scenes debates that unfolded in the Reagan administration, PEPFAR's public debate gave new prominence to American evangelical Christian positions regarding AIDS and humanitarianism more broadly. AIDS had long seemed a distant concern for evangelicals, even those focused on humanitarian causes abroad. In 1987 the conservative North Carolina senator Jesse Helms, who considered himself a fundamentalist Christian, infamously denounced federal funding for AIDS care and treatment, arguing that people living with AIDS were "perverted human beings" and that federally funded AIDS programs risked promoting "homosexual activities."[13] But by 2002, after years of resistance, even this staunchest of AIDS critics had changed his tune: standing alongside the evangelical humanitarian Franklin Graham, Helms reversed course and supported a new bill that sought to expand American funding to address the global AIDS crisis.[14]

This kind of rapid change of course typified many evangelical Christians' views of AIDS in the early years of the new century. In part this shift can be attributed to changing perceptions of the victims of the epidemic. By the early 'oos the most visible sufferers of AIDS were living in Africa and were widely perceived to be infected through heterosexual sex. Women and children were far more sympathetic victims in the eyes of social conservatives than the white homosexual men who had dominated American media coverage of AIDS during its first decade. But President Bush and his advisors were also successful in reframing AIDS relief as an opportunity to elevate faith-based approaches to humanitarian concerns. Rather than see sexual transmission as a reason to ignore the epidemic, AIDS was suddenly attractive for the ways federal AIDS policy could work to promote social policies long viewed as desirable to evangelical Christians, such as abstinence-only sex education and policies promoting and supporting heterosexual marriage. An editorial in *Christianity Today* from 2002 was representative of this position. In it, the authors argued that comprehensive sex education and condom distribution were "failed" efforts at AIDS prevention and what was needed was a "sea change" in policy, driven by Christians who could provide the kind of moral guidance about sexual behavior that was necessary to fully address AIDS risk.[15]

PEPFAR's policy guidelines for funding were a victory for Christians who campaigned for prevention methods focused on behavior changes, like abstinence and "faithfulness" to a single partner, over other approaches. The $1 billion pledged to support abstinence-only education and the promotion of monogamous marriages was a huge sum of money by any standards and resulted in a flood of support for these kinds of programs in donor-recipient countries.

In Uganda, one of the initial fourteen countries targeted for PEPFAR funding, AIDS had long been understood as a social and humanitarian crisis of almost unprecedented proportions. By the late 1980s and early 1990s, the country faced prevalence rates of nearly 15 percent of the population, a crippling statistic by any measure.[16] Despite the extent of the virus's impact, Uganda drew praise for its government's fast action in response to the devastation of the epidemic, especially for embracing culturally relevant interventions that involved local communities.[17] The Ugandan government initially supported a wide range of policies spearheaded by a broad sector of the population, from newly organized women's groups to government ministries. Religious organizations were not marginal to this response.[18] While AIDS was a morally fraught issue, associated with supposed sexual promiscuity, the mainline (Anglican and Catholic) churches generally worked alongside other health and social services providers during the first two decades of the epidemic, usually providing services that aligned with church priorities (never promoting condoms, for instance, but addressing issues like the children orphaned by the virus). Churches were neither high-profile nor absent from what is generally considered to have been a remarkably effective broad-based and multisector approach to AIDS prevention in Uganda during the 1980s and 1990s.

By the '00s, Uganda's religious landscape was being quickly transformed by the growing popularity and prominence of nondenominational and "born-again" churches.[19] While the country had been predominantly Anglican and Catholic throughout the twentieth century, these newer churches first proliferated in the 1980s and 1990s as the country emerged from two decades of war and political instability into a period of relative peace. A changing media sector, which brought with it satellite television that streamed American televangelists, along with the loosening of state regulations regarding the operation of independent churches, had hastened the growth of evangelical and nondenominational churches. Without the same bureaucracy and history within the country as that of mainline churches, independent churches did not, in the epidemic's first decades, have the infrastructure, or the motivation, to engage with the AIDS crisis in concrete ways. Many also had direct ties to Western missionary groups, which, as I noted, were unlikely to focus on the epidemic in its first decades. But, just as PEPFAR changed American Christian perspectives on AIDS, it also changed the landscape of Christian AIDS activism in Uganda. By the mid-'00s, sexual abstinence as AIDS prevention emerged as a popular topic for sermons and other church activities, and a new wave of AIDS activism was fostered within the Christian community in Uganda, shaped in part by PEPFAR's support and funding.

Born-Again Programs to Fight AIDS in Uganda

When I was doing anthropological fieldwork on AIDS in Uganda in the mid-'00s, there was a palpable shift in AIDS prevention initiatives, from the more expansive, multisector approach that characterized Uganda's initial response to the epidemic, to a new focus on and the greater visibility of abstinence-only education. The U.S. government's support for abstinence-only programming, and the widespread perception within Uganda that such programming was supported by America's born-again president, provided an opening for new kinds of AIDS activists and organizations in Uganda. This shift drew many smaller nondenominational churches into AIDS work for the first time.

One prominent example of this new wave of activists was Pastor Martin Ssempa, who headed a nondenominational born-again church in central

Kampala that welcomed many university students to its congregation. He had first become active in AIDS education in the 1990s, while he was himself a university student, but he rose to prominence as a Christian AIDS activist in the next decade, as he capitalized on his ties to U.S. evangelical leaders.[20] By 2003, when PEPFAR was proposed, he emerged as a vocal supporter of sexual abstinence as AIDS prevention. Ssempa, in a shift from earlier AIDS activists in Uganda, viewed AIDS as a problem that demanded not only consideration and funding but also a *Christian* solution. Ssempa was skilled at promoting his message in media-savvy ways, and he thrived on creating a sense of conflict that would draw attention to his work. He would often emphasize that abstinence was not one way but the *only* appropriate way to prevent AIDS. (In one infamous case, he burned a pile of condoms in the middle of Kampala's Makerere University campus to make this point.)[21] Ssempa characterized his church, in an interview with me, as one that was ideally positioned to address the AIDS epidemic because he had his hand on the pulse of the youth and knew how to attract them: "My church was founded intentionally to be a church that dealt with the problems of young people: that's sex, that's AIDS, that's entertainment." Ssempa's position highlighted the changing stakes of AIDS activism in Kampala in the wake of PEPFAR. No longer simply content to respond to an unfolding crisis or draw international attention to a humanitarian disaster, AIDS activists like Ssempa viewed their activism as a new kind of platform to argue for their vision of family and social life in Uganda—teaching young adults about sexuality in a way that was godly but also compelling, media friendly, and high-stakes.

Ssempa's church was also representative of another aspect that shifted under PEPFAR, which was the infusion of funding for religious organizations that sought to engage in AIDS work for the first time. PEPFAR was a giant global program, administered by a U.S. federal agency (the Office of the U.S. Global AIDS Coordinator), but in donor-recipient countries the impact of PEPFAR was often felt through the involvement of community-oriented, local programs that administered relatively small grants, like those received by churches and religious NGOs like Ssempa's.[22] There were large PEPFAR grants in Uganda, but these tended to fund treatment-access initiatives, which were directed by established multinational and national NGOs that engaged in clinical care work—like World Vision (a global humanitarian Christian organization), Population Services International (a reproductive health NGO), and Uganda's TASO organization (a national AIDS treatment project). Churches and small community organizations applied and received funding for smaller-scale educational projects, especially prevention education programs.

In Kampala, PEPFAR funded a university newspaper, written by members of a church-affiliated Christian community group, that focused entirely on promoting sexual abstinence. Martin Ssempa ran a weekly Saturday night gospel music entertainment event, where the focus was summed up by comical banners urging students to "keep your underwear on!" Another youth education program, this one aimed at high school students on school term break, sought to teach teenagers about the importance of "faithful" marriage and the dangers of youthful liaisons. In this lesson, marriage was described as a "fortress" that would keep a couple safe from the demands and threats (social, financial, and epidemiological) of extramarital relationships.

At the core of PEPFAR's emphasis on abstinence and faithfulness was a belief that personal self-control—the ability to abstain from sex until marriage and to remain faithful to one person thereafter—was the ultimate means of preventing AIDS. In the wake of the influx of funding for these programs and the involvement of Christian organizations that sought to promote this message, these behaviors took on a moral valence: if AIDS prevention was within one's control, infection was evidence of a personal and probable moral failure. This was, from a public health standpoint, the most problematic aspect of the abstinence-and-faithfulness focus. While these behaviors were effective on an individual level, on a societal level an emphasis on personal "behavior change" ignored the structural drivers of the epidemic, especially economic and gender inequality.[23] Some people, no matter their willpower or faith, would at some point find themselves in a position that put them at risk for infection. For Ugandan women, this would sometimes mean infection within marriages to which they themselves had been faithful.[24]

Despite these shortcomings, the abstinence-and-faithfulness message was deeply appealing for both Ugandan and American Christians because of this emphasis on individual responsibility and self-control. Abstinence was popular in many churches because it was part of a larger message that positioned Christianity as a path that allowed for new kinds of independence—of faith, but also of a new personal agency in relationships with others. It marked a significant break from older Ugandan models for family and moral selfhood that were rooted in an emphasis on social interdependence and relationships of spiritual, social, and economic reciprocity with an extended kin group. In church, abstinence talk went hand in hand with a new vision for personal relationships that were driven by individual choice and

The Politics of American Compassion in Uganda

self-control. This message also aligned with a theological orientation in char-ismatic and born-again churches that stressed personal spiritual growth—being "born again" in Christ—and that positioned born-again spirituality in contrast to indigenous or "traditional" spiritual beliefs. Spiritual work in these churches highlighted acts of deliverance—the breaking of spiritual bonds to the past that may hinder an individual's physical, emotional, and spiritual development. Abstinence was a lesson that fit well within a theo-logical context that encouraged believers to take control of their spiritual and material selves—breaking off ties with nonbelievers and focusing criticism on so-called traditional aspects of Ugandan life.

Of course, the limitations of this message were precisely in the ways it could not provide the structural changes—the tangible help—that would transform young people's positions within society or within their kin rela-tionships. Without jobs and financial independence, youth remained part of family and societal systems that restricted choices and options as often as they provided them. And without transformations to gender relations, women's ability to negotiate their status within marriage and manage their risk relative to their partners' behavior remained limited. Nonetheless, the message of "faith in the self"—an emphasis on personal accountability and self-control—ran through PEPFAR's prevention programs as it did other economic and political endeavors associated with American interventions in Africa during this decade. For many Ugandan young adults, abstinence's focus on self-empowerment was considered novel, modern, American, and Christian. But it was also shaped by a broader economic and political strategy that aimed to stress the individual as the solution to a host of structural and humanitarian problems and that under President Bush was animated by the sentimental ideals of Christian compassion.

Neoliberalism, Empire, and Christianity: Compassion's Role during the Global AIDS Crisis

PEPFAR's emphasis on the ability to self-manage disease risk—to privi-lege individual solutions to broader structural and social problems—was an approach that had been shaped by the neoliberal economic policies of the late twentieth century. In Uganda, these economic policies were felt most keenly in the form of structural adjustment programs (SAPs) that the state was forced to adopt in the late 1980s when President Yoweri Museveni accepted foreign loans of last resort to help stabilize the country after decades of civil war. SAPs demand that aid recipients deregulate private industry, privatize state industries, and decrease spending on social services, all in an effort to force open national markets to global investment and competition.[25] Under these "free market" conditions, where the state must retreat from direct investment in its population, it is the individual, rather than the community, who is positioned as the primary agent of "development" and transformation.

This faith in individual will as panacea was true as well for Western governments that embraced economic austerity in the 1990s and into the next decade, a time during which a new political rhetoric celebrating the citizen-volunteer was popularized.[26] President Bush's "compassionate conservativism" emerged alongside David Cameron's "Big Society" model in Great Britain during this period, both of which argued that newly emboldened free markets provided the space for individuals to step into the gap created by a retreating welfare state. Counterintuitively, this perspective on the relationship between the market and social welfare considers neoliberal governance not as an overly rationalized, amoral project but as dependent on the emergence of a new kind of citizen-subject who is encouraged to demonstrate care for fellow citizens in the face of abject need.

Bush's compassionate conservativism highlighted this dissonance at the center of neoliberal austerity. It was a political philosophy that emphasized not only fiscal discipline but also an ideal of self-empowerment that would translate into a new kind of citizenship, one where individuals, not governments, would take care of each other. Bush's government would "encourage people and communities to help themselves and one another," reminding Americans that "the truest kind of compassion is to help citizens build better lives of their own."[27] Compassion both stressed the new power of personal sentiment to address poverty and other pressing social problems and also celebrated the power of compassion to change the subjects of such care. In this model, social change is rooted not in strengthened infrastructure or other community-level investments but in personal changes to individual behavior. Recipients of aid would ideally become more responsible for themselves, eliminating social problems in turn.

For American evangelical Christians, Bush's emphasis on compassion aligned with a belief system that celebrated the power of faith to transform individuals and, by extension, society. Evangelicals view compassionate acts not only as "selfless" gifts of aid but as transformative acts of God's mercy. Compassion is a central tenet of evangelical belief: the demand that believers respond to the needy as an expression of God's work on earth. Demonstrations of compassion are ostensibly gifts, given without the expectation of return. But as acts of godly love, Christians also believe them to engender

The Politics of American Compassion in Uganda

change in the recipients of aid. More than simply an emotional bond with others, compassion was believed to do something to both giver and receiver of aid, who are both altered by the presence of God's love. This creates something of a catch-22 for recipients of aid, who must demonstrate need but also the capacity for successful change.[28]

The influence of this mindset is evident in Bush's political discourse in the ways compassion was often paired with a focus on results-based accountability. People are always worthy of compassion, according to this mindset, but, in response, they should demonstrate how they have been changed by this aid, becoming more capable and successful. The effects of compassionate care are shown in individuals who are more accountable for their actions, able to address the problems they face by demonstrating good judgment and self-control. This transformation of the self, ideally in response to the actions of others, was the engine of compassionate conservativism. Bush's administration emphasized this connection in its "Armies of Compassion" policy overview, noting that "government should help the needy achieve independence and personal responsibility."[29] More than a form of care, compassion was about creating measurable, results-driven change in persons and communities, placing the onus for such changes on the recipients of aid.

In many Ugandan churches during the mid-'00s, a similar language of self-help and personal empowerment was becoming familiar and popular. In some of the urban born-again churches that had taken up AIDS prevention in the mid-'00s, business acumen, entrepreneurial drive, and the capacity to help oneself were the themes of a powerful and popular rhetoric. At one leadership conference I attended in 2007, led by Pastor Ssempa and a visiting American pastor from Las Vegas, Kevin Odor, university students were told that they had the power to become leaders if they cultivated tools of self-management and developed the "willpower" to plan better for their futures. Held in a Catholic conference center on Makerere University's campus, the event had drawn students from college campuses around the capital city. More than just a church seminar, the workshop had the feel of a business school lecture series. Both pastors spoke about planning for success, evaluating one's strengths, and responding to setbacks. The emphasis in these lessons was on the ways one's material success was rooted not in the supernatural power of belief but in one's own capacity to work and improve. This message is one that I have elsewhere termed a "gospel of self-help,"[30] the celebration of an entrepreneurial ethos that many born-again churches in Kampala embraced in the '00s.

In this way, American evangelical compassion was helping to shape an emergent neoliberal subjecthood in Uganda, deploying a language of spirituality and moral action to craft a model of individual responsibility. The funding for abstinence education was generated by a broader shift in political and social discourse that was rooted in the United States and that had coalesced around Bush's "compassionate conservative" ideal: faith and fiscal policy would come together to celebrate personal self-reliance as the engine of social, economic, and epidemiological change. PEPFAR was just one way these ideas were engaging Ugandans.[31]

Yet, even as an American-influenced language of self-help was taking hold in the mid-'00s, Ugandans were not simply echoing their American partners. Self-help coexisted alongside other moral orientations to behavior and social obligation that were also influential during these years. In Uganda, independence and autonomy—especially breaking away from problematic ties of kin and asserting financial independence from others—are not necessarily celebrated goals. Scholars of Africa have long recognized the ways that relationships, especially hierarchical ones, are important mechanisms of social mobility in places like Uganda, where economic, political, and moral interdependence operates as a "mode of action" rather than simply a constraint on individual agency.[32] The importance of relationships of inequality and interdependence to Ugandan political and social life is reflected in historical and contemporary political connections,[33] attitudes about marriage,[34] and economic associations of patronage that still dominate certain sectors of workplace life[35] and help to shape perspectives on the meaning of economic "development."[36] This is to say that for Ugandans, the value of "self-help" and personal autonomy was not self-evident in the '00s. As I will discuss below, the continuing existence of alternative readings of moral behavior and social obligation created the opening for conflicts over how PEPFAR programs—perhaps especially the charitable relationships between American Christians and Ugandans—were interpreted.

Reciprocity and Other Perspectives on Humanitarian Care: Ugandan Reflections on American Charity

There was great hope on the part of both American Christians and Ugandan Christians that abstinence, and a broader message of self-empowerment, would solve a vast array of social and economic problems in Uganda. Many Ugandan born-again Christians were fiercely motivated by a belief in self-transformation and by a message that with good planning and willpower they could withstand the threat of HIV and succeed economically and personally. The primary problems with this plan were in the structural limitations that defined it. Despite a deep desire for success, without tangible changes to their circumstances (such as a job offer or secure housing), other material change was unlikely. Good intentions were in great supply, but this did not always translate into changing circumstances, or even changed behaviors.

The programs that PEPFAR funded also suffered from the broader limitations that typically characterized international aid. Grants were usually short lived, especially for small-scale education projects. A grant to print an abstinence-only newspaper provided a brief windfall for a small Christian NGO, but it did little to create long-term financial security for members of that community. For Ugandans, the fleeting nature of U.S. investment in what were perceived as Christian approaches to prevention was troublesome especially for the ways relationships between donors and recipients were fragile, open to the whims of federal funding but also open to political criticism and U.S. election cycles. Some of the most prominent churches involved in abstinence-only education in Uganda later became active in promoting anti-homosexuality legislation in that country in 2009, when a born-again member of Uganda's parliament introduced the Anti-Homosexuality Bill, which included a clause imposing the death penalty for certain infractions of homosexual sex. The politically volatile nature of this bill in the global realm threatened some of the aid relationships Ugandan churches had cultivated with partners in the United States, as U.S. churches, ceding to a new politics of sexuality at home, withdrew support for Ugandans associated with the bill.[37] This left many Ugandans critical of the seemingly arbitrary way that Christian doctrine would drive American policy, a position laid bare when Martin Ssempa denounced Rick Warren's efforts to distance himself from the legislation.[38]

The disagreement between Ugandan and American Christians over the Anti-Homosexuality Bill revealed some of the biggest problems with this humanitarian aid relationship for Ugandans. This was an association that demanded obedience—staying true to a message, demonstrating accountability for promised changes—but there was little agency for Ugandans to react to, shape, or speak back to American demands. This is not to say that the virulent hate that led to the Anti-Homosexuality Bill was in any way supportable, but it helps to highlight the ways that Ugandans viewed their ties to Americans and the problems they experienced once they embraced these connections. One problem with the U.S. evangelical emphasis on self-help was how U.S. relationships with Ugandans did little to radically alter economic conditions in ways that would foster new kinds of autonomy for youth and their communities. But these associations, which celebrated self-empowerment and personal will as the key determinants of successful behavior, also ran counter to how Ugandans typically viewed the value of dependency: not as burdensome and morally questionable but as a key aspect of a society defined by relationships of interdependence and mutual obligation.

In Uganda, relationships of dependence, even those defined by the abject need of the individual seeking help, are understood to be socially productive and morally redeeming for both the giver and the receiver of aid. Release from a relationship of dependence is not necessarily a social or personal goal. As China Scherz has written in her study of a western Ugandan charity, dependency on others is often viewed as a critical mode of social mobility, a morally redeeming position that—far from problematic—is considered socially necessary and essential to social reproduction in Uganda.[39] Similarly, Harri Englund, writing of human rights discourse and the tentative circulation of the ideal of "equality" in Malawi, has noted that the poor in that country are typically more successful making political demands by utilizing a language of mutual obligation between the powerful and the less so. It is *inequality*, rather than equality, that is believed to build social bonds and provide moral motivation. Englund argues that a liberal celebration of equality may obscure the alternative moral frameworks for social change that exist throughout rural Africa.[40] In Uganda, the obligation to give and support others is not only virtuous but a behavior that is thought to shape social hierarchies that provide support and enable social reproduction. Because of this, most Ugandans view opportunity and obligation in the position of both dependents and those at the top of social hierarchies. Those dependent on aid are not passive supplicants but are viewed as critical actors in socially productive relationships of inequality. This is to say that Ugandan Christians, for all their celebration of self-help and self-control, may have viewed their relationship to American benefactors differently than the way Americans viewed their own compassionate acts.

Many church communities involved in AIDS activism in the opening decade of the twenty-first century saw abstinence activism as a way to build connections abroad and to bring donors in contact with their communities in order to provide new kinds of financial support. PEPFAR was just one way this might happen. Independent American churches—like Kevin Odor's (of the leadership seminar above) or, perhaps most famously, Rick Warren's Saddleback Church, which had dubbed Uganda a "purpose-driven nation" and whose members set out by the thousands to solve problems of chronic poverty through their "church in a box" strategy[41]—often sought out Ugandan churches as partners in humanitarian and social projects, from abstinence to orphan sponsorship.[42] These were relationships that typically brought physical support, in the form of visits from American short-term mission volunteers, as well as financial support.

These relationships were welcomed by Ugandans. But what was often frustrating was how the dependency of Ugandan Christians led to a sense of disempowerment. American Christians may have sent money, but the terms of such an association were determined by Americans rather than by Ugandans. This seems typical of many aid relationships, but what made the terms of this one especially unsettling was the way compassion engendered a belief in the cultivation of autonomy and control without providing the means for recipients of aid to control or manage the relationships to which they were a part. The controversy over homosexuality was indicative of this frustration. Ugandan Christian supporters of the Anti-Homosexuality Bill argued that they were being stewards of Christian principles, upholding the word of God, and yet American Christians—who in supporting abstinence had seemed to demand that Christian morality take front and center—were now critical of Ugandans, withdrawing their financial support of many politically active churches.

Today, born-again churches remain important players in national politics in Uganda. And there continue to be many partnerships and donor relationships that tie American evangelicals to Ugandans. But the moment that PEPFAR created, with its American emphasis on Christian compassion as a mode of economic, social, and medical salvation, is no longer considered in entirely uncritical ways by Ugandan Christians. Ugandan born-again Christians, much like mainline Anglicans, came to view their own political aspirations as, at least in part, distinct from those of their American counterparts. This assertion of independence can be tied to doctrinal disagreements, such as those that divided the Anglican Communion in the mid-'00s, cleaving more conservative African congregations from the more liberal North American church.[43] But there was also a critical eye cast toward the nature of humanitarian relationships and the role played by Africans within these relationships. This wasn't a criticism over biblical interpretations; rather, it was one that centered on questions of dependency, agency, money, and power. Martin Ssempa, in a 2007 conversation with me, emphasized this narrative, explaining that Ugandans, too, are international actors, but their "stories" are always told by Americans and other Westerners who relegate

Africans to dependent partners, recipients of aid rather than actors in their own narrative: "There is this entire sense that an African cannot go beyond a certain barrier; it's like a sound barrier. I always envisioned myself as an international person. . . . So, I wanted to go out [abroad]. I wanted to run away from this country. But I did not. I decided to stay. But the problem for the African is that we never tell our stories."

Ssempa highlights here a criticism that many Ugandans—born-again Christian and not—shared with me during the 'oos: that while Uganda had successful HIV prevention efforts prior to the expansion of global funding under PEPFAR, it was now Americans rather than Ugandans who controlled and used this story to support policy and direct funding. While Ugandans like Ssempa supported abstinence, seeing it as aligned with other Christian frameworks, his frustration lay in the ways Ugandans had been sidelined in this humanitarian relationship, relegated to aid recipients rather than active agents in the shaping of community responses to AIDS. Like his American partners, he viewed himself as a globally oriented Christian believer but struggled against a persistent perception by these partners that he would always be a dependent in a one-directional relationship.

Ssempa is a complicated figure who has drawn deserved criticism for his homophobic views and vocal support of draconian criminal penalties for same-sex sexuality in Uganda. But he also articulates well the complicated dynamics of American approaches to global humanitarian aid under George W. Bush. Compassionate conservatism helped to change dramatically how American evangelicals viewed the global AIDS pandemic and their responsibility to help others far removed from their own communities. But compassion, while creating a sense of connection with other Christians, also disseminated an unfulfilled promise that individuals who received aid would be empowered to help themselves. Compassion presented difficult choices for Ugandan believers, who actively supported abstinence and the broader American emphasis on self-help. Approaches like abstinence demanded that believers change their behaviors, but young adults were given few tools beyond educational seminars to help them do so. And the moral message underlying compassion was that believers who remained in need of aid yet who failed to help themselves were less deserving, morally questionable, and (as Ssempa charges) not even in control of their own "story." This moral reading of dependent relationships ran counter to the ways Ugandans had long viewed relationships of charity or patronage, where recipients of aid were powerful agents of change and social mobility. Such a conflict revealed the divergent orientations to an emergent neoliberal subject held by American and Ugandan Christians. When fractures developed between American and Ugandan political goals, these differing views on the nature of interdependent aid relationships—the shape of obligation and agency and of power and inequality—were laid bare.

Conclusion

Popular accounts of Bush's presidency have tended to celebrate PEPFAR as a radical departure for the Republican Party, an investment in humanitarian relief that was targeted at mostly poor, mostly politically marginal communities in Africa.[44] Like Bush's most high-profile domestic social policies, PEPFAR emphasized the transformative possibilities of compassion, the belief that sentimental bonds between individual citizens could address endemic problems such as those of inequality, poverty, and health disparities. In this scenario, a government reshaped by the conservative economic principles that had enforced conditions of austerity was redeemed by the actions of individuals who could take on the work of the state by providing charitable care for their citizen-others.

PEPFAR is especially notable for the ways it engaged and mobilized evangelical Christians to take up the global AIDS crisis, an astonishing change in how conservative American Christians viewed their responsibility and obligation toward those suffering from the epidemic. This mobilization was in part dependent on a recognition that President Bush's interpretation of compassion was more than simply an emotional tie between citizen-actors and the recipients of aid but a Christian action, one that was ordained by God and driven by faith. In describing PEPFAR, Bush encouraged this interpretation, invoking biblical references to describe his program as one of moral obligation: "There is no way to quantify PEPFAR's greatest achievement: the spread of hope. . . . Spreading hope is in our moral interests—because we believe that to whom much is given, much is required."[45]

In many ways, PEPFAR heralded a new approach to humanitarianism and political action by American evangelicals. Christianity has long been tied up in broader political projects of empire building, central to European and American arguments that sought to justify colonial rule by characterizing state actions as moral, Christian projects and the civilizing visions of the colonial state as God-ordained.[46] The early twenty-first century marked a subtle but notable shift in this narrative. Bush's policies saw Christian sentiment and care not simply through a utilitarian lens. Christian sentiment helped to shape not only the details of federal policy—such as the decision to emphasize abstinence—but also an entire approach to humanitarian action. Compassionate conservatism stressed the necessity of affective ties between believers as key tools of social change, redefining the role of belief as one central to the remaking of behavior and, in turn, citizenship. Feelings, and in particular a Christian orientation to feelings, were key to the Bush administration's view of how neoliberal economic and political policies could function. Affective ties between individuals—being called to help the needy and the poor—made up a critical engine beneath his policies, impacting both domestic approaches to social services and a global vision of American influence.

Much of the criticism of PEPFAR has focused on the ways a Christian worldview shaped the policy in tangible ways, for instance by overriding the influence of many public health professionals to emphasize sexual abstinence over other kinds of AIDS prevention approaches.[47] In this chapter I have sought to cast a light on another issue with PEPFAR: the ways that compassion shaped the relationships between the givers and the receivers of aid. There is often an assumption that Ugandan Christians and American Christians viewed the problem of AIDS through the same eyes. And indeed, there were many similarities in the two groups' worldviews and support of certain social and health policies, like the abstinence-as-prevention model. But what is not often considered are the ways these two groups viewed humanitarian relationships and the nature of social obligation differently. American compassion, while celebrating the power of self-help and individual will, cast a negative moral light on conditions of dependency. This is a familiar perspective for Americans, who are taught to distrust social positions of dependency as morally objectionable and lacking in agency and social purpose. Ugandans have a different cultural orientation to the ways social bonds between unequals should work and to the moral and social purpose invested in positions of dependence. This led to rifts in the ways Americans and Ugandans viewed their positions relative to each other, especially as Ugandans increasingly saw that they were perceived as powerless and marginal players in American humanitarian projects.

The story of PEPFAR in Uganda reveals the ways American compassion traveled in the early '00s and the influence it had, especially within the United States, in reshaping American Christians' views of their own obligations to people far from home. But compassion's effects were not without limits. The vision of American compassion espoused by Bush was not a universal one within Christian communities globally. While it has greatly influenced the extent of ties between American and African Christians since

2004, African Christians have also sought to question the motives and influence of Americans, seeking to assert other views of what a global Christian communion may look like and the role of the "needy" within it.

Notes

1. "Is It Churlish to Criticise Bush over His Spending on AIDS?," *Lancet* 364, no. 9431 (July 2004): 303–4.

2. Vijay Joshi, "AIDS Conferees Prefer Condoms over Abstinence," *Spokesman-Review* (Spokane, WA), July 13, 2004, www.spokesman.com/stories/2004/jul/13/aids-conferees-prefer-condoms-over-abstinence (accessed May 28, 2020).

3. Christine J. Gardner, *Making Chastity Sexy: The Rhetoric of Evangelical Abstinence Campaigns* (Chicago: University of Chicago Press, 2011), 145.

4. State of the Union address, January 28, 2003, on *Washington Post* website, www.washingtonpost.com/wp-srv/onpolitics/transcripts/bushtext_012803.html.

5. Heather D. Curtis, *Holy Humanitarians: American Evangelicals and Global Aid* (Cambridge, MA: Harvard University Press, 2018).

6. Melani McAlister, *The Kingdom of God Has No Borders: A Global History of American Evangelicals* (New York: Oxford University Press, 2018).

7. Anthony Petro, *After the Wrath of God: AIDS, Sexuality, and American Religion* (Oxford: Oxford University Press 2015), 18.

8. Petro, 19.

9. Rebecca Sager, *Faith, Politics, and Power: The Politics of Faith-Based Initiatives* (Oxford: Oxford University Press, 2009), 4.

10. Jennifer Brier, *Infectious Ideas: U.S. Political Responses to the AIDS Crisis* (Chapel Hill: University of North Carolina Press, 2011), 80.

11. Brier, 80.

12. *Hearing before the Senate Subcommittee of African Affairs: Fighting AIDS in Uganda: What Went Right?*, 108th Cong., 1st sess., May 19, 2003, S. Hrg. 108-106.

13. Edward I. Koch, "Senator Helms's Callousness towards AIDS Victims," *New York Times*, November 7, 1987, sec. 1, p. 27, www.nytimes.com/1987/11/07/opinion/senator-helms-s-callousness-toward-aids-victims.html.

14. Adam Clymer, "Helms Reverses Opposition to Help on AIDS," *New York Times*, March 26, 2002, sec. A, p. 22, www.nytimes.com/2002/03/26/us/helms-reverses-opposition-to-help-on-aids.html.

15. Petro, *After the Wrath*, 47.

16. Justin O. Parkhurst, "Evidence, Politics and Uganda's HIV Success: Moving Forward with ABC and HIV Prevention," *Journal of International Development* 23, no. 2 (2011): 242.

17. Daniel Low-Beer and Rand Stoneburner, "Uganda and the Challenge of HIV/AIDS," in *The Political Economy of AIDS in Africa*, ed. Nana K. Poku and Alan Whiteside (London: Routledge, 2004), 165–90; Helen Epstein, *The Invisible Cure: Africa, the West, and the Fight against AIDS* (New York: Farrar, Straus and Giroux, 2007).

18. The country is predominantly Christian, with roughly one-third of the population identifying as Anglican and one-third Catholic and the rest split between

identifying as Muslim or as Pentecostal or a member of other Christian groups. The Anglican and Catholic Churches have long been important political institutions in the country, and both play key roles in the social services and humanitarian sectors of the country.

19. Ugandans use the term "born again" broadly, to refer to both mainline and non-mainline (independent and Pentecostal) Christians. Typically, it denotes Christian believers who have embraced more charismatic faith practices, believe the Bible to be the authoritative truth, and emphasize personal salvation experiences (being "born again" in Christ). While there are born-again communities within the mainline churches in Uganda and an influential history of faith revival within the Church of Uganda that dates back to the early twentieth century (see Derek Peterson, *Ethnic Patriotism and the East African Revival: A History of Dissent* Cambridge: Cambridge University Press, 2012), newer independent churches are now more closely associated with this term. The term "evangelical" is not as popular in Uganda as it is in the United States, but the term "born again" shares some similarities with the way the label "evangelical" is used in U.S. contexts. Ugandan born-again Christians are considered a political force in Uganda and have embraced all forms of media—including television, popular music, and the Internet—with vigor and savvy over the last two decades.

20. Ssempa is married to an American, whom he met while she was a missionary in Uganda. He acquired U.S. citizenship through marriage and has long-term relationships with several U.S. evangelical leaders and church communities, including several who stood by him during the controversy over Uganda's Anti-Homosexuality Bill (discussed below). See, for instance, Barbara Bradley Hagerty, "U.S. Church Lends Help to Anti-gay Ugandan Pastor," *NPR: All Things Considered*, July 13, 2010, www.npr.org /templates/story/story.php?storyId=128491183.

21. Epstein, *Invisible Cure*, 191–92.

22. Ssempa's church had an affiliated NGO, Campus Alliance to Wipe Out AIDS, that applied for and facilitated PEPFAR grants for abstinence education.

23. For one analysis of the failure of PEPFAR's prevention policies to emphasize structural change, see Anne Eascove, *Modernizing Sexuality: U.S. AIDS Prevention in Sub-Saharan Africa* (Oxford: Oxford University Press, 2016).

24. Shanti Parikh, "Going Public: Modern Wives, Men's Infidelity, and Marriage in East-Central Uganda," in *The Secret: Love, Marriage and HIV*, ed. Jennifer Hirsh, Holly Wardlow, Daniel Jordan Smith, Harriet M. Phinney, Shanti Parikh, and Constance A. Nathanson (Nashville, TN: Vanderbilt University Press, 2009), 168–96.

25. For one study of the effects and scope of structural adjustment in Africa, see James Ferguson, *Global Shadows: Africa in the Neoliberal World Order* (Durham, NC: Duke University Press, 2006).

26. Barbara Cruikshank, *The Will to Empower* (Ithaca, NY: Cornell University Press, 2019).

27. Office of the Press Secretary, "Fact Sheet: Compassionate Conservativism," The White House: President George W. Bush, April 30, 2002, https:// georgewbushwhitehouse.archives.gov/news/releases/2002/04/20020430.html (accessed May 26, 2020).

28. Omri Elisha, *Moral Ambitions: Mobilization and Social Outreach in Evangelical Megachurches* (Berkeley: University of California Press, 2011), 169.

29. "Rallying the Armies of Compassion," 107th Cong., 1st sess., January 31, 2001, House Document 107–36, 6–7.

30. Lydia Boyd, "The Gospel of Self-Help: Born-Again Musicians and the Moral Problem of Dependency in Uganda," *American Ethnologist* 45, no. 2 (2018): 241–52.

31. For instance, see Jörg Wiegratz, *Neoliberal Moral Economy: Capitalism, Sociocultural Change and Fraud in Uganda* (New York: Rowman and Littlefield, 2016).

32. James Ferguson, "Declarations of Dependence: Labour, Personhood, and Welfare in Southern Africa," *Journal of the Royal Anthropological Institute* 19, no. 2 (June 2013): 223–42.

33. Holly Hanson, *Landed Obligation: The Practice of Power in Buganda* (Portsmouth, NH: Heinemann, 2003); Mikael Karlström, "On the Aesthetics and Dialogics of Power in the Postcolony," *Africa* 73, no. 1 (2003): 57–76.

34. Parikh, "Going Public."

35. David Pier, *Ugandan Music in the Marketing Era: The Branded Arena* (New York: Palgrave Macmillan, 2015).

36. Susan Reynolds Whyte and Michael A. Whyte, "The Values of Development: Conceiving Growth and Progress in Bunyole," in *Developing Uganda*, ed. Holger Bernt Hansen and Michael Twaddle (Oxford: James Currey Press, 1998), 227–44.

37. Lydia Boyd, "The Problem with Freedom: Homosexuality and Human Rights in Uganda," *Anthropological Quarterly* 86, no. 3 (2013): 697–724.

38. Melani McAlister, "Homosexuality and Humanitarianism: The Case of Rick Warren in Africa," *Key Issues in Religion and World Affairs*, Institute on Culture, Religion and World Affairs, Boston University, September 2016, www.bu.edu/cura/files/2016/12 /mcalisterpaper.pdf.

39. China Scherz, *Having People, Having Heart: Charity, Sustainability, Development and the Problems of Dependence in Uganda* (Chicago: University of Chicago Press, 2014).

40. Harri Englund, *African Airwaves: Mediating Equality on the Chichewa Radio* (Bloomington: Indiana University Press, 2011), 48.

41. Katy Tangenberg, "Saddleback Church and the P.E.A.C.E Plan: Implications for Social Work," *Social Work and Christianity* 35, no. 4 (2008): 391–412.

42. Lydia Boyd, "Circuits of Compassion: The Affective Labor of Uganda's Christian Orphan Choirs," *African Studies Review* 63, no. 3 (2020): 518–39.

43. Miranda Hassett, *Anglican Communion in Crisis: How Episcopal Dissidents and Their African Allies Are Reshaping Anglicanism* (Princeton, NJ: Princeton University Press, 2007).

44. Erika Check Hayden, "An Unlikely Champion: Was Setting Up PEPFAR—a Massive HIV Treatment Programme—the Best Thing That President Bush Ever Did?," *Nature* 457, no. 7227 (2009): 254.

45. "Remarks on the Signing of the United States Global Leadership against HIV/ AIDS, Tuberculosis, and Malaria Reauthorization Act of 2008," July 30, 2008, Public Papers of the Presidents of the United States: George W. Bush, www.govinfo.gov /content/pkg/PPP-2008-book2/html/PPP-2008-book2-doc-pg1066.htm (accessed May 26, 2020). The biblical reference is to Luke 12:48.

46. John Comaroff, "Images of Empire, Contests of Conscience: Models of Colonial Domination in South Africa," *American Ethnologist* 16, no. 4 (1989): 661–85; Camilla Boisen, "The Changing Moral Justification of Empire: From the Right to Colonise to the

Obligation to Civilise," *History of European Ideas* 39, no. 3 (2012): 335–53; Peter J. Cain, "Character, 'Ordered Liberty,' and the Mission to Civilise: British Moral Justification of Empire, 1870–1914," *Journal of Imperial and Commonwealth History* 40, no. 4 (2012): 557–78.

47. Ilene Leventhal, "PEPFAR: Preaching Abstinence at the Cost of Global Health and Other Misguided Relief Policies," *Temple International and Comparative Law Journal* 24, no. 1 (2010): 173–212; John W. Dietrich, "The Politics of PEPFAR: The President's Emergency Plan for AIDS Relief," *Ethics and International Affairs* 21, no. 3 (2007): 277–92.

CHAPTER TWELVE

Bloody Kinship

Transnational Copts and American Persecution Politics

Candace Lukasik

In recent years, American politicians, think tanks, and NGOs have channeled their efforts into supporting ("saving") Middle Eastern Christians, especially in the wake of the so-called Arab Spring and the rise of the Islamic State. Over the past decade, Coptic Christians (the largest Christian community in the Middle East) have increasingly immigrated to the United States through the Diversity Immigrant Visa (or green card lottery), asylum, and family reunification programs. The growth of the Coptic community in the United States, along with lobbying efforts and a rise in ISIS-affiliated attacks on Copts' places of worship and pilgrimage in Egypt, have pushed them into the political spotlight. Since the 1990s, attacks on Egyptian Copts have been made legible to American (particularly evangelical) audiences[1] through the global, moral imaginary of the "persecuted church," which argues that Christians around the globe are persecuted more than at any other time in history.[2] Once the objects of American missionary efforts, Egyptian Copts have now been reconfigured as Americans' Christian kin in their suffering for Christ, and politically active and affluent American Copts have engaged this imaginary in their lobbying efforts, advocacy, and social interactions. American persecution discourse has restructured Christian kinship along these imperial lines.

Images of bloodied Egyptian Coptic bodies and their hagiographic accounts of witness to Christ have circulated among Western Christian religiopolitical networks in what I term an *economy of blood*: an imperial economy of Christian kinship that performs the double movement of glory and racialization. In *The Kingdom and the Glory*, Giorgio Agamben argues that media in modern democracies dispense "glory," a doxological aspect of power that functions to shape public opinion and consensus.[3] In one movement, the suffering of Coptic Christians in Egypt has been theologically engaged by American evangelicals and their kin as a triumphalist vision of Western Christendom. Thus, the persecuted church has positioned the strengthening of Western Christianity on the death of Eastern Christians, like the Copts, who purify the faith and bolster claims of besiegement.[4] In another movement, American Copts, of many different social classes, are also racialized as Arab/Middle Eastern/Muslim nonwhite Others by the actual administrative apparatus of government within war on terror itineraries of securitization.[5] The racialization of American Copts is a dual process oscillating between Christian kinship with white America and the optics of nonwhite suspicion. Racialization is a multi-scalar process that proliferates through these different religio-racial divisions within the geopolitics of persecution. Western Christians mobilize Eastern Christian suffering, yet those Christians ultimately remain "Eastern," nonwhite exemplars for imperial discourses of kinship. This double movement has placed American Copts in a bind, whereby indigenous Coptic collective memory of blood and persecution has intersected with the political, theological, and affective formations of this economy of blood.[6] These binds shape the contours of American Coptic politics as well as processes of communal formation and potential solidarities with other minority communities within the United States.

This chapter analyzes how the remapping of different Christian traditions produces effects on a global geopolitical scale and examines how this reconfiguration unfolds the complex religiopolitical enmeshment of Western Christianity and whiteness.[7] I argue that this newly geopoliticized, transnational economy of blood has altered older economies of blood in Christian conceptions of kinship and the broader political imaginaries such conceptions have traditionally authorized.[8] Coptic Christians have historically

Transnational Copts and American Persecution Politics

engaged the blood of the martyrs as a social imaginary that connects the community to past forms of persecution and contemporary contexts of political subjugation and sectarian strife in Egypt.[9] Such contexts reverberate in the diaspora, producing new kinds of political subjectivities among American Copts that place them into alliances with the Christian right. In spite of support for such an agenda among conservatives within the community, American Copts have also been racialized by war on terror power structures, in which the inclusion of their Egyptian kin's bloodied bodies has been an affective part.

By unpacking the theological polysemy and political binds of conservative Western Christian kinship, I show what becomes of Coptic conceptions and practices of kinship in the encounter with the evangelical and geopolitical economy of blood in post-9/11 America. By studying Coptic experiences of racialization in this specific context, we can better understand how the pervasive logics of whiteness alter everyday interactions and can reinterpret histories of trauma through new contexts of empire expansion.[10] Whiteness is the process of variegation: a bloody structure of parsing who belongs as kin and who is marked by suspicion. Racialization is the process of becoming a subject of this parsing. White supremacy and American imperial power discipline Middle Eastern diasporic life by rewarding the suppression of emblems of Islam and Arab-ness, even when one cannot phenotypically pass as white.[11]

Scholars of the earliest Middle Eastern migrations to the United States have examined how legal cases for naturalization of Middle Eastern Christian communities tended to stress their Christianity and its proximity to whiteness and the West.[12] While many Copts identify themselves on legal documents as white, Coptic Orthodox dioceses in America have also encouraged their congregations to racially identify themselves on the U.S. Census as "Coptic," in hopes that "Copts will be recognized as an important race within the American society."[13] Institutional strategies of distinction emphasize Coptic difference from Arabs/Muslims for communal identification and for advocacy and interest from American political power.

Grounding my analysis in twenty months of ethnographic fieldwork among recent Coptic migrants; first-, second-, and third-generation American Copts; and clergy members moving transnationally between Bahjura (a village in Upper Egypt) and the New York–New Jersey area of the United States, as well as Washington, DC, lobbying networks, I investigate how the economy of blood structures and obscures the everyday lived experiences of racialization. I first discuss the specificity of blood to a Christian economy of suffering and community to investigate why spilled Coptic blood resonates for American evangelicalism in particular ways. I focus on the tensions internal to such an economy and show how it parses kin through the dialectic of community building ("kin") and suspicion ("not kin"). Through this dissection, I analyze what kinship becomes in Middle Eastern Christian encounters with American racial formations. I then ethnographically attend to the ways Copts have interacted with and navigated post-9/11 racial infrastructures and explain how they shape Coptic perspectives on Christian-Muslim relations between diaspora and homeland.

Bloody Kinship

Pope Tawadros II, patriarch of the Coptic Orthodox Church, has publicly stated that Copts are not persecuted in Egypt. Within the framework of national unity, the Coptic Church has promoted Muslim-Christian coexistence as the essence of Egyptian national identity. Admitting otherwise is thought by members of the clerical hierarchy and Egyptian Coptic elite to threaten public order and disrupt the national fabric.[14] During his first visit to the New York–New Jersey area in September 2018, Pope Tawadros spoke at Rutgers University's athletic center to hundreds of American Copts. Joined by New Jersey politicians and clergy, Pope Tawadros finished the evening with a speech in English:

> Since Islam entered [Egypt], we have always lived peacefully together—Muslims and Christians. . . . Now, the population of Copts in Egypt is 15 million. We live among 85 million Egyptian Muslims. But all Egyptians are one. We consider our church to be a keeper of national unity of Egypt. . . . At the same time, the evacuation of Christians from the Middle East is very serious for the whole world. Evacuation of Christians from Iraq and Syria is very dangerous to the peace process in the Middle East. Therefore, we [the Coptic Church] are a strong keeper of the national unity in Egypt. There is a strong relationship between the church in Egypt, the president, the government, the parliament . . . with al-Azhar, with all churches.[15]

Only minutes before the pope's speech, however, U.S. representative Chris Smith of New Jersey's 4th District, a Catholic, spoke directly to the pope and discussed in explicit detail Coptic persecution in Egypt. Reading from his prepared speech, Smith proclaimed,

Thank you, Your Holiness, for radiating the love, compassion, and mercy of Jesus Christ. . . . Like so many people around the world, I am especially inspired by your courage and the bravery of your clergy and laity in the midst of persecution and terrorism. . . . Your Holiness, over the years I've chaired many congressional hearings on the plight of the Coptic Church and the indomitable spirit that you and others in this great church have shown. . . . As the prime sponsor of the Frank Wolf International Religious Freedom Act, a law that empowers the president of the United States, the Department of State and Defense, and other agencies with new tools including sanctions against individual abuses and a fresh mandate, a strategy to confront and combat religious persecution, I am confident that we together are going to more than ever stop religious persecution.[16]

American Christian politicians have increasingly interacted with American Coptic leaders and the patriarch himself and have connected histories of violence between Muslims and Christians in Egypt with the global war on terror and a geopolitical theology of persecution, which at times conflicts with the public political positions of the Coptic Church itself. This form of Christian kinship gathers around the blood of the persecuted, traversing theological divisions. Acts of Christian kinship around martyrdom and blood piety are nothing new to either Western Christian or Coptic traditions. Yet, in the contemporary moment, these genealogies intersect to form an economy in the service of American imperial interests.

Caroline Bynum has examined the different valences of blood piety and cult in late medieval Europe. Medieval motifs of dismemberment and pouring blood in fifteenth-century devotion were often about access, not partition, and this openness was the opposite not so much of violence as of corruption.[17] While the body of Christ within these medieval image economies tended to signify community and enclosure, blood gestured to an outflow. Drop by drop, a broader Christian community was unified into an immanent, organic whole: "the community of blood."[18] This process of inclusion dually involved the exclusion of others based on bloodlines, which drew radical distinctions between bloods. Non-Christians became the carriers of impurity, hostile persecutors and defilers of Christian blood, as well as a necessary Other for the purpose of revelation. Thinking about anti-Jewish host-desecration libels, Bynum argues that the stories do not merely evidence hatred of Jews and greed for Jewish property; rather, Christians needed Jews to produce miraculous blood. In Bynum's reading, devotional texts constructed these narratives to culminate not in a verdict of Jewish guilt (of which Christians were convinced) but in the wonderful blood of God made visible in matters of Jewish desecration.[19] The double movement of violation and sanctification within devotional images and text was part of an emerging moral imaginary of Western Christianity in its aesthetics and sensibilities and its imperial expansion and focus on the parsing of kin. This blood produces enclosures and is expansively territorializing in ways Coptic genealogies of blood are not.

In the Coptic case, the blood of martyrs has referred both to Christian triumph over death and spiritual belonging but also represents communal Otherness to ruling powers and society.[20] The Coptic calendar dates not from the birth of Christ or the beginning of Christian Egypt but from the "Era of the Martyrs" under Roman emperor Diocletian. During early Islamic expansion in Egypt, hagiographies and narratives of persecution became especially critical to the church's institutional coherence as the community's social constitution began to change. In Coptic material culture, graphic scenes of dismemberment, blood, and martyrdom emerged as discursive nodes of communal belonging and, in turn, reinforced Coptic difference from and perseverance under Arab and Islamic rulers. Narratives and images of death not only structured the Coptic Church's institutional legitimacy but also forged its indigenous character. By the eighteenth century, Febe Armanios argues, Coptic Orthodox clerics regularly deployed narratives of persecution and martyrdom in their sermons to prevent Muslim and interdenominational conversions increasing under Western missionary influence.[21] In contemporary Egypt, the church avoids issues that would create antagonism among Copts toward the Muslim majority and vehemently discourages any calls for the separation of the Copts or their isolation from Egyptian society. The modern Coptic Church has depended upon these commemorative acts of witness and death for the continuous making of both religious and national contours of belonging.[22] Within this genealogy, a Coptic moral imaginary emerges in the claims-making practices of difference that gesture to Christian endurance in Egypt.[23] Imperial subjugation and communal Otherness have historically mapped a Coptic genealogy of blood not as one of enclosure but as a practice of endurance. Thus, persecution and blood define a Coptic moral imaginary as an oscillation between similarity and difference, whether that be in contemporary relation to Egypt's Muslim majority or to America's white Christian right.

Following the Hart-Celler Act of 1965, Copts increasingly immigrated to the United States. The convergence of these two genealogies of blood and

Christian kinship comes in a context of this migration as well as in expanding Coptic political activism in Washington, DC, in the mid-1990s, at a time when the persecuted Christians movement was gaining steam. Scholars of early Christianity have described the Roman arena, where much martyr blood was spilled, as a public space in which the religiopolitical imaginary of the society was repeatedly constituted and acted out on bodies. Martyrs' blood was part of a larger ideological drama in which state power and social relations were repeatedly contested, reconstituted, and reinscribed.[24] In a parallel fashion, a growing interest in contemporary Christian martyrs among American evangelicals of the late 1980s and early 1990s intersected with increasing geopolitical attention to the Middle East, Islam, and terrorism. Narratives of Coptic suffering aided in the shaping of foreign policy on international religious freedom and the persecuted Christians movement.

Persecuted Bodies

Beginning in the early 1970s and flourishing in the 1990s, American evangelicals developed a set of foreign policy objectives that focused on human rights advocacy, which blended their spiritual and political beliefs, skillful lobbyists to promote their interests in Congress, and a strong network linking them with their coreligionists throughout the world. During this period, former Cold War think tanks like the Hudson Institute, Freedom House, and the Institute for Religion and Democracy partnered with evangelicals and consulted a few Coptic diaspora activists in shifting from the fight against godless communism toward the fight against fundamentalist Islam. Today, in such think tanks and other advocacy organizations, Copts now hold positions of power, shaping policy through the lens of human rights language and Christian-persecution discourse. As diasporic representatives, they engage and add authority to right-wing discourses, such as "dhimmitude," which argues that if the global war on Christians is not won, American Christians will resemble Middle Eastern Christians, subjugated under Islam, where their religion is kept private and care is taken so public acts do not offend the state religion. To this conservative coalition, Copts, as both symbols and actors in their own right, have offered a striking portfolio of bloody, convicting narratives and imagery, which reinforces persecution discourse.[25]

The Christian persecution movement has positioned Eastern Christians as martyrs for Western Christendom, in that their fate is not seen as negatively impacting Christianity as a whole because Western Christianity—in particular, white evangelicalism and its ecumenical proponents—benefits from this persecution. It is by the spilling of their blood that Western Christian kinship is opened to Eastern Christians, like the Copts. Coptic blood becomes shared Western Christian blood. The death of Copts in Egypt serves a "purifying function" for white evangelicalism.[26] Coptic racialization within American society is parsed from this religiopolitical formation. While Coptic martyrdom is included within the economy of blood, Coptic bodies are simultaneously remapped as suspicious. Both moves are variations of the same economy. It is also here, for example, that the Christian persecution movement can at once champion Christians who are oppressed while differentiating between that abstract suffering and the conditions that perpetuate it, such as destructive economic policies, support for authoritarian regimes and settler-colonial projects such as Israel, and the global war on terror.

Melani McAlister has argued that the suffering of Eastern Christian bodies is recounted and put on display in an evangelical public sphere.[27] The examination and presentation of those persecuted bodies has offered Americans a new kind of Christian selfhood.[28] This new "evangelical internationalism" is marked by fear and a sense of threat from Islam, but it is also defined by increased attention to the suffering and needs of Christians outside the United States.[29] In this fight, American evangelicals have made significant alliances with Catholics, Jews, Mormons, and, more recently, Eastern Orthodox Christians.[30] Evangelicals have found ways to work more ecumenically on issues they deem important to the overall project of "saving America," and part of the work in "saving America" has also been the work of "saving" Middle Eastern Christians from Islamic oppression. Through images, such as of the twenty Copts and one Ghanaian beheaded on the shores of Libya by Islamic State affiliates or of the spate of bombings that have ravaged large churches and cathedrals throughout Egypt, Copts have been assigned a unique role within this moral imaginary.

In December 2017, I attended the Third Archon International Conference on Religious Freedom, held at the Trump Hotel in Washington, DC. The Archons of the Ecumenical Patriarchate is a society of laity, chosen by the patriarch of Constantinople for their service to the Greek Orthodox Church and for their respect within the community. Titled "The Persecution of Christians in the Holy Lands and The Middle East: Consequences and Solutions," the conference's schedule was theologically eclectic, its speakers made up of politicians of evangelical backgrounds, Greek Orthodox influencers, Syriac and Coptic bishops, and upper-middle-class Copts involved in advocacy work in Washington, DC.

At registration, I received a tote bag filled with the typical conference materials, including a folder, schedule, notepad, and engraved pen. The bag also contained the book *Muslim: What You Need to Know about the World's Fastest-Growing Religion* by conference presenter Hank Hanegraaff, a convert from evangelicalism to Greek Orthodoxy, who gained fame through his radio show, *Bible Answer Man*, and his numerous publications on Christianity and American culture. While the book is concerned with the rising global demographic divide between Muslims and Christians, it is just as concerned with connecting global processes and contexts, forming them into an all-en-compassing narrative of Islam and terror. "Equally grave is the specter of global Islamic jihadism now exacting mass genocide on Christians in the East and ever-multiplying terrorist attacks throughout the West," he writes in the afterword.[31]

Hanegraaff's book and its message for such a conference stand at the crossroads of the defense of Western civilization and represent an offensive on Brown and Black bodies in the war on terror.[32] In this imaginary, Islam as a system of governance stands as an affront to Western political, social, and spiritual values. By deploying Copts and other Middle Eastern Chris-tians as exemplary victims of such a system, the audience of evangelical and Greek Orthodox elites (an otherwise unlikely alliance) instrumentalized their victimhood. [33]

Session 2, titled "Persecution of Christians and Possible Solutions," took place at an auditorium on Capitol Hill. The auditorium was dark, except for bright lights focused on a large stage projection of the twenty-one Libya martyrs of the Coptic Church, darkened to black and white, lined up on their knees in front of images of masked members of ISIS standing ominously behind them (fig. 12.1). Following opening remarks, clerical leaders from various Middle Eastern churches gave speeches regarding their positions on persecution and Western intervention.

Bishop Angaelos of London spoke on behalf of the Coptic Orthodox Church. In contrast to Pope Tawadros, Bishop Angaelos has explicitly described the persecution of Copts, appearing on the BBC and numerous other outlets following attacks in Egypt. During the panel, he commented,

> We come at a time when there are 200 to 500 million Christians per-secuted around the world. In scores of countries . . . they are suffer-ing at a time when we as humanity are in an era of our development that prides itself in international treaties, international conventions and a right to life. . . . The Christians of whom we speak are those

Coptic icon by Washington, DC–based iconographer Tony Rezk of the twenty-one martyrs of Libya receiving the crown of martyrdom. *Republished here with permission.*

that deny and reject minority status, for they are indigenous people. If what is happening in the Middle East were to happen to the indigenous people of America or Canada or the Aborigines of Australia, the world would be up in arms. They live the faith that was born in the region.[34]

Against the backdrop of the Libya martyrs on their knees, the bishop described how he was compelled by the image to mark his own body:

The twenty-one martyrs of Libya have changed the world. Typically, the Copts have a cross tattoo on their inner right wrist, just as a sign of who they are. I grew up in Australia. I didn't have one; I didn't see the need. But when I watch this video and the . . . man in the middle having to mask his face so we would not know who pointed that knife and said, "We are after the nation of the cross," I felt a need to get a cross for them. We hear the stories of the saints and the

Transnational Copts and American Persecution Politics

martyrs in our church every day. Another bombing, another martyr, another saint; it's still happening. It happened on our screens. We saw it before us.[35]

The persecuted body not only marks Christians as under global siege but argues that through the blood of persecuted (Eastern) Christian bodies, all of Western Christendom and its imperial formations are sanctified.[36] The icon of the persecuted body among Christians, across theological, racial, and national lines, has produced new kinds of affiliations defined by its embodiment, its global knowledge, and the marks of shared victimization. The global efficacy of the evangelical public sphere and its remapping of Coptic martyrology persuades even a Coptic bishop—who otherwise saw no need for an identitarian tattoo—to mark the Coptic cross on his right wrist.

In a ballroom at the Trump Hotel just down the street from the White House itself, President Donald Trump's closest associates were the keynote speakers and key figures of the conference dinner. The first remarks came from Jordan Sekulow, executive director for the American Center for Law and Justice. His father, Jay Sekulow, is a frequent commentator on the Christian Broadcasting Network and on Fox News, a Messianic Jew, and one of Trump's personal lawyers. Jordan remarked on the persecution of Christians around the world, but especially in the Middle East, as an American problem. By looking to the faith and tragic circumstances of the Copts, America should be inspired to carry the imperial light of religious freedom to all corners of the globe. Sekulow proclaimed,

> We cannot forget that our brothers and sisters in Christ, whether they be of the Orthodox faith or just the Christian faith generally, are facing immense persecution around the world. For all of us, do not forget those Coptic Christians who are in the heart of Egypt, worshipping on Christmas Day, worshipping on Easter, and hundreds are killed. And yet, next Easter, hundreds more show up. And that is a symbolism of their Christian faith, but it is also unacceptable in the world that we live in. . . . Here we are in the United States of America. . . . You have a government that accepts freedom. And we're unique. In the United States, we have to learn in a unique way how to take that understanding that we have been born into and ingrained into us, and take that to parts of the world where that is not ingrained, where the free exercise of religion is not the first right. We have so much to do for the persecuted church.[37]

In this discourse, America is the leader, the savior, the example for the world. America can bring freedom to other parts of the world, where persecution and devastation have prevailed. Coptic blood is shed and displayed as spectacle upon the world stage. Bombings, attacks, and shootings were brought to bear not only on Egyptian Copts but on all of Christendom. This economy of blood includes Copts in the role of martyr and maimed body, an imagery that the Coptic Church has also championed as a communal identity marker and as a contemporary relational node with the Egyptian security state. This constellation of conservative discourses that includes the Copts as persecuted figures at the hands of Muslim militants has bound American Copts into particular characteristics of racial-religious legibility that have mediated interfaith relations in the United States.

Suspicious Bodies

After 9/11, anti-Muslim assaults and intimidation rose significantly in the United States, with the number of hate crimes jumping from 28 incidents in 2000 to 481 by the end of 2001.[38] Islamophobia and anti-Muslim rhetoric affected not only American Muslims but also Sikhs, non-Muslim Arabs, and people of South Asian descent.[39] One of the early victims of this violence was the Egyptian-born Coptic Christian Adel Karas, who was shot dead by two white men inside his grocery store in San Gabriel, California, on September 15, 2001.[40] Scholars have argued that the racialization of Muslims in post-9/11 America has meant that certain bodies have been made "suspicious."[41] Copts have been included among these suspicious bodies, and many have tried to combat such suspicion through emphasizing their Christian faith, one particular strategy that Middle Eastern Christians have deployed to assert a claim of racial-religious misrecognition and declare allegiance to the persecuted body as racial-religious form.[42]

On a cold winter evening in Staten Island, I sat across from Abouna Girgis in the kitchen of the administrative center of the local Coptic diocese.[43] In his late thirties and recently elevated to the priesthood, Abouna grew up in Bayonne, New Jersey, and has strong ties to his clergy-filled family back in Luxor, Upper Egypt, visiting them regularly. We talked about protests that had stalled zoning board approval of Bayonne's first mosque. (The same zoning board approved the expansion of a Coptic church in 2011.) After the local Muslim community purchased the property in 2015, its proposal was denied by the zoning board in early 2017, which cited traffic and parking issues. The property was protested against and even vandalized, with crude

Transnational Copts and American Persecution Politics

phrases such as "F—— Muslims" and "F—— Arabs," in the name of Donald Trump, then Republican nominee for president.

Bayonne is a working-class neighborhood where historically many Italian, Polish, and Irish immigrant communities took up residence. More recently, Bayonne has become home to many Middle Eastern communities, including and especially Egyptians, both Muslim and Coptic Christian. When Abouna was growing up, though, his family was one of only a few Middle Eastern families. "You could tell, even at that age, that people weren't used to your complexion. They weren't comfortable with having people of your complexion around," he said. Now, the community has two Coptic Orthodox churches and is expanding with a new influx of Egyptian Coptic immigrants. Though the community also faces its own share of discrimination, Copts joined in the protests against the Bayonne mosque. Demonstrators held signs that said, "Stop the mosque!" "If the mosque comes, the mayor goes!" "No mosque, remember 9/11!" I asked Abouna Girgis what he thought about the protests in his hometown. "Look," he answered, "if you're Coptic, you're going to protest Islam. When you've seen and gone through the harassment, the persecution in Egypt and everything, can you blame them?" Coptic demonstrations against mosques and engagement in Islamophobic rhetoric are practices that aim to secure Copts' recognition as Christians and also reflect communal trauma manifesting itself in diaspora.[44]

For example, Copts continue to deal with issues of church construction and repair in Egypt.[45] Despite recent government efforts to streamline the process, Christians still face both official and social restrictions on building their houses of worship: officials are slow to issue permits, security agencies fail to protect churches from attack, and violence from Muslim neighbors has succeeded in preventing church construction in communities throughout Egypt.[46] These difficulties continue to affect this transnational diaspora in Copts' everyday interactions with Egyptian Muslims in New Jersey.

In early 2017, I sat in a packed room of parents and general Coptic congregants in Jersey City. Abouna Lazarus was explaining a multimillion-dollar new church project. The current church building, unchanged since the 1970s, was far too small for the influx of immigrants from Egypt and the growth of the second generation. With a map of the area on the television next to an icon of Christ, Abouna outlined how much of the land had already been purchased. However, there was a stumbling block: a key piece of land was yet to be purchased for the property because it was owned by a "non-Christian, but Egyptian man" (*howa gheyr mesihee bas masry*). "I won't say more than this" (*mish ha'ool aktar men keda*), Abouna smiled; I also saw recognition on the faces of congregants as to what this actually meant. I asked the priest later to clarify this exchange: "He simply will not sell this to us. What would that look like? A Muslim Egyptian selling a piece of land in the United States for the purpose of building a church? How would this news be received in Egypt by Muslims there?" Egyptian Coptic kinship, and its sectarian politics, is remapped onto new, imperial terrain. Diaspora plays kinship in and across migration, where Coptic *Christian* difference matters varyingly in an American Christian context.

Abouna Girgis and I continued our conversation. Abouna recounted how he and a group of friends had stopped at a local 7-Eleven on the evening of September 11, 2001. While there, he was heckled by a group of men (whom he took to be "Hispanic") who hurled insults at him. "We had the wrong complexion," he recounted. "They said to us, 'You f'in terrorists. Look what you did. We're going to get you!' [After 9/11], you felt like you were a target, and it wasn't your fault." A local priest in the days following 9/11 even went under house arrest because of his supposed resemblance to Osama bin Laden, another Coptic interlocutor later recounted. After 9/11, Copts changed their attire to sartorially distance themselves from Arabs/Muslims. Coptic clergy in New Jersey noted that Pope Shenouda III, the late patriarch of the Coptic Orthodox Church, allowed priests to wear a wooden cross similar to Catholic clergy and to trim their beards in the hopes that they would not be the targets of backlash or hate crimes. In Los Angeles since 9/11, Metropolitan Serapion has allowed clergy to forgo their traditional head covering ('amma)—an informal requirement throughout the Coptic Church—because, according to one priest, "they look like Islamic turbans." Coptic religious practices (such as priestly garb) have reformed in diaspora to reconcile with post-9/11 racial infrastructures that code such aesthetics as threatening.

The power of whiteness within American society is structured in and through such disciplinary measures and everyday relations, and the transformation of Coptic religious and social life in the United States gestures to the power of (white, Western) Christianity.[47] Copts are Eastern Christians, yet they must contend with and are transformed by an imperial and geopolitical form of Christianity, one that is intertwined with the power and privilege of whiteness. Such racial distinctions have never been tethered to a defined set of categories, whereby avoiding detection in those categories (name, dress, language) would somehow help to avoid the white gaze. Thinking with Karen Fields and Barbara Fields's notion of "racecraft," the racialization of Coptic Christians in American society is pieced together in the ordinary and extraordinary course of everyday doing. Racecraft governs racial imagination—"what goes with what and whom"—and guides imagination and human action.[48] Thus, the deference and dominance of racial distinctions lie in the dense set of prior representations and practices on which they build—the Muslim, the undocumented, the immigrant, the Jew, the Black person—their histories interweaving with one another.[49] The shifting gaze of racecraft in the United States can be traced in the ways the racialization of different groups circuits and overlaps.

Especially after 9/11, many Copts were identified by law enforcement as potential threats. Magdy Beshara was the Coptic owner of the St. George's Shell gas station in Bayville, New Jersey. Shortly after 9/11, the FBI came to the family's home in the middle of the night, questioning Beshara about whether Marwan al-Shehhi, one of the 9/11 hijackers, had worked at the gas station. Beshara's stepson Michael described to me in a personal interview on the aftermath of the initial FBI raid: "People would drive by and say, 'We're going to kill you terrorists' and throw a big liquor bottle at me and my sister." Under the PATRIOT Act, the government confiscated anything it desired from the gas station and their home. Their mail was opened and phones tapped, and Michael was followed to school by federal agents. The family faced death threats. Despite pleas to the police to intervene, the police refused. Michael described how the incident forced him to differentiate. "It made me feel weird to say out loud, but I always thought to myself, 'I'm not a Muslim, I'm a Christian.' I felt like I was putting them down to say, 'Hey, look, I'm the good guy.' I felt like we had to do anything to defend ourselves." At school, Michael was bullied and physically assaulted on dozens of occasions. At one point in the months following the raid, an unknown assailant set the family's house on fire while Michael and his little sister were sleeping. All of this took place even after the FBI notified Magdy Beshara that he was no longer a subject of investigation.[50]

As Junaid Rana has argued, cultural and institutional forms of discrimination interact with one another in a complex social system of racialization to create a racial infrastructure.[51] Yet, the process of racialization is never complete; identifying who is the "Muslim" is part of the apparatus of racialization. As Magdy Beshara noted during an interview after the FBI raid of his gas station, "Middle Eastern people, we all look alike, you know what I mean."

An important element in the contemporary racialization of Muslims is the historical context by which Islam has been understood as a theological and civilizational enemy of the Christian West. Tomaz Mastnak has argued that the Crusades represented an entirely new strategy of power in Christendom, a means of building new relations among Christians by directing outward a holy war against a contaminating enemy, an unclean race.[52] Mastnak and others have pointed to the theological conceptions of race that circulated centuries prior to the emergence of biopolitical racism.[53] In close proximity to Egyptian Muslims, Copts occupy a liminal space of difference within difference. Their theological and racial difference from the West has placed them into similar matrices of subjugation as other non-Christian peoples; yet, their new enmeshments with Western geopolitical imaginations of Christian persecution have positioned them as kin in the fight against Islamic terrorism. Within the colonial context of Egypt, Copts also had a complicated relationship to the British regime. Racial science in colonial Egypt set out to distinguish Copts from their Muslim neighbors, based on a shared Christian kinship, while at the same time denigrating the Copts for not being of an "enlightened" form of Christianity.[54] The imagined civilizational divide between a homogeneous Christian West and a Muslim East upended itself in the paradoxical logics of Coptic comprehension.

Colonial Legacies

Sitting in a Manhattan café, Nessim, a wealthy engineer, and I chatted about the study of Copts over tea. "The enemies of Edward Said are the heroes of the Copts," he said. Nessim lauded the Orientalists of colonial Egypt for their accomplishments for the Coptic community. Coptologist Gaston Maspero is noted as being partly (if not wholly) responsible for persuading elite Egyptian Copts that they are "descendants of the Pharaohs" and, most importantly, that they are "racially pure."[55] In Maspero's assertion that the bloodline of the Copts has remained pure from the time of the pharaohs, the Copts secured their place in the Egyptian nation.[56] Many Coptic intellectuals, politicians, and elite laypeople embraced this narrative of their timeless uniqueness and integral role in shaping Egyptian national identity, in contrast to a church-centered vision more congenial to clergy and working classes. Maspero also suggested that Egyptian Muslim populations were racially intermixed with Arabs but largely descended from Coptic Christians who had converted to Islam. "Egyptian Muslims, then, were a substandard Copt."[57]

Nessim continued,

> If you're trying to be a part of something, and you're a Copt, you sort
> of stepped over back to ancient Egypt because that was something
> to be proud of and the Europeans recognized it. There was always a

European standard that you lived up to. So, a lot of these Copts made the connection, not with Coptic culture—which they knew was inferior—but to the ancient Egyptian culture. But to do that, they needed to claim pure descent, and it fit neatly into the European attitude that Muslims were part of degenerate races, and only the pure Egyptians, these were the ones that were really a good race. All of these colonial thinkers understood the ancient Egyptians as comparable to the West. So, if you [as a Copt] can claim yourself to be ethnically pure [Egyptian], you place yourself on the Western scope and you bypass all that sort of mess.

European recognition of the Copts, so long as they were the pure descendants of the ancient Egyptians, meant that the Coptic elite had to distinguish themselves from Muslims and Islam, using the criteria and rhetoric provided by the colonial thinkers and rulers in order to gain recognition. Malcolm Reid has noted that Coptic elites of the time discovered the efficacy of ancient Egypt only by leaving their homeland for study in Europe.[58]

The legacy of these colonial racial-religious hierarchies persists. Anthony Shenoda has used the term "moral imaginary" to describe how some Egyptian Copts claim "moral" superiority and that they are "true Egyptians" for keeping their Christian faith, as opposed to Muslims who have "lost" their "Egyptian-ness."[59] Emerging out of Orientalist literature and colonial governance, "Muslim" countries were constructed as a geography that shared a common culture. In both *Mummies and Moslems* (1875) and *In the Levant* (1877), American writer Charles Dudley Warner differentiated "civilization" from "barbarism" or "savagery," always keyed to whiteness and its Others. In his writings on Egypt and the Levant, he described a meeting with a certain European traveler in Cairo: "We were civilized beings, met by chance in a barbarous place."[60] Copts were from this "barbarous" geography, but they were Christians. As Barbara Fields has pointed out, the division of peoples into Christian and heathen prior to the rise of modern racial science did not mean that all Christians were equal.[61] In British-occupied Ireland and in the American colonies, for instance, religious and racial systems of domination overlapped and interpenetrated. This logic operated in its own particular way in colonial Egypt among Coptic elites.

In *Modern Egypt*, Evelyn Baring, Earl of Cromer, described Copts and Muslims in Egypt in the early twentieth century as the same but different. Both Muslims and Copts had remained "stagnant." Yet Muslims were stagnant *because* they were Muslims, "because the customs which are interwoven with his religion, forbid him to change."[62] Copts were stagnant both due to their improper Christianity and because they were "Orientals," residing in a geography that prevented their progress because of its association with Islam. If they could refine their Christianity—make it modern and rational—they might be able to secure their path toward progress; yet they were still "arrested by barriers very similar to those which have applied in the case of the Moslem." Baring continued, "The Copt . . . has, without knowing it, assimilated himself to the Moslem. 'The modern Copt has become from head to foot, in manners, language, and spirit, a Moslem, however unwilling he may be to recognize the fact.' . . . For all purposes of broad generalization, the only difference between the Copt and the Moslem is that the former is an Egyptian who worships in a Christian church, whilst the latter is an Egyptian who worships in a Mohammedan mosque."[63] This complex structure of proximity and difference, articulated by Baring in an earlier colonial context, continues to affect Copts today in the United States as they navigate new binds of racial-religious power.

Proximities to Whiteness

Scholars of Islamophobia have pointed out that the post-9/11 era of the targeted profiling, racialization, and securitization of American Muslims only intensified and renewed what was already part of a long history of anti-Black racism, anti-Semitism, and xenophobia in the United States.[64] Measures of securitization such as the PATRIOT Act, the Countering Violent Extremism program, and the New York Police Department's Muslim Surveillance and Mapping Program signal a scalar shift in the targeting of racialized communities. The global reach of post-9/11 securitization is embedded within histories of Western conquest and imperialism that have disciplined bodies by the persuasive logics of whiteness, which include progress toward the "correct" kind of Christian politics and aesthetics. Middle Eastern Christian communities like the Copts contend with their racial difference yet are aligned in their religious affiliation with the majority of Americans. Studies of whiteness have documented how different European immigrant groups gained (and intermittently lost) white racial status.[65] Yet such studies have themselves most often operated on a Black/white dualism and rarely address the limits of such a binary or consider how Christianity configures racial difference.[66]

In the contemporary racialization of Arabs and Muslims in the United States, religion, national origin, and color articulate into complex subject formations that determine and differentiate the citizen and the terrorist.[67] The "Muslim" is not simply a marker of faith but rather a racialized designation.[68] As a racial-religious form, the Muslim is known through specifically racialized bodies, religious behaviors, and the amalgamation of many other attributes that go beyond phenotypical or sartorial markers.[69] The "Muslim" is not a definitive racial-religious form but rather understood through the racializing conditions that catch different groups into this racial net. Racial conceptions and structural conditions order such lives and delimit their human possibilities, placing such persons between the exclusionary conditions of a racial-religious form like the "Muslim" and the psychological and cultural strategies employed by racial subjects to accommodate themselves to everyday indignities.[70] Caught in the web of this racial-religious form, Copts attempt to reconcile communal histories of persecution, by Islamic regimes and everyday Egyptian Muslims, and colonial legacies with diasporic racial infrastructures that present new challenges to Coptic imaginaries.

One evening before a spiritual meeting, I met with a Coptic priest in a rural area of middle New Jersey. A new property had been purchased by the congregation, but the church had yet to be built. We sat in what appeared to be the old office of a two-story home, used temporarily as the liturgical space. Abouna is quite active on Facebook and had recently shared articles on President Trump's comments that Haiti and African nations (including Egypt) were "shithole" countries. Looking through the comments on the shared article, I noticed that many Copts voiced their support for Trump. I asked Abouna why many Copts expressed such views despite their Egyptian origins and kinship. "They support those comments," he explained, "because when they support them, they are essentially saying 'shithole' refers to Islam, not to them."

The work of differentiation done by some Copts gestures toward the power of whiteness, as a structure of assimilation, to mold sensibilities, relationships, and practices and avoid the gaze of suspicion.[71] Sarah Gualtieri has examined how the first wave of (primarily Christian) Syrian immigrants to the United States chose to stake their claim to citizenship on the basis of membership in the "white race" because "there was something compelling, even alluring, about whiteness that went beyond the strategic and the practical."[72] Gualtieri carefully attends to the logics of the new Syrian identity in American society, constructed around striving toward white acceptance. Their arguments were focused on Syrian connections to Christianity in order to reconsider racial difference along religious lines.

Following *Dow v. United States* (1915), which defined Syrians as white, anthropologist Franz Boas testified in 1925 in *United States v. Cartozian* that Armenians like defendant Tatos O. Cartozian were white because of their "European origin." The judge combined Boas's testimony with his own argumentation to rule on the division between Armenians and Turks. Ultimately emphasizing Armenian proximity to Europe and Armenians' Christian background, he ruled that they could be considered white.[73] In 1942, a judge in Detroit determined that a Muslim Yemeni immigrant could not be white. The judge noted, "Apart from the dark skin of the Arabs, it is well known that they are a part of the Mohammedan world and that a wide gulf separates their culture from that of the predominantly Christian peoples of Europe."[74] In the fall of 1943, however, Arab Muslims were deemed "white" by the Immigration and Naturalization Service, effectively casting them as partners with their Christian counterparts in the project of Western civilization. In their being designated as white, however, their religious identity was necessarily effaced. As Gualtieri writes, "Whereas the Christian identity of Syrian applicants in the racial prerequisite cases had been central to their argument for whiteness, and had indeed helped them secure it, Muslim Arabs were at their whitest when stripped of their religious affiliation."[75] Race and religion were closely tied together in the legal accession to whiteness.

The histories of other Middle Eastern Christians are relevant to contemporary discussions of Coptic identity in the United States. Within many naturalization cases that legally defined whiteness, the Christianity of such peoples was crucial to the logics of their belonging within American society. The Christianity of Middle Eastern Christians matters in different ways today, as their persecution is made visible by imagery, discourse, and policymaking efforts on their behalf. In everyday interactions, Copts emphasize their distinctiveness from "Arabs"—understood as an ethno-racial but also a religious identity in an America where Arab and Muslim continue to be intrinsically linked.

Strategies of separation evidence Coptic desire to disentangle from post-9/11 racial infrastructures—to not be identified as the enemy. But they also show how pervasive logics of whiteness work within marginalized communities, as they interweave with transnational histories of persecution and intercommunal violence. One interlocutor recounted how members of his New Jersey church told him he "looked Muslim" because of his beard. While members of this church are enmeshed in war on terror logics of "Muslim-ness" in the United States, the same comment was made to him by a monk visiting from Egypt. The symbolism of a beard in the United States is different from a beard in Egypt.[76] In Egypt, the beard varyingly symbolizes Islamist politics that have negatively impacted Egypt's religious minorities.

Particular fear has been directed toward the Muslim Brotherhood. Since the early twentieth century, the Muslim Brotherhood has been a major figure of Islamist opposition to the Egyptian state. During the 1970s, President Anwar Sadat facilitated the rise of Islamist politics that spun out of his control. Islamists became the ire of more-secular Muslims and were feared by Copts due to an increasing number of violent attacks. Over the past thirty years, the securitization and militarization of the Egyptian state has been constructed under the banner of fighting Islamic terrorism. The Mubarak regime and now the Sisi regime have deployed anti-Islamist rhetoric and charges of "terrorism" as a means to suppress all forms of political dissent. With the events of 9/11 and the war on terror, Egyptian security-state tactics have been rendered as a service to Egypt's prime geopolitical patron, the United States.[77] The Coptic Church has supported such regimes in the fight against Islamists, backing the 2013 coup and Abdel Fattah al-Sisi for the presidency in 2014 and 2018, as Coptic communities bore the violent brunt of postrevolutionary politics.[78] Coptic fear of the Muslim Brotherhood in Egypt manifests itself in transnational contexts and among different generations.

In March 2017, I drove back to Jersey City from a church meeting with Marie, Carol, and Justina, three Coptic women in their twenties. Carol asked me about my research, particularly on Coptic *shisha* bars and street vendors. Speaking about the recent influx of Coptic immigrants, I mentioned that many of them work for Muslim street vendors in Manhattan. Justina became agitated: "That just doesn't make sense to me. I thought all of the vendors were MB [Muslim Brotherhood]." Carol replied, "Okay, so that means the MB wouldn't hire them? How does that make any sense?" Justina asked, "Why would they hire Christians? Why would they want them to succeed? Giving these Copts jobs means you're helping their future. Why would they want that?" Carol refused Justina's argumentation as she continued, "Have you heard of the 100-year plan? That's the MB's plan to become the demographic majority. They're already on course to be the world's largest religion because they have more babies." While the fear of the Muslim Brotherhood's takeover of America has roots in Egypt, the particular rhetoric used by Justina on secretive plans and demographics is widely used and the conflation of Islamists with all Muslims is commonly done among the Far Right in the United States.

While Copts across generations are primed for such arguments from the Egyptian context, their manifestation in the United States is configured by domestic politics of Islamophobia and their export at a global scale. Tony, a Coptic-rights activist in his mid-seventies, came to the United States in 1969. Today, he is part of a broad network of Christian (mainly white) conservative activists aiming to demonstrate that "the fundamental teachings of Islam are incompatible with the Christian faith and the American way of life." At his home, Tony gave me copies of his books he has written under a more "Muslim-sounding" pseudonym. Inside one of the books, it reads, "Dedication: To my precious grandchildren: It is my prayer that you will never have to go through what I once did in my Islamic mother country; may you never have to flee America because it turned to Islam." The texts express his fear of America's conversion to Islam, a need to uphold traditional Judeo-Christian values, and arguments for Islam's inherent irrationality. Tony told me he does this work because he feels guilty for leaving Egypt: "Forty years ago, in Egypt, you couldn't tell the difference between a Christian and a Muslim; now all women are wearing hijab. The Islamization of Egypt is the culprit. I mean they were Muslims back then, but they have become Islamicized now."

In contrast to Tony's polemical writings on Islam, his own migration memoir describes a number of incidents of Muslim friendship that defined his upbringing. In one memory, he speaks about his Arabic teacher, Mr. Mohammed: "Mr. Mohammed was more than just a teacher, as he also supervised the class, paying attention to ethics and religion without any biases." One day, a fellow Muslim student made a joke mocking Christianity to the dismay of Tony and his Coptic classmates. The teacher proceeded to corporally punish the Muslim student, which Tony tried to fend off. The teacher insisted on giving the Muslim student a punishment. "That was the first time I ever heard of justice's rights in Egypt," Tony writes. "Never again did I hear about 'Madam Justice,' and I don't know if she has left the country or passed away." While much Western discussion on Egyptian Copts revolves around their persecution, Christian-Muslim life in contemporary Egypt is also centered on pedagogies of negotiation and ambiguity. The economy of blood incites American Copts engaged in advocacy and conservative politics into certain narratives and binds them into particular strategies of differentiation from the Arab/Muslim Other, ultimately effacing the fullness of transnational Coptic life.

The Time of Blood Has Not Passed

The sanguification of rhetoric has yet to produce a world of oceans without shores,
power without borders, blood without walls. —GIL ANIDJAR, *BLOOD*[79]

Michel Foucault and Piero Camporesi have argued that blood relations and bloody cruelty are marked as past tense. In that distant past, "power spoke through blood." And if "blood was a reality," it was so because it had a "symbolic function." European society was one of blood that oscillated between themes of wholeness and resurrection, as well as suffering and partition.[80] But is blood and its relationality truly a thing of the past? Does it not *still* function as a vehicle of imperial power to produce kin as well as racialized Others? Does blood, in the form of martyrs, not also incite inclusions and, simultaneously, produce exclusions?

The economy of blood discussed in this chapter circulates Coptic suffering to advance religiopolitical policies that exceed the direct needs of the Coptic community in the United States or in Egypt. Caught between whiteness and its racialized Others, American Copts connect Egyptian contexts to these new imperial formations. On the Upper East Side one August afternoon, I sat on a black crate next to the food cart owned by Wael, a Copt from Asyut, Upper Egypt, who came to the United States six years earlier through the green card lottery. "Everyone dreams of working abroad to make better money," he said with a tired smile. Wael explained how he felt marginalized back home and what made him ultimately decide to apply for the green card lottery: "Since I can remember, things are just not safe back home for us. . . . They kidnap Coptic girls and kill us. Recently, there's been even more violence against Christians . . . like the bombing [at Al-Qudiseen church] in Alexandria and the bus attack on the way to the monastery in Al-Minya. . . . Because of things like this I supported Trump's ban on Muslims to the United States." As halal food carts drove by us, Wael waved to his Egyptian Muslim colleagues but was quick to tell me about his dislike for them and their discrimination against him as a Copt, even in New York.

As more Copts immigrate to and build families in the United States, histories of persecution and sectarian violence in Egypt are remapped onto a transnational economy of blood, reconfiguring Christian kinship through American empire building. The blood of Coptic martyrs relates them as kin to Western Christians, building community in blood and by blood. Yet American Copts are placed into racial partition. Blood includes and simultaneously excludes in white Christian America. These different

Christian concepts of kinship and the broader political imaginaries that such conceptions have historically authorized require a multi-scalar approach to analyzing how Christianity and whiteness, as structures of global power, play out within a geopolitically important community like that of the Copts. For while the diaspora offers opportunities to form new solidarities and pathways of reparation and reconciliation with Arab and Egyptian Muslim kin, a geopolitical constellation of forces continues to suture Coptic Christians to itineraries of global Christian persecution and an economy of blood. Ultimately, liberation from these structures of recognition must include the transformation and revaluation of community beyond the geopolitics of persecution.

Notes

1. I deploy "evangelical" as a political construction and one connected to institutional power. Conservative white Protestants, led by Christian right organizations, have been key players in cultivating the "persecuted church" moral imaginary, especially as it pertains to Muslims and Middle Eastern Christians. Within the broader framework of American evangelicalism, Catholics, Jews, Eastern Orthodox Christians, Episcopalians, and other Protestants have also participated in such a coalition of faithful guided by evangelical aesthetics, sensibilities, passions, and politics.

2. Andrea Smith, *Unreconciled: From Racial Reconciliation to Racial Justice in Christian Evangelicalism* (Durham, NC: Duke University Press, 2019).

3. Giorgio Agamben, *The Kingdom and the Glory: For a Theological Genealogy of Economy and Government* (Stanford, CA: Stanford University Press, 2011).

4. Elizabeth Castelli, "Persecution Complexes: Identity Politics and the 'War on Christians,'" *Differences: A Journal of Feminist Cultural Studies* 18, no. 3 (2006): 152–80.

5. Nadine Naber, "Imperial Whiteness and the Diasporas of Empire," *American Quarterly* 66, no. 4 (2014): 1107–15; Leti Volpp, "The Citizen and the Terrorist," *UCLA Law Review* 49, no. 5 (2002): 1575–600.

6. Elizabeth Povinelli, *The Cunning of Recognition: Indigenous Alterities and the Making of Australian Multiculturalism* (Durham, NC: Duke University Press, 2002).

7. Ruth Marshall, *Political Spiritualities: The Pentecostal Revolution in Nigeria* (Chicago: University of Chicago Press, 2009).

8. Sarah Bakker Kellogg, "Perforating Kinship: Syriac Christianity, Ethnicity, and Secular Legibility," *Current Anthropology* 60, no. 4 (2019): 475–98.

9. Joseph Youssef, "From the Blood of St. Mina to the Martyrs of Maspero: Commemoration, Identity, and Social Memory in the Coptic Orthodox Church," *Journal of the Canadian Society for Coptic Studies* 5 (2013): 61–73.

10. Aisha Beliso–De Jesus and Jemima Pierre, "Introduction: Special Section: Anthropology of White Supremacy," *American Anthropologist* 122, no. 1 (2019): 65–75.

11. Naber, "Imperial Whiteness and the Diasporas of Empire."

12. Lisa Suhair Majaj, "Arab-Americans and the Meanings of Race," in *Postcolonial Theory and the United States: Race, Ethnicity, and Literature,* ed. Amritjit Singh and Peter Schmidt (Jackson: University of Mississippi Press, 2000), 320–37.

13. Fr. Moses Samaan, "Diocese Encourages Parishioners to Be Counted in 2010 U.S. Census," Coptic Orthodox Diocese of Los Angeles, Southern California, and Hawaii, March 20, 2010, http://lacopts.org/news/diocese-encourages-parishioners-to -be-counted-in-2010-us-census.

14. Vivian Ibrahim, "Beyond the Cross and the Crescent: Plural Identities and the Copts in Contemporary Egypt," *Ethnic and Racial Studies* 32, no. 14 (2015): 2584–97.

15. "HH Pope Tawadros Youth Meeting at Rutgers University, New Jersey," Christian Youth Channel, www.youtube.com/watch?v=dBUP2CVIvwE.

16. Matt Hadro, "Rep. Chris Smith Speaks at Rutgers in Defense of Coptic Christians," U.S. congressman Chris Smith website, https://chrissmith.house.gov/news /documentsingle.aspx?DocumentID=401450.

17. Caroline Walker Bynum, *Wonderful Blood: Theology and Practice in Late Medieval Northern Germany and Beyond* (Philadelphia: University of Pennsylvania Press, 2007), 11.

18. Gil Anidjar, *Blood: A Critique of Christianity* (New York: Columbia University Press, 2014), 145.

19. Bynum, *Wonderful Blood,* 81.

20. Carolyn M. Ramzy, "To Die Is Gain: Singing a Heavenly Citizenship among Egypt's Coptic Christians," *Ethnos* 80, no. 5 (2015): 649–70; Anna Dowell, "Landscapes of Belonging: Protestant Activism in Revolutionary Egypt," *International Journal of Sociology* 45, no. 3 (2015): 190–205.

21. Febe Armanios, *Coptic Christianity in Ottoman Egypt* (New York: Oxford University Press, 2011). See also Ramzy, "To Die Is Gain," 657–58.

22. Angie Heo, *The Political Lives of Saints: Christian-Muslim Mediation in Egypt* (Berkeley: University of California Press, 2018).

23. Anthony Shenoda, "Cultivating Mystery: Miracles and a Coptic Moral Imaginary" (PhD diss., Harvard University, 2010), 256.

24. Elizabeth Castelli, *Martyrdom and Memory: Early Christian Culture Making* (New York: Columbia University Press, 2004), 107.

25. Paul Sedra, "Class Cleavages and Ethnic Conflict: Coptic Christian Communities in Modern Egyptian Politics," *Islam and Christian-Muslim Relations* 10, no. 2 (1999): 219–35; Paul Sedra, "Writing the History of the Modern Copts: From Victims and Symbols to Actors," *History Compass* 7, no. 3 (2009): 1049–63.

26. Smith, *Unreconciled,* 118.

27. Melani McAlister, "The Politics of Persecution," *MERIP* 249 (Winter 2008), https://merip.org/2008/12/the-politics-of-persecution.

28. Omri Elisha, "Saved by a Martyr: Evangelical Mediation, Sanctification, and the 'Persecuted Church,'" *Journal of the American Academy of Religion* 84, no. 4 (2016): 1056–80.

29. Melani McAlister, *The Kingdom of God Has No Borders: A Global History of American Evangelicals* (New York: Oxford University Press, 2018).

30. Neil J. Young, *We Gather Together: The Religious Right and the Problem of Interfaith Politics* (Oxford: Oxford University Press, 2015).

31. Hank Hanegraaff, *Muslim: What You Need to Know about the World's Fastest-Growing Religion* (Nashville, TN: Thomas Nelson, 2017), 181.

32. Samuel Huntington, *The Clash of Civilizations and the Remaking of World Order* (New York: Simon and Schuster Paperbacks, 1996).

33. There are many Greek Orthodox communities throughout the Middle East. Thus, Greek participation in the economy of blood is akin to American Coptic involvement in think tanks and advocacy organizations mentioned in this article.

34. "Persecution of Christians and Possible Solutions," Session 2, www.youtube.com /watch?v=10iToAH4Z-k&feature=emb_imp_woyt (accessed March 1, 2022).

35. "Persecution of Christians and Possible Solutions."

36. McAlister, "Politics of Persecution."

37. "Grand Banquet, 3rd International Conference on Religious Freedom," www .youtube.com/watch?v=JMQqGkbiV4Q&t=1735s (accessed March 1, 2022).

38. Katayoun Kishi, "Assaults against Muslims in U.S. Surpass 2001 Level," Pew Research Center, November 15, 2017, www.pewresearch.org/fact-tank/2017/11/15 /assaults-against- muslims-in-u-s-surpass-2001-level/.

39. Jasbir Puar, *Terrorist Assemblages: Homonationalism in Queer Times* (Durham, NC: Duke University Press, 2007).

40. Joe Mozingo, "Slain Egyptian Was a Fixture in San Gabriel," *LA Times*, September 19, 2001, http://articles.latimes.com/2001/sep/ 19/local/me-47275.

41. Saher Selod, *Forever Suspect: Racialized Surveillance of Muslim Americans in the War on Terror* (New Brunswick, NJ: Rutgers University Press, 2018).

42. Yasmeen Hanoosh, *The Chaldeans: Politics and Identity in Iraq and the American Diaspora* (London: Bloomsbury Printing, 2019).

43. "Abouna" is the Arabic term for "Father," or priest.

44. Ghassan Hage, *White Nation: Fantasies of White Supremacy in a Multicultural Society* (London: Routledge, 2000), 60–61.

45. Paul Rowe, "Neo-millet Systems and Transnational Religious Movements: The Humayun Decrees and Church Construction in Egypt," *Journal of Church and State* 49 (2007): 329–50.

46. Ishak Ibrahim, "The Reality of Church Construction in Egypt," Tahrir Institute for Middle East Policy, June 27, 2019, https://timep.org/commentary/analysis/the -reality-of-church-construction-in-egypt.

47. W. E. B. Du Bois, "The Souls of White Folk," in *Darkwater: Voices from Within the Veil* (New York: Harcourt, Brace, and Howe, 1920): 29–52.

48. Karen E. Fields and Barbara J. Fields, *Racecraft: The Soul of Inequality in American Life* (New York: Verso Books, 2012), 25.

49. Junaid Rana, "The Story of Islamophobia," *Souls* 9, no. 2 (2016): 148–61.

50. Michael Winerip, "Our Towns; A Terrorist at the Shell Station? No, but That Goatee Looks Suspicious." *New York Times*, September 30, 2001, www.nytimes.com /2001/09/30/nyregion/our-towns-a-terrorist-at-the-shell-station-no-but-that-goatee -looks-suspicious.html.

51. Junaid Rana, "The Racial Infrastructure of the Terror-Industrial Complex," *Social Text* 34, no. 4 (2016): 119.

52. Tomaz Mastnak, *Crusading Peace: Christendom, the Muslim World, and Western Political Order* (Berkeley: University of California Press, 2002).

53. Keith Feldman and Leerom Medevoi, "Race/Religion/War: An Introduction," *Social Text* 34, no. 4 (2016): 1–17.

54. Malcolm Reid, *Whose Pharaohs? Archaeology, Museums, and Egyptian National Identity from Napoleon to World War I* (Berkeley: University of California Press, 2002).

55. Maspero quoted in B. L. Carter, *The Copts in Egyptian Politics* (London: Croom Helm, 1986), 96.

56. Carter, 119n38.

57. Carter, 119n38.

58. Reid, *Whose Pharaohs?*, 281.

59. Shenoda, "Cultivating Mystery," 8.

60. Quoted in Matthew Frye Jacobson, *Whiteness of a Different Color: European Immigrants and the Alchemy of Race* (Cambridge, MA: Harvard University Press, 1999), 145.

61. Barbara Jeanne Fields, "Slavery, Race, and Ideology in the United States of America," *New Left Review* 181, no. 1 (1990): 95–118.

62. Evelyn Baring, Earl of Cromer, *Modern Egypt*, vol. 1 (New York: Macmillan, 1908), 202.

63. Baring, 203–5.

64. Su'ad Abdul Khabeer, *Muslim Cool: Race, Religion, and Hip Hop in the United States* (New York: NYU Press, 2016).

65. Karen Brodkin, *How Jews Became White Folks* (New Brunswick, NJ: Rutgers University Press, 1998); Ian Haney-Lopez, *White by Law: The Legal Construction of Race* (New York: NYU Press, 1996).

66. Neda Maghbouleh, *The Limits of Whiteness: Iranian Americans and the Everyday Politics of Race* (Stanford, CA: Stanford University Press, 2017); Stanley Thangaraj, *Desi Hoop Dreams: Pickup Basketball and the Making of Asian American Masculinity* (New York: NYU Press, 2015).

67. Sally Howell and Andrew Shryock, "Cracking Down on Diaspora: Arab Detroit and America's 'War on Terror,'" *Anthropological Quarterly* 76, no. 3 (2003): 443–62.

68. Sherene Razack, *Casting Out: The Eviction of Muslims from Western Law and Politics* (Toronto: University of Toronto Press, 2008).

69. Sylvia Chan-Malik, *Being Muslim: A Cultural History of Women of Color in American Islam* (New York: NYU Press, 2018).

70. W. E. B. Du Bois, *The Souls of Black Folk: Essays and Sketches* (Chicago: A. C. McClurg, 1903).

71. Sonja Thomas, "Cowboys and Indians: Indian Priests in Rural Montana," *Women's Studies Quarterly* 47, no. 1 and 2 (2019): 110–31.

72. Sarah Gualtieri, *Between Arab and White: Race and Ethnicity in the Early Syrian American Diaspora* (Berkeley: University of California Press, 2009), 31.

73. Gualtieri, 49.

74. Gualtieri, 48.

75. Gualtieri, 51.

76. Walter Armbrust, "Media Review: *al-Da'iyya* (The Preacher)," *Journal of the American Academy of Religion* 82, no. 3 (2014): 841–56.

77. Saba Mahmood, *Religious Difference in a Secular Age: A Minority Report* (Princeton, NJ: Princeton University Press, 2015), 85.

78. Mariz Tadros, *Copts at the Crossroads: The Challenges of Building Inclusive Democracy in Egypt* (Cairo: AUC Press, 2013).

79. Anidjar, *Blood*, 18.

80. Foucault and Camporesi quoted in Anidjar, *Blood*, 22; Bynum, *Wonderful Blood*, 15.

CHAPTER THIRTEEN

Just Like Us

Evangelical Missions, Empathy, and the Neoliberal Subject

John Corrigan

Affect and Global Missions

The American evangelical project of global missions wagered that Americans would invest their personal and material resources in the grand vision of a world converted if those investors were repaid in emotional currency. Urging Americans to cultivate feelings for strangers abroad, missions proponents fashioned an emotions program around images of faraway others. That program constructed for its participants a sense of connectedness to persons they had never met nor would meet. It grounded in an affective economy the logistics of mission enterprise and above all the securing of funds and the enlistment of volunteers to travel the globe. Its success as a program was proportional to the steadiness of American evangelicals' affect-rich identification with evangelized populations whose lives they imagined.

American evangelicals felt for the yet-to-be converted alongside the recently converted and were glad that they did.

Beginning in the nineteenth century, American evangelical designs on bringing the "heathen" to Christ rested partly on a view of foreigners as victims of oppression. The leading edge of mission reports and the affective core of recruitment lectures was the lament that people suffered under political, social, and religious systems that kept them from knowing and freely worshipping Christ. As the mission project ramped up at Andover Theological Seminary and elsewhere in the early nineteenth century and reports from overseas were published in missionary magazines, the renewed genre of persecuted innocents lent dramatic gravity to discussions of evangelical roles and responsibilities.[1]

The persecution narrative made its resurgence in the annals of American evangelical missions with the rehearsal of a number of well-known stories and grew progressively richer in detail and more fervent in tone. A foundational incident for the genre was the account of Franciscan missionaries and their allies crucified at Nagasaki in 1597, after which there was "widespread persecution" there.[2] The victims were Catholic, but the drama of the story, and especially the means of execution, spoke dearly to evangelical Christians. Other chapters, such as the "massacre of native Christians" in Husang, China, were added to the picture over time.[3]

Some Americans overseas suffered along with the natives. Antebellum biographies vividly detailed the bravery and hurt of nineteenth-century American missionary exemplars Adoniram (1788–1850) and Ann Hasseltine Judson (1789–1826). The *Life of Mrs. Ann Judson, Late Missionary to Burmah* was first published in 1829 and was republished almost every year thereafter until 1856. Its descriptions of her efforts in the face of severe trials struck the evangelical heart deeply, gaining a wide readership and prompting Lydia Maria Child to remark that it was "a book so universally known that it scarce need be mentioned."[4] Francis Wayland's subsequent companion biography of Adoniram Judson proffered vignettes of imprisonment, torture, and loss, all concluding in pain, which was described in many different ways in dozens of instances.[5]

While effective imagistically because of their simple plots and affective resonance, pain-rich stories of government-administrated violence were read by missionaries as epiphenomena issuing from the more profound problem of corrupt heathen "systems": not merely repressive political orders and dehumanizing social structures but, most importantly, a canopy of ideological systems built upon superstition. Asia, "the stupendous empire of

Evangelical Missions and the Neoliberal Subject

superstition," like Africa was a place in thrall to heathen "religious systems, whose direct and powerful tendency is to pollute, rather than purify mankind—to enhance, rather than mitigate the sufferings of life."[6] American evangelicals pronounced their dismay as they would "look out upon those regions of superstition, and crime, and idolatry, and moral desolation, where 'the heathen, in his blindness, bows down to stock and stone,'" lamenting the "poor victims of superstition" confined therein.[7]

Repining over the "poor victims of superstition" remained a standard feature of evangelical reporting on missions throughout the twentieth century and into the twenty-first. The issue of persecution indeed earned both a heavier gravity and deeper valence in the wake of the Holocaust and as genocidal brutalities behind the Iron Curtain came to light. During that period, the broader human rights movement gathered momentum, both in the United States and Europe, and its communicative strategy of cultivating empathy for those who suffered from political tyranny dovetailed with the long-standing evangelical approach to drumming up support for foreign missions.

As Mark Philip Bradley has shown, the twentieth-century human rights movement built cases for reform based on the testimonials of witnesses who related their experiences, and especially their suffering, in public displays that appealed affectively to audiences who audited them. Bradley explained how first-person accounts of detention and torture, of witnessing brutality, executions, and disappearances, became the truth that grounded reports of human rights violations. Truth was an affectual truth, part, again, of the "circulation of affect,"[8] as emotionally charged stories made their way from the mouths of witnesses to the ears of persons distal to the suffering itself. Media were crucially important in that process, as conveyors not only of words but of images and sounds that contributed to the credibility of the testimony.[9]

Evangelical efforts to spark emotional response from potential missions supporters were manifested in various ways, and not least so in highly publicized bids to influence the U.S. government to intervene in cases of religious persecution overseas. Such evangelical ventures began in antebellum America but were more concerted and systematic in the mid-twentieth century. The evangelical campaign to locate and decry religious intolerance overseas was a key part of the American Protestant view of "world Christianity" that blossomed postwar from a century of Protestant commitment to the promotion of Christianity in foreign lands. Taking advantage of the development of air travel, the promoters of the evangelical cause abroad flew witnesses to Washington, DC, and elsewhere, so that those persons could deliver their accounts of religious persecution and torture to live audiences. In the same way that published missionary reports once transmitted word of the pain suffered by the tyrannized—whether the victims were converted or yet-to-be converted—the dramatically staged in-person retellings of suffering by non-Americans (mostly Asians, initially) further infused the problem of overseas persecution with affect. Just as importantly, the pragmatics of the evangelicals' cause were reinforced by the fact that their crusade took the same approach, employing the same tactics of persuasion, as the broader human rights movement that focused on political prisoners and refugees. That shared stratagem—the focus on testimonies to pain—enabled evangelical organizations to offer a vision of their operations as collaborations with other human rights campaigns.

Typical of evangelicals' affectual politics in promoting their overseas interests to an American audience was their management of the discussion of the cases of several East Asian clergy who came to America to talk about persecution in their homelands. In the spring of 1959, five Protestant church leaders testified before the House Un-American Activities Committee: Peter Chu Pong was from Hong Kong; Shih-Ping Wang, Tsin-tsai Liu, and Samuel W. S. Cheng were from Taiwan; and Kyung Rai Kim was from Seoul. All were witnesses to persecution, either in Red China or North Korea. Their testimonies were widely publicized in the press and reprinted for years in evangelical publications.[10]

All of the visiting Asian Christians stressed their experiences of physical torture. Pong discussed, among other things, how he had been imprisoned and beaten repeatedly and how "they slapped our faces, kicked our bodies, and poured cold water on our heads." Pong related how "they made my children stand and watch. If they cried the Communists beat them," reporting that "if I had confessed [to Christian belief] they would have killed me immediately."[11] Tsin-tsai Liu recounted similar suffering after the Chinese "began wholesale persecution of Protestant churches in 1950." He described in detail one torture that Christians endured that would return as a topic of debate in America a half century later: "They stop the noses of the people and pour water in their mouths. Every time the person breathes he swallows water."[12] Cheng provided further detail, describing the murder of his Christian sister-in-law: "They used five horses. One horse was tied to her neck and the other horses were tied to her arms and legs and they went in all directions. The biggest horse ran and it just tore her body into pieces. The blood streamed all over the public square, and the people shut their eyes and cried."[13]

Evangelical Missions and the Neoliberal Subject

The disseminated stories of the persecuted, in these instances and numerous others, gave the appearance that the Asian societies in which such things could occur were vastly different from the United States. Investigators in Washington and elsewhere used scalding rhetorical flourishes to characterize Asian overlords and their superstitious enablers as devils. They were brutal, barbarian, barely human monsters. They were the opposite of evangelical Americans, appearing as evil, demonic, miscreated Others. HUAC director Richard Arens described the Asian scene as sketched by the visiting clergy as "raw, ruthless terrorism as practiced by the perpetrators of the most monstrous conspiracy against humanity in all recorded history."[14]

Over the course of generations, evangelical Christians pictured the cultures of Asians, Africans, and others as perverse. Evangelical depictions of the populations of those cultures—collectively referenced as the heathen—accordingly cast them as people who inhabited that perversity and who needed saving from their terrible predicament, but who were in vague ways also responsible for it. Just as much academic analysis of religiously inspired terrorism later posited a mentality that strictly separated good from evil, right from wrong, the righteous from the infidels, so did evangelicals order the globe as an arena in which the godly were at war with the wicked.[15] And there was much wickedness among the heathen.

Empathy, Alterity, and Similarity

In 1759 Adam Smith wrote about sympathy in *The Theory of Moral Sentiments*, wherein he defined it as "fellow-feeling," a part of human nature.[16] More specifically, sympathy means feeling as another feels, and especially feeling sorrowful or sad when confronted with another's difficult circumstances. Edward Titchener, in translating a word from German to English, in 1909 subsequently coined the term "empathy," signifying broader and more complex meanings—beyond feeling *for* another—that eventually became the standard for psychologists, philosophers, and other academic writers.[17] Recent research has investigated empathy in various ways, including its manifestations as motor mimicry (parallel affect in mimicking the physical movements of another), emotional contagion, perspective taking, role taking, and feelings of nurturance; empathy as both cognitive and affective; and, in work that joins psychological research to philosophical and social scientific research, the complexities of "self-other merging."[18]

Empathy involves imagining how another feels and specifically how one would feel in another's situation.[19] But more fundamentally, it is "other-focused personal imagining" that requires a trick of simulating the cognitive and emotional state of another while also differentiating oneself from the other.[20] As such the empathizing actor represents "a living oxymoron," taking another as "being like me" as well as being a different subject.[21] If the trick works, empathy can lead to generosity and altruism.[22] Narrative can help, by prompting the imagination to psychologically emplace a person in situations acted by others.[23] In fMRI brain imaging experiments, even reading stories of others' actions results in increased activity in mirror neuron areas of the brain, and high-empathy persons show strong levels of activity in that specific neural substrate. Reading narratives is an especially powerful prompt to empathy.[24]

The coalesced genre of American evangelical missions literature, beginning with the antebellum surge of evangelical publications, accented the differences between American Christians and foreigners who inhabited alternate religious worlds. Literary depictions of terrible relations between English colonists and Native Americans supplied a precedent for subsequent evangelical classifications of overseas Others that relied upon starkly drawn differences. But even early Anglo-Americans believed that there was some measure of kinship with the Indians. Colonists accepted the emanant message of appealing but tortured historical narratives that Indians were, after all, lapsed Christians, or at least descended from Jews.[25] Similarly, nineteenth- and twentieth-century evangelical renderings of Asian, African, and Middle Eastern cultures, while condemning those cultures for their heathen ways, superstitions, corrupt political systems, barbarian social customs, and inbred distemper, also allowed for a view of persons inhabiting those cultures as people who were similar in important ways to Americans.

Evangelical missionary publications remained unrelenting in their condemnations of perversion—they sustained their diligent policing of boundaries—but at the same time they portrayed overseas populations as much like Americans in their hopes for community, security, spiritual advancement, family, and productivity. Empathy requires a share of identification with the other while still keeping one's distance. Evangelicals sustained their denunciations of foreign cultures at the same time that they cultivated in their readers a sense of kinship with the people who had built those cultures. Their approach accordingly did not melt one side into the other. Rather, it sharpened a sense of difference while dramatically overreaching in pronouncements of how foreign others were "just like us." There was a paradoxical aspect to evangelical missionary reports to match the paradoxical experience of empathy.

In the fall of 1912, the American missionary Josephine Davis, having previously read that heathen culture was the antithesis of her own, reported from Canton. She wrote that she was aware of the possibility of her demise when she left home for overseas, having "decided that hardships of every kind, persecutions and probably sudden death would come to me." Once in country, she gave the other version of the story: "Nothing has seemed strange or horrible to me," and the Chinese "are essentially just like us." She enjoyed eating the rice and discovered that "some of their customs are more sensible than ours."[26]

Helen Lee Richardson, stationed in Shanghai at the end of the previous century, had protested equally that "people do not realize that the Chinese are just like us." Richardson claimed that "we can come to love a people so that their native land may be, in a sense, our native land. What affects them affects us."[27] For the Baptist missionary Jennie Bixby Johnson, the Shan in Burma likewise were "folks, just like us." She offered that estimation specifically in summary of her discussion of everyday life in a Shan community. "We went to their houses and watched the women drying grains and weaving. They were ready to talk and said that their way of dressing was much better than ours, and their clothes much prettier." For Johnson, the everyday lives of others were like the everyday lives of "us," centered around common projects and shared interests.[28] Margaret A. Wright, in Manila, wrote that "their appreciation of jokes made me marvel more than ever." Decamping from a meeting with Filipinos, she exulted, "All the way home I thought of those words of Scripture, 'God hath made of one blood,' and over and over I said to myself, 'They are just like us.'"[29] Evalyn Toll in India had "already learned to love some of the people" because "they are just like us."[30] And Mary Elliot Fitch Tooker cast her own observations in verse: "Ah, the Chinese streets are dirty, and the Chinese people queer; / But after all, they're just like us, and the Master holds them dear."[31] The certainty of synonymity animated nineteenth- and twentieth-century evangelical missionary literature that equally reported on foreign places as strongholds of Satan: corrupt, evil, and dangersome.

Marriage and Romance

American missionary literature that conjointly promoted the image of foreign evil and the notion that people overseas were "just like us" did so with references to the everyday lives of people. Just as women missionaries such as Johnson and Wright conceptualized their relations with others through their exposure to the daily routines and local rhythms of life abroad, so also did missionary literature in general pay close attention to activities and behaviors that identified others as people who seemed to do as Americans did. Locals made food and sewed clothes, built shelters, laughed at jokes, celebrated births, mourned their dead, tended their animals, sang, loved their children, and entered into marriages. Americans read about those daily activities, thought about them, and even enacted them in parlor tableaux that were construed as informative entertainment and functioned as means to cultivate American feeling for people abroad. One afternoon in 1910, at the Alabama Street Presbyterian Church in Memphis, some congregants performed renditions of everyday scenes from the lives of several Asian populations "in the interest of missions." They staged a mock Korean wedding, replete with a procession, ceremony, feast, costumes, songs, and "salaams," "which were faithfully copied and successfully carried out." Other enactments that day included "the native women at work," the "coolie with his pack on his back," and "a mourner," among several others, all "according to the customs of the country."[32]

The partnering of men and women was of particular interest to Americans and had been for a long time. Euro-Americans, beginning with the Spanish, had focused closely on Native Americans' sexual behaviors in their efforts to Christianize them. Courtship, marriage, and child-rearing always were core concerns of the missionary endeavor and remained priorities of evangelical reckonings with societies that Christians sought to convert. Those core concerns defined familiar fields for moral reform, which was a large part of the business of missionizing. But they also mattered because they invited empathetic engagement. American missionaries and their supporters could feel their way into other societies by imagining others as people who married and raised children just as they did. The performative immersion into the setting of a Korean marriage as orchestrated by the members of the Alabama Street Presbyterian Church was one means, among others, of nurturing affectual attachments to evangelized populations.

For Christians, marriage as the harmony of bodies bespoke marriage as a harmony of souls, with each other and with God. Historian Kristin Mann observed of missionaries in Africa, "Investing domestic behavior with great significance, as the outward sign of inward religious conversion, they made marriage a pivotal resting ground of individual religious faith."[33] But that formula in practice was hard to apply when the data were strange. Evangelicals' extensive writing about marriage consequently illustrates the convolutedness of American endeavoring to empathize with persons from places abroad. One complication was the fact that American evangelical missionary understandings of marriage were constructed around beliefs about feeling. For Americans in the nineteenth century, marriage was for the most part companionate marriage, a relationship between a man and woman built on mutual attraction and feelings of affection. The couple expected the marriage to be happy and to endure because it was based on love. Moreover, evangelicals broached the message of love as a crucial part of the Christian tidings, and they affirmed that love of God for humanity was mirrored in the married love between a man and woman and in the love of one community for another.

According to many evangelical observers, romantic love in marriage suffered badly in Asia, Africa, and elsewhere. Missionary reports from overseas painted dismal pictures of marriage as political schemes that discouraged or denied romantic love. Dispatches from every region of the world anguished over the issue. As part of a broader characterization of Asia and Africa as places where superstition, cannibalism, human sacrifice, the worship of idols, and other abominations reigned, missionary communiqués unrelentingly bemoaned the sad state of marriage. Women were severely oppressed, immoral men candidly indulged their lust with many wives, and children suffered.[34] A sacramental relationship that was supposed to reflect the love of God was a tragic parody of the order of things given in scripture. It was a deep wound to the soul and a revelation of the demonic underbelly of heathen life.

Missionary grapplings with the problem of marriage signaled the complexity and polyvalency of the notion "just like us." Evangelicals in their appraisals of native marriages betrayed anxiety about alterity at the same time that they ventilated heartfelt Christian hopes to discover that Africans and Asians really were just like them. For evangelicals, love was a universal emotion naturally present between men and women in their intimate relationships with each other. Marriage as such was an everyday example of the Christian love of others that as ideology defined the agenda of missionary work for generations of volunteers. Trust in universal romantic love in marriage was necessary to the evangelical view of the world. But so also was the belief that yet-to-be Christianized cultures were toxic, polluted by sin, ignorance, and superstition. The evangelical imaginary was anchored in speculative play between those two ways of seeing the heathen world. To feel connected to foreign others, to experience the bonds of feeling that always defined evangelical missions programs, American actors—students, pastors, idealistic women, money givers, writers, churchgoers—were enjoined to emplace themselves in that imaginary, to love strangers overseas as they were (because they were just like us) while making them into what they should be (because their immorality made them so different). Missionaries' empathy was a conspicuously challenging exercise in endeavoring to feel like Africans (or others) while feeling like themselves. Religious ideas abetted the paradox, offering language and categories that structured the effort and worked to naturalize its mystery.[35]

In several instances during the mid-nineteenth and early twentieth centuries, evangelicals championing the right to legal Protestant weddings overseas persuaded the U.S. State Department to intervene in several countries on their behalf.[36] In general, however, Protestant missionary publications focused on reforming the local institution of marriage itself, laboring to keep before their readerships an ominous view of the state of marriage among the heathen. The *Methodist Review* struck that tone for much of the ink in its 1886 article "Women and Missions: Female Degradation in the Heathen Lands." It pictured indigenous marriage as representative of the larger problem of the treatment of women in overseas societies. The *Review* raged that "'wife-capture,' wherein women have been stolen, speared, clubbed, or otherwise half-killed in the process, has been, or is, too wide-spread to allow of even the enumeration of the peoples who have practiced it." Such behavior was linked to female infanticide, which had warped population ratios throughout heathen lands: "The Baboos of Bhudawar Kalan live in ten villages, in seven of which were found one hundred and four boys and one girl. Their other villages are said to contain two girls." More specifically and directly, it was polyandry and infant betrothal—"the greatest evil in India"—that fully poisoned marriage and were responsible for the destruction of women's lives in non-Christian societies around the world.[37]

American Baptists in India warned that "polygamy, with its attendant evils, is one of the chief causes of the deep degradation and wretchedness of this whole population."[38] The American Board of Commissioners for Foreign Missions was clear that "polygamy is one of the strongholds of heathenism" in Africa, and a Methodist article, "Polygamy and Christian Missions," identified polygamy (it actually was polygyny) as "an evil which, unless stamped out immediately by the use of strong measures," would ultimately subvert the entire Christian mission enterprise.[39] The *Missionary Herald* boiled down the problem in Africa to a familiar trope: "Marriage here is but little different from the slave trade; and the wife is treated but little different from the slave."[40] In a capitalist misreading of the notion of bridewealth, such commentary simply concluded that "wives are bought and sold."[41]

Evangelical Missions and the Neoliberal Subject

Missionaries, again, were close (but not unbiased) observers of everyday life among the people they visited. The alarm in their admonitions was rooted in their everyday contacts with their hosts. There sometimes was a sunnier viewpoint, however, and it emerged, also, out of their immersion in the lives of the people with whom they had settled. Missionaries, whose ranks included a large number of unmarried women,[42] paid keen attention to marriage ceremonies, whether they were in native custom or among converts. They passed their observations along in letters to magazine and book publishers. Readers subsequently engaged with what appeared to be the everyday lives of others as espied in what ostensibly were ceremonial joinings of two persons as they might be joined in America.

Sometimes the upbeat tone of marriage reports was well suited to leading readers to a sense that others were enthusiastic about marriage "just like us." "We attended a very interesting marriage ceremony performed according to the Brahmo ritual," wrote one observer from India, who then filed the specifics. A report from Burma noted "the excitement occasioned by a marriage feast which took place on Tuesday" among Buddhists, where amid an arrangement of flowers there was great feasting, the author taking care to detail the menu. Many observers noted the role of music in marriage ceremonies, and some mentioned dancing.[43] In many accounts, there was a strong note of enchantment. A meticulous account from Ceylon enthused in its conclusion that "all the ceremonies generally occupy four days, and are too numerous to be mentioned. The principal part is conducted in the night, and, when the lights are numerous, has a very splendid appearance." It is not hard to imagine how such accounts might have appealed to American readers who saw something of themselves in the impressive marriage ceremonies of persons in other parts of the world.[44]

But then again there always was the problem of bride-sale and polygamy. As beautiful and seemingly merry as some of the marriage ceremonies described by missionaries might have been, in the long term those events nevertheless were no match for Christian marriages, according to observers. When missionaries were married, sometimes to other American missionaries and sometimes to native converts, the weddings were longingly described and celebrated in missionary publications. The language of such stories generally differed from that found in descriptions of non-Christian marriages. Where comments in summaries of native ceremonies might be qualifiedly positive, narrations of missionary weddings plainly gushed with gaity and warmth. A letter from China in 1866 enthused that "today has also been to us a day of much joy" because of the marriages of several converts. "Who can estimate the gracious influence that may go out from these seven Christian households?" The letter informing of the marriages remarked that one spectating member of the local community, an "aged brother, more than eighty years old, remarked that it was the happiest day of his life."[45] Similarly in Kyoto ten years later, a converted man married a woman who had been baptized the day before. It was a brilliant marriage, as the "wife is perhaps best fitted to be a helpmeet for him of any woman in Japan, and her acquisition, by him and for the truth in this great city and in this empire, is a joyful and truly providential event."[46] God's hand was mightily evidenced in missionary marriages. But while emphasizing the distinguishing joy and providence of the marriage, the reporter appeared oblivious to the language of ownership in the account and to the problematic similarity of the idea of acquisition to local practices of "bride-buying" that missionaries vehemently condemned.

The odd language in the account of the Kyoto marriage was a way of discursively elevating Christian rites above non-Christian. Similar wordings are found in other missionary discussions of local marriages. In some such accounts, missionary writing comes across as strained. The seams show; the ragged edges are visible. "Do they really understand what marriage is, and are they really like us?" are unspoken questions that hound the reports. In Central Africa in 1859, a marriage of converts was an occasion to showcase the superiority of Christianity, but the statement declaring such difference was haunted by special pleading: "At the conclusion of the marriage ceremony, which was in the Mpongwe language, the guests presented their salutations to the newly married couple, after which they partook of cake and lemonade, and then dispersed, evidently feeling that Christian marriage is superior to their heathenish system of polygamy."[47] Missionaries wanted to believe that Christianity was better than heathenism and that their hosts agreed with them. But they were uncertain at times of where to draw the line separating the two. That could be a problem when published field reports that aimed at cultivating reader empathy had to perform the exacting gymnastics of disclosing how others were just like them but yet quite different. What did it mean for Africans to enjoy an afternoon of wedding cake and lemonade just like Americans and then go back to their "heathenish system of polygamy"?

The knotty dynamics of feeling that drove the evangelical enterprise can be glimpsed in an early twentieth-century missionary's remarks about marriage in Africa.[48] "I think it is fair to say," he wrote, "that the average African is less immoral than the average European, and that marriage in pagan Africa is more binding and produces far fewer divorces than in Christian Europe." Like

Evangelical Missions and the Neoliberal Subject

Westerners, Africans were invested in the idea that "marriage is a process, progressive and accumulative; both in duties and status." Through a long betrothal process that could last years, "the man and woman grow gradually into a new relationship . . . marked by mutuality and reciprocity." Africans, indeed, appeared much like Christians. Yet, even in view of that, African cultures were immoral because they were not Christian. They retained damaging superstitions and edged toward abomination in their polygyny, and, rightfully, "the whole of missionary work has been an interference with African society and African marriage," and "we cannot abdicate it." In the end, "we are not concerned with an idealization of African society . . . but with changing it until it is Christian."[49]

If missionaries tacitly entertained questions about whether Christian marriages were truly categorically superior to heathen marriages, their frequent mentionings of ceremonies in which native rites were joined with Christian liturgy suggest that they were trying to come to terms with hybridity in a way that likely produced further ambiguity. In late nineteenth-century Japan, Buddhist "Endeavor Societies" developed "a distinctive marriage ceremony" that joined Buddhist and Christian practices. A Methodist writer remarked of the societies, "They have carried their modifications of faith and practice so far as to have been spoken of as 'Christianized Buddhists.'" In such an instance, empathy might have been easier, a sense of identification stronger because they were closer to being "just like us." But at the same time, they were not "just like us." There was distance, and that distance did not go unnoticed.[50] In a parallel instance in China, the bride and groom in the course of a Christian wedding performed a local ritual of "knocking their heads." The Christian minister emphasized that "this part of the ceremony we hope to see done away with."[51] Similarly, at a Zulu ceremony, local and regional practices were woven into the Christian service, including one that struck the officiating minister as "quite in imitation of the old custom in Bible lands." But Bible or not, he "saw what I consider an element of danger in the disposition of some to allow heathen customs at Christian weddings."[52]

Evangelical missionary narration of marriage among people in distant lands presented it as an aspect of everyday life. Marrying was, purportedly, something that everyone did or yearned to do. It made "them" like "us." But missionary publications wove their stories about marriage back and forth through a field of variant depictions of life in Asian and African villages. The people living in those villages were clearly not "like us" at all when the topic was polygyny, dowry, or child betrothal. The affectual affinity of American evangelicals for those they aimed to convert, the feeling of empathy that evangelicals cultivated, was dynamic and unstable. At times it led to collaborations and at other times to impositions executed in keeping with the mentality of colonial entitledness.

Romantic Love and Heteronormativity in Africa

All empathy is not the same. Empathy involves feeling what another feels while remaining oneself. It is always that paradox. But the way that empathy is practiced differs from one context to another. For the great many evangelicals who administrated or otherwise supported the colossal program of world conversion from their congregational homes in America, empathy was the practice of cultivating feelings that others felt by reading about those others and especially about their everyday lives. American evangelicals read that Chinese sewed clothes; so did they. Africans mourned their dead; so did they. People in Burma got married; so did they. Indians suffered, and Americans ventured to feel their pain. It was possible to be generous toward those others who were "just like us." Empathy led to a certain kind of altruism. But in the case of evangelical missions, that performance included the levying of evangelicals' own beliefs on the people with whom they empathized. Empathy served empire.

The imperial impulse in evangelicals' empathy can be glimpsed in their promotion of the ideal of romance in marriage. Romantic love was part of a matrix of interconnected ideas about how humans should live their lives. Evangelicals yearned to see that matrix implemented among the people they befriended. Their altruism, which led them across oceans and, as Josephine Davis imagined, possibly to suffering and sudden death, became their crusade to free people from what they saw as the tyrannies of superstition and brutish traditions. Their focus on marriage was central to that crusade. They understood marriage to be in its essence a matter of romantic love, and they worked hard to persuade the people they visited to make their marriages on that model. Extrapolating from their understanding of the relationship of a person to God through love, "they insisted that Christian marriage united two individuals" and "that it should be based on Western ideals of love and companionship."[53]

Scholars who have studied the shifting African cultural landscape of the past few decades conclude, for example, that romantic love has in fact become an ideal for many Africans as well.[54] Valentine's Day is celebrated throughout Africa, a credible sign that "Africans have long remade affective ideals and practices by engaging those from elsewhere," including, most prominently,

Evangelical Missions and the Neoliberal Subject

those prescribed by Christian missionaries and European colonial regimes.[55] But as a visibly public embrace of romantic love has grown, African scholars as well as European and American writers have complicated that story. They have challenged the narrative that had been constructed by missionaries that marriages made in keeping with local and regional practices were crude transactions bordering on sex work. Romance was strongly present in Swahili poetry in the nineteenth century, love letters and art expressed passionate and romantic feelings, and romantic love appears to have been important in relationships between men and women, even if persons then ended up in marriages executed as unions of families. It may also be the case, as some have argued, that recent African claims on indigenous traditions of romantic love emblemize an African aspiration to appear modern.[56]

It nevertheless is likely that evangelical missionaries' promotion of romantic love in marriage evidenced a measure of emotional imperialism. Some scholars suggest that missionaries forced it upon Africans, and others, as a part of their evangelizing program.[57] But it was not only romantic love that preoccupied missionaries. Romantic love, as part of a larger view of Christian life, was joined to a Christian view of the family. Family was the product of romantic love between a man and a woman. Missionaries wanted that for those they converted, but their vision of local cultures was clouded. Missionaries overlooked the stability of those African families that were constructed in traditional ways, including through early betrothal, polygyny, and the exchange of lobola, or dowry. Such marriages were alliances between families, and over generations these unions built extended networks of interrelationships among parties that not only lent stability to the social order but also established frameworks for the transmission of knowledge and skills from older to younger members. Focused closely on sexual behaviors, missionaries missed much of the larger picture. They saw what they believed was suffering and empathized with the victims. What missionaries felt was braided with what missionaries saw through American lenses.

There has been much recent discussion of empathy among scholars and in government and business circles. Barack Obama's widely read *The Audacity of Hope* urged an American recommitment to empathy in a nation that was suffering from an "empathy deficit." Dev Patnaik followed with *Wired to Care: How Companies Prosper When They Create Widespread Empathy*.[58] Such books represent a growing literature that recommends empathy because it makes sense as a framework for the expansion of neoliberal agendas. When Naomi Head writes about "the political character of empathy" in international relations, she means to address "a certain teleological aspect to empathy."

And for her and other investigators, there is an approach to empathy that "tends to exclude sufficient acknowledgment of the relations of power which structure context-specific and situated conflicts."[59] Empathy is a humanist value that does ideological work.

Empathy can be transformative. It can disrupt habits of engagement and exchange between parties in ways that lead to questioning of assumptions about how such relations should be structured. It can lead to insight. Empathy equally is affective capital that can be invested by neoliberal regimes seeking to exploit for profit existing gender, racial, social, and sexual hierarchies. It can be deployed to reinforce those hierarchies. It functions as a means to construct the neoliberal subject.[60]

As Carolyn Pedwell has argued, the international aid apparatus is a particularly vivid illustration of how "empathetic self-transformation can become commodified in ways that fix unequal affective subjects."[61] Neoliberal technologies of governmentality exploit empathy as a skill useful to the aligning of global economic ambitions with local resources. Pedwell offers a view of how international "immersion" programs, through which corporate, governmental, and NGO representatives visit societies targeted for "development," treat empathy as an investment in reproducing asymmetrical power relations favorable to profit making. Immersed visitors imagine themselves, through their cultivated empathy, to be justified in speaking for their hosts. That means informing them of the "right ways" to do things, namely, according to canons ensuring regulation, disciplining, and domination by global hegemons.[62]

Evangelical missionaries' efforts to foster Christian marriage among converts demanded a "right way" of marriage. In the case of Africa, evangelicals empathized with the people they visited and concluded that marriage, as a union of a man and a woman, was one part of a larger divine design for African societies. In the global calculations of neoliberal economics, the subject is heterosexual. The neoliberal empathies of Christian missionaries guided them to promote that view of sexuality in Africa and, in the case of sub-Saharan nations such as Uganda and Nigeria, to speak forcefully about the criminal nature of homosexuality.[63]

Homosexuality is dangerous in such a worldview partly because it threatens the traditional Christian family. The heteronormative family is a major component of neoliberal assumptions about the conditions most favorable to the accumulation and circulation of capital in late modernity. Privatization, open markets, strong international banking systems accompanied by national defense infrastructures to protect them, and globalization all are imbricated with the productivity of citizen-subjects. Those citizens best serve the ends of development and profitability when they form kinship groups ideally arranged as heteronormative families. "Good families" are those wherein personal responsibility and initiative are in evidence, a healthy distance from the state is observed, and skills are transmitted via family lines vertically and horizontally throughout the kinship group.[64]

Numerous evangelical groups, which in some instances allied with other Protestant groups and Roman Catholics, helped to force the issue of homosexuality in Africa. Their efforts overseas increased as the visibility and political will of LGBT groups in the United States rose and as the issue of gay marriage became increasingly more important in American politics. Among those evangelical organizations that fought hardest against gay rights was the Family Research Council (FRC), which, since its founding in 1983, has been a leader of conservative Christian efforts to develop technologies of exclusion aimed at gays and lesbians. The FRC also has been vigorously engaged in campaigns against same-sex-desiring individuals in Africa, including famously lobbying against a U.S. congressional resolution condemning an Ugandan anti-homosexuality law that authorized life in prison and, initially, the death penalty in some cases.[65]

The FRC promotes a neoliberal homophobic discourse. The African projects of the FRC and other conservative evangelical groups are built upon an ideological platform that upholds romantic love between a man and a woman, their Christian marriage, and the family that is built around that marriage as crucial to the organization of human resources for global capitalism. A FRC policy statement asserts, "Family Research Council believes, and social science has now clearly demonstrated, that children do best when raised by their own biological mother and father who are committed to one another in a lifelong marriage. Indeed, the data demonstrate that adults also thrive in this same family structure." The policy is elaborated with regard to a dedicated section on "Family Economics," which explains further: "The family is the great generator, and the intact family the greatest generator, of human capital (knowledge, attitudes, skills and habits of the individual), and of much financial savings and capital as well. The vast majority of small businesses (out of which eventually grow the large businesses of the nation) begin as family businesses."[66] Regarding heterosexual marriage, the FRC said, "We need to persuade not just with logical argument or irrefutable fact but with empathy and stories."[67]

Neoliberals Just Like Us

American evangelical missions to Asia, Africa, and other foreign lands brought two gospels. One was a gospel of Christianity. The other was a gospel of global capitalism, of liberalism that became neoliberalism. One was overt and explicit, the other less obvious. They were intertwined.

Missionaries tried to empathize with their hosts. Their reports, published in magazines and newspapers in America, served as narratives that cultivated the empathy of readers. They related that others were just like them, just like American Christians. They also complained incessantly about the corruption, sinfulness, and blatant evil they discovered overseas. Their empathy kept a distance even as it aimed at closeness.

Marriage, as a pivotal facet of the everyday lives that missionaries reported on, was central to evangelicals' conceptualization of their mission. Missionaries rejected indigenous systems of family making as oppressive and wicked. They promoted what they believed was the sublime alternative of romantic love, monogamy, and the nuclear family of man, woman, and child.

Informed by their practice of empathy that they knew what was best for the people they engaged, missionaries imposed upon those people an anti-homosexual view. In so doing, they served as major vectors of neoliberal views. Their insistence on heteronormativity contributed significantly to the construction of neoliberal subjects who would carry forward the economic and political agendas of global capitalism. One of the ironies of missionary involvement in Africa is that African same-sex-desiring relationships, which are not fitted into traditions of marriage there, can dramatically represent precisely the ideal of romantic love that evangelicals insist upon as the reason for and bulwark of marriage.

Empathy enabled evangelical missionaries to locate—that is, construct—populations that were "just like us." Empathy paradoxically led evangelicals at the same time to recognize how others differed from them and to believe that they, the evangelicals, through feeling the lives of others, knew what was best for those others. I have endeavored here to illustrate that the process was complex. The fostering of neoliberalism, as it grew out of roots put down before scholars began to utilize that term, was bound up with other things—not just marriage and sexuality but also gender, class, and race. But it is possible to see, in the example of evangelical efforts in regard to marriage, how empathy functioned in an assortment of ways. Even as empathy produced a great effect upon tithe-pledging evangelicals at home in America, the result was that "the whole of missionary work has been an

Evangelical Missions and the Neoliberal Subject

interference with African society and African marriage." Yet, as James W. Welch observed, the work of the missionaries in Africa, driven by empathy, would go on "until it is Christian."[68]

Notes

I thank Joseph Hellweg for his careful reading of the manuscript and for the thoughtful suggestions that have improved it.

1. On the key role of Andover and the American Board of Commissioners for Foreign Missions, see Emily Conroy-Krutz, *Christian Imperialism: Converting the World in the Early American Republic* (Ithaca, NY: Cornell University Press, 2015).

2. Marquis Lafayette Gordon, *Thirty Eventful Years: The Story of the American Board Mission in Japan, 1869–1899* (Boston: American Board of Commissioners of Foreign Missions, 1901), 2.

3. M. C. Wilcox, "Kucheng District," in *Seventy-Seventh Annual Report of the Missionary Society of the Methodist Episcopal Church* (New York: Missionary Society of the Methodist Episcopal Church, 1896), 53.

4. Lydia Maria Child, *Good Wives* (Boston, 1833), 246. Historian Amanda Porterfield has written that by 1833, the book had become "constitutive of American Protestant culture" (*Mary Lyon and the Mount Holyoke Missionaries* [New York: Oxford University Press, 1997], 56).

5. Francis Wayland, *A Memoir of the Life and Labors of the Rev. Adoniram Judson, D.D.*, 2 vols. (Boston: Phillips, Sampson, 1853).

6. "Burning of Widows in India," *Missionary Herald at Home and Abroad* 25, no. 4 (April 1829): 130.

7. J. N. Murdock, "A Century of Missions and Its Lessons," *Baptist Missionary Magazine* July 1892, 190; William Heathcote Delancey, "Annual Sermon," *Spirit of Missions* 23 (1858): 513. "The poor victims of superstition" is a recurring phrase in American evangelical missionary literature, here drawn from "Opening Fields—The Address of Dr. Maclay," *Fifty-Fourth Annual Report of the Missionary Society of the Methodist Episcopal Church* (New York: Missionary Society of the Methodist Episcopal Church, 1873), 39.

8. Sara Ahmed, "Affective Economies," *Social Text* 22 (2004): 17–39; and Sara Ahmed, *The Cultural Politics of Emotion* (London: Routledge, 2004). This is my claim, not Bradley's.

9. Mark Philip Bradley, *The World Reimagined: Americans and Human Rights in the Twentieth Century* (New York: Cambridge University Press, 2016), 137–48.

10. A more detailed discussion of this is in John Corrigan, *Religious Intolerance, America, and the World: A History of Forgetting and Remembering* (Chicago: University of Chicago Press, 2020).

11. Pong, *Communist Persecution of Churches in Red China and Northern Korea . . . March 26, 1959* (Washington, DC: Government Printing Office, 1959), 1, 2, 3.

12. Pong, 5, 6.

13. Pong, 28–29.

14. *Issues Presented by Air Reserve Center Training Manual. Hearing before the Committee on Un-American Activities. Eighty-sixth Congress, Second Session. February 25, 1960* (Washington, DC: Government Printing Office, 1960), 1289.

15. Twenty-first-century discussion of terrorism has taken several analytical positions, but an influential argument (even though it is overstated) remains the one made by Mark Juergensmeyer, among others, that religious inspired terrorism is grounded in belief in cosmic polarities and especially in a view stressing war between good and evil ("The Logic of Religious Violence: The Case of the Punjab," *Contributions to Indian Sociology* 22 [1988]: 65–88).

16. Adam Smith, *The Theory of Moral Sentiments* (1759), part 1, section 1, chapters 1, 2, and 3.

17. A discussion of the several ways Titchener understood the term is in Edward Bradford Titchener, "Introspection and Empathy," *Lectures on the Experimental Psychology of Thought-Processes* (New York: Macmillan, 1909).

18. Mark H. Davis has argued that both cognitive and affective outcomes are central to empathy ("Empathy," in *Handbook of the Sociology of Emotions*, ed. Jan E. Stets and Jonathan H. Turner [New York: Springer, 2006], 443–66). See also Daniele Marzoli, Rocco Palumbo, Alberto di Domenico, Barbara Penolazzi, Patrizia Garganese, and Luca Tommasi, "The Relation between Self-Reported Empathy and Motor Identification with Imagined Agents," *PLoS/ONE*, January 26, 2011, https://doi.org/10.1371/journal.pone .0014595; Neil Roughley and Thomas Schramme, "Empathy, Sympathy, Concern and Moral Agency," in *Forms of Fellow Feeling*, ed. Neil Roughley and Thomas Schramme (New York: Cambridge University Press, 2018), 3–58; C. Daniel Batson, David A. Lishner, Jennifer Cook, and Stacey Sawyer, "Similarity and Nurturance: Two Possible Sources of Empathy for Strangers," *Basic and Applied Social Psychology* 27 (2005): 15–25; and C. Daniel Batson, Karen Sager, Eric Garst, Misook Kang, Kostia Rubchinsky, and Karen Dawson, "Is Empathy-Induced Helping Due to Self-Other Merging?," *Journal of Personality and Social Psychology* 73 (1997): 495–509.

19. C. Daniel Batson makes the point that these are two kinds of empathetic imagining that are not necessarily joined in the experience of empathy ("Two Forms of Perspective Taking: Imagining How Another Feels and Imagining How One Would Feel," in *Handbook of Imagination and Mental Simulation*, ed. Keith D. Markman, William M. P. Klein, and Julie A. Suhr [New York: Psychology Press, 2009], 267–79).

20. Murray Smith, "Empathy, Expansionism, and the Extended Mind," in *Empathy: Philosophical and Psychological Processes*, ed. Amy Coplan and Peter Goldie (New York: Oxford University Press, 2011), 100; Amy Coplan, "Understanding Empathy: Its Features and Effects," in Coplan and Goldie, *Empathy*, 3–18.

21. Vittorio Gallese, "'Being Like Me': Self-Other Identity, Mirror Neurons, and Empathy," in *Perspectives on Imitation: Mechanisms of Imitation and Imitation in Animals*, ed. Susan L. Hurley and Nick Chater (Cambridge, MA: MIT Press, 2005), 101.

22. Jorge A. Barraza and Paul J. Zak, "Empathy towards Strangers Triggers Oxytocin Release and Subsequent Generosity," in *Values, Empathy and Fairness across Social Barriers: Annals of the New York Academy of Science, Volume 1167*, ed. Oscar Villaroya, Scott Atran, Arcadi Navarro, Kevin Ochsner, and Adolf Tobeña (Boston: Blackwell, on behalf of the New York Academy of Sciences, 2009), 182–89; C. Daniel Batson, *Altruism in Humans* (New York: Oxford University Press, 2011); C. Daniel Batson, "The Empathy-Altruism Hypothesis: Issues and Implications," in *Empathy: From Bench to Bedside*, ed. Jean Decety (Cambridge, MA: MIT Press, 2012), 41–54; C. Daniel Batson, "Empathy and

Altruism," in *The Oxford Handbook of Hyper-egoic Phenomena*, ed. Kirk Warren Brown and Mark R. Leary (New York: Oxford University Press, 2017), 161–71.

23. Murray Smith notes, "The human mind amplifies its capacities by exploiting the world beyond the physical boundaries of the body; empathy may be both a mechanism and a beneficiary of such extension, its power being enhanced through the practice of narration." He argues that "the domain of representation, and especially the practice of narration, constitutes the 'environmental support' created by the mind to drive its amplified performance. Public narration—exemplified above all by the narrative arts—is the anvil on which such extension is forged" ("Empathy, Expansionism, and the Extended Mind," 99, 108–9).

24. Marco Tettamanti, Giovanni Buccino, Maria Cristina Saccuman, and Vittorio Gallese, "Listening to Action-Related Sentences Activates Fronto-parietal Motor Circuits," *Journal of Cognitive Neuroscience* 17 (2005): 273–81; Suzanne Keen, "A Theory of Narrative Empathy," *Narrative* 14 (2006): 207–36; Suzanne Keen, *Empathy and the Novel* (New York: Oxford University Press, 2010).

25. A relevant summary is in John Corrigan, "Amalek and the Rhetoric of Extermination," in *The First Prejudice: Religious Tolerance and Intolerance in Early America*, ed. Chris Beneke and Christopher S. Grenda (Philadelphia: University of Pennsylvania Press, 2011), 64–67.

26. S. Josephine Davis, "Joy in Service," in the October 1912 issue included in the collection *Mission Studies: Woman's Work in Foreign Lands*, vol. 6, *1911–1913* (Cleveland: no publisher, 1915), 298, 299.

27. Helen Lee Richardson, "Woman's Work in China," in *The Student Missionary Appeal. Addresses at the Third International Convention of the Student Volunteer Movement for Foreign Missions, Held at Cleveland, Ohio, February 23–27, 1898* (New York: Student Volunteer Movement for Foreign Missions, 1898), 341.

28. Jennie Bixby Johnson, "Pioneering among the Shans," *Helping Hand* 40 (July–August 1911): 140.

29. Margaret A. Wright, "Just Like Us," *Woman's Missionary Friend* 48, no. 5 (May 1916): 158.

30. "From Foreign Letters," *Woman's Missionary Friend* 46, no. 6 (June 1912): 215.

31. Mary Elliott Fitch Tooker, "The Furloughed Missionary," *Woman's Work: A Foreign Missions Magazine* 33 (January 1918): 11.

32. F. Rica Straeffer, "A Missionary Entertainment," *Christian Observer*, January 9, 1910, 27. The article included the notation, "Directions which can be easily followed, with sample costumes will be sent to anyone applying to Miss F. Rica Straeffer, 597 Poplar Ave., Memphis, Tenn" (27).

33. Kristin Mann, "The Historical Roots and Cultural Logic of Outside Marriage in Colonial Lagos," in *Nuptiality in Sub-Saharan Africa*, ed. Caroline Bledsoe and Gilles Pison (Oxford: Oxford University Press, 1994), 167.

34. A useful overview of these problems, and especially child marriage, as they appeared in evangelical missionary writing is Joan Jacobs Brumberg, "Zenanas and Girlless Villages: The Ethnology of American Evangelical Women, 1870–1910," *Journal of American History* 69, no. 2 (September 1982): 347–71.

35. Religion additionally provided inspiration and a salve for the missionary, because empathizing with the heathen husband of multiple victimized wives—the very figure

of the monster in so much American overseas reportage—was not an easy assignment. The success of empathy was never assured. And the possibility that it could fail was evidenced, in one instance, in the general reluctance among the evangelical churches in America to organize campaigns to convert Mormons—also passionately denounced for their practice of polygamy. Evangelicals had little empathy for Mormons.

36. American evangelical concerns about marriage in other parts of the world coalesced in the antebellum period. Angered that Protestant marriages were not allowed in some parts of Catholic South America, Protestants pressed the State Department to intervene. A long series of treaties between the United States and other countries already had pronounced American interest in securing freedom of worship for Protestant Americans visiting those countries. Under Secretary of State Lewis Cass in the 1850s, and then in periodic official actions, the United States undertook to force other nations to make room for Protestant marriages in their legal systems. The most impressive victories of evangelicals on that front came as a result of the late nineteenth- and early twentieth-century agitations of the Chicago Methodist Ministers Meeting, an ad hoc organization that demanded the State Department "secure in these South American republics the fullest civil liberty for American citizens and native-born Protestants, especially by the legalizations of marriages performed by others than clergy of the Roman Catholic Church." Secretary of State John Hay communicated the official directive to the U.S. ministers George H. Bridgman in Bolivia, Archibald J. Sampson in Ecuador, and Irving B. Dudley in Peru. He copied it from a demand sent to him by the Methodist Ministers Meeting ("Mr. Hay to Mr. Bridgman, September 1, 1899," in *A Digest of International Law*, ed. John Bassett Moore, vol. 2 of 8 vols. [Washington, DC: Government Printing Office, 1906], 180). The State Department responded by forwarding the demand to its ministers in South America. Peru came to heel in 1897, Ecuador in 1902, and Bolivia in 1906. The efforts of the Chicago Methodist Ministers Meeting are reported in John Lee, *Religious Liberty in South America* (Cincinnati: Jennings and Graham, 1907).

Evangelicals did not press for official U.S. government action regarding marriage only in South America. Nineteenth-century American Protestant complaints about religious freedom in Europe in general, which could include concern about Protestant marriage, were focused largely on the Catholic nations of Spain, Portugal, larger Austria, and parts of Germany, with occasional reference to Italy. Evangelicals nevertheless also found reason to complain about Norway and Sweden. In the early twenty-first century, the issue of Christian marriage in Muslim countries became a topic of public debate in places such as Morocco (Ahmed Eljechtimi, "Christians Want Marriages Recognized in Morocco," Reuters, June 8, 2018, www.reuters.com/article/us-morocco -religion/christians-want-marriages-recognized-in-morocco-idUSKCN1J4231 [accessed July 6, 2019].)

37. "Women and Missions: Female Degradation in the Heathen Lands," *Methodist Review* 2 (September 1886): 650, 651, 652.

38. "Letters of Mr. Bronson: Labors at Nowgong," *Baptist Missionary Magazine*, September 1844, 267.

39. "South Africa: Letter from Mr. Bryant, September 28, 1846," *Missionary Herald*, May 1847, 146; "Polygamy and Christian Missions," *Methodist Review* 1 (November 1885): 942.

Evangelical Missions and the Neoliberal Subject

40. "Intelligence from the Missions. Gaboon. Journal of Mr. Bushnell," *Missionary Herald*, July 1855, 198.

41. "Eastern Africa. Letters from Mr. Burgess, Dated September 12, 1839," *Missionary Herald*, April 1840, 119.

42. By the early twentieth century, women constituted about 60 percent of the missionary population. Joan Jacobs Brumberg though that even in the early mid-nineteenth century, among Congregationalist and Baptists, the percentage of women missionaries who were unmarried at the time they began service was 60 percent. Among Methodists it was as much as 98 percent (Brumberg, "Zenanas and Girlless Villages," 350). See also Barbara Welter, "She Hath Done What She Could: Protestant Women's Missionary Careers in Nineteenth-Century America," *American Quarterly* 30, no. 5 (1978): 624–38.

43. Some evangelical missionaries did not approve of dancing, but reports generally referenced it as representative of the felicity of the event.

44. Alternatively, reports from overseas occasionally denounced heathen marriage ceremonies. One missionary witnessed an event he censured as a rude and dirty gathering of drunks, and he concluded, "But we had seen enough, far too much, save for its value as a study of genuine heathenism" (H. E. Safford, "A Heathen Wedding: A Marriage Ceremony among the Kachins," *Baptist Missionary Magazine*, December 1909, 443). Marriage ceremonies that might seem similar to American readers could also, for some, be the epitome of what was strange and dangerous about the people among whom missionaries lived.

45. "The Chiu Mission: Letter from Mr. Johnson," *Missionary Magazine*, April 1866, 1.

46. "Japan Mission: Further Evidence of Progress," *Missionary Herald*, May 1876, 159.

47. "Gaboon Mission. West Africa. Letter from Mr. Bushnell," *Missionary Herald*, March 1859, 65.

48. Missionaries in their overviews of African lives did not usually point out that what was true for one community in Africa might not be true for another: Nigeria was not Kenya, and so on. This account did state that.

49. James W. Welch, "Can Christian Marriage in Africa Be Christian?," *International Review of Mission*, January 1933, 21, 20. Welch was a missionary to Nigeria in the late 1920s to early 1930s. I am unable to confidently identify the author's native country and religious denomination. A Presbyterian (U.S.A.) missions report lists a James Welch as a missionary to the Natoma and Shiloh Indians in Kansas in 1905 (*Home Missions: One Hundred and Third Report of the Board of Home Missions of the Presbyterian Church of the United States* [New York: Presbyterian Building, 1905], 232).

50. "The Influence of Christian Missions on Buddhism in Japan," *Methodist Review* 10 (May 1894): 485.

51. "Soochow Mission. A Chinese Wedding," *Missionary Herald*, August 1885, 320.

52. "Zulu Mission. Southeastern Africa," *Missionary Herald*, October 1875, 304.

53. Mann, "Historical Roots and Cultural Logic of Outside Marriage in Colonial Lagos," 169.

54. Corrie Decker notes that "by the mid-1990s, literature on love in Africa began to challenge the colonial notion that romantic love did not exist in precolonial Africa" ("Love and Sex in Islamic Africa: Introduction," *Africa Today* 61 [2015]: 2).

55. Lynn M. Thomas and Jennifer Cole, "Thinking through Love in Africa," in *Love in Africa*, ed. Lynn M. Thomas and Jennifer Cole (Chicago: University of Chicago Press, 2009), 5. For introductory discussions of some of the issues at stake, in a global frame, see Mark B. Padilla, Jennifer S. Hirsch, Miguel Munoz-Laboy, Richard G. Parker, and Robert Sember, eds., *Love and Globalizations: Transformations of Intimacy in the Contemporary World* (Nashville, TN: Vanderbilt University Press, 2008); and William Jankowiak, *Romantic Passion: A Universal Experience?* (New York: Columbia University Press, 1995).

56. Natasha Erlank, "The White Wedding: Affect and Economy in South Africa in the Early Twentieth Century," *African Studies Review* 57 (2014): 29–50; Mark Hunter, *Love in the Time of AIDS: Inequality, Gender, and Rights in South Africa* (Bloomington: Indiana University Press, 2010); Megan Vaughan, "The History of Romantic Love in Sub-Saharan Africa," *Proceedings of the British Academy* 167 (2010): 1–23; Douglas J. Falen, "Polygyny and Christian Marriage in Africa: The Case of Benin," *African Studies Review* 51 (2008): 51–75; Elisabeth McMahon, "'Marrying Beneath Herself': Women, Affect, and Power in Colonial Zanzibar," in "Love and Sex in Islamic Africa," *Africa Today* 61 (2015): 27–40. The entire special issue of *Africa Today* (Summer 2015) is relevant. Many Christian-affiliated African scholars have positively addressed the mingling of Christian marriage traditions with African; for example, see Del Chinchen, "Valentine's Day Comes to Africa," *Missio Nexus*, April 1, 1998, https://missionexus.org/valentines-day-comes-to-africa; and Kristina Karanja Matua and Del Chinchen, "Dowry in Africa: A Wife Purchased or a Wife Cherished?," *Missio Nexus*, January 1, 2006, https://missionexus.org/dowry-in-africa-a-wife-purchased-or-a-wife-cherished.

57. Elizabeth Povinelli, *The Empire of Love: Toward a Theory of Intimacy, Genealogy and Carnality* (Princeton, NJ: Princeton University Press, 2006). Megan Vaughan offers qualified criticism of the idea in "Romantic Love in Sub-Saharan Africa," 2–5.

58. Barack Obama, *The Audacity of Hope: Thoughts on Reclaiming the American Dream* (New York: Random House, 2006), 105; Dev Patnaik, *Wired to Care: How Companies Prosper When They Create Widespread Empathy* (New York: Pearson, 2010). Carolyn Pedwell analyzes the neoliberal aims of both books in *Affective Relations: The Transnational Politics of Empathy* (Basingstoke: Palgrave Macmillan, 2014), 44–69.

59. Naomi Head, "A Politics of Empathy: Encounters with Empathy in Israel and Palestine," *Review of International Studies* 42 (2016): 95, 96–97. Head believes that empathy can transform self-other relationships. See also Andrew Linklater, *The Transformation of Political Community* (Cambridge: Polity Press, 1998); and Andrew Linklater, *The Problem of Harm in World Politics* (Cambridge: Cambridge University Press, 2011). International relations scholar Richard Ned Lebow, while recognizing a politics of empathy, writes that "affection builds empathy, which allows us to perceive ourselves through the eyes of others. Empathy in turn encourages us to see others as our *ontological* equals" ("Reason, Emotion, and Cooperation," *International Politics* 42 [2005]: 304, emphasis added).

60. Pedwell, *Affective Relations*.

61. Carolyn Pedwell, "Affective Transformations: Empathy, Neoliberalism, and International Development," *Feminist Theory* 13 (2012): 163; Pedwell, *Affective Relations*, 70–92.

62. Pedwell, *Affective Relations*, 120. Pedwell observes, "What liberal ethics of empathy often fail to address" is that efforts to think and feel like others "may be more likely to enable and perpetuate the inequality and violence of neoliberalism and neocolonialism than it is to resist or transform these realities. In other words, most liberal injunctions for greater affective knowledge avoid confronting how a positivist rhetoric linking empathy, accuracy, and prediction can become fully complicit with the interconnected logics of Western imperialism, capitalist accumulation and war" (Carolyn Pedwell, "Carolyn Pedwell on Empathy, Accuracy, and Transnational Politics," *Theory, Culture, and Society*, December 22, 2014, www.theoryculturesociety.org/carolyn-pedwell-on-empathy-accuracy-and-transnational-politics/).

63. Discussions of Christian homophobia that address the issue from several different perspectives are in Adriaan van Klinken and Ezra Chitando, eds., *Public Religion and the Politics of Homosexuality in Africa* (London: Routledge, 2016); and in Chitando and van Klinken, eds., *Christianity and Controversies over Homosexuality in Africa* (London: Routledge, 2016). On the issue of whether homosexuality was foreign to Africa, see the excellent overview with bibliography in Joseph Hellweg, "Same-Gender Desire, Religion, and Homophobia: Challenges, Complexities, and Progress for LGBTIQ Liberation in Africa," *Journal of the American Academy of Religion* 83 (2015): 887–96; Kapya Kaoma, "The Paradox and Tension of Moral Claims: Evangelical Christianity, the Politicization and Globalization of Sexual Politics in Sub-Saharan Africa," *Critical Research on Religion* 2 (2014): 227–45; Stephen Murray and Will Roscoe, *Boy Wives and Female Husbands: Studies in African Homosexualities* (New York: Palgrave, 1998); and Robert Baum, "Homosexuality in the Traditional Religions of the Americas and Africa," in *Homosexuality and World Religions*, ed. Arlene Swidler (Valley Forge, PA: Trinity Press International, 1993), 1–46.

64. Eliza Garwood, "Reproducing the Homonormative Family: Neoliberalism, Queer Theory, and Same-Sex Reproductive Law," *Journal of International Women's Studies* 17 (2016): 8. I draw here on Michel Foucault, *The History of Sexuality*, vol. 1, trans. Robert Hurley (New York: Pantheon, 1978).

65. The Ugandan Anti-Homosexuality Act of 2014 was thrown out by the Constitutional Court of Uganda that same year. On U.S. support of it, see David Weigel, "Family Research Council Lobbied against Resolution Condemning Uganda Anti-Homosexuality Law," *Washington Post*, June 4, 2010, http://voices.washingtonpost.com/right-now/2010/06/family_research_council_lobbie.html. For discussion of conservative Christian involvement in African sexual politics, including mention of the role played by the FRC, see Marcia Oliver, "Transnational Sex Politics, Conservative Christianity, and Antigay Activism in Uganda," *Studies in Social Justice* 7 (2013): 83–105; and John Anderson, "Conservative Christianity, the Global South, and the Battle over Sexual Orientation," *Third World Quarterly* 32 (2011): 1589–1605.

66. The FRC statement on "Family Structure" can be found at the FRC's website, www.frc.org/family-structure. The statement on "Family Economics" that immediately follows is at www.frc.org/family-economics (both sites accessed July 6, 2019). An insightful discussion of the FRC in these regards is in David Peterson, "Neoliberal Homophobic Discourse: Heteronormative Human Capital and the Exclusion of Queer Citizens," *Journal of Homosexuality* 58 (2011): 1–16. See also John D'Emilio, "Capitalism

and Gay Identity," in *The Lesbian and Gay Studies Reader*, ed. Henry Abelove, Michèle Aina Barale, and David M. Halperin (New York: Routledge, 1993), 467–76.

67. Rob Schwarzwalder, "Why the Age of Spiritual Ambivalence Is Also the Age of Opportunity," Family Research Council, www.frc.org/op-eds/why-the-age-of-spiritual-ambivalence-is-also-the-age-of-opportunity (accessed July 6, 2019).

68. Welch, "Can Christian Marriage in Africa Be Christian?"

ACKNOWLEDGMENTS

This volume has its origins in the conference "Global Faith and Worldly Power: Evangelical Encounters with American Empire," organized by the Obama Institute for Transnational American Studies at Johannes Gutenberg University in Mainz, Germany. This three-day event in October 2018 brought together historians and social scientists from the United States, Germany, the UK, and Ireland who in recent decades have used transnational perspectives to challenge standard narratives in the history of both evangelicalism and U.S. international relations. The meeting in Mainz, famous for being the home of the inventor of the movable-type printing press and the creator of the Gutenberg Bible, featured keynotes, panels, and roundtable discussions that investigated larger historiographical and theoretical issues at the intersection of religion and international relations. Participants examined American evangelicals' interactions with Asia, Africa, Europe, and South America in the nineteenth and twentieth centuries. They also explored the relationship between American evangelicalism and the consolidation as well as the contestation of U.S. global political, economic, and cultural power. The editors would like to gratefully acknowledge the financial support provided by the Obama Institute, the Henry Luce Foundation, the Freunde und Förderer der Universität Mainz e.V., and the Zentrum für Interkulturelle Studien Mainz.

The scholarly network that came together in Mainz first emerged from a series of conferences in 2014 and 2015 organized by the Centre for Imperial and Post-Colonial Studies (University of Southampton, UK), in cooperation with the David Bruce Centre for American Studies (Keele University, UK), the Institute of North American Studies at King's College London, and the Roosevelt Study Center, Middelburg, the Netherlands (now Roosevelt Institute for American Studies). We would like to thank Kendrick Oliver, Uta Balbier, and Hans Krabbendam for facilitating these conversations and for inspiring a body of fresh scholarship on evangelicals and their interventions in society, culture, and politics both at home and abroad. Their pioneering efforts to direct attention to evangelical engagements with the world beyond the United States resulted in the publication of a special issue of the *Journal of American Studies*, "Exploring the Global History of American Evangelicalism," in November 2017.

It has been a pleasure working with Elaine Maisner at the University of North Carolina Press. She proposed the idea of this book and enthusiastically advanced it through the various stages of assembly and editing. Her critical reading of the manuscript resulted in many improvements, and her prompt and engaged responses to our questions and concerns made this an enjoyable process from beginning to end.

We are grateful to Sneeha Bose, an MA student at George Washington University and research assistant for the project, for her utterly reliable handling of the logistical chores of keeping track of contributions, organizing them in an online document forum, and managing many details of the submissions process. We also thank her for her thoughtful comments on the introduction.

We have very much enjoyed collaborating with the authors of the chapters in this book and thank them for their patience, intellectual investment, good cheer, and dedication to producing an integrated collection of studies on evangelical global missions. We likewise thank the two anonymous peer reviewers for UNC Press for careful, informed readings of the manuscript. Their remarks, on matters of detail as well as in terms of overarching conception, were invaluable.

John Corrigan thanks Hans Krabbendam for his generous reading of work in progress and for his ready conversation about American evangelicals and their missions during a Fulbright residency in Middelburg. He also thanks Joseph Hellweg, who brought his deep knowledge of religion in Africa to a critical reading of a draft of the chapter included here, offering excellent suggestions for clarifications and enlargements. He likewise is grateful to Devin Burns, his research assistant at Florida State University, for her collaboration.

Melani McAlister thanks the University Facilitating Fund and the Humanities Facilitating Fund of George Washington University for research support and Carl Conetta for reading a draft of the introduction, and especially for engaging in conversations about evangelical internationalism for so many years.

Axel R. Schäfer is grateful to Michaela Hoenicke Moore (University of Iowa) for her friendship and encouragement in pursuing this project and her thoughtful feedback on drafts. Her inimitable style, combining profound scholarly insight with an infectious enthusiasm, was a tremendous inspiration in working on this volume.

Julie Bush did a truly exceptional job copyediting the manuscript, and Mary Carley Caviness made the production process smooth and easy. We thank them for their help. Derek Gottlieb expertly indexed the book.

Finally, the editors would like to thank each other for the energy, focus, and largesse that made for a model of collegial alliance. Coediting across the Atlantic during the Covid crisis posed particular challenges, but the spirit of cooperation, efficiency, and good humor that prevailed throughout this project was a timely salve for many of the privations of the pandemic.

CONTRIBUTORS

Editors

John Corrigan is Lucius Moody Bristol Distinguished Professor of Religion and professor of history at Florida State University. His most recent book is *Religious Intolerance, America, and the World.*

Melani McAlister is professor of American studies and international affairs at George Washington University. Her most recent monograph is *The Kingdom of God Has No Borders: A Global History of American Evangelicals.*

Axel R. Schäfer is chair of American history at the Obama Institute for Transnational American Studies at Johannes Gutenberg University in Mainz, Germany. Among his monographs are *Piety and Public Funding: Evangelicals and the State in Modern America* and *Countercultural Conservatives: American Evangelicalism from the Postwar Revival to the New Christian Right.*

Contributors

Lydia Boyd is associate professor of African, African American, and diaspora studies at the University of North Carolina at Chapel Hill. She is author of *Preaching Prevention: Born-Again Christianity and the Moral Politics of AIDS in Uganda.*

Emily Conroy-Krutz is associate professor of history at Michigan State University. She is author of *Christian Imperialism: Converting the World in the Early American Republic.*

Christina Cecelia Davidson is an assistant professor of history at the University of Southern California. She is completing a book manuscript on religion, race, and U.S. empire in the late nineteenth-century Dominican Republic.

Helen Jin Kim is assistant professor of American religious history at Emory University and author of *Race for Revival: How Cold War South Korea Shaped the American Evangelical Empire.*

David C. Kirkpatrick is assistant professor of religion at James Madison University and author of *A Gospel for the Poor: Global Social Christianity and the Latin American Evangelical Left.*

Candace Lukasik is a postdoctoral research associate at the John C. Danforth Center on Religion and Politics at Washington University in St. Louis. Her current book project is tentatively titled "Martyrs and Migrants: Coptic Christians and the Persecution Politics of U.S. Empire."

Sarah Miller-Davenport is senior lecturer in twentieth-century U.S. history at the University of Sheffield. She is the author of *Gateway State: Hawai'i and the Cultural Transformation of American Empire* and has written about evangelical missionaries for the *Journal of American History.* She is currently working on a project on the reinvention of New York as a global city after 1975.

Dana L. Robert is William Fairfield Warren Distinguished Professor and director of the Center for Global Christianity and Mission at Boston University. She is a member of the American Academy of Arts and Sciences.

Tom Smith is Keasbey Research Fellow in American Studies at Selwyn College, University of Cambridge. He is currently working on a book manuscript examining the historical thinking of American Protestant missionaries in Hawai'i and the Philippines in the late nineteenth and early twentieth centuries.

Lauren F. Turek is associate professor of history at Trinity University in San Antonio, Texas, where she teaches courses on modern U.S. history, U.S. foreign relations, and public history. She is the author of *To Bring the Good News to All Nations: Evangelical Influence on Human Rights and U.S. Foreign Relations* and has published articles and chapters on religion in American politics and foreign relations in *Diplomatic History*, the *Journal of American Studies*, *Religions*, and several edited volumes.

Gene Zubovich is assistant professor at the University at Buffalo, SUNY. He is author of *Before the Religious Right: Liberal Protestants, Human Rights, and the Polarization of the United States.*

INDEX

communism, 13, 15, 19, 23, 157, 160–62, 189, 196, 201–2, 208, 236, 241–43, 246, 273. *See also* capitalism; Cold War
Compassion International, 275
Congo, 8–9, 15, 185, 279
Congregationalism, 130, 149, 151–52, 160, 164, 167n27
Conroy-Krutz, Emily, 10, 179
consumerism, 34, 185
Contras, 21, 241, 243, 246–47, 249, 252. *See also* Sandinistas; Nicaragua
conversion, 1, 9, 12, 55, 60, 98, 107, 130, 139n18, 181, 186. *See also* evangelicalism; missionary work
Copeland, Kenneth, 23
Coptic Christians, 323–25, 328, 330–33, 335–38, 341, 343
Coptic Orthodox Church, 326, 336
Corrigan, John, 27, 36, 180, 248, 267, 283
Costas, Orlando, 18, 217–18, 223–24, 226–27, 229, 232–33, 237n1
Criswell, W. A., 16
Crosby, Albert, 271
Cru (Campus Crusade), 37, 275
Cuba, 26–27, 104, 219–20, 235
Cumings, Bruce, 200
CUNY (City University of New York), 145, 158, 162
Curtis, Heather, 180

DACA (Deferred Action for Childhood Arrivals), 27
Darrow, Clarence, 4
Davidann, Jon, 135
Davidson, Christina Cecelia, 8
Davis, Josephine, 357
Day, I., 86
Daystar, 30
Dead Men on Furlough (Pierce), 196, 207–11
DeBayle, Anastasio Somoza, 246
decolonization: and capitalism, 35–36; commitments to, 106–8, 127, 153, 235–36 (*see also* Cold War; colonialism; imperialism); legacies of, 13–17, 98–99, 174–76, 186–88, 231, 242–44;

and race, 3–6, 188–90, 288; and transnationalism, 270
Deferred Action for Childhood Arrivals (DACA), 27
Dellums, C. L., 152
de los Reyes, Isabelo, 113
Derrick, William B., 83
dhimmitude, 329
Dickerson, William F., 84
Diocletian, 328
Disciples of Christ, 116
Dochuk, Darren, 159, 266
Dominican Republic, 8, 80, 226. *See also* Hispaniola
Dominican War of Restoration, 77
Doran, George H., 112
double consciousness, 272
Douglass, Frederick, 74
Dow, Philip E., 274, 279
Dow v. United States, 342
Du Bois, W. E. B., 152, 154–55, 168n41, 272
Dugan, Robert P., Jr., 245
Dulles, John Foster, 153, 202, 214n36
Dumke, Glenn, 163, 1763
Dunker, Marilee Pierce, 197–98

East India Company, 177
Eckhoff, K. M., 129
Ecological Imperialism (Crosby), 271
economy of blood, 324–27, 330
ecumenicalism (or ecumenism), 11–13, 71–72, 85–89, 98–99, 103–5, 109–10, 114–17, 145–47, 149, 152–53, 180–81, 274, 330. *See also* evangelicalism; missionary networks
Eddy, G. Sherwood, 103
Edinburgh Missionary Conference of 1910, 10
education, 10, 53–54, 57, 109, 125, 130–32, 150, 161–62. *See also* literacy
Egypt, 335
Eisenhower, Dwight D., 196, 214n36, 274
empathy, 355–57, 361–64, 366, 370n17
Englund, Harri, 314
entanglement, 138n5
epiphanal spaces, 278

imperialism, 6, 13, 15, 37, 78, 98, 105–6, 263–64, 269, 281–82, 286, 336; critics of, 105–6; role of missionaries in, 6, 13–15, 263–64, 269, 286, 336; strategies of, 37–38, 281–82. *See also* colonialism; decolonization; missionaries

Imperial Rescript on Education, 136, 138n14

Inboden, William, 266

India, 10, 53–54, 56, 113, 180, 186

indigenization, 107–8, 264

indigenous people, 7, 11, 23, 98–99, 117n12, 204, 284, 356

industrialization, 132

Institute for Religion and Democracy, 249, 329

International Christian Leadership, 274

International Congress on World Evangelism. *See* Lausanne Congress

International Fellowship of Evangelical Students, 227

International Missionary Council, 149

International Religious Freedom Act of 1998, 25, 275

International Students' Missionary Conference, 122

Inter-Religious Task Force, 249

InterVarsity Christian Fellowship, 14, 17, 26, 31, 37, 221, 278

In the Levant (Warner), 338

Iran-Contra scandal, 260n63

Iraq War, 284

Isé, J. T., 127–28, 136, 139n18

ISEDET (Instituto Superior Evangélico de Estudios Teológicos), 233

Islam, 25, 273, 328–29, 331, 334–35, 339–40, 342–43. *See also* Muslim-Christian relations

Islamic State, 323

Islamophobia, 24, 284, 334, 337, 340, 345

isolationism, 148, 271

Israel, 18, 330

Jackson-Vanik amendment, 20

Jakes, T. D., 29

Janes, L. L., 127

Japan, 12, 14, 63, 122–23, 126–27, 130–31, 133, 135–36, 138n14, 182–83, 198–99

Japanese internment, 151

Jenkins, E. C., 107

Jenkins, James, 29

Jenkins, Jerry, 31

jeremiad tradition, 285

Jesus to the Communist World, 249

Jim Crow, 150–51, 153–54

Johnson, Anson Burlingame, 62

Johnson, Charles S., 152, 167n27

Johnson, Jennie Bixby, 357–58

Johnson, Lyndon, 265

Johnson, Sylvester, 265

Johnson, Torrey, 184

Jones, Bob, 223, 225–26, 239n36. *See also* Bob Jones Academy

Jones, E. Stanley, 277

Jones, Howard, 17

Jones Law, 106

Joshua, T. B., 31

Judaism, 20, 203

Judson, Adoniram, 352

Judson, Ann Hasseltine, 352

Kalu, Ogbu, 23

Kantzer, Kenneth, 241–42

Kaplan, Amy, 7

Karas, Adel, 334

Kaub, Verne, 160–61

Keeley, Theresa, 250

Kenya, 269, 285

Kim, Helen Jin, 17

Kim, Kyung Rai, 354

Kim Ch'anghwa, 196–97, 205–11

Kim Il Sung, 200–201

King, David, 267

Kingdom and the Glory, The (Agamben), 324

King, Martin Luther, Jr., 17

Kirk, Andrew, 233

Kirkpatrick, David C., 18, 279

North Korea, 200, 354. *See also* Korean War

nuclear weaponry, 269

Oakland General Strike of 1946, 156

Oakland Tribune, 157, 162

Oashard, Paul, 88

Obama, Barack, 276, 365

Ockenga, Harold, 15

Odor, Kevin, 311, 314–15

105 Persons Incident, 198

One World (Willkie), 153

Open Doors News Service, 249

Operation Blessing, 251

Operation Mobilization, 11

Organization of Economic Cooperation and Development, 265

Oriental Exclusion Act, 154

orientalism, 9, 202. *See also* racism

Oriental Mission Society, 204

Ortega, Daniel, 250, 252–53

Osías, Camilo, 110–12

Other Side, 220, 235

Ottoman Empire, 3, 10

Oxnam, G. Bromley, 159

Pacific School of Religion, 151, 156

pacifism, 175, 268

Padilla, René, 18, 221–22, 227, 231, 234, 238n12

Paek Okhyŏn, 196–97, 205–11, 215n54

paganism, 185

Paine, Stephen W., 158–59

Painter, David, 247

Palau, Luis, 29

Panic of 1837, 57

Paris Basis, 104–5. *See also* Portland Basis; Young Men's Christian Association

Parker, Peter, 63

paternalism, 135, 154, 188, 229

Patnaik, Dev, 365

PATRIOT Act, 337, 340

patriotism, 60, 133. *See also* nationalism

Paul, Thomas, 76

Payne, Daniel Alexander, 73, 81, 85

Pearson, Carlton, 29

Pedwell, Carolyn, 284, 366, 375n62

Pence, Mike, 3

Pentecostalism, 21–23, 26, 34–35, 37, 279

People of the Philippines, The (Laubach), 108–9, 112

People's Christian Coalition. *See* Sojourners

Perry, Samuel L., 147

persecution, 341, 352, 354–55; of Christians, 3, 10, 275, 323, 329, 333

Petro, Anthony, 302

Philippine Council of Evangelical Churches, 116

Philippine Organic Act, 102

Philippines: Catholic rule in, 98; colonization of, 201; independence of, 103, 106–8, 112, 115, 173, 179, 185; military power in, 183; missionaries in, 172, 177, 282; politics in, 101–2; social reform in, 180, 191n30; spiritual culture of, 111, 113

Picot, Thomas Richard, 86–87

Pierce, Bob, 17–18, 187, 195–96, 198, 203–5, 207–11, 215n54, 218, 279. *See also* Han, Kyung Chik; World Vision

Pinochet, Augusto, 221

Pittsburgh Courier, 15

Point Four Program, 275

Politics of Jesus, The (Yoder), 233

polygamy, 360–61

Pompeo, Mike, 25

Pong, Peter Chu, 354

Population Services International, 307

Populorum progressio, 228

Portland Basis, 101, 104–6, 108. *See also* Paris Basis; Young Men's Christian Association

Post-American, 18

Potsdam Conference, 200

poverty, 77, 218, 228

premillennialism, 160

Presbyterian Board of Foreign Missions, 53, 59, 64

Presbyterian Church of East Africa, 22

President's Emergency Plan for AIDS Relief (PEPFAR), 33, 207, 299–305,

308, 312–13, 315–17. *See also* AIDS
    programs
Press, Torrance, 209
Pressoir, J. C., 76
Preston, Andrew, 266
Prohibition, 181–82
prosperity gospel, 22, 35, 283
Protestant-Catholic relations, 15, 88,
    98, 108, 113. *See also* Catholicism;
    Protestantism
*Protestant Ethic and the Spirit of Capitalism,
    The* (Weber), 33–34
Protestantism: and egalitarianism, 27–28;
    and evangelicalism, 10, 98, 112; and
    humanitarianism, 28; in local contexts,
    12; perceptions of, 1, 3–4, 280; and
    race, 17, 89; spread of, 73–74. *See also*
    evangelicalism; fundamentalists;
    Protestant-Catholic relations
Prudential Committee, 57
Puerto Rico, 13–14, 103, 177, 224
Pugh, Theophilus, 76
Purpose Driven Life, The (Warren), 300

Quakers, 75–76

racecraft, 336–37
racial categorization, 338, 341–42. *See also*
    racialization, racism
racialization, 324–25, 336–37
racial solidarity, 77
racism, 7–9, 16, 87, 128, 133–34, 150–53,
    162, 179, 189–90, 197, 209–10,
    222–26, 284, 288, 340. *See also*
    colonialism; imperialism; orientalism;
    white supremacy
Rana, Junaid, 337
Randolph, A. Philip, 150
Rankin, Henry, 60, 63–64
Reagan, Bruce, 163
Reagan, Ronald, 20–21, 164–65, 242–46,
    249–51, 254n8, 266–67, 303–4
Reagan Doctrine, 217
Reconstruction, 79
Reed, Ralph, 5
religion and sports, 124–25

religious freedom, 13, 21, 23, 25–26, 127,
    183, 199, 245, 249, 251, 253, 275. *See
    also* human rights
Religious Roundtable, 20
religious-secular divide, 51–52, 62, 101, 155
Rescue Mission, 29
Re-thinking Missions (Hocking Report),
    11, 181
Rezk, Tony, 332
Ribuffo, Leo, 265
Richardson, Helen Lee, 357
Rich Christians in an Age of Hunger (Sider),
    233
Robert, Dana L., 12
Roberts, Jacob, 75
Roberts, Oral, 15, 22–23
Robertson, Pat, 5, 20, 29, 251
Robinson, Richard, 75, 92n17
Rockefeller, John, 181
Rockefeller Foundation, 11
Rodger, James B., 103
Roosevelt, Eleanor, 158
Roosevelt, Franklin Delano, 150, 156
Rosenberg, Emily, 6, 273
Ross, Dick, 207
Rowlinson, Frank, 10

Sager, Rebecca, 302
Salvadoran civil war, 220, 235
Salvation Army, 275
Samaritan's Purse, 32, 275, 301–2
Sanders, Frank K., 132
Sandinistas, 21, 246–52. *See also* Contras;
    Nicaragua
Scandinavian Student Movement, 129
Schaeffer, Francis, 11, 15
Schäfer, Axel R., 24, 37, 116
Scherz, China, 314
Schulten, Susan, 147
Scofield Reference Bible of 1909, 4
Scopes trial, 4, 181–82
scripture, 4, 18–19, 55, 75, 134, 223
segregation, 146, 151, 162
Sekulow, Jay, 333
Sekulow, Jordan, 333
Selassie, Haile, 279

Seminario Bíblico Latinoamericano (SBL), 229–31
SEND International. *See* Far Eastern Gospel Crusade
September 11, 2001, attacks, 25, 325, 334–37, 343. *See also* war on terror
700 Club, The (television show), 251
Seventh-Day Adventists, 275
Sharkey, Heather, 279
Sheldon, Charles, 179
Shenoda, Anthony, 338
Shenouda III (pope), 336
Sheppard, William H., 9
Sherman, John, 62
Shorter, James A., 80–81
Sider, Ron, 221, 223, 233, 277
Sierra Leone, 74, 84–85, 89
Singapore, 50
Sino-Japanese War, 61
Sisi, Abdel Fattah al-, 343
Skinner, Tom, 15, 277
slavery, 73–74, 77, 154
Smith, Adam, 355
Smith, Chris, 326–27
Smith, Murray, 371n23
Smith, Shepherd, 304
Smith, Tom, 7–8, 282
Social Gospel, 50, 149–50, 180, 202–3
socialism, 149, 159, 200, 208, 231
Sojourners, 18, 268
Sojourners, 220, 234, 249–50
South Africa, 5, 21–22, 89, 177
South Berkeley Community Church, 152
Southern Baptist International Mission Board, 27
Southern Baptists, 10–11, 16, 20–21, 37, 278. *See also* Baptists
Southern California Republican Women's Club, 161
South Korea, 200. *See also* Korean War
Soviet Union (USSR), 23–24, 173–74, 188, 200, 245. *See also* Cold War
Spanish-American War, 98, 101, 124, 177–78
sports, 124–25, 138n8

Spreading the American Dream (Rosenberg), 6
Springfield Daily Union, 124
Sproul, Gordon, 158
Ssempa, Martin, 306–8, 311, 313, 315–16
Stagg, Amos Alonzo, 125
Stalin, Joseph, 200–201
Steele, Irwin W., 160
Steward, Theophilus Gould, 80
Stott, John, 223
St. Peter's Union Methodist Episcopal, 80
Student Volunteer Missionary Union of Great Britain and Ireland, 129
Student Volunteer Movement, 100–101, 123
Sullivan, Leon, 21
Sullivan Principles, 21
Sutton, Matthew, 266
Swaggart, Jimmy, 5
Swartz, David, 277–79
Swift, John T., 127–28, 135–36
Syngman Rhee, 200

Tabitha Mojawon (Tabitha Widows Home), 197, 206
Taft, William Howard, 177
Taft-Katsura Agreement, 201
Talladega Civic League, 150
Talladega College, 149
Tanner, Sarah E., 82
TASO organization, 307
Tawadros II (pope), 326, 331
televangelism, 29–30, 306
Tener, William A., 102–3
10/40 Window campaign, 24
Teología de la liberación (Gutiérrez), 219, 228
"Teólogo en la encrujijada" (Costas), 224
Thanksgiving Workshop of Evangelical Social Concern, 221
Theory of Moral Sentiments, The (Smith), 355
Things Fall Apart (Achebe), 6
Thompson, Michael, 147
Thurman, Howard, 152

Weaver, Galen, 151
Weber, Max, 33–34
Welch, James W., 369
Wells, Ida B., 8
Wesleyans, 76–77, 86–87
Westad, Odd Arne, 19
White, Paula, 28–29
White, Walter, 151, 158
white evangelicals, 3–4, 36. *See also* evangelicals; white supremacy
Whitehead, Andrew L., 147
White House Office of Faith-Based and Community Initiatives, 301–2
white supremacy, 16, 153–54. *See also* racism; white evangelicals
Whittlesey, Faith Ryan, 248
Wilder, Robert, 139n33
Williams, Roger, 285
Williams, Samuel, 63
Williams, Smallwood, 15
Williamson, John Rutter, 123–24
Willkie, Wendell, 152–53, 155
Wills, George, 268
Wilson, Woodrow, 3, 106
Wired to Care (Patnaik), 365
Wishard, Luther M., 128, 131, 133–34
Witness for Peace, 250
Wittner, Lawrence, 183
Women's Christian Temperance Union, 10
Women's Missionary Union, 278
Women's Parent Mite Missionary Society, 79, 81–82, 84–86
World Alliance of Young Men's Christian Associations, 131
World Bank, 32
World Christian Database (World Religion Database), 31

World Congress on Evangelism, 254–55n10, 278
World Council of Churches, 22, 149, 160, 164–65, 265
World Relief Corporation, 275
World Religion Database (WRD), 31
World's Student Christian Federation, 129
World Vision, 17–19, 28, 32, 165, 187, 195–97, 205–12, 218, 270, 275, 278–79, 300, 307; and Vision Fund, 32. *See also* Han, Kyung Chik; Pierce, Bob
World War I, 97, 99, 106–9, 124, 181
World War II, 11–13, 115, 146, 150–51, 172–88, 195, 201, 231–35, 244, 264–69, 273, 353
Wright, Margaret A., 357–58
Wurmbrand, Richard, 218
Wuthnow, Robert, 280
Wycliffe Bible Translators, 11

Yangco, Teodoro, 104, 110–11
Year 2000, 24
Yi Sŭnghun, 198
Yoder, John Howard, 233
Young Men's Christian Association (YMCA), 12, 100–108, 114, 124–26, 128, 130–33, 135–36, 151, 151n49, 221. *See also* Paris Basis; Portland Basis
Young Women's Christian Association (YWCA), 161–62
Youth for Christ (YFC), 175, 184–85, 187, 203
Yun Chi'ho, 199

Ziemtsma, David, 266
Zipp, Samuel, 147
Zubovich, Gene, 13

CPSIA information can be obtained
at www.ICGtesting.com
Printed in the USA
LVHW102149271022
731795LV00005B/439